NOW PITCHING
FOR THE
YANKEES

SPINNING THE NEWS
FOR MICKEY, BILLY, AND
GEORGE

Marty Appel

SPORT CLASSIC BOOKS

For information about permission to reproduce selections from this book,
please write to:
Permissions
Sport Media Publishing, Inc.,
21 Carlaw Ave.,
Toronto, Ontario, Canada, M4M 2R6
www.sportclassicbooks.com

Cover design: Paul Hodgson
Cover photo credits:
Mickey Mantle (Martin Blumenthal, The SPORT Collection);
Reggie Jackson (Louis Requena);
Billy Martin (Daniel Baliotti, The SPORT Collection);
George Steinbrenner (author's collection);
Yogi Berra & Thurman Munson (Kevin Fitzgerald, The SPORT Collection).

Interior design: Ann Sullivan & Greg Oliver

ISBN: 0-9731443-5-1

Library of Congress Control Number: 2002116810

Printed in United States of America

For Brian and Debbie, the best parts of my life.

CONTENTS

FOREWORD

Being in baseball for a long time, you get to meet a lot of people. I've met quite a few in my years with the Yankees, as a player, coach, and manager. You don't forget the good ones—the players, the trainers, the clubhouse guys, the front office guys, and so on.

I've always liked Marty Appel. He's one of the good ones in baseball. I guess I've known him for almost thirty years, when I came back as a coach and he was the PR man. There was a lot of craziness in those days, but nothing really seemed to faze Marty. Even with all the controversy that came up, he always acted real professional. The players and coaches liked him—I remember Thurman Munson and Elston Howard, two great guys, really trusted him a lot.

What I also liked about Marty was that he was a real student of the game. He was knowledgeable and would always tell you something interesting that you didn't know—and he was pretty funny, too.

After I got fired as manager in 1985, I lost some of my old connections. I hadn't seen Marty in some time until they told me they were building a museum and education center in my honor at Montclair State a couple of years ago, and Marty was going to do PR for it. I was happy about that. And he showed he still must be a pretty good PR man, because the museum got an incredible amount of publicity—even before it opened.

For example, the Toms River kids who won the Little League championship visited the unfinished building, and it was all over the papers; I guess that was a good story. But Marty has a lot of great stories to tell after all he's seen and been a part of. That's what's so great about baseball—all the great stories. And I promise you this book has a lot of them.

YOGI BERRA

ACKNOWLEDGMENTS

My monthly sportswriters lunch group of Larry Ritter, Ray Robinson, Bob Creamer, Al Silverman, Stan Isaacs, Lee Lowenfish, Darrell Berger, Brian Silverman, David Falkner, and the late Mike Gershman always let me try out this material on them, and I am grateful. Likewise, the annual Hot Stove League dinner party of Barry Halper, Bill Madden, and Moss Klein.

Special thanks to those who aren't part of the anecdotes in this book, but have been important in my life, including: Donna Anastasio, Bob Aniello, Kurt Ascherman, Pat Austin, Andrea Axelrod, Raquel Barrera, Peter Bavasi, Geoff Belinfante, Kathy Bennett, Alice Benson, Barry Berger, Brian Berk, Ira Berkow, Mike Berkus, Jay Black, Hal Bock, Neill Cameron, Ed Camp, Phil Carter, Jim Charlton, Thea Chassin, Mike Cherkasky, Pam Cecil, Renata Circeo, John Coppinger, John Corporon, Joe D'Ambrosio, Jack Danzis, Joe Durso, Bruce Fabricant, Bill Finneran, David Fishof, Frank Fleizach, Red Foley, Marilyn Funt, Stan and Bernice Gedzelman, Rick Gentile, Patricia Gitt, Bill Gladstone, Laurie Goldberg, Liz Goldberg, Michael Goldberg, Joe Goldstein, Bert Gould, Ross Greenburg, Bud Greenspan, Joe Grippo, Ernestine Guglielmo, Colin Hagen, Janie Hamilton, Doug Hearle, Bill Heyman, Bob Hollander, Zander Hollander, Lesley Hunt, Bob Ibach, Steve Jacobson, Rob Johnson, George Kalinsky, Dave Kaplan, Jacqui Kartanos, Billy Keresey, Ira Kotler, Paul Kurtz, J Langdon, Rex Lardner, Hannah Lee, Mel Leventhal, Bill Liederman, Bill Littauer, Bruce Lowitt, Carl Lundquist, Gene Luntz, John Margaritis, Cheryl Mason, Charlie McCabe, Ellen Mednick, Janet Mines, Stan Moger, Carol and Paul Muldawer, Mark and Lydia Neubart, Dave Oliver, Pat Olsen, Neil Offen, Dale Petroskey, Arthur Pincus, Dave Polinger, Sy Preston, Linda Purgess, Joyce Quandt, Ed Randall, John Rawlings, Louis Requena, Arthur Richman, Jonathan Rinehart, Yale Robbins, Sandy Robinson, George Rosenberg, Jay Rosenstein, Fred Rothenberg, Chris Russo, Rich Sandomir, Mari Santana, Elna Seabrooks, Richard Seidlitz, Bill Shannon, Kathy Shepherd, Pete Silverman, Frank Simio, Mike Slaff, Bob Solomon, Jordan Sprechman, Rusty Staub, John Sterling, Marc and Barbara Stertz, Andy Strasberg, John Tagliaferro, Alan Taylor, George Vecsey, Mike Wach, Suzyn Waldman, Charles Waterman, Eve and Chad Weller, Irv and Eileen Welzer, Bob Wilke, Jack Wilkinson, Pat Williams, Bob Wolff, Rick Wolff, John Woodward, Mara Young, Vic Ziegel, friends at Beckett and Krause Publications, and the extended Appel family, especially Norm, Jackie, Scott, Andrew, and Brad.

At Total Sports, John Thorn, Rob Wilson, Jed Thorn, Ann Sullivan, Chad Lawrence, and Dave Weiner.

At SPORTClassic Books, Wayne Parrish, Jim O'Leary, Wes Seeley, Peter Grucza and Greg Oliver.

YANKEE FAN
FROM BROOKLYN

I was an accidental Yankee fan.

It was all a mistake.

I was seven years old and didn't know what I was doing.

And since much that has happened in my life since has been determined by that most important decision we make as children—who we root for—I have to wonder whether perhaps I chose the wrong path when I came to that particular fork in the road.

If so, it was a lucky accident.

I turned seven in the summer of 1955. Baseball hadn't entered my life yet. But by October there was something called a Subway Series in town. The Dodgers against the Yankees. A World Series. My baseball awakening.

Had I known my baseball history, I would have realized that this was not their first meeting. They had played each other in 1941, 1947, 1949, 1952, and 1953. Each time, the Yankees had won.

It came to be expected. The Dodgers, the team of the common folk, where even those who sat in cramped box seats at Ebbets Fields were actually "bleacher bums," were the lovable losers whose rallying cry had become "wait till next year!"

The Yankees, the team of Wall Street fans, of the businesslike precision that had brought them endless pennants, won so often and predictably that not once did they get a ticker-tape parade in Manhattan, as is so common today.

Had I really known the Dodger players—Jackie and Pee Wee,

Campy and Furillo, Snider and Hodges, Erskine, Newcombe, Gilliam—
the later-named "Boys of Summer" (from the book by Roger Kahn)—I
would probably have loved them, as did most of my neighbors on St.
John's Place in Brooklyn.

But I didn't know the players. All I came to know was the celebration in the streets when Johnny Podres beat the Yanks in the seventh
game for the first world championship ever in Brooklyn.

I guess I just wasn't educated enough in the game to understand the true
significance of that Brooklyn victory over the Yankees. I was confused, and
something within me made me suddenly feel sorry for the losers.

Amidst all the excitement, my heart went out to the poor Yanks.
Surely they must have tried their hardest and come up short. How sad
they must feel!

And so on that day, October 4, 1955, I became a Yankee fan. I was
going to be a champion of the underdog. I was going to root my little
heart out for these poor guys in pinstripe uniforms until they could get
back on their feet and hold their heads high. I would not be like all my
neighbors. I was going to go it alone in the borough of Brooklyn.

Nearly half a century later, having gone on to become the Yankees'
public relations director and the executive producer of their telecasts,
having written books and represented clients within the Yankees' world, it
is still the Yankee box score that I check first in the morning paper. They
have won another 10 world championships since 1955, and I have come
to accept that they are anything but underdogs. But there is nothing like
the fan loyalty that develops when you're a kid, and nothing like the
undying devotion of a man to his team. A lot of wonderful adventures
have flowed from that fateful day in '55, along with a lot of fascinating
people I've been fortunate to work with.

Had I become a Dodger fan, like most people in Brooklyn were
supposed to be, I would have lost my team to Los Angeles two years later.
Sometimes things happen for a reason.

I was born on August 7, 1948. Nine days later, Babe Ruth died. I'm told that
when I heard the news I cried like a baby.

The Brooklyn I remember was one in the final years of trolley cars and
of great military parades on Armistice Day along Eastern Parkway, the
model train set in Prospect Park, our brownstone at 1215 St. John's Place,
our black 1950 Chevy with the gray top, and stoop ball with pink
Spaldeens at Aunt Goldye's house.

My father took great pride in that Chevy. He had taken a train to
Detroit to pick it up, and he kept it immaculate, especially the light gray

interior. Then we paid a visit to his mother-in-law in the Bronx, my grandmother, and she insisted that he take home a jar of her homemade borscht—the dark red, made-from-beets, European specialty of hers. "No, please, thanks just the same, but we'd rather not," he said. To no avail.

When we got home he discovered that it had spilled all over the Chevy's upholstery. My grandmother never lived down the borscht story, partly because that remained the family car until 1959, and she remained his mother-in-law until she died in 1994 at the age of 94.

My family moved to Maspeth, Queens, soon after the Dodgers won the '55 Series. We bought a two-bedroom co-op for $79 a month. Topps baseball cards were a nickel a pack, and a quart of milk was a quarter—I was entrusted to go to the milk machine in the basement to make that purchase on occasion. I now had a younger brother and roommate, Norman, who went on to become a chemist but not much of a sports fan.

I got a Yankee jacket around that time, along with a Yankee cap, and a road-gray flannel Yankee uniform, made so by my mother ironing the words NEW YORK onto the front, except for the R being backwards. It came with real stirrup socks and knickers, and what a total thrill that was to wear.

It was in Queens that I first learned to play ball. We played punch ball and slap ball and box ball in the playground, and then hardball in the Police Athletic League sandlots of Maurice Park. Richie Zisk, who later played for the Pirates and White Sox, was part of that league. We had green caps with PAL buttons on them, and no uniforms, but the games were on real diamonds and I loved them.

Like every other Yankee fan, I loved Mickey Mantle, but Bobby Richardson was special to me. I felt he was a favorite player uniquely my own, not to be shared with everyone. I loved his game. I kept both his daily and career stats updated on my bulletin board, and I could practically recite the names of all 35 pitchers he touched for home runs (Arnie Portocarrero twice), including Clem Labine (grand slam) in the 1960 World Series. I knew that John Buzhardt was the pitcher who ended his longest hitting streak at 18 games, and I knew that a Los Angeles Angels infielder named Billy Moran had beaten him out to start an All-Star Game, which fries me to this day. I also knew that when I needed to bear down and get a hit, I would drop my knees a little like he did, hold the bat high and level, and tell myself, "I'm Bobby Richardson," and hit the ball better than I might have.

Inspired by Bobby, I learned to play second base; and to this day, in my fifties, I am totally at home there, no matter how seldom I play. Somehow, I seemed to have an instinct for it. Even at 10 or 11, I knew all the moves. I could make the pivot, knew how to signal to the outfielders how many outs there were, how to determine who was covering second on a force (mouth open or closed), when to play in, how to whip that ball around the infield after an out, how to cover first on a bunt, how to execute the cutoffs, how to sift the dirt with my foot after an error, as though a pebble had found its way there, and, of course, all the big league moves like tossing the ball onto the mound if you caught the last out, which I loved doing. Very cool.

I wrote him a fan letter in 1959, his first season as a regular, and I got home from school one day to find a black-and-white postcard of him, signed on the back, saying, "Really appreciated your letter. Sincerely, Bobby Richardson." That was the best autograph I ever got. My memory of how our apartment in Queens looked includes where that postcard was on the Formica kitchen counter.

I soon joined his well-organized fan club, as posted in *Sport* magazine, and although the mailings from the club always included religious tracts, I still couldn't wait to get them. Bobby may have been an ardent Baptist, but he also hit .301 in 1959 and made the All-Star team, which counted for a lot where I came from.

In 1962 the fan club held a contest. We had to guess in which game he would get his 100th hit of the season.

I hit it right on the nose (I think it was the 81st), and I received a Western Union telegram the next day saying, "Congratulations, you have won an autographed baseball in the 100 Hit Contest!"

Later that season, I met the co-presidents of the fan club at Yankee Stadium, Candy and Jimmy Lindstrom, and they in turn walked me to the front-row boxes near first base during batting practice and called Bobby over. I had never been so close to a real Yankee! I had never really seen the heavy flannel cloth of the uniform up close. I had never even been in the box seats before! I was introduced as the winner of the contest, and, although I don't remember what we said, I was so in awe of the moment that it couldn't have been very profound.

Bobby was truly a special person. His teammates liked him because, although he may not have been "one of the boys," he did command respect. They didn't swear around Bobby, although it was said that when Yogi Berra became manager, that was a bit of a sore point between them. Yogi spoke not only "Yogi," he spoke baseball—and that can be a colorful language. When a remorseful Mickey Mantle lay dying in a Dallas hospital, it was Bobby Richardson who sat with him, talked him through the life he had led, and brought him in touch with God. Richardson and Mantle respected each other, which speaks volumes about them both.

I was not just an anonymous fan club member to Richardson. When I went to work for the Yankees two years after his retirement, I wrote to Bobby and told him I was now answering fan mail in the basement office near the clubhouse. He immediately phoned me, let me know that he remembered me, and wished me good luck. And then, a few years later, when it fell to me to plan Old Timers Days—well, Bobby was always first on the list. And when we opened the new Yankee Stadium in 1976, I made sure Bobby delivered the invocation on the field.

When I left the Yankees, Bobby stopped going to Old Timers Days. He said it wasn't the same, which was a compliment to me because he included me among the "old guard," even though I came along two years after he had retired.

Each year we exchange Christmas cards, and I always make note of another year passing and his record of 12 RBIs in a World Series still standing. As of 2000 it had survived for an unbelievable 40 years, longer than the Ruth or Maris single-season home run records.

When I went to work for the Atlanta Olympic Committee in 1992, Bobby called from his home in Sumter, South Carolina, and asked if he could come down and have lunch with me one day.

So we had lunch in Atlanta, and I brought the ball he had signed for me when I won that contest in 1962. And he signed his name again, 30 years later.

Maybe we'll do it one more time in 2022.

My dad and his twin sister, Sydell, were the fifth and sixth children of Ukrainian immigrants who had come to the United States after the turn of the century. All of the seven children were Brooklyn born, and, although Yiddish was my grandparents' language, the kids were all English speakers.

Every few years, rather than pay an extra $5 a month in rent, the family would move to another Brooklyn brownstone, generally in the Williamsburg neighborhood, where many Jewish people settled. My grandfather had a rag business—he would collect rags and resell them in bulk to garment manufacturers. At another time he operated a shaved ice business off a pushcart, where customers could get lemonade or orangeade from a large tank, beautifully polished and lined with lemon or orange slices. Because there were no paper cups, he used glasses, and you had to consume it there and return the glass on the spot.

My grandfather had been a horse soldier in the Russo-Japanese War of 1904–05, and this knowledge certainly helped me conjure up the image of a dashing, heroic young man on horseback.

But I only knew him as an elderly man; frail, Yiddish-speaking, and seldom rising from his recliner as he watched television hour after hour when we visited. I don't think he understood anything he saw, but I marvel today to think that he was only in his sixties at the time. He wasn't ill—people just became elderly at an earlier age back then. To borrow a Yogi-ism, "it gets late early out there."

His wife, my grandmother, died when I was just a baby, but he lived until 1963. I was always close to all of my father's brothers and sisters, and we used to have a "cousins club" at which the whole extended family would gather. My generation failed to keep that up, and I miss the regular contact with my cousins.

None of my aunts or uncles was particularly interested in sports, with the exception of Uncle Phil, who loved the ponies. He was not a betting man; he just loved the atmosphere at the track, loved standing along the rail and admiring the horses.

Aunt Syd, my father's twin, was a five-foot dynamo who, despite being among the youngest, was the matriarch of the clan. She was a dynamic businesswoman who drove big Cadillacs, dressed to kill, wore the spikiest high heels, and held opinions on everyone and everything. She was a figure to reckon with.

My father was the only one of the four boys to get drafted in World War II. He had graduated from Boys High and had gone on to work in the dispensary at Jacobs Shoe Factory in Brooklyn, distributing bandages when needed.

The Army deemed that enough of a qualification to make him a medic. So off he went to the European theater, part of General Patton's army, reaching the rank of corporal, and landing at Normandy in the great invasion.

I think the war years were the best years of his life. For a kid from Brooklyn to be off to Europe for this great adventure, with the safety of the Red Cross around his sleeve, with a French girlfriend named Trudy, to fight "the good war," it must have been a thrill. War as a thrill? To hear him tell his stories, it surely was. Yogi, who also landed at Normandy (the only major leaguer to do so), called the first night of the invasion "beautiful," with the skyrockets going off. I saw *Saving Private Ryan*; it wasn't beautiful. Maybe we were looking at two different wars.

My dad is a great and loyal friend and truly one of the biggest-hearted and nicest men you would ever want to meet. It says a lot about him to know that he and his Brooklyn buddies—Louie and Artie and Hermie and Jack and Jake and Kivie and the rest—remained friends for all of their adult lives, when most of them resettled in Florida. These were friendships of more than 75 years! One day during the war, the whole bunch of them managed to meet up at Trafalgar Square in London—they had somehow all arranged for one-day furloughs at the same time. And they all came home from the war in one piece.

After the war, my father's older brother Bill took him in and taught him the insurance business. For the next 34 years he worked as an insurance broker, a job that never created much interesting dinner conversation. He was a suit-and-tie sort of guy, one who would even keep his tie on when he mowed the lawn. The hustle and bustle of working in Manhattan could try anyone's nerves, and in his younger years he could be a little stressed out after a day's work and commute.

In 1972 he was held up in his office, the gun-toting robber throwing an overcoat over his head as he rifled the drawers for cash. (Cash in an insurance office?) My father thought he was a goner, and just a few months later he moved his office up near our suburban home in Rockland County. From that point on, he became a much mellower figure. Everyone who knew him thought he was one of the most easy going people they had ever met.

He met my mother soon after returning from the war. A mutual friend introduced them—Kivie, from that boyhood crowd of his. My mother, Celia Mann, lived in the Bronx with her parents and her two younger sisters, Selma and Ruth. If you've ever traveled by subway from Brooklyn to the Bronx, you will understand why, after two or three dates, my father had had it with the trip and asked her to marry him. He was, after all, already 30 years old.

My mother was nine years younger than my father but liked to say, "Girls mature much faster than boys." In her case, it was certainly true. Her mother worked, first in Germany and then in the United States, and as the oldest sister she had the responsibility of helping raise her two siblings. This created in her a strong work ethic and a very serious nature. She had a pretty face, which radiated when she smiled, but she did take life very seriously, and it was hard to ever find her totally relaxed.

She was born in Germany in 1925, and thus was old enough to remember seeing Hitler parade through her city, Karlsruhe, and to understand the rise of Nazism. Christian friends told her she could no longer enter their homes through the front door. Once the brightest student in her class, she was relegated to the back of the classrooms and never called upon when she raised her hand.

By the mid-'30s her parents knew it was time to leave. They had relatives in Canada and in the U.S. who could vouch for them and put up the guarantees of employment in the States, but getting an exit visa was difficult. There were a few occasions of raised hopes followed by disappointment. And the stakes were high. As history would prove, their lives could well have ended in concentration camps had they not managed to escape. But they received their approvals just before the curtain came down on emigration, which would likely have doomed them to the death camps. And so, although one could say that by leaving in 1937 they escaped Nazism and the ravages and horrors of all it represented, the Holocaust was very much a part of my mother's legacy. She was a survivor of a living horror, a survivor of one of the supreme villains of history. And as much as her life changed when she came to America, it was always a part of her.

My mother's family traveled aboard the *Aquitania*, leaving from France, and my mother's tale of awakening early in the morning to go on deck and see the Statue of Liberty could bring tears to anyone's eyes. I have videotaped both of my parents' oral histories, and she didn't disappoint—the Statue of Liberty story was a classic.

Not all her family was so fortunate. Her grandmother had actually come to the U.S. in the 1920s and then returned to Poland. She was an older woman, she found it difficult to understand new ways, and she felt compelled to return to the simpler ways of Szinewa, her hometown.

Years later, the SS rounded up the Jews in her village for shipment to a concentration camp. Despite her frailty and old age, she tried to run from the SS—and was shot and killed.

Determined to assimilate into American society and not be viewed as foreigners, my mother and her sisters decided to lose their German accents, and did. That was a remarkable achievement, followed by my mother's amazing feat of winning the English medal at Taft High School, as well as the French medal. She was a serious student who placed education above all else, and she later became an executive secretary for the school board in Rockland County, a perfect position for her. She could use all of her talents: organization, conscientiousness, and leadership, and many felt she actually ran the whole operation. (I was always aware that these were very Germanic traits, but she would never acknowledge the cultural link.)

My parents retired to Florida in 1980. One day in 1988, my mother was reading one of her many Jewish newsletters when she came upon an item inviting displaced Jewish citizens of Karlsruhe, West Germany, to visit, with a guest, all expenses paid, courtesy of the city government. An act of reparation.

My mother's eyes brightened. Despite Hitler, her memories of Karlsruhe were happy childhood ones of beautiful cobblestone streets, a town square, a pond at which you could rent a rowboat, colorful merchants, bicycles, and flowers everywhere.

"Irv," she said, "we're going."

She also rounded up her two sisters, Ruth and Selma, along with their husbands, and made it a party of six. Her mother, still active at 88 and living in Beverly Hills, would have none of it. Her memories were bitter. She had divorced her husband not long after my mother married, and every memory of her past was, sadly, a bad one.

When my mother called and told me of her plans, I knew a good story when I heard one. I immediately dashed off a letter to *People* magazine, pitching this as a story idea, and they loved it. They assigned a writer and a photographer to accompany them from Miami Airport through the whole journey. The result was an eight-page feature in the November 7, 1988, edition.

The trip was the crowning moment of my mother's life. The whole group received extraordinary red-carpet treatment. The German people were sincere in their repentance. My mother was accepting of the gesture. "It wasn't the people," she said. "It was the government, and people are taught to follow their leaders."

She was given a book on the history of Karlsruhe, which included (in German of course) a section on how the best Jewish students were suddenly mistreated and ignored—and her name was cited in the book.

They visited the site of the long since-destroyed synagogue in Karlsruhe, and my uncle Abe, a part-time cantor, led a teary-eyed group in prayer. *People* was capturing all of this.

My mother led the group to the site of their home. Remarkably, despite heavy bombing during the war, it still stood. It was a three-story building with a courtyard in front, and as the group spoke in the courtyard, an old woman on the top floor shouted down in German, "What is all of this commotion?!"

My mother looked up, apologized for the noise, and said, "Forgive us, but we used to live here."

The woman stared down and said, "Cilly Mann?" (It was my mother's name in German.) "Jacob Mann's daughter?"

"Frau Golling?" my mother responded. "Oh, my God."

The old woman had in fact been their neighbor, a lifetime ago. She hurried down the steps and they all embraced and they all cried for what should have been.

"She was a wonderful woman," my mother told *People*. "She would turn on our lights on the Sabbath, and we would give her Passover matzo, which she loved. But her husband was a very stern guy, tough, anti-Semitic. When she was with him, she avoided us all."

For sentiment, it was hard to top the meeting with Frau Golling, but another sweet moment came when my mother went rowing on the city's lake, just as she had as a little girl. Her life had come full circle. There was a sense of completion to the unfinished childhood.

When she returned, she told me that she would like to visit again.

"Mom," I said, "I wouldn't do it. It could never be the same as this trip."

And she never went back, which was just as well. It was a perfect, perfect memory.

Four years after her return, she was diagnosed with ovarian cancer. It is a horrible cancer, for it is hard to detect and moves quickly.

The doctors told us that she had "two to three years" to live. But being Celia Appel, she was determined to beat it. She did what she had done with every challenge ever thrown at her—she read everything she could read, overruled doctors, loaded up on vitamins, sought alternative medicine, became totally knowledgeable about her illness, and fought it like the warrior she was.

And every now and then, the blood counts and all of those other numbers they record to measure your health would turn good. On at least two occasions, the doctor shook his head and said, "I think you are on the road to beating this."

But in the end, she lived with it for two and a half years, exactly what the original prognosis had been. The disease was stronger than even my mother's incredible will.

Her final weeks were spent in her Florida condo, resigned to her fate, bringing things to closure. She read the manuscript I had written on 19th century baseball star King Kelly. As the end drew near I made a final visit with my children to see her. She asked me to close the door. And she said, "I would like to hear the eulogy you've prepared for me."

"Oh, Mom," I said. "I haven't prepared a eulogy—you're gonna beat this."

But we both knew better, and Mom took no bullshit, even though she would never use that word.

We looked at each other and I knew I was in a corner. I nodded; I went to my suitcase and took it out. She was going to give me one last edit.

I stood at the foot of her bed. I smiled and told her that "these things tend to be pretty positive, you know." She smiled for the first time during the visit.

And I read her the eulogy. *How many of us would like to hear our eulogies?* I thought. Why not give her this moment?

She had a few corrections, a few dates were wrong, but she was pleased. And in this odd moment, so was I. Pleased that I had had the good sense to grant her this wish.

The kids and I went back to New York, but just a few days later, she knew it was time to leave her bed for the trip to the hospice, which cared for her in her final hours. She had loved her retirement in Wynmoor Village, and although her voice was weak, she asked the ambulance driver if he could take her on one last drive on the road that circled the peaceful retirement community. She was on a gurney and could only see the sky, but it was her last wish.

She died the next day at 69.

She was, as we say in sports, an impact player.

After my discovery of baseball with the 1955 World Series, my mother brought home an unofficial 1956 Yankee Yearbook from the corner candy store when I was home from school with the measles. I devoured every page, particularly those with the Mick. This was my team.

Mel Allen, on WPIX, Channel 11, began to teach me the game. He may not have known I was listening, but he always seemed to know he had new fans just discovering baseball. He could point out that the umpire raises his hand for a strike, and does nothing for a ball, and I don't think it patronized his longtime listeners. For an awakening young fan, he was the professor, and a grand one he was. It was like learning democracy from Jefferson and Madison.

I loved Mel, just as Dodger fans hated him. His delivery was as effortless as a Whitey Ford changeup, as smooth as the ice-cold Ballantine Beer he would lovingly describe. He'd get excited about the ball rolling "all the way to the auxiliary scoreboard!" He'd explain the infield fly rule in perfect detail and tell us that no one had ever hit a fair ball out of Yankee Stadium. He'd tell us the story of Yogi Berra dropping Ted Williams' two-out foul ball in Allie Reynolds' no-hitter (only to catch the next one and save the day), and he'd tell us about Williams playing a doubleheader on the final day of the '41 season rather than sit on his .400 average (he wound up at .406), and . . . well, I just went out and got my Ph.D. in baseball from Professor Allen.

When I went to work for the Yankees in '68, he had been sacked four years earlier, and still everyone was asking, "Why!?" It was the most asked question I encountered in my time with the Yankees, until it was finally surpassed by "What's it like to work for George Steinbrenner?"

In his exile, Mel became a far humbler man than the one seasoned Yankee employees remembered. He had been, it seems, somewhat of a tyrant and fairly difficult to work with. But the firing had leveled him, and the Mel Allen I came to know as an adult was a sad figure—still with a great voice, very emotional, and very likeable, but clearly very humbled. "I wear my heart on my sleeve," he said to me, not long after I had introduced myself and expressed my childhood admiration. This was a far cry from the man I had learned might have rapped his statistician over the head with the *Little Red Book of Baseball* if some fact had been given in error.

I didn't always know where I was going during conversations with Mel, but the adventure was usually worth it. One year he had heart surgery at the University of Alabama Medical Center, not far from where he was born. It was a fine facility, but there were plenty of good ones in New York, and Mel had lived in Connecticut for decades. So when I next saw him and asked him how he was doing, I asked, "Why did you go to Alabama for the surgery, Mel?" I thought he was going to say something about going back to his roots.

"Oh, that's a great, great medical facility," he answered. "In fact, you know who had surgery there just a few years ago? Milburn Stone, you know, the actor."

"Milburn Stone?" I said. "You mean the guy who played Doc on *Gunsmoke*? You thought it was a good place because the actor who played Doc on *Gunsmoke* trusted it? And isn't he dead?"

"Well, yes," said Mel, "but it's a helluva place."

Mel died in June 1996. I don't know any other media figures who could have drawn Joe DiMaggio, Phil Rizzuto, Yogi Berra, and Whitey Ford—in yarmulkes—to a funeral in Connecticut, but he did. The great voice of my youth lived to overcome the anguish of his firing, to bask in the love of his fans, and to even earn the admiration of those players he had broadcast. He had been just as important to the legacy of the great Yankee franchise, in his own way, as they had each been.

Another event that secured my passion as a baseball fan was the day my father brought home a full box of Topps baseball cards. Dad knew someone who worked for Topps, and here was a box of '56 cards. I treasured them. To this day, if you name a player from that era, the image of his card flashes through my mind, whether it is Ted Lepcio or Dave Pope or the great Mickey himself. I would invent all kinds of ways to sort my collection. I'd play imaginary games with them, and I'd flip them with friends, and I'd put them in my bicycle spokes, and I'd scale them against walls. I'd keep "standings" based on which team had the most cards in my collection. There seemed to be no limit to what you could do with the cards, and the last thing we ever thought about was their cash value.

But one day, I decided to sell them. I don't know what got into me, but a burst of eight-year-old entrepreneurism overcame me. I set up a cardboard box on the street and sold my collection for probably $5, a lot of money back then.

It took about an hour for my folly to sink in. I started to cry. My precious cards were gone, I had this stupid bunch of coins to show for it, and no interest in starting a coin collection.

I suppose my mother could have practiced "tough love" and taught me the hard lesson about making my bed and lying in it, but instead she was moved by my tears, and God bless her, she began calling every mother on the street whose son's name I could recall, and she bought back as many cards as she could for me. I may have lost a Mantle or two in the transaction (maybe a quick $10,000 today), but I had certainly learned a lesson in life—some things are far more important than money, especially if you have no critical need for it.

So I got my '56 cards back, and yes—I've still got them. I've got all of my childhood cards, because my mother was the one who *didn't* throw them out. And although I have sold other memorabilia to help finance my children's college educations, the cards haven't moved. I learned my lesson.

And when I would, years later, serve as a spokesman for Topps, I would find myself explaining why there were cards that were worth hundreds—thousands, in fact—and I would say, "If not for all the mothers who threw out cards, this might never have been."

When it was apparent that my interest in baseball was getting serious, my father decided it was time to take me to my first game. I have long forgotten the date or the opponent, but the site was Ebbets Field. Egad, we were going to see the Dodgers!

I was pretty smug about it. He had picked up reserved tickets at the Dodgers office on Montague Street, which happened to be the very street on which his insurance business was located. Larry King likes to tell the story of that Montague Street ticket window "where no matter when you went, or who was behind the glass, the name tag always said 'Shaughnessy.'"

My father was born in Brooklyn in 1916, which was, coincidentally, a pennant-winning year for the Brooklyn Robins, managed by Wilbert Robinson and featuring an outfielder named Casey Stengel. Babe Ruth had been a pitching star for the Red Sox against the Brooklyns.

Despite the fact that he had grown up as a native-born Brooklynite, spoke the language, and was surrounded by other native sons, baseball sort of bypassed my father and his crowd. So, as it happened, my first game at Ebbets Field in 1956 was also Irving Appel's first game at

Ebbets Field, at the ripe age of 40.

I have three memories of that visit. The first was finding the rotund Roy Campanella very amusing, since we were seated behind him all afternoon.

Second, I remember how very white the Dodger uniforms were, something that to this day I admire. It is a shade of white that is almost off the charts.

Finally, there was the grass. St. John's Place had little grass, just patches on the front courtyards, and while we did go to Prospect Park on occasion, I was wholly unprepared for the expanse of the green outfield in Ebbets Field. As we walked up the ramps to get to our seats, the green slivers kept unfolding, teasing us as we climbed, with still another turn up another ramp to our seats, and still more green revealed. When I later discovered the much larger green of the Yankee Stadium outfield, I was in total awe. I had never seen anything so beautiful. I later came to marvel at the vastness of the real estate—how three men covered all of that territory on which a dozen or more homes could have been built. To this day I am always swept away by the beauty and vastness of major league outfields. And I have never much liked the style of mowing the grass in patterns. It always looked better to me as one vast carpet.

I don't know whether the Dodgers won or lost that day, but I do know that it was my only time in Ebbets Field. I went on, of course, to embrace the Yankees and ultimately to work for them. But what I missed with the Dodgers haunts me to this day. I can see now that if ever there was a team to fall in love with, it was "Dem Bums." Ebbets Field has taken on a nostalgic charm, which romanticizes its actual discomfort, but the aura was genuine.

In 1960, Aunt Syd, my father's twin, was ready to move to a bigger house with Uncle Jerry, and they sold their home in Monsey, New York, to my parents. It was about 25 miles northwest of New York City, across the Hudson River in Rockland County. There we settled into what I came to consider my hometown.

At Spring Valley High I was sports editor of the school paper, and it was apparent that my aptitude was much greater in this area than as a laborer. In shop class, while everyone was constructing elaborate pieces of furniture, I was building bookends—one piece of wood nailed to another to form a perfect L. It took me an entire semester, and then they didn't work. I couldn't make bookends that worked.

The hamlet in which we lived—Monsey—was evolving into an ultra-orthodox Hasidic Jewish settlement. Today it is fully converted; then, it was about 20 percent Hasidic. There was no intermingling—they thought of us as unworthy sinners, a disgrace to the religion. We thought of them as strange aliens in black coats, and we went to public school and they to Yeshiva. They would stare at us when we broke Sabbath laws and drove the car or played ball on Saturday. We stared back at their odd fashion and messy lawns. We should all have been more ecumenical, but it wasn't to be.

My move to the suburbs made me no less of a Yankee fan, for there was still Mel Allen, with Red Barber and Phil Rizzuto, the "three-ring team" (for Ballantine Beer's logo), teaching me the game on channel 11. In those days the Yankees televised about 136 out of 154 games. You couldn't watch 136 games with those announcers and not come away an expert. Rizzuto was just starting out after his playing career ended, and tended to defer to the two powerful broadcasters, but he was fun and brought his love of the game to the booth and passed it on to his listeners. I can still remember his work in the Yankees' 22-inning victory in Detroit on a Sunday evening in 1962, and how he made it so entertaining.

There were early signs that I was going to be involved in baseball and, somehow, in telling its story. I'm sure a lot of kids had my passion, but I think I took it to deeper levels than most did at an early age.

I think it became clear that I was going to write more baseball than I was going to play when a friend and I took it upon ourselves to compile a list of every Yankee there ever was.

Today, such a list is easily found in the Yankee press guide, but then, it did not exist and was very difficult to assemble. We managed to discover old rosters and booklets and did the best we could, but we probably got only about 40 percent of them. Still, it was a good exercise for projects I would one day do for a living!

There were some big changes going on with me when we moved to the suburbs in 1960 and I entered my teen years. For one, I stunk in Little League. Reaching the majors was no longer an option if I couldn't even connect off a Steve Berman slowball.

In school, I was no longer a whiz. Although in elementary school in New York I had probably been at the very top of my class, suddenly in seventh grade I took French and didn't have a clue to what was going on. In fact, I wasn't exactly tearing up the course in my other subjects either. I was becoming an average student, not especially motivated.

I liked to read, was developing a deep interest in current events, and began to compile my own encyclopedia of important facts in my head. Name the presidents in order? No problem. I even got all the fat ones in order from the turn of the century. Actor who starred in *Life of Riley* before William Bendix? Jackie Gleason. Original seven Project Mercury astronauts? Knew 'em. Only actor to star in three different television hits in three decades? Robert Conrad. Kennedy's cabinet? Knew them all, even the Postmaster General. First year the World Series movie was shot in color? 1960, of course. Gold supply in the world? Enough to build 20 percent of the Washington Monument from the base—and no more.

I had a mind born to play *Jeopardy*. Give me a gift certificate to a bookstore and I'll come home with an entertaining reference book.

I came to realize that I was a walking collection of factoids but was not really as smart as they had led me to believe in sixth grade. I can name all the defeated vice presidential candidates back to the New Deal, and I can tell you what year every number one song on the *Billboard* charts was recorded. But I haven't understood the plot of a James Bond movie since *Goldfinger*, have no idea how planes fly, ships float, or CDs give us music. Spellcheck is the best invention for mankind since penicillin, a word that makes my point at once.

I knew my baseball. I managed to learn so much about the game that it didn't matter if the player had been dead for 50 years or was the starting right fielder on the Senators—I knew them all. I could have conversations with men who had seen Bill Terry play and could hold my own with them. The most important books that launched me on this kick were the Turkin–Thompson *Encyclopedia of Baseball*, John Rosenberg's *The Story of Baseball*, The Elias Sports Bureau's *Little Red Book of Baseball*, and *The Mickey Mantle Story* by Gene Schoor, from which I did book reports in four consecutive years. There were also the Chip Hilton baseball novels by Clair Bee.

I was also a *Sporting News* subscriber beginning in 1962, and I haven't missed an issue since. It cost $12 a year to subscribe when I started, and you got a free *Official Baseball Guide* thrown in. The first *Guide* I got was in '62, and I have since built the collection backward and forward so that it now ranges from the first issue of 1876 to the present. I don't think there are too many individuals with the full run.

My best times were ballgames on summer nights. With Ricky and Jeff Krebs, and with Steve Berman, we would pair off for hundreds of games of stickball (with a tennis ball, on the street), or wiffle ball (on the lawn next to the Krebs' house). I more than held my own at that level, and they were nights that would go on long past sundown, playing only by the glow of streetlights.

One summer Steve agreed to feed Rusty, our German shepherd, while we went on a family vacation around New York State. Our trip took us to Cooperstown, my first visit to the Hall of Fame, where, in appreciation for feeding Rusty, my mother bought Steve a Willie Mays figurine made by Hartland Plastics. Mays was Steve's favorite player.

If you are a collector, you might know that those Hartland figures can now sell for nearly a thousand dollars each.

In 1992, when I was living in Atlanta and working for the Olympics, I got a phone call one day from an old neighbor who was now working in Atlanta as well. He had seen my name in the newspaper.

"Marty? Hey it's me, Steve Berman!"

It had been about 20 years since I'd heard his voice.

"Berman?" I said. "When are you planning on returning my Hartland Mays? That was just a loaner, you know!"

He laughed, and said he still had it and he knew how much it was worth. And he said that if I wanted it back, I'd have to produce Rusty.

Unfortunately, Rusty the Wonder Pooch was no longer with us. Berman still has the Hartland Mays, and it continues to appreciate in value.

Jeff Krebs and I got involved in a writing project in 1963 that would become my first book. Although I still supported the Yankees, and his roots were with the Dodgers, both of us could not help but be captivated by the early New York Mets. Casey Stengel had made them such a loveable bunch of losers that they had stolen everyone's hearts. And so, for their second season, we put aside our loyalties and decided to watch or listen to every single Mets game and write a diary of the '63 season. Marvelous Marv Throneberry, Choo Choo Coleman, Jimmy Piersall, Duke Snider—they were all there.

I pick it up today and still laugh out loud. It was never published, but a delightful British editor at Doubleday, Naomi Burton, found it so interesting that two teens would write this book that she insisted on meeting with us. She said the book wasn't quite ready for prime time, but she gave us Stan Musial's new autobiography as a gift and told us to look up a top literary agent in town, Sterling Lord.

Lord represented Jimmy Breslin, who had written *Can't Anybody Here Play This Game*, a terrific book about the Mets' first season; the title came from a Stengel quote.

It seemed that Breslin's book was about to come out in paperback, and he didn't have time to update it for the '63 season. "Would we," asked Lord, "agree to let Breslin use portions of our book to update his?"

Well, that sounded pretty first-class to us, and we said, "Sure."

So the manuscript was passed to Breslin at his *Herald-Tribune* office. And there it sat for over a year. He never looked at it, his paperback edition was never updated, and when the *Herald-Tribune* folded, a nice secretary called to say she had found it and was sending it back.

The manuscript still exists, but the closest it ever came to notoriety was to reside in Jimmy Breslin's desk for a year, unopened.

Around this time I also began to think that I wanted to be a baseball announcer. Mel Allen, Red Barber, and Phil Rizzuto were my influences, although I confess to enjoying the work of Lindsey Nelson, Bob Murphy, and Ralph Kiner of the Mets. When I hear Murphy on the radio today, it takes me back to my early teen years, when it seemed that all that mattered was baseball in the afternoon, with puffy cumulous clouds hovering over the ballpark.

I started to practice this craft. I would turn down the sound on the television, set up a tape recorder with all my reference books and even a three-minute egg timer, which Red Barber said he used in order to remember to give the score. It never sounded very authentic without crowd noise in the background, but I thought I was getting pretty good at it, and really felt this might be my profession one day.

In fact, in my junior high school yearbook it said "Mel Allen Step Aside" next to my photo. That was 1963. Mel did step aside the following year, too soon for me. But 25 years later I became executive producer of those same Yankee telecasts. Not a bad junior high forecast, all things considered.

I became interested in journalism through the *New York World Telegram & Sun*, a broadsheet that my father brought home from work each day. I would spread it out on the living-room floor and expand my baseball knowledge through its pages. Willard Mullin was their brilliant cartoonist, and he had a different comic character for each of the 20 teams. I loved sports cartoonists—I collected Charlie McGill's work from the *Bergen Record*, and I so enjoyed Bill Gallo in the *Daily News* that I later asked him to draw my kids for a Christmas card, which he did!

Dan Daniel was the writer I first connected with. In addition to his columns, he would write a regular "Ask Daniel" column, from which I learned a great deal about baseball. He never seemed to tire of answering the same questions ("Has anyone ever hit a fair ball out of Yankee Stadium?"), and he seemed to know his stuff. He had been the baseball editor of the *Telegram* since 1924 and was respected as one of the game's great historians.

Although the *Telegram* was my "paper of choice," I had a love for the diversity out there. I knew the *Daily News* style, with its small Beacon Wax ads on the page with Ed Sullivan's column; its great centerfold with exciting pictures; its "Bulldog" edition, featuring partial line scores of night games still in progress at press time; its *Sunday Magazine* with color shots of the Yankees; and its must-read columns by Dick Young and Jimmy Powers.

The *Magazine* gave you colorful home-team schedules each spring to hang on the wall, and every other year they would give you "Casey at the Bat," including a wonderful illustration of mighty Casey whiffing.

The Yankee color shots were usually taken during spring training, and I came to recognize the trees in the background as the Yankees' St. Petersburg training site. When I first visited St. Petersburg with the Yankees years later (it was then home for the Mets' spring training), I made a side trip to Miller Huggins Field, where those trees still resided. It required a special trip, because the exhibition games were played at Al Lang Field, and only practices were held at what by then was called Huggins-Stengel Field. But I found the trees.

The *New York Post* had great sports columns and a different slant on the game, being an afternoon paper. America's afternoon papers are one of the great casualties of the latter part of the 20th century.

I found the *Times* a little over my head, and it didn't become an important part of my day until college. Now, no matter where in the country I am, my day starts with *The New York Times*. It has become a bit of a running joke, in fact, that people always seem to spot me carrying it.

I finally came to realize that I was becoming only as smart as the *Times* would permit me to be. That was a little confining. My day still begins with the *Times*, but I have done my best to listen to other voices as well.

I took my interest in journalism with me to our school newspaper. In high school, our style was to have headlines "flush left and right," meaning that a careful character count had to be employed to make sure all the heads filled the width of the columns, and that lines were still grammatically broken in the proper manner.

Somehow, I had a gift for this. I not only presided over sports coverage but wrote all the paper's headlines, and I did them all in one take. I could feel the character count and could get SENIOR PROM SLATED FOR JUNE 6 to fit perfectly in one try.

I attended high school journalism seminars at Columbia University and received journalism certificates from the National Quill & Scroll Society and from the *Bergen Record*. I felt very comfortable in this world and, for a long time, assumed that journalism would be my career.

In 10th grade I became Spring Valley High's "stringer" for both the *Rockland Journal-News* and the *Bergen Record*. That meant I covered all our team sports and phoned in the results to the papers. The first game I ever had to cover in this capacity was Spring Valley at Sleepy Hollow football in Tarrytown, New York. With no one having prepared me for the assignment, I chose to cover it from the sideline rather than the press box. Closer to the action, I thought.

Well, from field level, I surrendered all my perspective and was hopelessly lost. I had the final score right, but not much else. It was an inauspicious start, but I got through it and grew more comfortable, whether I was covering soccer or wrestling or track or basketball.

Track meets were surprisingly fun. So much going on, all at once, and all very intense. We had a track star at Spring Valley named Dave Mumme (pronounced "Mumy") who set a state pole vault record, which was a thrilling moment in my coverage. Mumme was heroic even as a teenager. He had that star quality that I would later find in Mickey Mantle and few others. Walking the halls of the high school, he had a presence. He came from a military family, and he went to Air Force Academy after Spring Valley, scored a touchdown on a nationally televised game, and then I never heard about him again. But I consider him to have been the first "star" I covered.

The *Journal-News*, the Gannett daily in Rockland, liked my work, and although I was still in high school, I was elevated to a bylined reporter. This was a pretty amazing feat for 16. The work took me into the office in Nyack, and I began to feel the excitement of a newsroom and to understand its workings. When the Associated Press machine would ring, you knew a bulletin was coming in. They were heady times.

I'd work the sports desk at night, taking bowling scores or whatever else came across. In bowling, if a player was absent, he was credited with his average for each game, so that a full team would "compete." I didn't know this. So one day I got the bowling results and saw that two players on the same team had bowled the exact same scores in three consecutive games. I thought this was pretty amazing, and, not only did I write a little story about it, I thought I would phone it in to the AP, thinking they would find it quite unusual as well. Fortunately, I had a senior editor over me who managed to catch my ignorance in time.

I also began to work at a commercial radio station when I was 16— WRKL, Rockland's first radio station. It was owned by a former engineer from WNEW radio in New York, Al Spiro, and this had been his dream: his own station. During a class visit to the station, I told him I'd love to work in radio someday. He said, "You'll start Saturday; be here at eight."

And there I was, co-host with him of "Teenage Hot Line," during which callers could phone in and discuss teenage concerns. It was the very early days of talk radio—the technology of bringing calls in (and of the seven-second delay) was quite something, and the show was a bit of a hit. I was on it for 67 weeks.

Al Spiro was great; he would let me try anything. I read the five-minute hourly newscasts during the show, prepared by our news director (who did not like my doing this at all), and one day Al let me interrupt regular programming with the bulletin that Winston Churchill had died.

Then he sent me out to do "Man in the Street" interviews, such as, "What do you think of Governor Rockefeller's plan to impose a state sales tax?" And I covered an antiwar march in Spring Valley. (I got there at 10—but it had been changed to noon. No one told me, and there was no one to ask, so I phoned in my report that the parade hadn't attracted many marchers.)

A big assignment was a powerboat race on the Hudson River. I worked with the station's sports director, and we broadcast from a light-house in Nyack. I hated ladders and heights, and was happy just to reach my perch safely. The sports director only wanted to read the commercials, and he trusted me with the race reports.

As predicted in the morning paper, the leader for most of the after-noon was the favorite, and each time he'd whiz by, I'd mark him off on my clipboard and broadcast that "Pee Wee Della Russo remains the leader."

Late in the race, I was ready with my report but hadn't seen Pee Wee go by. I figured I had missed him—it was a little foggy and getting darker—so I reported that he was still ahead, nearing the end. We had no telephone communication with race officials, and I sure wasn't going to go up and down that ladder any more than I had to.

We signed off declaring Pee Wee the winner, and with the sports director patting me on the back and reminding listeners to enjoy their Thanksgiving dinner at the Mt. Ivy Diner on Route 202.

It was a nice feeling of accomplishment—my first live sports broad-cast and the thrill of radio. Unfortunately, my mood turned grim the next day when the *Journal-News* reported on page one that a horrible accident had occurred and that Pee Wee Della Russo had drowned.

I expected to be reprimanded or perhaps fired, but nobody ever said anything. Not even the sports director. I finally concluded that no one was listening—not at home, and not even at the station. And not even my sports director. He was just polishing his ad copy for the Mt. Ivy Diner!

So I got away with one there. Poor Pee Wee. At least he had one last victory before he left us.

BASEBALL
GRANDFATHERS

People don't always realize how spoiled we New York fans were back in the '50s and '60s. Assuming that there was still a lot of New York interest in the '59 Los Angeles Dodgers, and even a carryover to the Dodgers of '65–'66, there was a New York–based team in every single World Series between 1949 and 1966, a span of 18 seasons.

In 1967 the streak ended when Boston played St. Louis, and around that time it was common to hear that baseball had become stale, passe, second to football, no longer the national pastime. In fact, I was in college then, and I remember going to the dorm basement to catch Game 2, only to find that everyone was watching an early-season Giants football game and I had no support to switch channels. What a shock that was. But I always tried to remove myself from the "national pastime" debate, because I always felt that for a New Yorker, of course the game had declined! No New York team in the World Series? Beam me up, Scottie!

But make no mistake about it: baseball in the late '60s *was* a declining game. The great stars of the '50s and '60s were fading away—Mantle, Mays, Banks, Maris, Mathews, Frank Robinson, Koufax, Drysdale, Clemente—all would be gone within a few years of one another. Only Henry Aaron seemed to linger. Yes, stars like Reggie Jackson, Tom Seaver, and Johnny Bench were coming up, but other great young athletes were moving to basketball or football. The talent pool was no longer going to baseball. You could make a lot of money in other sports.

The All-Star rosters contained a number of players who in another time might have been considered journeymen. And with that came diminishing fan interest.

While I was working on a book project with Bowie Kuhn in the mid-'80s, he even suggested that baseball's comeback in the late '70s and '80s had been accomplished "without us ever finding another Mickey Mantle."

It is almost impossible to explain to someone born after 1960 the difference between baseball's hold on society "way back when" and its position today. There was a time in this nation when no one could dispute that baseball was the national pastime. When you see photos of thousands of fans standing in the centers of their towns watching scoreboards tell them the progression of the World Series via Western Union; when you think of how so many people knew the names of all 400 major leaguers (and their batting averages), or how deeply into our culture the game penetrated—not even momentary resurgences like the McGwire-Sosa season of '98 approach it.

The term *keeping score at home* was real. People kept their own box scores when they took in a game, whether in the ballpark or in front of TVs or radios. Today, only the crowd in the press box keeps it up. Fans may have a general awareness of what 6 *to* 4 *to* 3 means, but not in the sense that they ever write it onto a scorecard.

I often met many people who told me that for them interest faded when "the great DiMaggio" retired. I met many who left the game after the Dodgers and Giants left town.   Baseball wasn't quite the shared experience it had been.

Expansion began to make it impossible to know all the players, and, later, free agency made it nearly impossible to have the same players back each year. Football, basketball, and hockey, plus the competition from dozens of television stations, many with live sports from around the country, eroded the "home team" concept and made rooting an occasional event, often saved only for championship seasons.

It was, in short, a tough period for baseball when I entered college in the fall of 1966.

My college years were spent in the small central New York city of Oneonta, at the state university. Oneonta was home to a Yankee farm team in the New York–Penn League, run by the town's former mayor, Sam Nader. Sam ran the only team in organized baseball that didn't serve beer to the fans.

"It's not that I'm a prohibitionist," he said. "I just didn't like the fans getting rowdy and saying bad things to the players. It's a small park, the players hear everything. We're a family town."

I had no connection to the team when I was in school, because the New York–Penn League was a summer league, and the games were played during our summer breaks.

Nor did I have much connection to the Baseball Hall of Fame, 19 miles northeast in Cooperstown. Baseball was passe in the '60s when I was in school, and I never found many people interested in visiting the Hall with me. I may have been the only student to take a date to the Hall of Fame.

Still, I hadn't lost my interest in the game. I had first visited the Hall in 1962 while on vacation with my family (the trip when Berman got the Mays Hartland statue). As a souvenir, I purchased the full set of black-and-white postcards of the plaques. I hung them over my bed in order of election. I looked forward each year to mailing off a quarter and getting the new batch. It's amazing to think that I would later have a hand in writing them.

I went to the Hall of Fame one day during college and met Lee Allen, the historian. Lee was one of the great students of the game and, although he died before its publication, one of the guiding lights behind the massive baseball encyclopedia, which Macmillan published in 1969. Having read a number of Lee's books—100 Years of Baseball, The World Series, The American League, The National League, and his "Cooperstown Corner" columns in The Sporting News, I was well prepared to chat him up about the game. He was thrilled that he had such an interested listener, and we shared a very pleasant afternoon together.

"Come any time you want," he said. "Call first—I'll make sure to leave you a ticket."

I continued to visit the Hall of Fame from time to time with my roommate, Buddy Mandell, who was also from Spring Valley High School and who had been my friend for years.

At Oneonta I became aware that only three students received subscriptions to The Sporting News. Buddy and I were two of them. The fact that we were roommates didn't matter; there was no way we could have shared a copy. It consumed us. Our favorite columnist was Joe Falls of the Detroit Free Press. We could keep up with Dick Young and Jim Murray through its pages as well.

Buddy and I were swept up by the powerful news events of 1968. Our obsession with baseball didn't prevent us from being aware of the volatile world of that time.

I was, in fact, the editor in chief of the weekly campus newspaper, which was a very political position to hold at that time. You couldn't put the White Rose Ball on page one—you had to pay attention to the draft and the war and the assassinations and civil rights—and growing student demands for the right to be treated as adults.

One week brought so many changes to our remote campus—the elimination of curfews, permission for women to visit men's rooms, students on disciplinary panels—that I just ran a tabloid-sized headline, MASSIVE REFORMS SWEEP CAMPUS.

Although I was liberal by upbringing and by conscience, I was lapped many times over by the campus radicals, who were small in number but vocal in their outrage over the war and assorted domestic atrocities, mostly matters of basic human rights. I was determined to run the newspaper as I was brought up thinking a newspaper should be run—the who, what, when, where, and why, presented thoughtfully and fact-checked. My influence was, of course, *The New York Times*. I edited each week's paper with an image of the *Times* in my mind. I interviewed Bobby Kennedy when he visited the campus. I covered a riotous appearance by American Nazi Party leader George Lincoln Rockwell. (When he was assassinated a few years later, I did a front-page story about his Oneonta appearance for the *Journal-News*.)

The radical bunch wanted to use the paper to decry Lyndon Johnson and his advisors, to attack the Vietnam War, and to fight other global issues. I maintained that the campus paper was not the proper instrument for this. But by the spring of my year as editor, they managed to bring me up on censorship charges before the Student Senate. The senate cleared me, but it was an enlightening moment. I came out feeling not vindicated or heroic, but actually questioning my own principles. I was awakening to the concept that the events going on "out there" were in fact going on "here" too, and that perhaps there was a place for them in the student paper. I won the "impeachment," but I came out of it a broader thinker. They had made some valid points, and perhaps argued them better than I had.

At Oneonta, Buddy was my sports editor on the *State Times*, so we were not only roommates but also working partners on the paper. At the start of the year, the sports editor was a fellow whom everyone called Fumunda John. Fumunda John had the greatest baseball memory I have ever seen in my life. He memorized schedules!

"Fumunda," I'd say, "Cincinnati Reds, 1958."

"Easy," he'd reply. "Starting April fifteenth, home opener, Philadelphia. Two off days. Then three in Pittsburgh. One in Philly. Home for two with Milwaukee. Four-game weekend series with the Pirates, doubleheader on Sunday. Off day. Two with the Cards at home. You want May?"

I never saw anything like it. He simply cracked the code. He understood the East–West movements of the schedule makers. He had an incredible mind for this. He got two subscriptions to *The Sporting News*— one to read, one to save in mint condition. He looked like John Belushi. He could be pretty scary-looking in the morning. It was in the morning that I chose to fire him as sports editor and replace him with Buddy.

It was justified. He was my sports columnist and he hadn't written a sports column—or edited the sports page—in over a month. But it was one of the scariest moments of my young career. And Fumunda John never spoke to me again.

So Buddy and I moved on. Sometimes important things would keep our minds active. One night, the lights were out when I said, "Mandell, for the life of me I can't think of the name of the Phillies relief pitcher from a few years ago, when they almost won the pennant."

Buddy's mind was similarly blocked. After about three or four minutes we had pretty much decided that we weren't going to come up with the name, nor were we going to lose any sleep over it.

"Well, good night."

"'Night."

About three hours later—three hours of total silence—a voice came out of the dark from his corner of the room.

"Was his first name Jack?"

"BALDSCHUN!!!" I screamed, and we both jumped out of bed and danced around the room in total happiness. Now we could sleep.

One cold night in Oneonta, temperature well below zero, Buddy and I were driving home on a dark and deserted road well past midnight. Suddenly, his car got a flat tire. The ground was frozen, the snow was piled high, and here we were, in all our misery, about to attempt to change the tire. A real "Dad?" moment.

One big problem—the lug nuts were machine bolted on and were determined not to move. The frigid air enhanced their seal, and the two of us could not make them budge. We were, it seemed, doomed.

Suddenly, headlights appeared in the distance, the first car in more than 15 minutes. The car pulled up alongside us, the window opened, and a friendly voice said, "You guys need any help?"

In a tribute to the manners taught by our parents, we answered in unison, "No, thanks just the same, we're fine."

Idiots. We were nowhere close to fine. We were in big trouble. As the window closed and the car began to pull away, I said to Buddy, "Wasn't that Coach Fodero?"

It was. Coach Fodero was Oneonta's gymnastics coach. His biceps were legendary. He could have loosened the lug nuts with his toes while doing an iron cross.

Idiots.

I was a political science major in college and was giving some thought to moving toward pre-law. My favorite course was Constitutional Law. I loved the logic of the writings of the Supreme Court justices, whether they were writing a minority or a majority opinion. I thought that if law school could give me a mind like that, it wouldn't even matter if I practiced law. It might even make me a better journalist.

But after my freshman year, my course would forever change.

I was home for the summer, listening to *Sgt. Pepper's Lonely Hearts Club Band* and preparing for a three-week visit to relatives in Los Angeles, when I got the idea to write a letter to the Yankees asking for a summer job.

Everything that has happened to me since, including the opportunity to write this book, comes from that afternoon at our Royal typewriter, when I prepared the following letter to Bob Fishel, the Yankees' public relations director.

7 Lenore Avenue
Monsey, New York 10952
August 5, 1967

Mr. Robert O. Fishel
c/o Yankee Stadium
Bronx, New York 10451

Dear Mr. Fishel:

This letter may set some sort of record for "earliest application by a right-handed typist," but this is more of a preliminary inquiry than a formal application.

I am currently 19 years old and a sophomore at State University College at Oneonta. I am Editor-in-Chief of our weekly campus newspaper, after having been a sports editor for six consecutive years, dating back through junior high, high school, and my freshman year. In addition, I have worked under my own byline as a sportswriter for the Rockland Journal-News—year round during my final two years in high school, and currently as a summer employee before I return to college.

I have long had an interest in public relations and journalism (I used to do a weekly broadcast of telephone conversations over WRKL radio), and I was now wondering if the Yankee Public

Relations Office might have room for, if I may use the word, an "ambitious" worker for next summer.

I realize that it is quite a while before next summer appears, but, as I will be returning to Oneonta shortly, I was wondering if I might be able to set up an appointment with you either this summer, or on a convenient time during the school year so that I may plan to come to New York and discuss it with you. Primarily at the moment however, I was just interested in knowing whether such a job might be available, so that I may compete for it.

Thanking you for your time, and hoping to hear from you shortly, I am

Respectfully,
Martin Appel

Frankly, I never thought I would get a response. I mean, these were the Yankees. They must get hundreds of letters like this. So certain was I of no response that by the time I got back from Los Angeles, I had forgotten about the letter.

Then the phone rang. Connie Fernandez, Bob Fishel's long-time secretary, was calling to see if I could come in to visit on August 29.

"Yes," I told her, "I can do that."

I wore my only suit, and a properly conservative tie, borrowed from my father. I headed down the Palisades Parkway with my mind racing. Would I be expected to do all the talking? How would I begin?

I was probably an hour early, so I just walked around the block a few times. Down Babe Ruth Plaza, across Ruppert Place, over by the Jerome Cafeteria, Manny's Baseball Land, under the El, past the bleacher entrance, past the Yankee Tavern. The Red Sox were in town, the "Impossible Dream" Red Sox of '67, but that game was hours away. There was stillness to the morning. The walk was not calming me down.

I reported to the switchboard, an old-fashioned black switchboard as in a Jimmy Cagney movie. Anne and Rita were the operators. They took a phone message for Steve Whitaker, a young outfielder of whom much was expected. Another was a call for Arthur Dede, a veteran Yankee scout, whom only someone like me, who read all the scouts' names in the Yankee Yearbook, would consider a celebrity. Then they summoned Kathy Adams, an adorable redheaded secretary in the PR office, to fetch me.

Down the stairs I walked—the concrete stairs to the basement of Yankee Stadium, where the public relations office stood apart from the other offices. I had a black loose-leaf binder with me, containing my clippings from the *Journal-News*. The Yankees had only put offices in the ballpark a year before. Prior to that, the organization was housed near the Plaza Hotel, in the Squibb Building at 745 Fifth Avenue, and the executives would commute uptown for the game after the workday. Out of loyalty to the landlord or whatever, Bob Fishel spent many of the years I knew him searching drugstores around the American League for any remaining tubes of Squibb toothpaste he could find.

Fishel's office was about 10 x 12, with a large desk, and a messy credenza behind it. On a small stand was a baseball signed by Babe Ruth, commemorating a 700-foot home run he had hit in St. Petersburg one spring. There were scorecards on Fishel's desk and lots of carbon copies of letters written. He had a trap door in the wall to his right, behind which he kept boxes of autographed baseballs for business purposes, such as charitable requests.

I was, surprisingly, very comfortable. I hadn't expected this, but I somehow felt at home among the Yankee logos and Yankee literature.

Bob stood and shook my hand. I recognized his face from Yankee Yearbooks. He wore a custom-tailored white shirt with an ROF monogram, and his tie was held in place by a Yankee tie chain. His handshake was firm and businesslike, but comforting.

I pointed to a scorecard on his desk and said, "I was one of your scorecard contest winners last year."

He gave me a broad smile. "You were? That's great," he said. He wrote on my letter "Fan won scorecard contest."

"Yes, I won two tickets to a game. They were good seats—thank you!"

I had his interest.

"Another thing you might like to know," I ventured, "is that when you started High School Sports Editors Day here in '64, I asked the very first question of Yogi."

"You did?" Now he had a wide smile. "What did you ask?"

"I asked what the managers talk about at home plate; I saw that he and Bill Rigney had been laughing when they exchanged lineups the night before."

Now Bob was curious. "What did Yogi answer?"

"He said, 'We just shoot the breeze.'"

We both laughed. The ice was clearly broken.

"Well," he continued, "we have an ongoing problem with fan mail getting backed up. We try to help the players keep up with it, but it's a never-ending battle. And we like the fans to get a response. It's good PR. When your letter arrived, I was thinking that we could use some help in this area. Now, it wouldn't pay much, about four hundred a month, maybe a little more than you get at the *Journal-News*. We could use you from around June first through Labor Day, if you'd be interested. Oh, and you'd get tickets to the games, as well."

If I'd be interested? Oh, brother!

I told him I most certainly was, and he told me that he would give me a final word shortly. When I looked in the file cabinet years later under "employment applications," I saw that he had written "Tentatively hired 8/29/67."

I didn't know for sure that I was in. So, after we shook hands and I left his outer door, it occurred to me that I might never again be this close to the Yankee clubhouse. And that door, right over there, must be the Yankee clubhouse door. If I opened it, I could always apologize for opening the wrong door, and I would get a look at the clubhouse. So I went for it.

But when I opened the door, no clubhouse. Instead, I was met with a large sign that said ABSOLUTELY NO WOMEN BEYOND THIS POINT. I pretty much figured out that that was the right direction, but I was no longer going to push my luck.

I drove home feeling successful for having handled myself well. I felt I had gotten the job. And about a week later, just before I returned to Oneonta, Bob called me and told me I had indeed been hired.

The enormity of it was almost overwhelming that day. A job in any facet of baseball would have been terrific. But this was the Yankees, my own team, the franchise that had spotted the rest of the league 21 years before winning its first pennant—and then would wind up with 36 over the rest of the century. It was Ruth and Gehrig and DiMaggio and Mantle . . . and now, me! Look out!

If you are a young reader, I would encourage your lesson from this to be—go for it! Never be overwhelmed by the thought of a dream job. I had no relatives with the Yankees, no "ins," no special favors due me. I wrote my letter and gave it my best shot. It worked. I was on my way.

I had three years of college to go when the Yankees hired me. Was it going to keep my interest?

Oneonta was a progressive school, part of the state university system, which had been enormously expanded by Governor Rockefeller. The course offerings were strong, and I managed to make the dean's list a few times as I moved forward in my major. Besides Constitutional Law, I particularly enjoyed two courses from the speech and theater depart-ment—Argumentation and Debate, and Group Discussion, both of which would prove enormously valuable in the decision making that lay in front of me.

Eager to begin work with the Yankees, I called Bob Fishel during the winter of my sophomore year and asked him if I could come in during my spring break in April. He was happy to hear from me and said, "By all means!"

I arrived for my first day of work on a rather controversial morning. Dr. Martin Luther King Jr. had been assassinated on April 4, 1968. His funeral was scheduled for April 9—Opening Day.

Had baseball been left to its own devices, there would not have been any delay to the season. But a group of black players, many on the Phillies, made it quite clear that they would not play on the ninth.

Other teams followed, and pretty soon the commissioner, General William "Spike" Eckert, was faced with the reality that he had better shut the game down on the ninth out of respect for Dr. King.

It was probably pointed out to him that one of Pete Rozelle's big mistakes as NFL commissioner was failing to cancel games on the weekend following President Kennedy's assassination five years earlier. But the argument must have developed that King was not a president, and the nation did not quite know how to deal with the assassination of an unelected official.

In the end, baseball got it right. And that was what was going on in Bob Fishel's office when I arrived for my first day of work on April 8. He was busy arranging to move the Cardinal Hays High School band from Tuesday to Wednesday, arranging for the first-ball thrower to move up a day, and juggling a host of other assignments. I was pretty much a distraction when I showed up. He greeted me with haste and turned me over to the next office, shared by his assistant, Bill Guilfoile, and the elderly head of the speakers' bureau, Jackie Farrell. The office was a little larger than Fishel's, but the two facing desks made it seem smaller. On the wall was a huge portrait of Babe Ruth.

There were two sportswriters in the office at the time—legends, to me. One was Maury Allen of the *New York Post*, who stepped right up and extended his hand and introduced himself. I was very impressed. Maury was one of baseball's "chipmunk" writers, inquisitive, sensitive, and funny.

The other was Harold Rosenthal, a retired *Herald-Tribune* writer who was now doing public relations for the American Football League. He would claim to be the only writer to ever shut down three *Tribunes*—the *Herald-Tribune*, the *World Journal Tribune*, and the *New York Tribune*. Harold and Maury would remain my friends for life. Even in his mid-80s,

Harold was one of the keenest wits I have ever met. Profane yet tactful all at once, his letters (bearing multiple postage stamps from the 1930s) were treasures. He could at a moment's notice recall the beginnings of Yankee airline travel, the politics behind it, who the good guys and the bad guys were, who drank what on the flights, and why the Yankees were either first or last at doing something. His memory was impeccable, but it was his appreciation of the little things behind the scenes that made him so interesting. And he could always cut to the chase when describing friends and foes.

In Bill Guilfoile I was meeting a bright and efficient professional who treated everyone with respect and dignity. A former boxer at Notre Dame, he had been Fishel's assistant since 1960. Five pennants in his first five seasons was a pretty good start for Bill, but, like many veteran Yankee employees, he had now adjusted to losing seasons.

Bill was meticulous, even-tempered, helpful, kind, generous, and bore no ego despite his seniority with the Yankees, and I took an immediate liking to him. It is another friendship that continues to this day. There are times I refer to him as "America's nicest man."

Bill helped me fill out my tax forms and handed me a box of letters to be answered. He walked me past the No Women sign and down into a basement corner of the stadium, next to the mailroom. This would be my office, or the one I would share, at least, with the television producer, who would just stop by to review commercial rundowns, and with the parking lot general manager, who would come in and count the day's cash.

The room was wood paneled with a slanted ceiling, and beneath the lower deck of the first base stands. It had a serviceable typewriter, and Bill arranged for me to get a supply of stationery. When he explained some of the form letters to send out ("Thank you for your letter and your interest in the Yankees. We receive so many similar requests during the year that it is impossible to accommodate everyone . . ."), I asked him who should sign the letters.

"You should!" he said. And so, on my very first day, I was signing my name on Yankee stationery.

The Yankees were owned by CBS. Each letter had to conform to a particular CBS style, in terms of paragraph setup, form of greeting, and so on. This being my first office job, that was how I was trained, and, to this day, my letters bear the CBS style, learned on day one of my Yankee career.

Most of the fan letters were addressed to Mickey Mantle. Most asked for his autograph, and most received a black-and-white photo with a facsimile signature. I pretty much had the knack of this within an hour. It wasn't brain surgery. And the secret proved to be saving up a batch of mail that I'd have to "personally review" with Mick, in order to get some quality time with him. Those meetings at his locker were great; he'd read some letter, look at me quizzically, and crumple it with one hand. We'd laugh.

And so went the work. Reading a pile of letters, 90 percent of them for Mantle; typing the envelopes; occasionally writing a letter; and meetings with Mickey.

Baseball had, for many, bottomed out by 1968. Pitchers were dominating the games, while offense was what people had always preferred. The American League batted .230 that season (the Yankees .214!), and there was only one .300 hitter—Carl Yastrzemski at .301.

One day that summer, Bill Kane, our statistician, came in to announce that Mantle's lifetime batting average was about to drop under .300—probably that very afternoon.

"You mean he won't get back over it?" I asked.

"No, not the way he's going," sighed Bill. And indeed, he finished at .298 because of that .237 final season and considered it his greatest disappointment.

If Bob Fishel was my mentor, Bill Veeck was my baseball grandfather.

Now, before I go any farther with this, you should know that his name rhymes with wreck, and, in fact, he always introduced himself that way. "Veeck, as in *wreck*."

I call him my baseball grandfather because he was the man who first hired Fishel, and then, some 20 years later, Fishel hired me.

Fishel took a chance on me, as Veeck had taken a chance on him. It gave me a pretty good lineage in the game.

Veeck grew up in baseball, his father having been the president of the Chicago Cubs, and, as a young man, he helped plant the ivy on Wrigley Field's walls.

He went on to run the Cleveland Indians after losing a leg in World War II, brought Satchel Paige to the big leagues, took home the 1948 pennant before record crowds, and learned to promote the game while others were just opening their gates and hoping the little one-inch ad in the morning papers would get people to come. This was still a time when George Weiss, the Yankees' general manager, when offered an opportunity for the team's first-ever "cap day" pounded his fist on the desk and barked, "Do you think I want every kid in this town walking around in a Yankee cap?"

Veeck, however, was a master of promotion. As far as baseball is concerned, it can be said that he invented it. Except for an occasional "day" to honor a player, the words *baseball* and *promotion* never met before he got there.

Sometimes Veeck's efforts backfired, his "Disco Demolition Night" in 1979 being a classic example, when the White Sox had to forfeit the game as disco records were hurled onto the field. But that was late in his career and largely his son's idea. Usually, to the consternation of his fellow owners, he got it right. He put names on the backs of uniforms, created pyrotechnic scoreboards, and even had his White Sox wear short pants for a game or two in '75. What a sight it was to see Paul Richards, their ancient manager, dressed in knee-length shorts.

My time with Veeck was often educational and always entertaining. In later days, while working for George Steinbrenner, I might get a call in the Chicago press box. George was unable to receive the games in Florida and wanted me to give him a play-by-play over the phone. This was not only a three-hour assignment but tied up the only line in the press box.

Veeck watched with curiosity as the conversation dragged on. He always parked himself in the press box during games, for he enjoyed being among the journalist crowd. To kill the dead time between pitches, I would sometimes go into short promos for upcoming games or for the Yankee Yearbook. Anything to kill the awkward silence, even in jest. Finally Veeck asked a New York writer, "Who's he talking to?" When he found out, he hobbled over to the phone and decisively pressed his finger down on it, disconnecting us. He loved hanging up on George. He told his operator not to put any more calls through from the pest.

"But, Bill," I said, "he's going to think I was the one who hung up on him!"

"You'll always have a job here," he answered.

Steinbrenner assigned Gene Michael to Comiskey Park that year to be his "eye in the sky," using a walkie-talkie to communicate to the dugout with defensive observations. Veeck barred him from the press box for being "annoying" and possibly illegal. So Michael bought a ticket and sat in the stands. The next day, Veeck hired a clown, in full Bozo attire, to sit next to Michael for the whole game.

I enjoyed picking Veeck's brain about the game's subtle changes, for by now he had really seen a lot—some of it of his own making.

"What about the dirt path from home plate to the pitcher's mound?" I asked him one day. "How was it decided to eliminate that?"

"Oh, that would have been Phil Wrigley," he said. "He was always concerned with the aesthetics of the game. He wanted Wrigley Field to look good. The dirt path was there because otherwise catchers wore out the grass walking to the mound. But history proved you could go a whole season without wearing it out, just by reseeding during road trips. Wrigley suspected that. He did it."

When the Arizona Diamondbacks put the path back in at the opening of Bank One Ballpark in 1998, I laughed to myself, thinking Veeck would find it funny, too. They did it as a throwback. Had they known it was chucked out because Wrigley felt it was ugly, they might have reconsidered.

Veeck, of course, liked my connection to Fishel. "Roberto," he called him. We would just talk baseball, and he would sit there smoking and then stub out the butt on his wooden leg. At Comiskey Park he gave himself an unpretentious office—just a desk, really—and he'd answer the phone himself.

Veeck hired Fishel in the late '40s to help publicize the Indians. Bob was not their PR director, but rather worked for the advertising agency associated with the club. Sometimes those outside positions are key within the team's structure, even if they are not listed in the team directory. (Another example of this was Tom Villante, who headed the Schaefer Beer account for the Brooklyn Dodgers, and later for the Yankees.)

Fishel was in his mid-30s when he went to work for Veeck but looked pretty much as he did until the day he died. He was about 5´6″, slender, neatly dressed, and quick in his stride. He parted his hair in the middle, wore thick glasses, and had an engaging smile. He spoke in a husky and authoritative voice, and often with the charming phrases of polite society from another time, such as "Hello, old boy!" His hairstyle and those phrases made you feel as though he were a gentleman from the Gatsby era.

He never married, but the entire baseball community was his family, and everyone should have a family as concerned and caring as he did. He was respected, well liked, intellectual, and a man about town when it came to the theater, fine restaurants, and custom-made shirts. He had an inner wisdom that gave him a decisive sense of right and wrong—an understated but necessary talent when he worked for Veeck, Weiss, Steinbrenner, and Gabe Paul over the years. How someone with such integrity could navigate those waters was often a wonder in itself. But he was also a master at negotiating baseball's politics.

Veeck hired Bob to do PR for the hapless St. Louis Browns when he bought the club after the big years in Cleveland. Bob loved baseball, was loyal to Veeck, and saw it as a great adventure. He had been stationed in

New Orleans during World War II, so leaving home was not especially traumatic, and off he went to St. Louis.

One of Veeck's stunts there was Grandstand Manager Day, when the fans behind the dugout would hold up signs saying BUNT or STEAL or HIT AND RUN. The manager didn't have to take the advice, so it wasn't as though any strategy was being revealed, but it was a classic Veeck stunt, and Bob had to manage it. It was one of those cutting-edge Veeck moments, when a purist would have to pause and think, *This game counts in the standings?* He had a lot of those.

Bob was also the fellow who signed Veeck's midget, Eddie Gaedel—an idea inspired by a James Thurber short story. He signed him in the back seat of his Packard to a one-day contract, which was never filed with the league. When the story of Gaedel's one at bat is told, it's often followed by, "After that, they banned midgets," or something to that effect. Actually, what came out of it was simply a rule stating that contracts had to be filed with the league for approval. There's no clause in Major League Baseball's rules that prohibits clubs from signing midgets.

For many years, I have been involved in helping to write the plaques for new Hall of Famers headed for Cooperstown. This involvement goes back to 1979, and I love being part of the process. In 1991, we were preparing the Bill Veeck plaque, and the question arose of whether or not the Gaedel stunt should be included in the biographical text.

I didn't for a second think it should; it was the kind of thing that keeps you *out* of the Hall of Fame! Still, it may be the moment he was best known for, besides his general reputation as a populist, anti-establishment kind of guy.

Anyway, if you should have a chance to walk by Veeck's plaque in Cooperstown some day, read the last line. It is my personal favorite:

A CHAMPION OF THE LITTLE GUY.

Mission accomplished.

In 1954 the Browns moved to Baltimore, Veeck sold the team, and Bob was a free agent with a growing reputation, working again for an ad agency. Remarkably, the Yankees—baseball's polar opposite of the Brownies—hired him.

Red Patterson, the first man to hold the title of public relations director for the Yankees, bolted from the club in the first inning of a summer doubleheader at the Stadium, incensed that Weiss would question his leaving two tickets for the elevator operator at the Yanks' offices in the Squibb Building. He jumped to the Dodgers (he had obviously been talking to them already), and the plum position of PR man for the five-time consecutive world champions was open.

If the elevator man hadn't asked Patterson for tickets, I might not have become the PR director myself some day. But he did. Life is a series of "what if" moments. And the affable Patterson, who was still working for the Dodgers when I entered baseball, became another "grandfather" in my career.

Red had joined the Yankees in 1946 after a year in the National League publicity office. He had been a writer for the *Tribune* before the war and had covered Lou Gehrig's final game in Detroit. Red, Jackie Farrell, and Maggie Regerts were the PR department when he came over from the NL, and it wasn't any bigger when he turned it over to Bob.

Bob told me that his interview with Weiss was businesslike and didn't really cover any of his past pranks with Veeck. Weiss wanted to make sure he would represent the team in a professional manner, and Bob was at his best with such a task. The signing of Gaedel in the back of his Packard had, of course, been done in a professional manner. He was much more the Yankee type than the Brownie type. But he must have made Weiss squirm: the guy who did PR for Veeck inheriting a legacy of DiMaggio and McCarthy and Dickey, such solid citizens?

"In the end," Bob laughingly told me, "Weiss hired me because I was Jewish. A lot of the writers covering the club then were Jewish—Dan Daniel of the *World-Telegram*, Milton Gross of the *Post*, Harold Rosenthal of the *Herald-Tribune*, Ben Epstein of the *Mirror*, Louis Effrat at the *Times*, even Dick Young at the *News* was half Jewish. He thought it would go over well."

The irony was that Bob was a nonobservant Jew who didn't even take off for the high holidays. He wasn't exactly an atheist, but his religion, like his family, was baseball. His Ten Commandments included, Never swing at the first pitch after someone has walked on four consecutive pitches, which fell just after "Thou shalt not kill." But if that's why Weiss hired him, so be it.

After replacing Red Patterson, Bob succeeded in gaining the confidence of the writers while pleasing his bosses. He always delivered the company line but still managed to form genuine, lifelong friendships with many in the press. (The word *media* hadn't come along yet.) His Christmas card list exceeded 1,500. He sent hundreds and hundreds of birthday cards each year—not only to members of the press, but to their wives and children. He was a wonderful dinner companion, with interesting views on current events. He never cheated the team a nickel on his expense account and dutifully submitted a letter of resignation each time team ownership changed, feeling that new management had a right to hire its own spokesman. Fortunately for the Yankees, Bob's resignation was never accepted.

And oh, he loved his baseball. He was one of those in the game with whom you could talk politics and theater and literature and art, but the splendor of the national pastime was what really got into his blood. He derived genuine enthusiasm from each game, loved the Yankees' glory years, and suffered their decline.

And baseball people respected him. He used to give check marks and Xs for good plays and bad plays that didn't result in errors, and each year Lee MacPhail would ask him for this summary, just to get a better overall picture of a player. An infielder might have 65 checks and eight Xs that never showed up on his fielding records, and Bob's judgment was highly credible.

Reflecting later in his life, Bob gave himself a failing grade for the 1961 season, when Maris and Mantle were belting all those home runs. Maris later said the Yankees did nothing to help him. He would be hemmed into his locker stall by a crowd of writers, pinned and questioned endlessly until he'd lose his patience.

Years later the NFL developed interview rooms apart from locker rooms to provide a more organized setting for press conferences. Baseball followed this practice in the World Series, but, as in many cases, the NFL set the trend from a PR standpoint. Bob felt he should have thought of it in 1961, and he was pretty tough on himself for it. Maris did not have good feelings toward the Yankee management and, sadly, lumped Bob in that category.

The truth was Maris was hemmed in by not more than 10 or 12 writers, none with microphones, no video—just a dozen guys with notepads. It wasn't that terrible, and Roger contributed to the pressure himself. Sometimes he would retreat to the training room and put a little hand statue, with its middle finger extended, on his stool. It wasn't the best way to win over the press.

But Bob always felt bad about it. He appreciated the respect he had from Mantle and Berra and Ford and all the other greats, but he was saddened by Maris's feelings. And he saw and totally accepted Roger's point. He was pretty hard on himself over it.

When Bob left the Yankees for the American League office, he proved an able administrator who had the respect of everyone in the game. But when I asked him one day about the possibility of his one day becoming the league president, he said, "Oh, I couldn't see myself presiding over a meeting with people like George and Edward Bennett Williams and Gene Autry. You need someone of much higher stature."

He was wrong, but it was a typically self-effacing comment.

Such was the love that people had for Bob that when he died in 1988 of an asthma attack in the back seat of a Manhattan taxi, he was eulogized in a ceremony on the field at Yankee Stadium, on a day the team was on the road. Hundreds of people sat behind the Yankee dugout in 100-degree heat, while a number of speakers, myself included, spoke of his career and of how much he was appreciated. I mentioned in my remarks that I believed that only Babe Ruth, 40 years earlier, had been memorialized in Yankee Stadium in a moment that did not simply precede a ballgame with a moment of silence.

We established a scholarship in Bob's name at his alma mater, Hiram College in Ohio, that day. The Yankee pressroom came to be called the Bob Fishel pressroom, and an annual award bearing his name is given to a public relations person in the game.

And each year since 1989, on May 15, his birthday, Lee MacPhail (Bob's good friend and boss at both the Yankees and the American League), Howard Berk (another former Yankee vice president), and I, along with a guest, have had lunch in his honor to remember his many great qualities.

THE BABE'S
BIG SECRET

At the time I entered baseball, the front offices of the game were stocked with what I called lifers. They were people who intended to devote their entire working lives to the game, even if salaries in the "outside" would have given them fuller lives in a material sense.

Many were descendants of the titans of the game—the Rickeys, the MacPhails, even the Dunns. Jack Dunn III was in the Baltimore Orioles' front office; his grandfather had signed Babe Ruth out of St. Mary's orphanage a half-century earlier. It was fascinating to learn about this lineage.

Some were merely occupational descendants—they had worked in the front offices of Branch Rickey or Larry MacPhail, or in Bob Fishel's case, of Bill Veeck.

I loved these people. They were there when baseball was still sort of a mom-and-pop shop, when Calvin Griffith in Minnesota could employ all of his relatives and run a major league team on a shoestring. But they were characters who had grown up in the game and were there for the love of it.

Calvin was himself the adopted son of Hall of Famer Clark Griffith, longtime owner of the Washington Senators, and the first manager of the New York Highlanders.

"Calvin was my first boss when I was the scoreboard boy in old Griffith Stadium," Bowie Kuhn told me, when we worked on his autobiography together. Then he laughed to himself.

"Maybe I shouldn't say this, but we used to say that one of his responsibilities was to go around after the game and collect all of the unsold hot dogs, which the Griffiths would then consume for dinner."

Baseball was like that then. Those people were in baseball for the love of the game, hardly for the money. Lee MacPhail had been president of the Baltimore Orioles shortly before I entered baseball, and he earned a salary of $35,000 a year. This was not unheard of, and the lifers never complained.

Today's front offices are populated more heavily by marketing and business gurus, who enjoy the game but see it as another stop in their career before they move on to market another product.

By those standards, I arrived almost uneducated. (I would later take a course from 98-year-old Edward Bernys, considered the founder of the public relations profession. He told us about his recollection of people hanging black crepe over their doors when President McKinley was assassinated, and about how you had to do "Research, research, research!" to make PR claims that the media liked.)

It's fine for baseball to attract the MBA types; the game needs the best marketing people it can attract. But the sense of community that existed when I arrived in the '60s has faded. Even the general managers are seldom in for the long haul.

The hours were long, but the life was good because the people in the game were so interesting. The camaraderie of the game was its lifeblood. Although Gabe Paul would later tell me "This is war!" when building the Yankees, in truth no general manager ever really wanted to fleece another. It was all a grand fraternity, and today's fleecing would surely come back to bite you in the ass, for there would be another trading deadline, another waiver claim just around the bend. At the end of the day, everyone wanted everyone else to do just fine in front of his ownership.

One year the Yankees dealt Danny Cater to the Red Sox for Sparky Lyle. It was a sensational deal for the Yankees, and Dick O'Connell, the Red Sox general manager, felt the wrath of the Bosox fans. It was what it was, a straight up, one-for-one deal. The Sox had simply overrated Cater, who we knew as one of those .300 hitters who wasn't strong in run production, and would be forever expendable for the right price.

MacPhail, our general manager by then, felt for his Boston comrade. So, some months later, he sold infielder Mario Guerrero to the Sox and let it be called a "player to be named later." Mario wasn't a savior, but it helped O'Connell; he had gotten another body besides Cater. These things were not uncommon. There had been no "player to be named later," and suddenly there was Guerrero in the Red Sox infield. It was a quiet courtesy, and the record books reflected that Guerrero was part of the deal. There would be no gloating over a one-sided deal in baseball. MacPhail felt O'Connell's discomfort and sought to right it.

During my time in baseball's front offices, I never lost sight of the fact for a minute that we were all being granted a rare privilege: a chance to serve, in a small way, as caretakers for our national pastime. And as a true fan, maybe I had a special appreciation for the "other side"—the fans, and what it meant to them. I think it helped make me an effective Yankee spokesman.

For example, in 1974 I walked into Gabe Paul's office to find samples of new Yankee road uniforms draped across his sofa. They were the opposite of the home pinstripes—they were navy blue with white pinstripes. The NY logo was in white. Gabe liked them. I nearly fainted. Although the drab gray road uniforms were not exciting, with the plain NEW YORK across the chest, they were just as much the Yankees' look as were the home uniforms. I think my dramatic disdain helped saved the day and saved the Yankees from wearing these awful pajamas on the field.

I lobbied hard for day baseball on the summer schedule, and I think I helped add a few dates along the way. Back in the summer of 1964, just after I'd turned 16, I stayed home and watched a day game on TV. It was Mel Stottlemyre's Yankee debut. The weather outside was beautiful, but the Yankees were fighting for a pennant, and this was an important debut for this thin, highly regarded righthander up from Richmond. It was a wonderful game, a Stottlemyre victory aided by a titanic center field home run by Mantle over the batter's-eye screen at Yankee Stadium. And to this day, whenever I find myself just watching a midweek day game, often the Cubs from Wrigley, I think back to that afternoon and how it was all that mattered in the world. The feeling is still there, and those lazy summer afternoons needed some day baseball in them.

I can even recall a historic moment in communications, when America launched the Telstar communications satellite, which would be the first to provide satellite transmission of television signals. Because the transmission began a few moments earlier than expected, the Cape Canaveral engineers switched to the only live television signal they were receiving at the time, a Cubs game on WGN, broadcast by Jack Brickhouse. It was only a few seconds long, but I was watching, and I saw the July 11, 1962, Cubs for a fleeting moment along with the rest of the television-viewing northern hemisphere. What a concept, I remember thinking—imagine being able to watch games other than my home teams'! The fans were all asked to wave to the satellite by PA announcer Pat Piper.

Neither the Yankees, major league baseball, nor I were at the top of our games when I entered the Yankees front office in 1968.

As thrilled as I was to be a part of the New York Yankees' public relations department, I was basically unskilled in the craft of PR. Today, college students can major in public relations or marketing—or even in sports marketing—and come to a job with a formal set of skills.

As a political science major, my skills were heavy on the baseball knowledge side but uninformed on the art of public communications, especially before the sophisticated New York media. Fortunately, I was in a position to learn from two of the best: Bob Fishel and his assistant, Bill Guilfoile. It became clear in short order that I was going to learn this craft with Yankee Stadium as my classroom and with a couple of professors who knew more than a little bit about sports PR. I was going to be all right, even without a marketing degree.

Guilfoile had joined the Yankees in 1960 out of Notre Dame and the Navy. He was a model of efficiency and possessed the kind of decency and courtesy one would expect from someone from Fond du Lac, Wisconsin. He was athletic, thoughtful, soft-spoken, and a gentleman.

He also had a great sense of Yankee tradition, despite not being raised as a Yankee fan. He used to recount for me that one of his greatest thrills was the Old Timers Day that Joe McCarthy entered the Yankee clubhouse for a rare appearance. He had not been back to the Yankees in some time but was revered by those who played for him.

The clubhouse—awash with fellows greeting old friends, reporters, the current players—went silent as Marse Joe walked in. And then suddenly, spontaneously, his former players just began to applaud for him, giving him a standing ovation in his old clubhouse, a terrific tribute. Bill told the story well.

Bill and I did a joint project for the Yankee press guide in the summer of '69, the dark ages of research. He decided it would be a terrific addition to include the all-time top 20 in the major hitting and pitching categories as a special page in the book.

Today, computers at the Elias Sports Bureau or Stats Inc. can churn out the most unbelievable information in seconds. It amazes me. When the Mets and Rockies faced each other one day in 1999 and both starting pitchers had the same name (Bobby Jones), Elias was able to report—within hours—the last time that had occurred. It was uncanny, but not unlike some of the miracles this great stat bureau regularly performs, such as the time they were able to report—again, within hours—that when Mickey Tettleton batted against Andy Pettitte, it was the first time two players with four t's in their last names had ever faced each other.

But in 1969 when we embarked on this project, it was a major undertaking. We pulled out the old *Baseball Registers* in the office—hardbound, with the name ED BARROW engraved on the covers—and began to extract the Yankee totals from the career totals of Yankee greats. If a player split a season between the Yankees and another club, the records were combined, leaving us in a bit of a fix. Occasionally the *Baseball Guide* would give you the split records, but not always. We were doing what now seems like an easy project in a painstakingly slow way.

However, in 1968, Macmillan was preparing to issue the first computer-generated baseball encyclopedia. "Big Mac," as many of us called it, was to be issued for 1969, professional baseball's centennial season. It would knock out the classic Turkin–Thompson *Encyclopedia of Baseball* and became a sensational gift for baseball fans for years.

Macmillan had the information we were lacking—the split-season records that would give closure to our project. Working in pencil on accounting stationery, we polished up our list and were ready to put it into the 1970 press guide. There it still appears, three decades later, Frank Crosetti having long dropped off the top 20 home run list, and every year I see it I think of Bill and me cranking it out on accountant's stationery. Now every team has this feature; press guides have become 300-page "media guides," and creating them is as easy as dialing it up on a computer. Then, it was heady stuff.

Press guides were "media only" in those days. The fans never saw them. It was felt that the media deserved the courtesy of some knowledge that the fans couldn't access. Today, the teams sell their guides for $15 or more. Then, they were free, and 48 pages was considered quite substantial. Some teams managed with less. Bob Fishel would keep the last eight years' worth in his coat pocket for quick reference.

Mike Burke, the team's CBS-appointed president, was a thoroughly dashing figure who around the time I joined the Yankees, was a candidate for commissioner of baseball. The owners had sacked William Eckert, who, they felt, knew nothing about their game—a tribute to their fine interviewing process in the first place. I remember being on the field for Old Timers Day at Yankee Stadium in 1968 and finding myself in conversation with General Eckert. The introductions had ended, preparations were being made for the Old Timers Game, and there we stood, face to face. We talked about the nice crowd, the nice weather, and soon we were talking about the bad weather I experienced in Oneonta. Suddenly I realized that this poor man, the commissioner of baseball, had no one to talk to at a Yankee Old Timers Day except for the kid in the fan mail office about the weather in Oneonta.

It was a blessing that they put him out of his misery after the season ended.

Burke was a candidate because he looked like a man for the times, a marketing guru when baseball needed marketing skills. In truth, Mike was dashing. He wore great suits and had a grand collection of wide neckties, although, oddly, his shirts were few and often frayed around the collar. With his longish gray hair, it was thought that he might be able to connect with young people. That was, in large measure, why he was a candidate. He was also viewed as brilliant, if not a tad extreme, advocating a designated hitter rule and the end of league offices. But in truth, the baseball establishment was still in crewcuts and couldn't really warm up to his sort. At a winter sports banquet that year, M. Donald Grant of the Mets donned a Beatles wig to mock Burke's appearance. It was embarrassing.

But the owners were viewing their declining attendance figures and were prepared to listen to new ideas, at least in the early ballots.

Burke had been an OSS operative in World War II, the same war Ralph Houk had fought. For years we thought Houk had won the war; now it appeared it might have been Burke. His war adventures in Italy had in fact inspired Gary Cooper's role in *Cloak and Dagger*. Some of Burke's background was larger than life, and he was a damned fascinating guy. He rode horseback, he knew Hemingway, he drove a Datsun 240Z, his hair was long enough to annoy conservatives, his suits were dark and pinstripe enough to please the CBS crowd, and his girlfriends were the tall and thin model types.

One year we had a hot minor league prospect named Charlie Spikes. Because he had been a number one draft pick, most who followed the club had heard of him.

Burke was at this time dating an actress and model known as Sam. She would sit with him in his private box on the mezzanine level over first base, enjoying the cloth-napkin food and beverage service, and hanging on his every word.

We used to put Charlie Spikes progress reports in our daily press notes, and, one evening during a game, our direct phone line, Burke to PR, rang in the press box. Fishel picked it up, first ring as always.

"Bob, does this fellow Charlie Spikes have a nickname?" Burke asked.

"Not that I'm aware of," replied Bob.

"Well, how about, starting tomorrow, we call him Sam Spikes in the notes, okay?"

Bob paused, thought better of what he was probably about to say, and said, weakly, "Okay."

He turned to me and said, "You're not going to believe this."

We actually did use "Sam Spikes" for a day, but Bob found it so awkward he just stopped and hoped Burke wouldn't bring it up again. He didn't. "Sam Spikes" was a one-day wonder.

Fishel asked me to write a little bio for the press guide on Burke and sent it upstairs to him for approval. At the mention of two award citations he had received during the war, the Silver Star and the Navy Cross, Burke drew arrows out to the margins and inserted "for gallantry" and "for heroism." Indeed, those bold, thick, hand-written missives became his trademark, so much so that Bob had him write an annual introduction to the Yankee Yearbook, in his own distinctive Magic Marker style.

I wish I could say that I got to know Burke well, but, as Fishel's assistant, I was once removed, even in a front office that numbered barely sixty people. He would say, "Hi, Marty," but I always hoped he would stop and ask me about myself, or solicit my opinion on some subject, figuring I was the lost demographic in his sport! But we never really had an actual conversation, and I'm afraid I was always the fan mail kid in his eyes, even after I had become Bob's assistant.

As for the battle for commissioner, Burke's National League "opponent" was the league president, Chub Feeney. Chub was an affable good ol' boy, truly one of the pack, a guy who could hold his liquor and smoke a cigar, and would certainly have had the support of most clubs had there not been an AL–NL rivalry. But that rivalry had generated a compromise candidate: National League attorney Bowie Kuhn. And that put an end to Burke leaving the Yanks. We at the Stadium were relieved that he was staying.

Around this time, I was becoming aware that there was a booming sports epicenter in New York, and that the Yankees were barely a part of it. There was a very popular saloon at 150 West 52nd Street, just down the street from CBS, and it was owned by, and named for, Mike Manuche.

This was the place for power drinking in the days when men were still measured by their capacity to consume and somehow drive home safely. And a strange phenomenon was taking place at Manuche's—the convergence of the staffs of the National Football League, the New York football Giants, *Sports Illustrated*, and CBS. The offices of all four were within blocks of the tavern. The young, handsome, rising stars from these offices would congregate there, along with people like Frank Gifford, Kyle Rote, and Pat Summerall. From these days emerged a synergy of media, executives, and athletes, coming together as the NFL was taking the lead in American sports, as *Sports Illustrated* was becoming an important voice in American sports, and as CBS Sports was becoming a Sunday afternoon fixture for American men.

Manuche's was taking the place of Toots Shor's, which was still favored by the older crowd, the crowd of Jimmy Cannon and Joe DiMaggio and Mickey Mantle. As baseball was becoming less important as a topic of discussion, the new power elite was moving to a new watering hole. And baseball wasn't tagging along, not even the CBS Yankees.

The best representation the Yankees could muster at Manuche's was to have the CBS salesmen, who had some small interest in Yankee telecasts, on the scene. But the conversation was always about football, and the glamor sport was changing. Baseball people felt out of place and, as Shor grew older and lost his restaurant, almost orphaned. There was no real baseball gathering place, just as the old beat writers, who covered baseball year round, were fading. A new generation of bright columnists was learning to cover the interplay between social issues and baseball, and beat guys were pleading to get off the road and lead normal lives. The assignment was no longer a lifetime assignment. Now the writers would burn out quickly and have no interest in running downtown to drink. The landscape was changing.

Some of the players whom I developed a fondness for in my first year were, aside from Mantle, Steve Whitaker, Bill Robinson, Bobby Cox, Dick Howser, Ruben Amaro, and Bronx-born Rocky Colavito. Amaro was the first player after Mantle to learn my name.

Colavito joined the team in the summer—his final weeks as a major leaguer—and he wowed the crowd one Sunday afternoon by pitching in relief and winning the game.

Rocky stayed on as a batting coach in the minors for a couple of years, and I heard that the players took well to his coaching. But Lee MacPhail said to me, "Oh, minor leaguers are just like fans—if a coach was a big star, they think he's better than he is. The best coaches are the guys who weren't stars, who they never heard of."

Rocky dropped out of the coaching ranks shortly thereafter, but so many years later, there he was again, coaching for Dick Howser and the Kansas City Royals the day George Brett went nuts after being called out for using his pine tar–laden bat.

I liked Howser a lot. He was in the last year of his career as an infielder in '68 (we had a lot of "final season" guys that year, Mantle among them), and in '69 he succeeded Crosetti as our third base coach. Howser wore a small shoe—7 ½—and, because that was my shoe size, I was on a few occasions given his old spikes when he wore them out. I still use them when I play softball, and they still say 34 on the tongue, his number.

Dick was a good-humored guy with a great baseball mind, and I thought he could be a manager one day. Our statistician Bill Kane liked Howser too, but didn't agree with me.

"It's tough to say this, here in the 1970s," he would say, "but to be a successful manager, I think you have to have a physical presence, as though you could level a player who wasn't listening to you. Sort of that unspoken threat. Alston's got it. Houk's got it. Bauer's got it. That sort of thing."

Howser certainly didn't have it. And historically, neither did Miller Huggins, who was often on the humiliating end of Ruth's jabs; but he made the Hall of Fame and got the first monument in Yankee Stadium.

But Howser did make it. The Royals gave him a chance, and he took them to the 1985 world championship, before he got cancer and died a few years later, a great loss for us all.

One year Dick and I had to drive to upstate New York for winter sports banquets in Oneonta and Syracuse. Through my skilled navigation we got very lost, and, caught in a developing snowstorm, we were not in the best of moods. We were hoping to spot someone—anyone—for directions back to the road we were supposed to be on.

Finally we saw a figure shoveling his driveway on our left. As we got closer, I couldn't believe my eyes.

"Isn't that Al Salerno?" I asked.

Salerno was a former American League umpire. Here in the middle of nowhere, Al Salerno was our snow shoveler and potential directions provider. It was a one-in-a-zillion shot.

Howser, though, was just like any old ballplayer would be when meeting an old umpire.

"Salerno?" he said. "Screw him. Keep driving."

Steve Whitaker and Bill Robinson were marked as stars of the future on the '68 Yankees. Both had good looks, great tools, and impressive minor league stats. It's hard to believe today, but, for a time, Whitaker was so popular that only Mantle got more fan mail. Robinson was more intellectual, a quiet student of the game, much like Bernie Williams today. Mike Burke had a special interest in wanting Robinson to break through as a major star. Burke carried the burden of the Yankees' history of being slow to sign black players. He felt Robinson could be his ticket out of the purgatory of defending the organization's past. Plus, he genuinely liked Bill and his wife, Mary, and continued to socialize with them long after Bill left the Yankees.

Bill had been acquired in a trade with the Braves for no less than Clete Boyer and came with great expectations.

By 1968, 14 seasons after African American players were first signed by the Yankees, only Elston Howard—the first—had become a star. The franchise had continued to be selective. Vic Power, an early prospect, was shuffled off to the Athletics when he was thought to be "too flashy" and, it was whispered, "dated white women."

As for being too flashy, no prospects, black or white, had much of a chance with the Yankees if that was their tag. The Yanks were equal opportunity disqualifiers if flashiness was the problem. If you weren't flashy, you might stick around. Tom Tresh, not flashy, was permitted a four-year batting slump before he was finally dispatched.

So, 13 years after Elston Howard's debut, there was still not another black star on the horizon, and Burke—very liberal in his politics—wanted Robinson to be the man. Bill did indeed have the talent—it just wasn't going to come through on the Yankees, for whatever reason. Some thought it was the pressure. He only played three years for the Yanks, and batted just .206 with 10 homers. He went on to play 12 more years for the Phillies and Pirates, went to the World Series in '79, and had a good career.

Burke was always interested in getting a minority star for the melting pot that was New York. For several years he tried to get Lee MacPhail to swing a deal for Mike Epstein, the muscular Washington Senator first baseman who called himself Super Jew. One season we were close to trading Mel Stottlemyre for him.

It never happened, and it was probably for the best. But Epstein was a good guy who went on to become a Jewish cowboy in Wyoming after he retired, far more rare than being a Jewish Yankee.

Steve Whitaker asked me if I wanted to play pepper with him in the outfield early one afternoon, which surely exceeded my usual duties. But of course, I said yes, and for a half-hour or so, using his glove, I soft tossed as he slapped the ball back at me with his bat. That pretty much marked Whitaker as my personal favorite for some time, but, sadly, his time was running out. Although he sat next to Mantle in the team photo that year, he hit .117 in 28 games and was a Seattle Pilot in '69, hardly heard from again. We had a lot of guys like that in those years.

Bobby Cox, the enormously successful manager of the Atlanta Braves, was our third baseman in '68, the only year he was ever a regular in the big leagues. He looked then as he looks today—as though he were in his 50s. He was a heady player, a gutsy player, but small on talent, and his ascent up the coaching and managing ladder would come along soon after.

One day I watched him signing baseballs at the clubhouse table. This was a regular routine—players were obligated to stop by the table and sign a few dozen balls. Often the boxes belonged to other players, who needed a batch at home for family, friends, garage mechanics, postmen, etc. Everyone wants autographed baseballs.

So there was Bobby, signing a six-letter autograph, *Bob Cox*, grumbling and complaining as he did it. And across the table, silently and uncomplainingly signing, was Bill Monbouquette, owner of one of the longest names in baseball. I thought it was a very funny scene.

Bob Cox was not, by the way, the shortest autograph in history. Neither was Mel Ott. The honor went to Ed Ott, the Pittsburgh catcher. It will be a tough record to beat.

I always enjoyed my time with Cox. One year we arranged for him to be a guest speaker at a senior citizens center near Ft. Lauderdale. I went along partly because I liked these things and partly because he had pretty much commandeered my rental car for the spring, and I was landlocked without him.

Anyway, he made his speech about supporting the Yankees, told a few anecdotes, and then took questions. It was immediately apparent that everyone in the room thought he was Billy Cox, the third baseman of the Brooklyn Dodgers in the '50s.

Bobby decided to make no effort to correct them. If they were going to get a thrill out of actually meeting Billy Cox, that was the way it would be. He talked about what great guys all the Dodgers were (he had actually come up through the Dodger organization himself), and then he said goodnight, signed a lot of autographs as "B. Cox," and we had a good laugh driving home, knowing that we had given those nice people a night to remember.

But I'm getting a little ahead of myself.

After working for two summers in the fan mail office, it was time to return to Oneonta for my senior year.

Toward the end of the summer Bob Fishel and I sat in some empty seats near the Yankee dugout for a chat about my future. I used to love going into the empty ballpark at midday. The grounds crew, really good guys, most of whom were related to each other, were always taking care of their beautiful field—each was a skilled gardener in his own right, and each loved being part of the Yankee organization.

The guys were hosing down the infield with a graceful arc of water, a rainbow forming in the mist, as Bob and I chatted. To talk in an empty stadium is an odd experience. With fans crowding the stands, you have to raise your voice to be heard by your neighbor. But when the stands are deserted, you can almost speak in a conversational tone with someone all the way over by the other dugout.

I knew that the following summer I would need a real job, and he acknowledged that he might not have one for me. He said he might be able to get me into a CBS sales training program, which did not sound especially interesting to me. But I had to admit that with no other prospects, it would be something to consider.

I could always go back into sports journalism, I felt, and I think that I would indeed have done that. I did love journalism, loved the deadline pressure, loved being able to interpret the game quickly, and loved to write. But it was a rather sad conversation in the end. It seemed as if my days with the Yankees were coming to a close.

Back in Oneonta for my senior year, I fell in love with a girl named Donna. She was Dutch, she was from Long Island, she was a junior, and she was beautiful. She also had an exotic look to her that some found enticing and some found, well, just unusual. You either got it or you didn't.

I fell for Donna in a big way, but, unfortunately, it was not reciprocal—at least not the way I would have wanted it.

We spent a few days of the Christmas break at her parents' home on Long Island, but it was clear that the relationship was wilting.

When I returned home on December 29, I had a message from Bill Guilfoile. He told me that he had accepted a job as public relations director of the Pirates—and that I ought to see Bob and let him know I was interested in succeeding him.

I was torn. My normal, orderly instincts were taking control. I had another semester of college. I was right on schedule to graduate in June, and, sorry, I don't do things out of order.

But this was something I couldn't dismiss.

"Hello, Bob?"

I went in the next day at 11. We talked. He was pleased that I had called. "What do you think of Bill going to Pittsburgh?" he asked. I said it was a great opportunity, and I knew he would do well. From Mantle to Clemente, he was covering a lot of greatness. When I finished my response, Bob looked at me and said, "Want his job?"

I said, "Yes!"

Now that didn't mean I had it, only that I was interested and would be a candidate. Bob did have others in mind. I explained my obligation to one more semester, and Bob explained that he did need someone right away. He was comfortable with me, knew that I knew my stuff, had observed me learning at every turn, and had been impressed by my writing the Old Timers Day programs and other chores outside the fan mail area.

I asked him to give me a week.

I drove back to Oneonta on January 4. I called four professors whom I liked personally and who knew about my summer job with the Yankees. They were fans. And yes, they would be perfectly happy to structure independent study courses for me, which would give me the missing 12 credits and allow me to graduate on time.

That part was done. I could do this.

Then came another call from Bill Guilfoile.

"What would you think of coming with me to Pittsburgh to be my assistant?"

Could this be? Two offers?

Suddenly, I had more decisions to make than I could handle.

The best thing the Pirates had going for them, as far as I was concerned, was that Guilfoile was one of the finest people I had ever known. Most people who have dealt with him over the years would agree. At the Yankees for 10 seasons, at the Pirates for 10, and then at the Baseball Hall of Fame for the final third of his career before retirement, he was loved by all he worked with.

So respected as a friend was Bill that one of his proudest moments grew from Roberto Clemente's trust and admiration for him in Pittsburgh. Clemente had 2,999 hits with one game to play in 1972. He decided to sit it out, in order to generate excitement and anticipation for the following season.

Not that Bill had a premonition, but he went to Roberto, as a friend, and urged him to play. Bill told him, "Roberto, you never know what can happen—an injury, whatever; you just never know."

No one knew that Clemente would die in a plane crash on New Year's Eve. But at Bill's urging, he played in that last game and got his 3,000th hit.

Bill offered me a $10,000 salary. If that sounds small today, consider that the Yankees were offering $8,000. And the difference represented big numbers when a new car cost $3,500.

I had to admit to myself that as much as I admired Fishel, I was a little intimidated by him. Guilfoile was going to be easier as a boss. But then again, it was the *Yankees!* My team! Twenty teams out there, and the one I grew up with was offering me a job. The most glamorous, historic team in the world, the Ruth team, the Gehrig team, the DiMaggio team, the Mantle team.

I weighed all the pros and cons. My parents drove up and we went to dinner at Molinari's in Oneonta, which was a restaurant owned by Frank Malzone, the old Red Sox third baseman. Two friends joined us. By the end of the meal, it was going to be the Yankees. That was where my heart was. And of course, I was still just a candidate. But if Bob hired someone else, I now had the Pittsburgh option.

That night, Bob called me during a meeting break in Philadelphia. He said the job was mine, and that I could think it over for a few days. He never did learn of the Pirates' offer. I think he might have been a little upset with Bill if he knew, but he never did.

So, on a Friday I was in Oneonta, cleaning out my room, shaking hands with friends, and saying a hasty goodbye to classes. In truth, people weren't that impressed by my new job—it was baseball and this was 1970. Dull. On Monday I was at my desk—Bill's old desk—in the public relations office at Yankee Stadium. In the desk was a note from Bill that read, "Give 'em hell." I didn't know Bill ever used that word.

It reminded me of a great baseball story involving Birdie Tebbets, a baseball lifer. He had been let go as a manager and had left his successor two envelopes, with instructions to open them "when the going gets tough." One said "open first," the other, "open second."

After a losing streak, with the press screaming that the new man was no improvement at all, he opened the first envelope and it read, "Blame it all on me."

Some weeks later, still stuck in the second division, he opened the second one. All it said was, "Prepare two envelopes."

So Monday, January 26, 1970, was day one of my adult working career. It should have been a spectacular day, but I was in a daze. I was even mourning the breakup with Donna in the middle of all of this. There was a surreal quality to it. Guilfoile called around noon and, disguising his voice, said, "Can you tell me whom the Yankees traded to get Red Ruffing?" It was typical of the sort of call that might come in at any time to our office. And of course it was Cedric Durst; I didn't have to look it up. That was why I belonged there.

That very afternoon, an Associated Press photographer came by to take a picture of our clubhouse man, Pete Sheehy, packing for spring training. I was in the clubhouse accompanying the photographer, and he asked me to get on the other side of the trunk where the uniforms were being packed. And I did. The resulting photo ran everywhere, with my name, and many people who thought I had become assistant director of public relations now thought I had made it all up and was in fact Pete Sheehy's clubhouse assistant. It was not a photo op intended to advance my career. But it proved I had found my way to the clubhouse.

Pete was a quiet sort, a legend, of course, having worked in the clubhouse since 1927. He had been just a street kid, peering through a window, when Pop Logan hired him to help out. He was a family man, but you wouldn't know that, because he spent most of his waking hours in the Yankee clubhouse. He smoked Camels, and the ashes would never fall from the cigarette. I don't know how he did that. Sixty to seventy percent of his cigarette was ash, and he would never flick it off.

He also seldom clipped his fingernails. They would be an inch and a half past his fingertips. No one ever mentioned this as being unusual.

One spring he lost his false teeth while packing for the trip north. They had apparently fallen into one of the many trunks that get shipped home. "Pete," I said, "get some teeth! How can you be like this?"

"Oh, they'll turn up," he said.

They never did.

He was a great kidder, a wonderful keeper of secrets, and a great confidant to generations of players. No one ever had a bad word for Pete. His assistant, "Little Pete" Previte (about half an inch shorter than "Big Pete"), was very talkative, very gossipy. People thought they got along well, living together for months on end in the clubhouse, but they actually made fairly wide circles around each other. Truth be told, the job was not all glamor. Picking up dirty laundry and cleaning the toilets were not glamorous. But they also managed the equipment, set up a postgame buffet, and bore the important responsibility of assigning uniform numbers.

Big Pete also had a wonderful memory. One day I had a 1932 team photo in my hands, but I needed the "left to rights," as we called them, to identify all the players. Walking 90 steps to the clubhouse was in order, and I plopped it on the table. "Pete, can you give me all the names?"

Not only could he do that, but he said, "Oh, '32, that was the year Gomez and Ruth showed up late for the picture."

Sure enough, if you look carefully, there are Lefty Gomez and the Babe, clearly wearing only their untucked jerseys hastily thrown over street clothes. To Pete, it might just as well have been yesterday.

After a couple of years I thought I had sufficiently earned Big Pete's confidence that he might actually break his famous silence and give me some inside scoop. I sat down at the ebony lacquered picnic table in the middle of the clubhouse and said, "Pete, today is the day. Today is the day you have to tell me all about the Babe."

He took a drag on his Camel and looked at me. I wondered if I had crossed the line and destroyed our growing friendship.

And then he uttered what might have been his best-kept secret. I never heard anyone else say that Pete told him the same thing.

"Never flushed the toilet."

That was it. And maybe that was all you needed to know about the Babe.

The one person who always understood and shared these stories with me was Thad Mumford, our right field ballboy, and the first African American ballboy in the majors. The son of a Washington dentist, he would commute to the Bronx for the joy of this job, and he loved Pete, even though Pete always called him Tad.

Thad would go on to a great career in Hollywood and, with Dan Wilcox, was the producer of the M*A*S*H television series, even slipping my name (well, "Martin Appelski," he used) into an episode. "Tad" and I started at the bottom of the ladder in the Yankee organization, fan mail clerk and right field ballboy, but we both could appreciate Big Pete.

Spring training was coming up, and I was to go to beautiful Ft. Lauderdale as part of my responsibilities. But first I had to deal with another gnawing matter.

The military draft.

As had everyone, I had been assigned a lottery number, a number low enough that it would certainly be called at some point. I had registered with a draft board in Oneonta rather than downstate, thinking that the quota would be more enthusiastically filled there by others.

Just a few weeks into my Yankee tenure, I was called for a physical. If I passed, I could have been in Oneonta on that Friday and Saigon a few weeks later. I was not, in truth, the soldierly type.

I drove to Oneonta and got on the bus to Albany with other men my age. They were mostly from farm families, and they took this as a great adventure. One guy even played a harmonica on the bus. It might even have been his first bus ride. I sensed that they were looking forward to passing the physical and getting those M-1 rifles. I kept to myself.

In Albany, it was looking bad. I was passing every stage of the physical. I had submitted a doctor's note, which had the word *asthma* in it, but no one was taking note of it. Pass, pass, pass, pass, next station. This wasn't good.

I passed them all. Then came a final interview with a doctor named Johnson. Johnson was about to become my personal war hero, right there with Generals Sherman, MacArthur, and Eisenhower. In seconds, he looked at my doctor's note, wrote "asthma" on my papers, and classified me 4-F. Unfit. Go home.

Bang, I was out of there. Everyone on the bus back to Oneonta was gleeful. They were all selected, I flunked out. And when I got home late that night, there in the mailbox was a letter accepting me into the Army Reserves. So, even had I passed, I would have made it to reserve duty and would have been a weekend warrior. But that was all unnecessary now. I was excused. Back to reality, back to the Bronx.

And just one more thing to clear up. Donna.

Donna was now student teaching in Albany. We had no contact. But inspired by the scene in *The Graduate* in which Ben (Dustin Hoffman) drives up unannounced to Berkeley to see Elaine (Katherine Ross), I got into my 1970 Plymouth Barracuda and headed up the thruway to confront Donna and put everything right.

I did chicken out about a mile from her apartment and elected to call first from a pay phone. She invited me over but made certain that her roommate never left. We had dinner, we talked, and then it was apparent that I was going to be on my way, accomplishing nothing.

I got in my car and started driving back home. As the exits passed— Kingston, New Paltz, Newburgh—I began to feel a burden lifting. I was over her! It wasn't what I expected, but it had brought closure to the relationship and I could get on with my life. The trip had no real plan, and no real accomplishment, but suddenly it all made sense. I needed to make that trip to move past her.

About 10 years later I got a call from the alumni office at Oneonta. They were going to honor me as the Graduate of the Year. In chatting with them, I asked if they happened to have a current listing for Donna. I guess I was just curious.

After an awkward pause, the voice said, "Um, gosh, we show that she passed away in 1974."

I was stunned. They had no other information. I was stunned because someone I had once cared for so deeply had died years before and I had never heard.

I did a little research and discovered that she had died of progyria, the disease that causes rapid aging in humans. I was sad for Donna and wondered if she had always known that this gene was in her. It will always be a source of wonder to me.

SHHH! MICK
CRIES AT MOVIES

Ballplayers like meeting actors, and actors like meeting ballplayers. At the turn of the century, both were considered undesirables and banned from the better hotels. They might not be aware of this common bond, but they get a kick out of mingling and even exchanging autographs.

On occasion a movie would be shot at Yankee Stadium, and these were always pretty special days. Some of the best historic footage of old Yankee Stadium lives on in the cinema, even in awful movies like *The Babe Ruth Story*—or in great ones like *Pride of the Yankees*.

One day Frank Sinatra was at our place, doing a movie called *The Detective*.

Now Jackie Farrell, our pint-sized head of the speakers' bureau, had been an old New Jersey buddy of Frank's. He'd had a chance, he said, to be his manager, but passed on it. Instead Jackie got into the fight game, then made his way to the Yankees, and was one of Ruth's best friends. Because Jackie was barely five feet tall, and also raised in an orphanage, Babe actually remembered him by name—a rarity—and they had a great friendship. Eventually Jackie ran the speakers' bureau, meaning if he wasn't personally delivering a speech and winning friends for the Yankees, he would accompany a player on this mission. Everyone loved Jackie, and there wasn't a Moose Lodge within 200 miles he hadn't visited, winning friends for the Yanks.

I would later share an office with ol' Jackie, who was well past 70 by then. His desk was back-to-back with mine, and I have no idea what color it was, because the papers and newsclippings on his side were seven inches deep and covered with dust.

He had a habit of shuffling in on game days and going through his "mail" as though he'd never seen it before. He would review all of these letters from the '40s and '50s, just piled on his desk. He had a letter from Sally Rand, the famous fan dancer of the '30s, and his friend. He would thoughtfully pick up this letter, read it, say to me, "Getta load of *this*!" and flip me the letter. This was repeated on more than fifty occasions.

He had a lot of friends among New Jersey politicians, but, unfortunately, a good many of them were doing time at various penitentiaries around the country. Jackie corresponded with them all. Friendship ranked higher than political virtue with him.

The day Sinatra was at the Stadium, all the secretaries went nuts, just as in the days of the old Brooklyn Paramount shows, and then one remembered that Jackie had always claimed to be his old friend, and nearly his manager. Informed of his presence, Jackie said, "No kidding; I gotta say hello."

Now, not everyone had believed that Jackie really knew Sinatra, and, to be kind, many felt that even if he did, Sinatra would have long ago forgotten him. So a lot of people were holding their breath for little Jackie as he walked up a ramp and toward the empty field to say hello. No one wanted Jackie to be embarrassed here.

Jackie went down to the railing by the Yankee dugout. Sinatra was near the third base dugout, huddled with his crew.

"Hey, Frank!" yelled Jackie, full of confidence. All the secretaries were standing near him.

No response.

"Hey, Sinatra!" he shouted.

Frank turned around. He looked over at the cluster of people.

"Jackie Farrell!" he screamed. And he trotted over to the rail and gave Jackie an enormous hug.

Ever the gentleman, Jackie wasted no time in saying, "I'd like you to meet our Yankee secretaries, Frank." And one by one, he introduced them all. Frank shook hands with everyone, talked about the old days in Hoboken with Jackie, embraced him again, and went back to shooting.

Jackie Farrell stood six feet tall that afternoon.

The most interesting film shot at Yankee Stadium during my time there was *Bang the Drum Slowly*. It starred Michael Moriarty and Robert De Niro, although Vincent Gardenia pretty much stole the film as the team's manager. Neither Moriarty nor De Niro were well known at the time, so there wasn't a big fuss over the presence of Robert De Niro on our grounds. But there was an excitement to the filming process, and our old Irish doorman, Mahoney, was given a bit part on the spot, so perfect was he to say "You all have to leave now" in his Irish brogue.

They shot this film at both Yankee and Shea stadiums, moving equipment back and forth depending on which team was on the road. In the movie you'll see pitches being delivered in one park and fielded in the other. Or players in the Yankee dugout running onto the field at Shea. But aside from those technicalities that only perfectionists would care about, it was a good baseball movie.

The opening scene, under the credits, was Moriarty and De Niro taking a lap around the warning track. This being "old" Yankee Stadium, before renovation, it is the best Technicolor, 35-millimeter record we have of the old place.

The home clubhouse set was actually the visiting team's clubhouse, so that is better preserved on film than the rather spacious and splendid home clubhouse was.

About thirty years after this film was made, I was introduced to Danny Aiello during a cocktail party at Sardi's, honoring my friend Irv Welzer, a Tony Award winner as producer of *Annie Get Your Gun*.

"Danny, this is Marty Appel."

At once, Danny gave me a big bear hug and said, "I don't need an introduction to Marty Appel! He was the Yankees PR guy when I made my first movie, *Bang the Drum Slowly*."

I was shocked.

"Danny, I never met any of the actors, how would you know me?"

"Hey, I was a huge Yankee fan," he said, "I knew everybody there!"

Such is the enduring power of the Yankees. I had a similar introduction to Spike Lee. "Spike, this is Marty Appel."

"The Yankee guy?"

Yankee fans are everywhere. And moments like this made me realize that the association with the team carried far beyond my imagination.

I mention all of these films because in the first week of my first summer's employment, another one was being shot at Yankee Stadium: *Paper Lion*, starring Alan Alda as George Plimpton. *Paper Lion* was actually a football movie, but it recalled Plimpton's first "Walter Mitty" effort, when he pitched to big leaguers in Yankee Stadium (for a book called *Out of My League*).

To back up Alda ("Plimpton") on the mound, extras were needed who would look athletic enough to pass for ballplayers. And so a casting call went out to real Yankees, and about a dozen signed up, earning about eighty dollars for the day. One was Bobby Cox, another was Steve Barber, and I think Steve Whitaker was in it. Maybe even Tom Tresh. Players would do a lot for eighty bucks then.

Another was Jim Bouton.

Bouton was in his final days with the Yankees. He had burst onto the scene in 1962 as one of four terrific Yankee rookies—with Tresh, Joe Pepitone, and Phil Linz—and had turned into a 20-game winner and a World Series hero. He was never "one of the boys"—in fact, he was not like other players at all. He was a fan who had sat in the bleachers as a kid and who had somehow become a big leaguer. But he was far too politically left to ever be one of the boys, and anyone who got along so well with the writers was never trusted. So the Bulldog was often left by himself.

Now it was 1968, and Jim was battling back from the minor leagues. He had spent most of '67 at Syracuse, trying to learn a knuckleball. He would make only three starts with the '68 Yankees and then would be off to the Seattle Pilots the following year, taking notes along the way for what would become *Ball Four*, the bestselling baseball book of all time.

And here he was on this sunny morning, during a break in the shooting, sitting by himself in the Yankee dugout. Alone.

I wandered over to him during a break from answering fan mail. I introduced myself, and he greeting me pleasantly. It turned out that both of our minds were elsewhere.

Robert Kennedy had been shot earlier in the day, following his victory in the California primary. He was still clinging to life, but it was apparent from the news reports that he would die. Just as my first week on the job, in April, had been marred by the shooting of Dr. King, my first week of the summer coincided with the RFK shooting.

I had done volunteer work for Kennedy just weeks before in college. This shocking assassination had effectively shut down the electoral process for 1968. And that is what Bouton and I began to speak about— how our political system was moving closer to a third world country's, with opposition candidates being killed, and how, by eliminating Kennedy, the likelihood of the election serving as a referendum on the Vietnam War was pretty much disappearing.

It was a very stimulating conversation, and I was of course fascinated that I was having it with a real Yankee, sitting there in his uniform, in the Yankee dugout! Bouton and I connected nicely that day. He was, as I mentioned, alone, which was both a metaphor for his Yankee career and a forecast of his future. Somehow he connected with a kid from the fan mail department and found someone to talk to.

This didn't grow into a special friendship, for, a week later, he was gone, sold to Seattle of the Pacific Coast League, his Yankee career over.

But he did remember me over the years when we occasionally met, and he did remember that we had had that conversation in the Yankee dugout the day of the RFK assassination.

When Jim wrote *Ball Four*, he couldn't seem to understand why it was considered such a breach of conduct to reveal what went on in the club-house. When he was banned from ballparks while trying to earn a living as a broadcaster, he didn't get it. When his old teammates ignored him, he expressed disbelief. When old opponents whom he didn't even know personally attacked him, he would say, "He doesn't even know me!"

Ball Four was a very important book. Co-authored with Leonard Shecter, an iconoclast New York sportswriter, it was important because it took you into the mind of a big league ballplayer who was literate enough to tell you what that experience meant. When Bouton wrote of getting out of bed in the middle of the night and delivering a phantom pitch next to his bed, with a fear that he had somehow "lost it" in his sleep, he was taking us through a thought process that might have been momentarily experienced by every pitcher in baseball history. It was wonderful for those moments.

It was entertaining for others—the nighttime habits of ballplayers, the mischief of his celebrated Yankee teammates.

The publication of *Ball Four* did take baseball books to a new level, and did break old taboos. When Mantle and Ford collaborated with Joe Durso on a book of personal anecdotes, they told many of the same stories Bouton had told. It was as though, once the story was out there, a barrier was lifted and it became fair game.

So whereas baseball literature had been fanciful and easy for 70 years, whereas Gene Schoor's Mickey Mantle biography could be the subject of my book reports for several years running, the game had now changed. Baseball writing had matured, and the fans were going to be taken along whether they wanted to be or not.

When I worked with Bowie Kuhn on his autobiography many years later, we came to the Bouton affair. Kuhn had called Bouton onto the carpet for poor conduct when he wrote the book, and being called to the principal's office had helped make *Ball Four* a bestseller. But Kuhn did not want to describe the moment. One of our few areas of disagreement was over the treatment of the Bouton matter. I thought it was a very significant event for baseball and for the Kuhn administration. He felt otherwise and didn't want to mention it at all.

In the end, he agreed to four paragraphs at the end of a chapter, concluding with Mickey Mantle's own review of the book: "Jim who?"

Bouton had no invitations to Yankees Old Timers Days for 30 years. Thirty years! True, early on, players like Mantle and Ford and Ellie

Howard had said they didn't want him there. And it was felt that if he were invited, others might boycott. I thought that was an exaggerated fear, but he was not invited, nor would Pete Sheehy give any player Bouton's number, 56. It was ignobly "retired."

Finally, in 1998, Bouton was invited back. His daughter had been killed in an auto accident. His son wrote a guest column in *The New York Times* saying how much it would mean to him. Steinbrenner was in a forgiving mood. Everyone was, after all, getting older. Mantle was gone. Howard was gone.

And so the Bulldog returned for Old Timers Day in 1998. He was, it turned out, in better shape than most of his teammates and still pitching in pickup games when he could find one. He had also become a successful businessman. Because his daughter's devastating death had played a part in the invitation, it was a very emotional day for Jim. And I looked at him in the Yankee dugout, the very dugout where we had sat together 30 years before on the day Robert Kennedy was shot, and I thought that grudges should never last this long.

There is not one thing about my first spring training that I've forgotten. I remember every restaurant I ate in, whom I dined with, every journalist who visited, every author who stopped by, every player's gait, every ritual—from the hardboiled eggs and the soup of the day in the clubhouse to the day when Pete first put the team in pinstripes so we could begin taking better pictures for the Yearbook, scorecard, and publicity stills. We stayed in a beautiful Schrafft's Hotel on Sunrise and A1A right on the beach, and our offices, adjacent to a hospitality room, were in the hotel. There were few night games in spring training, so the day ended around four—time to get back for a quick swim and then plan dinner.

The shrimp cocktail on the rooftop restaurant was the best. I often dined with Tony Solaita, a sumo-sized first baseman from American Samoa who was as gentle a man as there ever was. He had hit 51 home runs in a Class-A league the year before, and Pete gave him uniform number 51. He was not ready for the majors yet, but he was one of the people everyone wanted to watch develop in a big league camp. Tony was serious when he said that his motivation for playing ball was to make enough money to help his father, a minister, build a new church on the island.

Tony would only play one game for the Yankees in 1968, but he saw action in parts of six other seasons with the Royals, Angels, Expos, and Blue Jays. He hit 50 home runs in 525 games before his final release, one short of that magical 51 that got everyone's attention. He was fairly popular in Kansas City but never made it as a star. He went back to American Samoa, I hope with enough money to build that church, and the next time I saw his name in the newspaper was in February 1990. He had been murdered in a robbery. Such a gentle man.

Ft. Lauderdale was like paradise to me. My first day there, Bob Fishel picked me up at the airport, along with our team photographer Michael Grossbardt, and gave us a guided tour. The inland waterways gave the city the nickname "The Venice of America." It was popular for spring break with college students, and had been immortalized in bikini movies. The nightclubs were dazzling. Joe Namath had opened a Bachelor's 3 restaurant downtown. It was the place to go.

The hospitality room in Schrafft's was a key stop for all visiting baseball people, and sometimes for drop-ins like Jesse Owens, the Olympic hero. Jesse had been hired by the American League as a baserunning instructor. Usually there is some personal connection at work when such hires are made, perhaps a tie to Joe Cronin, the league president. I didn't know that to be the case, but it was a treat to sit with him and listen to his tales. I found it especially interesting to hear him tell of his adventures in the '36 Olympics, winning in front of Hitler, because I was sure he would have been sick of telling the story after almost 35 years. But he wasn't, not a bit.

Jim Turner, our pitching coach, frequently dominated the conversations in the hospitality room. Turner spent more than a half century in uniform, a record at the time (Connie Mack did not wear a uniform—there is always some catch to baseball trivia), and had strong opinions on everything. I remember a long argument he mounted, to the effect that a manager was not "fired" if his contract wasn't renewed, he had simply fulfilled the contract. It was not a firing. Okay, Colonel. (The record books will tell you that Turner's nickname was "Milkman Jim," because of an offseason job he once held. Never once was he ever called Milkman when I was around. It was always "Colonel.")

I also liked the Colonel's old baseball expressions, brought forth from another age. Occasionally I would be near the Yankee dugout toward the end of a game, preparing to grab a player for a postgame television interview or something, and I would be able to listen in on the sounds from the dugout. Some of it was surprisingly trite, right out of Little League, things like "Hang in there, man" or "You can do it!"

My favorite was Turner's gleeful reaction to a big, sweeping curve that baffled some poor hitter. He would whoop and erupt with "Kansas City Kitty!" It conjured up images of ball fields from a very long time ago. But then again, Jim Turner dated back to 1925 in pro ball.

Years after he retired, I had reason to call him for a magazine story I was writing. He still lived in Nashville, Tennessee, with the same phone number I'd had for 20 years. I remembered that he lived with his wife, Pauline, and two grown, unmarried daughters.

As one does, cautiously, I gently asked how Pauline was, not quite sure if she had passed on.

"Oh, she's fine, just fine, thanks for asking," he said. "But she passed away last year."

Turner had put in his baseball time, but his fellow coach, Frank Crosetti, was truly a Yankee legend. He had broken in as Yankee shortstop in 1932 and remained as a coach through 1968, my first year. Talkative, wiry, and peppery even in his later years, he used to jump into the stands and run after early-arriving concession boys who had caught a batting practice foul ball and refused to toss it back. Oh, was the Cro ever faithful about guarding the ball supply! What a sight to see old No. 2 at full gallop in pursuit of some 18-year-old who had caught a lucky foul.

Ralph Houk presided over all of this. He was not a hospitality room guy, because his home was in Pompano Beach, but as manager he was a commanding presence. That he had fought heroically in World War II was not a surprise, for he was clearly a well-chosen leader. So respected was he that, fearful of his being lured away to manage the Red Sox, the Yankees dropped Casey Stengel after the 1960 World Series to promote Houk. And of course, Houk responded with three straight pennants before moving up to the front office.

As general manager he had hired Yogi Berra to manage in '64 and then took part in the firing of Yogi after the team lost the World Series. Yogi never verbalized this, but how ignominious it must have been to have his onetime backup catcher—a guy who could never crack the lineup—become his boss, and then fire him.

With Berra's dismissal came the imploding of the Yankee dynasty: the debacle of the Johnny Keane hiring and firing, and then the return of Houk to the manager's job. He was still "the Major," still a commanding presence, but suddenly his teams were very ordinary and he was no longer looking quite like the genius who had coaxed the '61 Yankees into successes Stengel never dreamed of.

Within the Yankees he had unyielding respect up and down the organization, and I think he could have managed forever, even if with a .500 ballclub. He didn't do it with charm—he could be ferocious and intimidating with the press—but the players all loved him (except for Curt Blefary, who thought he should be playing more). "I'd run through a wall for Ralph Houk" was the common phrase. Or did we create that in the PR department?

One of Houk's strengths was loyalty, and this may have also been one of his failings. As the seasons of mediocrity plowed forward, with little sign of progress from the farm system, the fans began to take things out on Horace Clarke.

Horace was a victim because he was there so long. He succeeded Bobby Richardson at second base, and although you will find that he led the league in putouts, chances, and double plays several times, he was pretty gun-shy at second and not one to stand in and take his lumps, as the keystone guy has to do. Fans saw this, the media saw it, but Houk stuck with him. And as others came and went, Horace stayed, so that the whole era began to become the Horace Clarke era.

Hoss was a good offensive player, a good baserunner, and an easy-going, mellow kind of guy from the Virgin Islands. I would kid him about wearing long-sleeve sweatshirts on the hottest of summer days, and he would say, "Ah, mon, this is a cool snap where I come from."

But his presence on the field was irritating the fans, who saw it as a lack of effort to improve the club.

In fact, however, such an opportunity came along in successive spring trainings in the person of Fred Francis Frazier of Fresno, California. Fred was a fourth-round draft pick in 1969 and had caught people's attention by hitting .286 at Kinston in 1970 and .261 at Syracuse in '71, respectable marks for a second baseman at that time. He was smooth in the field, had a head for the game, and had a self-confidence that said "big leaguer." He was built like Richardson and was often compared to him.

Some—including Fishel, who was looking at it from a marketing standpoint—felt that in another organization the manager would have just taken the bold step of saying, "This kid is going north with us as my second baseman!" It would have been an exciting story—a 20-year-old, the job his to lose, a statement about shaking up the pattern of losing, a statement about recognizing that with Horace Clarke, mediocrity was the order of the day.

But Houk, more than most managers, was loyal to veterans and was not the sort who would ever do anything like that. Many felt he made up the 25-man roster before anyone reported to spring training. In all his years, I think he kept one non-roster player from spring training, a pitcher named Fred Beene. (The players used to think I knew the roster, too, because I would have been told whom to feature in the Yearbook. In truth, I was often coached as to whom to put on the pages that could be changed in the "revised edition.")

Fred Frazier never played a single game in the major leagues. Disheartened, he went back and hit .216 at Syracuse in '72 and soon dropped off the radar screens. He was a big leaguer to me, and, as Fishel said, his promotion would have given the team a dramatic shot in the arm when we needed it. But that wasn't Houk's style.

The most dramatic presence in our spring training camp was certainly Mickey Mantle, who was enlisted as a special instructor. He was certainly special, but hardly an instructor. It was doomed to failure, for the players were too much in awe to ask him for tips, and he was too shy to just walk up to someone and offer them.

Joe DiMaggio had been a special instructor until 1967, but then Charlie Finley hired him to be a full-time coach (and vice president) with the Oakland A's, ending his Yankee tenure. That tenure was remembered mostly for the occasional presence of Marilyn Monroe.

In 1993 I was on business in Ft. Lauderdale and decided to stay at the Sheraton Yankee Clipper Hotel, where the team had first stayed when it moved there from St. Petersburg in 1962. As an older bellman was taking me to my room, I was telling him that I had never stayed there during my Yankee days, because by then we had moved to Schrafft's.

It turned out that he had worked there all those years.

"Ah, yes," he said. "Room 134 was always Mr. Bruce Henry. And room 138, that was Mr. Fishel. And room 234 was Mr. DiMaggio. And 227 was Miss Monroe and her hairdresser when they would visit."

One of my favorite old stories involved those innocent roommates, Bobby Richardson and Tony Kubek, models of perfect behavior. The phone in their room rang, and it was the unmistakable whispery voice of Marilyn.

"Is Joe there?" she asked. She had misdialed.

"Nope, not here," said Tony. "See ya."

Richardson, according to legend, could not believe Kubek had simply hung up without starting a conversation. Kubek said Bobby almost insisted that they call her back to see if she needed help with something. Good old Marilyn could touch the heart of even Bobby Richardson.

Harry Harris, a crusty but likeable photographer with the Associated Press who once had a fistfight with Ernest Hemingway over some woman in a Key West saloon, once happened upon Joe and Marilyn on the Ft. Lauderdale beach outside the Yankee Clipper. Harry was not what you would call an autograph hound, but he had a baseball with him, and something told him to get it signed by the two of them. What a treasure that would become! A ball signed by the two of them is rarer than . . .

well, the modern joke in the collecting world is, "rarer than a baseball *not* signed by Bob Feller!" I was told that Harry's son turned down a mid–five figure offer for the ball.

With DiMaggio having moved to Oakland, the arrival of Mantle as a special instructor brought some needed glamor to the camp. And because Mantle knew me from my days as his fan mail handler, we had a nice friendship in those spring camps. One of my jobs, since he wasn't really instructing, was to arrange for him to pose for photos with rookies—they would be too shy to ask him, so they would ask me. Mick would always be happy to pose. How many Steve Grotemyers, Larry Gowells, Rick Earles, Dave Cheadles, Gerry Pirtles, and Jorge Maduros have those pictures today, I don't know, but I hope they had the good sense to save them.

My favorite ritual each spring was the day Mickey arrived in town. I would pick him up at Ft. Lauderdale Airport, which in those days required that you descend from the plane onto the tarmac rather than walk directly into the terminal. I would wait for him at the bottom of the steps and we would walk briskly toward the luggage carousel. Heads would turn in a moment of recognition, and occasionally he would sign an autograph, but once the bags came, whoosh, we were gone.

We'd go to some beachfront restaurant off a hotel on the Galt Ocean Mile (Mick would order his "breakfast of champions," a Bloody Mary), and then we would get him a rental car and register him at Schrafft's. In the car we would talk about life. He would ask if I had a girlfriend, and once I said I was hoping to find one who was also "a friend." He said, "Hell, Merlyn's my best friend." I thought it was a wonderfully sweet comment about his wife, a partner in what would develop into an enormously complicated relationship.

A remarkable moment came one evening when a few of us, Mantle included, decided to walk a few hundred yards from Schrafft's to the local theater on Sunrise. They were showing *The Last Picture Show*, a black-and-white study of life in a small Texas town in the 1950s. Of course it could have been the '40s as well—things didn't change very much—and it could have been Oklahoma as well as Texas. Could have even been Commerce.

Mick must have heard something about the movie, because I didn't take him for a guy who just went to the cinema to pass the time or who loved Peter Bogdanovich's films. Whatever the reason, when the film ended and the lights went on, there he was, wiping tears from his eyes.

"That reminded you of home?" I asked.

"Hell, we even had a village idiot like that one," he said, starting to smile now.

During spring training of 1972, Mayor John Lindsay of New York came to camp. He was campaigning during the presidential primary season, and Florida was a key state. A drop in at the Yankees camp seemed essential, even if he knew nothing about baseball. Not a thing. I was told he would sit next to the Yankee dugout during Mayor's Trophy Games—torture for him—and ask an aide, "Is this good, should I cheer?"

In any case, he was as lost in a baseball clubhouse as he would have been in a mosque, and his campaign aides, desperate for a photo op and trying to ease the discomfort over none of the players caring one drop about the candidate, found Mantle on the left side of the clubhouse, munching on a sandwich. "Ah, Mantle," they said, "a guy he's heard of."

Mick was in his role as an instructor, of course, and the fact that he had retired four years before was not among Lindsay's facts on hand. The aides walked him over to Mantle, and Lindsay reached out his hand, shook it warmly, and said, "Luck, luck, luck!"

Mantle looked at him quizzically. "Luck, luck, luck?" What the hell was that supposed to mean? Does he think I'm a player on this team? Does he mean digesting the sandwich?

It should be noted that politics was for Mantle what baseball was to Lindsay. I doubt that Mantle ever voted or could name one senator or the three branches of the federal government. What a moment in photo op history this was.

So Mickey accepted the "luck, luck, luck," finished his sandwich, and Lindsay, photo accomplished, went on to get slaughtered in the primary, drop out of the campaign, and essentially finish his political career.

Mantle had chosen to retire in Ft. Lauderdale in the days before spring training opened in 1969. He wore a houndstooth jacket and spoke to a barrage of microphones, admitting, "I just can't hit anymore." For years people would say, "Jeez, Mick, if they only had the DH rule when you were playing, you could have gone on." They were missing the point.

Mick was the first to admit that to retire at 36—and to have his last good season at 32—was not the way it should have turned out. He blamed it on carousing too much, as he saw Mays and Aaron and Rose play into their 40s. Of course, he'd had horrific injuries right from his rookie season that severely hampered him as well.

Since I did my share of Mantle watching in '68, it did bother me that he seldom took batting practice. It was as though he had already moved on to another level. His buddies from the great teams were all gone; here he was sitting next to Steve Whitaker in the team photo. It took him a long time to wrap his legs with long Ace bandages for support each day, bandages that hung over a hook in his locker. He was watching his batting average drop below .240 in that final season—the year of the pitcher—and saw his career mark drop under .300, which always killed him. He seemed to lack motivation, and the fans were never seeing him take BP.

Some felt the decision to retire was made in the summer of '68 (Dick Young reported it in the *Daily News*, in a front-page headline), but it wasn't official until February of '69. Some accused the Yankees of delaying the news so as not to affect ticket sales. It turned out that it didn't have much effect at all. Attendance for 1969 dropped only 58,000, and in 1970 it actually surpassed the '68 total. In those days of course, we were making a big deal out of passing a million "for the twentieth consecutive year," and today 3 million has become the goal.

The high point of the 1969 season was Mickey Mantle Day, scheduled for June 8. I always liked these special "days," even if they were sometimes just excuses for sponsors to get free plugs by donating gifts.

Of course there were lesser ones as well—I remember we had a Danny Cater Day in 1970. Cater's wife was from Williamsport, and the good people of Williamsport decided they wanted to honor Danny with his own day.

"How many tickets will you be buying?" we asked the organizers.

"About six hundred," they said.

"You've got a Danny Cater Day."

Before the game, everyone was kidding Danny about whether he would give a "luckiest man on the face of the earth speech" and bring back memories of Lou Gehrig. No one took this very seriously.

But then we had the pregame ceremony—the fans barely paying attention, Danny getting a case of Dr Pepper and other special gifts—and suddenly he's at the microphone, crying like a baby. We had all overlooked the fact that he might actually be moved by this, and he was. It caught him by surprise and embarrassed him, too.

It must have embarrassed the good people of Williamsport a few years later when Danny changed wives, leaving his bride from the home of Little League baseball for the Holiday Inn desk clerk in Winter Haven, Florida . . . but these things happen.

Anyway, Mantle Day was a meticulously planned event, brilliantly choreographed by Bob Fishel.

Mantle had never looked more handsome. The fans had never poured more love from their seats. When he was introduced, the cheering went on for seven or eight minutes and might never have ended had not Mickey, at Mike Burke's urging, simply begun to speak. He evoked the names of his great predecessors. DiMaggio presented him with a plaque for the center field wall, and, to Joe's surprise (and probably relief), Mantle in turn said, "A few minutes ago Joe gave me a plaque, and if I'm going to have one hanging out there, he has to have one hanging just a little higher than mine."

A nice moment, Joe giving Mickey his plaque, Mickey giving Joe his plaque. And when we took those plaques down during the renovation of Yankee Stadium and re-hung them in the new Stadium in 1976, I walked to Monument Park with the construction people and made sure that Joe's plaque, for the first time, did in fact hang one inch higher than Mickey's.

I was proud of my little maneuver, even if from a distance you really couldn't discern the difference. Sadly, after I left, it was decided to remove all the plaques for a good cleaning, and when they were re-hung, my little maneuver was erased. Someone noticed that one was higher than the other.

Mantle Day brought back not only Mick's family, including his mother, his four boys (I had them sign a Yankee Yearbook with their family picture in their little boy handwriting), and Merlyn, but also his scout, Tom Greenwade; his former general manager, George Weiss; representatives of all of his pennant-winning teams; his minor league managers, Harry Craft and George Selkirk; and a move that really brought down the house, Mel Allen, in his first return to Yankee Stadium, to formally introduce Mickey from the dugout.

Mel had returned to the Yankee family, and for many it was the grandest moment of the whole day.

I don't know how Mick felt about Mel, other than that Mel had recommended a bad doctor to him late in '61, which caused him to miss most of the season's final weeks and lose the home run race to Maris.

Mick arrived early, looking great in a conservative blue suit. He saw me and said, "See if you can rustle me up my 'breakfast of champions'—Louie will know what I mean." Lou Napoli, the bartender in the pressroom, did know, poured the liquid into a cup, and I dutifully carried it back to the clubhouse for him. He proceeded to deliver a wonderful speech to the adoring crowd, and then, in a masterful Fishel touch, boarded a golf cart, with ground crew member Danny Coletti driving, and made a slow "last lap" around the Stadium, waving respectfully to the crowd. It was as moving a ceremony as any Yankee Stadium had ever staged—thankfully, free of gifts—and full of memories of an 18-year career in which the height of Mantle's popularity was attained in his declining seasons. From 1965–68 he was the most cheered player in baseball, whether playing at home or on the road.

For nearly thirty years, I held a very special memento of his career. It was his last bat. It was severely cracked, which added to its legend. All during 1968, the Yankee batboy, Elliott Ashley, had promised me a broken bat. The summer ended, and I still didn't have one. The Yankees concluded the '68 season in Fenway Park. Mantle batted in the first inning in the Saturday game and broke his bat popping out to Rico Petrocelli in short left field. He never took the field. It was a final at bat, except no one realized that it was. He didn't play Sunday, the final day of the season.

Elliott had remembered that he owed me a broken bat. I never expected it would be a Mantle, but he secured it for me, brought it back from Boston, and held it for me until we saw each other. Neither of us knew it was the "last bat" until Mantle retired five months later.

Bob Fishel gave me a great deal of autonomy for a rookie and pretty much turned over management of the Yearbook to me. I worked daily with Michael Grossbardt on our photo needs and with the design studio in New York on the layout. Before the days of FedEx, or even fax, we were dependent on the mail to check copy and design from 1,200 miles away in Florida. But as a fan who had never missed getting a Yearbook, I was loving the process of editing one.

Sure enough, I was getting coaching on who should get two-page spreads, who should be on the pages we could revise in a second edition, and who should just slip into the "on the way up" section rather than be granted a half-page of his own.

Some of our players were veterans who had started in the '50s and were running out their careers. Lindy McDaniel was our relief star. He gave the impression of being old before his time, certainly not one to enjoy the goings-on of immature teammates. He did his best, distributing "Pitching for the Master" religious tracts to everyone from time to time, but it didn't seem to reform anyone, except for an occasional batboy. Lindy may not have been "one of the boys," but he had a nasty forkball, and achieved tremendous success with the team.

Steve Hamilton was a tall, gray, amusing, and educated lefthander who was terror against lefthanded hitters, and a one-batter specialist long before such things were fashionable. He too was seemingly older than everyone else and was in fact the senior player on the team after Tresh and Pepitone were traded. I loved Hambone. He had an Andy Griffith sense of humor, chewed these huge wads of tobacco, and had a great compassion for the game. He was the American League player rep, the team's player rep, and he foresaw the coming of some sort of free agency. He was a thoughtful, diplomatic ambassador for the cause, and had he remained in the players union after his 1970 retirement, he would have been an effective and reasonable voice in what became a hostile environment, remaining so to this day.

Steve became famous for throwing the "Folly Floater," a blooper pitch that soared high into the air and was nearly impossible to hit on its downward trajectory unless you timed it just right. It was a bit of a burlesque pitch, and, in truth, he threw it perhaps 25 times in all. But it became his trademark.

The two most memorable occasions on which he used it were in retiring Cleveland's Tony Horton, who proceeded to crawl back to the dugout in embarrassment, and in a "B squad" minor league spring training game, where he was just getting his work in. A minor league umpire was working the plate, and, being unfamiliar with the pitch, he stepped in front of the plate and caught the floater, thinking Hamilton just wanted a new ball.

The Horton episode took on a sad hue when Tony had an emotional breakdown shortly thereafter and his career crashed to a close.

A terrific photo shoot we did one spring involved Pete Sheehy, who was normally quite camera-shy. When he casually mentioned to me that he had a photo "someplace" of himself with Ruth and Gehrig, I wouldn't let him alone until he produced it. Finally, he did. It was taken in St. Petersburg. He was seated between them on a backless bench in front of those distant, dense, St. Pete trees.

I decided to recreate the photo with current Yankee stars and do a Pete tribute in the Yearbook. I got a bench, found a spot with trees in the background, and all I needed was our current Ruth and Gehrig.

Well, it might have been Murcer and Munson in a year or two, but Thurman was still a rookie, so I had to turn to pitching, and I got Mel Stottlemyre and Fritz Peterson, who, like most Yankees, loved Pete and got a kick out of posing. We shot the thing in the deep recesses behind the right field fence, with trees in the background, and it was a nice tribute, which Pete appreciated. Not long after that, I finally persuaded him to join in the team photos, and he came to appreciate his small celebrity late in his career.

I had the idea to name the clubhouse in his honor when we moved back into the new Yankee Stadium in 1976. George Steinbrenner concurred and we had a sign made for the entrance. Thus, he had a chance to preside over "The Pete Sheehy Clubhouse" while he was still alive.

His funeral, in 1985, was in a small church in his hometown in New

Jersey, although it would have been perfectly appropriate to bury him under the Yankee clubhouse like popes are buried in the Vatican and cardinals at St. Patrick's Cathedral in New York. Billy Martin, in tears at the funeral, noted, "I've known the man for thirty-five years; he was like a father to me. Today was the first time I ever met his wife."

While we were pressing on with our 1970 Yankee camp, we were in the unusual position of being the less interesting team in town. The New York Mets had shocked the world by winning the 1969 World Series. As much of a Yankee fan as I was, and as much as this was a setback for our attendance and interest, I have to admit that for me, the '69 Mets was the most exciting sports story of my life. To have come from where they did, to have pulled off this miracle with a bunch of young and ordinary players, made you feel as though some heavenly being was watching over this. When Ron Swoboda made his incredible catch off Brooks Robinson—a ball that Clemente might not have caught—you knew this team was blessed. That was the play that said "Miracle Mets" for me.

And it was the play that said, "This is a sad time in Yankee history": second in attention from the New York fans, recovering from the end of the Mantle era, and no good fortune in sight.

AVOID THE BACK
OF THE BUS

I don't know why we didn't win more in the early '70s. We had an all-star team—in the front office, at least. Some of the best people to ever run baseball clubs were there.

Some were holdovers from the glamor years of Topping and Webb, which gave me a link to the front office that went back to the late '40s. I could talk to the guys in the ticket office, or on the grounds crew, about life in the Casey Stengel and George Weiss era, and for them it was yesterday.

Bill Kane was the statistician for the team. He had joined the club in 1961—a pretty magical year—out of St. Bonaventure's. The statistician in those days reported to Mel Allen, who could be a tyrant as a boss. On more than one occasion, Mel would smack Bill over the head with his scorecard if he felt Kane had bungled something. The biggest smack, the Bobby Thomson of smacks, came while a no-hitter was in progress against the Yankees. It seems Kane had missed the last-minute pitching change Minnesota made and had poor Mel giving the wrong pitcher for most of the game. Smack!

Bill had a good baseball mind and argued his points well. He always maintained that a pitcher's won-lost record told you more about him than his ERA, contrary to what many would argue.

"Is the guy a winner?" Kane would ask. "That's where you find the answer to the question."

Bill had battled polio as a child, leaving him with a limp and with one leg noticeably thinner than the other. He had an Irish face, but in the darkness of a bar, late in the evening, he could be mistaken for Mantle, especially if he was sitting with Whitey Ford. (Good for him—the only player I had ever been mistaken for was Thurman Munson.)

One night he was sitting at the bar with Ford, and a Yankee fan approached.

"Mickey?" said the fan.

Kane looked up.

"Umm, Mr. Mantle, excuse me for disturbing you, but you cannot believe what an honor it is for me to meet you. I mean, you have been my hero since you first came up. I know everything about you! I have pictures of you all over my house! This is unbelievable."

Whitey started to chuckle, but Kane said nothing.

"And the thing is, Mick, the COURAGE! The way you play with those bad legs, day after day, it's unbelievable!"

With that, Kane finally spoke.

"You don't know the half of it," he said. "Look at this."

With that, Bill rolled up his pant leg on his bad leg. The leg was barely eight inches in circumference.

The fan's eyes almost popped out.

"Oh, Mickey, I had no idea! God, how in the world can you play on that!"

And off he went into the night, shaking his head. I suspect that to this day he is telling the story of the night Mickey Mantle showed him his bad leg.

Kane eventually was named traveling secretary. At one time in baseball history, this job was like being an assistant general manager. It certainly was at the time Gabe Paul held it with Cincinnati in the late '30s and early '40s. And it was Gabe who promoted Kane (without a salary increase) to the position, when it was decided that there was really no need to have a full-time statistician.

Kane put up a good argument for a raise, but failed. He had no choice but to take the demanding job, or be out on the street.

He was succeeding Rob Franklin, who had served briefly following the retirement of long-time Yankee favorite Bruce Henry, one of the most engaging men in all of baseball. Bruce, who called everyone "coach," was as personable as he was capable, had a great sense of humor and a great friendship with Ralph Houk, and knew everyone in every town.

Franklin—much younger, much more cerebral—was filling big shoes. He was very bright (educated at Oberlin), befriended the team's brighter players, and thus was not as popular as Henry.

He did a great job, and he went through the entire 1973 season without ever losing a bag. Oh, except one: Mary Paul, Gabe's wife, had her makeup case lost on a flight to Texas.

And that was pretty much it for Rob. You could lose the team bats, you could lose the manager's suitcase, but not the general manager's wife's makeup case. So Bill Kane became the traveling secretary, and Rob went on to management positions at Madison Square Garden and Miami Arena.

Because Bill Virdon was now the Yankee manager, and because you couldn't have two Bills sitting at the front of the bus, Kane became "Killer Kane."

The players liked Kane. You could tell by all the kidding he took. But there was an honesty about him and he could put a player in his place if he needed to.

One guy who really took a liking to him was the surly Alex Johnson, who joined us late in '74 with a reputation for not getting along with anyone. He would go to dinner with Kane and converse with him, though many people had never even heard him speak. They stood side-by-side in team photos. No one could quite figure out what this bond was, unless it was about horseracing, which they both enjoyed.

I was never a big fan of gambling—or "gaming," as they now call it (hey, I'm a PR man, and I salute the guy who said, "Let's call it gaming"), but I was in love with Secretariat, the beautiful champion who won the Triple Crown in 1973. Months after that stirring last race, he was going to be walked around Belmont Park one last time before being retired to stud.

"Bill, where's Belmont?" I asked. "Queens?"

I wanted to go to "Secretariat Day" to see the horse in person.

So the two of us snuck off for the afternoon so I could applaud and take some pictures of the great racehorse, while Kane slipped up to the pari-mutuel windows to put a few bucks on the fourth race.

Killer and Gabe had an arm's-length relationship, which was fortunate for Gabe because there were days Kane wanted to put his nickname to good use. When Gabe rewrote the rules to get Kane excluded from a winning share of World Series money—a tradition that went back as far as baseball did, and certainly as far as when Gabe won with the Reds—the two of them came close to battle. Kane knew he could win the battle and lose the war. He could fight for what was rightfully his but ultimately lose his job. Gabe had put him in a terrible position, and it soured his tenure, which was otherwise efficient and professional.

I made my first road trip when Bruce Henry was leading the troops. It was at the end of the 1970 season, a trip to Boston and Baltimore. I think Fishel saw it as a reward for me, because he truly enjoyed traveling and was giving up a lot to send his assistant. But the year was almost over, and he felt I had earned the trip.

I was 22. I hadn't had a lot of travel experience myself, let alone with a baseball team. I had the responsibility of serving the press's needs as well as making sure I learned the routine, made the buses on time, and so forth.

Little did I know what the press's needs would entail on this trip.

Joining the team at such a young age, I was privileged to encounter some of the baseball writers whose roots went back to the '20s and '30s. I knew John Drebinger, who wrote the front page of *The New York Times* World Series coverage for every game between 1929 and 1963. I knew Jimmy Cannon, who started covering baseball in 1940 and was one of the few close friends Joe DiMaggio had among the press. I knew the brilliant Harold Rosenthal and the kindly Hy Goldberg and mischievous Til Ferdenzi and enterprising Dick Young and the regal Arthur Daley and other giants of their times in New York journalism. I even knew Fred Lieb, who began covering baseball in 1911.

With Drebinger, I would almost have to pinch myself, to think I was sitting in the press box next to the guy who covered the opening of Yankee Stadium, Ruth's called shot, and the Gashouse Gang of '34.

He was a brilliant writer, *New York Times* style, of course, and his coverage of Maris's 61st home run is textbook journalism. But what a character!

He was nearly deaf, saved only by his hearing aid, which he would selectively turn off or on depending on whether he was interested in listening. He was known as a guy who could figure the angles—he was said to have taken his dirty laundry on road trips with him so that he could do it in the hotel and charge it to the *Times*.

When the Vietnam War heated up and we invaded Cambodia, his young *Times* colleague, George Vecsey, disgusted by the events, decided one day not to stand in the press box during the national anthem. Drebinger walked over and proceeded to swat him repeatedly with a rolled-up newspaper as if he were training a puppy.

After the *Times* retired Drebby, the Yankees gave him a job in our own public relations department. He didn't have to do anything, but he was at every home game and was a delight to have around. And he took a liking to me, so I could listen to his stories and he could tell me about his debate with Casey Stengel over who had knocked the most years off his actual birth year.

And I knew Joe Trimble. A gruff, overweight, unkempt, crewcut-bearing bull of a man who kept his cigar in the center of his mouth, drank too much, and never, in my memory, showed much in the way of humor. He was the beat reporter for the *Daily News* in the days when that was as good a job as any sportswriter could want—except, perhaps, the day in the '40s when Nick Etten chased him through the Yankees train, determined to pulverize him.

Trimble's finest moment was covering Don Larsen's perfect game in the 1956 World Series.

"The imperfect man pitched a perfect game today," he began. It was one of the great leads of all time.

But Joe was not a perfect man, either. In parks where the pressroom was adjacent to the press box, he might slip in for a drink during the game. On a few occasions, he would get the winning hit or the losing error wrong in the paper the next day, totally missing pinch hitters or defensive replacements.

He also spent a lot of time hustling off to the shanty that served as a lavatory in the Yankee Stadium press box and, if serving as official scorer and missing a play, would just open the door and wave his index finger for a base hit, or make the "OK" sign for an error, reacting to little more than the crowd noise. We would look to the right to see Joe's call; if he wasn't there, all heads turned left toward the john, waiting for his fingers to emerge. He got the call right about half the time.

Fenway Park was one in which the pressroom was just steps from the press box.

We were in our final day in Boston on my first road trip. After the game, we had 90 minutes to get on the bus for Logan Airport. Getaway days were tough on the writers, particularly since a mad dash to the clubhouse was required for some quick quotes. In Boston, that was a long haul.

There was a story in this game—Fritz Peterson, our bright but flaky lefthander (Pete Sheehy would shake his left wrist to indicate someone who was flaky), was going for his 20th victory. He was 19–11 going into the game, and at the Statler-Hilton he had been assigned room 1912. He saw that as a horrible omen and demanded that his room be changed, which it was.

Fritz left the game with a lead and headed for the clubhouse. There, hardly evoking the spirit of former 20-game-winning Yankees like Ruffing, Gomez, Raschi, Reynolds, and Ford, he hid under Houk's desk in the manager's office, listening to the Red Sox announcers call off the final inning. The Yanks won, and Fritz was 20–11. He won his 20th while crouched under a desk.

The press headed for the clubhouse to get their story. All except for Trimble.

Joe had spent the first seven innings in the pressroom. He hadn't seen a pitch. In the eighth, he staggered into the press box, unzipped his portable typewriter's case, took some puffs on his cigar, and proceeded to urinate in his pants. A puddle formed under his seat, and the Red Sox PR director, Bill Crowley, came to me and said, "You have to do something about Trimble; this is a disgrace."

He was right, but what was I supposed to do? I spotted Bruce Henry and said as much to him. To my relief, he had no answer. I really didn't *want* to do anything. This was *my* responsibility?

"Fishel would have handled this," laughed Clif Keane, the acerbic Boston writer. Peter Gammons, just a kid like me, new to the scene, was laughing. The whole new generation of Boston writers—Dan Shaughnessy, Bob Ryan, Leigh Montville—were all getting an eyeful of the habits of the passing generation.

The game ended; Trimble popped the yellow Western Union paper into his typewriter and began to type. Maury Allen, my buddy from the *Post*, leaned over to me and said, "What in the world could he be writing? He didn't see a thing!"

I walked behind Joe. Sure enough, the page in his typewriter was all gibberish—#$$%E*%&*(%*). Jim Ogle of the *Newark Star-Ledger*, part of our traveling band of writers, took a deep breath and told me to just let him be.

"I'll take care of it," he said. And Jim, who always would say, "I may not be the best but I'm the fastest," proceeded to write his stories—all different—for the *Star-Ledger*, the *Staten Island Advance*, the *Long Island Press*, Associated Press, and UPI. Then, for good measure, he wrote Trimble's story for the *Daily News*, simply as a professional courtesy—two guys who had traveled the road together for years, one helping the other. Except I had a feeling it was always Jim helping Joe.

It was a remarkable performance.

Briefly, I was distracted. When I turned my attention back to Trimble's corner of the press box, he was gone. His typewriter was still there, but his seat was empty. We had about 15 minutes to get on the bus, and I knew he was in no shape to negotiate the ramps down to the clubhouse level where the bus was parked.

"You see Trimble?" I asked Johnny McCarthy, the press box attendant.

"Nope."

I went into the pressroom and asked the bartender. No Joe.

I went back to the press box and feared the worst. I looked over the front and onto the field. I thought perhaps he had tumbled out of the press box and rolled down the screen, perhaps landing on that big slice of protective covering that looks like a big turkey roll, used to cover home plate after a game. Was Joe splattered down there?

I didn't see him.

I was now alone in the press box, with five minutes till departure. Was it my job to find him? I took one last look around and raced down the ramps to the bus. Standing room only, but I made it. I mentioned to Bruce Henry that I had lost Trimble, but he said, "He's a big boy; we've got to go." Houk was more direct: "Screw him."

As the doors were closing, he appeared. Somehow he had found the bus; somehow he had counted off the 90 minutes perfectly. He got on and the doors closed behind him.

No one offered him a seat. And we rolled off to Logan with Trimble and his cigar in the front of the bus, he swaying back and forth with the movement of the vehicle. He smelled of urine. I could see the disgust on Houk's face in the front seat.

When we got to the airport, Joe was, of course, the first one off. And as perfectly as he had negotiated his way to the bus, there the precision ended. He missed the bottom step and landed, *plop*, on his belly, on the pavement.

Houk stepped over him. So did the coaches. Bruce Henry and Ogle helped him up. And he got on to that plane for the late-night trip to our next destination, somehow appearing for breakfast the next day as fresh as a daisy, as though nothing had ever happened. I wondered what he thought when he read his story in the *Daily News*.

"How was the trip?" asked Fishel.

I grew 15 years from the experience.

In late August 1970, Mickey Mantle returned to the Yankees as a coach. This would be his last regular-season stint with the team. He had been doing *Game of the Week* appearances for NBC but decided that he missed the camaraderie of baseball, and accepted a longstanding offer from Houk to return.

NBC was not very pleased that he never even told them about this; they read it in the newspapers.

Mickey was to be our first base coach—but only for the middle innings. Elston Howard, enduring the humiliation of this, was sent to the bench for those middle innings so that Mantle could pat guys on their rumps after a base hit, remind them how many outs there were, and yell "get back" on a pickoff.

But we were all thrilled to have Mantle back with us. Just his presence added majesty to the pinstripes once again.

Since I had worked out a friendship with him, which was comfortable enough for me to kid him, I put an office memo in his locker on his first day back. It read:

> Nice to have you back. . . . We have worked out the following schedule for you, knowing how anxious you were to get back into things:
> 11–11:30   Autograph room
> 11:35–12:00   Clinic for Con Edison Kids in bleachers
> 12:05–12:20   Meet 40 handicapped children, pose for photos
> 12:25–12:40   Speak to season box holders in Stadium Club on the value of their boxes to business
> 12:45–1:00   Interview with assistant sports director, WDOS, Oneonta, NY
> 1:00–1:15   Promotional tapes welcoming Yankee fans listening to our games on the Yankee radio network
> 1:20–1:30   Greet new employees of Yankee front office who have joined team since you left
> 1:35–1:45   Take batting practice for benefit of NBC, who will have a camera on the pitcher's mound
> 1:47–2:00   Interview with Marv Albert on WHN to discuss "What Jim Bouton's book has added to my life"
> 2:03   National anthem. This season, to encourage respect for the flag, we have a different Yankee lead the fans in the singing of The Star-Spangled Banner each day. The microphone is at second base.

Mickey read this in total shock and completely believed it. He took it in with him to Houk's office to say he just couldn't do all of this. "Maybe a few of these," he said, trying to be a good guy. Houk was in on the gag and spilled the beans. It was a fun moment.

Mantle's stint as first base coach only lasted through the end of the season. It really wasn't fun for him, after all. No Ford, no Berra, no Skowron, no Maris, no Boyer, no Bauer. It just wasn't the same. This was the period in his life in which Mick had a lot of trouble finding a place for himself. He was a young man (38) with nothing to do when he woke up each day but think about golf and vodka. He would limit his Yankee involvement now to spring training.

I got a pretty good souvenir out of his short stint as coach. When he joined the club, Pete had hastily created a number 7 jersey for him. Although it was a retired number, the guy it was retired for could, of course, wear it. Pete took Munson's jersey, which was pretty worn now from his wearing the chest protector all year, and had the 15 removed and a 7 sewn on.

Mantle used the uniform the following spring, and then Pete was going to toss it, it being pretty well worn. I asked him if I could have it, and he said sure. So I got not only Mantle's last uniform to be worn in a Yankee team photo but also the jersey that had been Munson's rookie uniform. I held on to it for almost 30 years, until it was time to sell off some stuff to help pay my son's college tuition. I put it up for auction through Leland's Auctions, and the uniform's cash return quickly found its way into the treasury at UMass. A very good trade.

Lee MacPhail was our general manager. Although his father had been flamboyant, bombastic, hard-drinking, and a battler, Lee was quiet, studious, thoughtful, and reserved. He had grown up in baseball, had been an Executive of the Year, and had recently returned to the Yankees to help redirect the team's fortunes. Although Lee went on to become president of the American League, it saddened him that he was unable to bring a pennant to New York. He had the skills to make the trades, but things never worked out as he wished.

The man who helped to bring Frank Robinson to the Orioles in 1965, laying the groundwork for one of the most consistently successful franchises in the American League, just couldn't find that magic in New York.

The Yankees were victims of their own success, in some ways. Ironically, MacPhail—while serving a term in the commissioner's office as special assistant to General Eckert—actually helped to craft the free agent draft that put an end to the Yankees' dynasty. No longer would the Yankee glamor help to lure seemingly every good prospect in the country. The draft began in 1965, and the Yankees picked Bill Burbach, a lumbering pitcher who would win six games in 1969 and never another. In 1966 the team selected Jim Lyttle, a right fielder with a great throwing arm but not much pop in his bat. He hit .310 in 87 games for us in 1970 but only drove in 14 runs and was not well liked by his teammates.

In 1967, following a last-place finish, the Yanks drafted Ron Blomberg with the number one pick in the country. Boomer was like a cartoon character, a Li'l Abner in pinstripes. Always first at the buffet table, and always good humored even when you were supposed to be upset—after defeats—he was enormously popular with fans because of his outgoing nature and zany interviews. (Bad start? "Don't worry," he'd say, "sugar always rises to the top.")

He liked the media, even if he garbled their names, with Dick Schaap coming out as Jack Snap, and they liked him.

And oh, could he mash a fastball. *If* it was delivered by a righthanded pitcher. In batting practice, on several occasions, he nearly cleared the upper deck in Yankee Stadium, and he dented the façade in right field more than once. The problem was, he never really grew beyond that singular skill, which he had had as a student at Druid Hills High in Atlanta. Till the end of his career, which concluded with a .293 lifetime average, he mashed righthanders' fastballs but grew little in other areas.

Assigned to first base, he never was able to make the throw to second on bunts. He once dropped a throw at first that would have been a triple play. ("It was the first triple play I ever *saw*, and I dropped it!" he said.)

The Yankees retarded his growth by platooning him in the minor leagues so that he didn't face lefties while coming up. We were frequently attacked for this strategy. But his minor league manager, Frank Verdi, would explain, "When we play him against a lefty, he gets so screwed up it takes two weeks to straighten him out against righties!"

So Blomberg—who loved his bagels, lived down the road from me in Riverdale, was an usher at my wedding, and remains a friend—never became what number one draft picks are supposed to become. It was sad, given all of that talent; and damned if he didn't power a home run at a Yankee Old Timers Day in '94 at age 46, never losing that sweet swing. Yes, there was a righthander on the mound.

Blomberg was another unfortunate mark on MacPhail's record as general manager. Lee knew a popular Jewish player could be huge in New York, and for a time Ron *was* huge: He shared a *Sports Illustrated* cover with Bobby Murcer the year he was still flirting with .400 on July 4. But the popularity only went so far, and he wasn't moving the team forward.

After the 1971 season, MacPhail made a big trade, dealing Stan Bahnsen to the White Sox for Rich McKinney.

Bahnsen had been Rookie of the Year in 1968 and looked like a Yankee. He had an ERA of 2.04 that season and was a steady presence in our rotation. He wasn't Christy Mathewson, of course, so trading him wasn't unthinkable, but to deal him for McKinney was one of the worst fiascos the Yankees ever experienced.

The team needed a third baseman. No one had really secured the position since Clete Boyer was traded in '67. Five years of Charlie Smith, Bobby Cox, and Jerry Kenney—and it wasn't happening.

McKinney had played third base five times in 1971 with the White Sox. He had batted a soft .271 (eight homers, 46 RBIs) but had hit well against the Yankees. He had somehow impressed our scouts. Some thought he was ready to reach new levels. They were right. Wrong direction, but they were right.

Bahnsen got the news of his trade in a phone call from Marv Albert, who was doing a radio talk show. It was a tough blow for Stan, who liked New York. He was pretty shocked that McKinney was the only value he could bring in return.

McKinney was our offseason big news, our new face, our new marquee star. He would take over third base.

I am often amazed at how easily managers, coaches, general managers, and scouts think a guy can change positions just like that, after a lifetime of training at another position. It's just not that easy at that level. There were people who truly believed Todd Hundley could move from catcher to outfielder with the Mets, and he turned out to be the worst outfielder New York may have ever seen. What goes into this thinking?

I saw an early sign of trouble with McKinney when we had our winter promotional caravan before the '72 season. This was a week-long bus caravan in which we visited outlying pockets of Yankee country—Wilkes-Barre, Albany, Cheshire, Connecticut, and other areas—introducing our latest and greatest to the local media. They were popular but wearying journeys, and we'd return to the Bronx each evening and start out fresh again the next day, traveling for a week. The caravans ran until 1974, when the nation's fuel shortage gave us an excuse to cancel them—and they never resumed. Gabe Paul wasn't a big fan of the rides.

Anyway, McKinney was our shining new face on the '72 caravan, and he wandered onto the bus the first day and sat near the back, across the aisle from me. I was looking forward to getting to know him better. Up front were MacPhail, Fishel, Houk, and other club officials.

Rich was 25, curly-haired, and sort of delicate in his manner. He seemed pleasant enough, and I introduced myself to him. It was clear to him, I'm sure, that I was the team's assistant director of public relations—a club official, so to speak, although a back-of-the-bus one. I was in my usual caravan outfit—wide tie, polyester sports jacket, bellbottom slacks, big sideburns, and mustache. Hey, it was 1972.

"So, Marty," he said, as we pulled out of the Yankee Stadium parking lot, "where can I get some shit?"

I looked at him, understanding what he was asking, but not quite believing it.

"You know, some weed."

Oh, boy. What a mess I was in now.

In the first place, even if I knew, I wasn't about to become a player's drug advisor. That would be all I needed. In the second place, what the hell was he doing, telling a *team official* that he smoked grass? Was he nuts? Did I command so little respect that he could never take me seriously as a team official?

And now, what was I supposed to do with this information? Was I supposed to go to MacPhail and say, "Lee, about this guy you got for Stan Bahnsen . . ."?

Was I supposed to keep it quiet to protect McKinney, who, 10 minutes earlier, I didn't know from Honus Wagner?

This was a tough one. I could confide in Fishel, but he would probably be the good corporate soldier and tell MacPhail, probably selling me out in the process. And if McKinney got busted, you knew he would mention *my* name to his teammates, and, even if they objected to his using marijuana, they wouldn't think much of me. What was I to become, the team narc?

No, that wasn't going to work. I was going to have to keep this to myself, under the assumption that if he was that open with me after 10 minutes, he'd sell himself out to others in short order. I kept my mouth shut.

It turned out that McKinney played himself out before anyone had a chance to suspect anything about him at all. His Yankee career lasted 37 games—33 at third base, where he was awful. When he made three errors in one game at Fenway in April, we knew we had big trouble.

He batted .215, hit one home run, and drove in seven runs. It was down to Syracuse with him, never to be seen again in Yankee pinstripes. Bahnsen won 20 for the White Sox.

Lee was hurt by this horrible trade, but these things happen in baseball. He was often able to poke fun at himself for such a screw-up. He even wrote a poem once about his career, in which he lampooned himself over the deal. But this wasn't the Yankees. Trading Bahnsen was one thing; getting nothing in return was a disaster. The only thing that saved us in '72 was that Lee purchased a third baseman from the Mexican League named Celerino Sanchez. Cellie didn't speak a word of English, but he had a great smile and a chest made of concrete. He played every hard smash off his chest, chased it down, and fired a bullet to first. The fans fell in love with him in the first week, partly because of his defense and partly because he was the anti-McKinney.

He saved us that year, because there was no one else. I went with him to a Harlem street fair during the summer—there weren't a lot of Mexicans in Harlem, but he was warmly received—and he and I spent a great afternoon as guys do who don't speak the same language. We smiled at each other every time a sexy girl walked by—the universal language.

That winter the Yankees made a great trade and got Graig Nettles from Cleveland, which gave us a real third baseman at last. Cellie's translator during his contract negotiation with MacPhail was Lou Piniella. He didn't come out of it feeling so good, and, before we knew it, he was on a flight back to the Mexican League. But he had pretty much saved our skin in '72.

MacPhail always said his toughest negotiation each winter was with Gene Michael. Stick was personable, cunning, and believed in his abilities far beyond what the stats showed. He managed to talk himself up to almost double what his second base partner Horace Clarke was making, something like $75,000 to $39,000 annually. No way was he twice the player Horace was, but, in the final years before agents, if a player (Clarke) wasn't able to speak up for himself, he would have to settle for whatever the club wanted to give him.

I had my own moment of negotiation with Lee, a chance to see how it all played out.

I had been working as Bob's assistant for two years, and, although I knew I had found my dream job, the pay was so low it was getting hard to have a life other than the Yankees. I was still living with my parents!

I finally decided that I had to move. I found a studio apartment in the Riverdale section of the Bronx, about 12 minutes from Yankee Stadium. It was on the top floor, overlooking the Hudson River, the George Washington Bridge, and, further south, the World Trade Center under construction. It was splendid, and it cost $279 a month, parking included.

I filled out the paperwork and told Bob I needed to run up there at lunchtime to make my first payment. He asked if he could come along and see it. This was nice; it was one of those "son I never had" moments we would sometimes experience, and I was delighted to have his experience and wisdom.

We got to the rental office, I introduced Bob, and the agent said, "I'm so sorry, Mr. Appel, but we can't let you have this after all. We don't feel your salary would support it."

What an embarrassing moment for Bob. He looked at his shoes and coughed a few little nervous coughs. I hardly knew what to say myself.

Finally, after a horrible few moments of silence, Bob said, "Well, I'm his employer, and I am sure that his salary will be going up shortly."

I got the apartment, and Bob had saved the day. Unfortunately, the salary did not go up for a long time, and I asked him about it.

"It may be the most we can pay at that level, Marty."

I gulped. *This was it? The end of the line?*

"Do you mind if I speak to Mr. MacPhail about it?" I asked.

He must have minded, since I was "going over his head," even with his approval. But he said okay.

I made an appointment with Lee, and he saw me promptly.

"So," he said, "I understand you would like to discuss your salary. Give me a little history of your salary progression."

"Little history" was an apt phrase. I had started at $8,000. After 12 months, I was increased to $9,000. Now, nearly 24 months later, I was still at $9,000.

"I see," said Lee, taking careful notes. He was so gentlemanly and kind that I was tempted to offer to go back to $8,000 if it would help the club.

"Well, this is interesting," he said. "Thanks for sharing it with me; we'll see what we can do."

And sure enough, seven months later, I was increased to $10,000. And that was my experience negotiating with Lee MacPhail.

Oh, Lee could be a little tight. Poor Bob Fishel was in Columbia Presbyterian Hospital one winter for eye surgery. He had had a detached retina, just months after Mike Burke had had the same thing. I told Lee I was going to visit Bob that afternoon and he said he'd like to join me.

I tucked him into my Plymouth Barracuda and we drove to the hospital, which was on the very site where the Highlanders had played their first games at old Hilltop Park at the turn of the century. It was only a 10-minute drive from Yankee Stadium.

I parked in a lot across the street. When our visit had concluded and we were exiting, the attendant looked at my ticket and said, "Eighty cents, please."

In a flash, Lee was reaching into his pocket and counting out change. He handed me 40 cents. We had split the parking.

It therefore must have killed Lee to have parted with a signed blank check, but that's what he did during our "hostage crisis" of 1971.

The White Sox and Yankees had made arrangements to play a series of exhibition games in Venezuela during spring training of '71. Significant financial incentives were built into the deal to make the trip worthwhile. The hook was that Luis Aparicio, a Venezuelan hero, was on the White Sox, and the Yankees, of course, were the best-known team in America, even if it had been a while since the glory years.

One problem that developed, however, was that the Sox had traded Aparicio to Boston with little care for the Venezuelan series. They had made the trade on December 1, 1970, but contracts for the games were already in place.

To accommodate the Venezuelan hosts, in a really unique gesture, the Red Sox agreed to loan Luis back to the White Sox for the trip. He would don his old uniform, play with his old teammates, and then return to the Red Sox camp. It was a remarkable adjustment, but not unlike many of the odd things we used to see in spring training.

One year, the Yankees were playing the Washington Senators just down the road in Pompano Beach. Our two training camps were minutes apart, and we used to play the Senators a lot—A games, B games, last-minute games that were almost "pickup" games. We lived in the same town, and in the evenings it was almost one big family. Dave Nelson, the Senators infielder, became one of my best friends in baseball after we sat next to each other watching the first Ali–Frazier fight in a movie theater.

In this one exhibition game, we went into extra innings but had run out of pitchers. No problem. The Senators simply lent us Bill Gogolewski, one of theirs, for the rest of the game. He needed the work, we needed a body, and the fans wanted to see the game played to conclusion. So there was Gogolewski, in his home Senators uniform, pitching against his teammates with Yankee players behind him.

Aparicio to the White Sox for three days? Not a problem.

The real problem arose when the teams were leaving to fly back to Florida. The local authorities decided that there were unpaid taxes that needed to be calculated before the teams could depart.

This was not acceptable; it was clear that the authorities, knowing they had the teams over a barrel, were about to demand huge taxes on the monies earned, despite all of this having supposedly been prearranged.

Some last minute negotiating at the airport brought about a temporary resolution. Don Unferth, the White Sox traveling secretary, and Bob Fishel would be "detained" in Venezuela until the matter was settled, and the teams would be allowed to leave.

MacPhail pulled out a Yankee check and signed his name. He handed it to Fishel and said, "Bob, use your best judgment, but whatever it takes, obviously, pay the money."

Poor Bob, and poor Don. From Ft. Lauderdale, where I had stayed behind, I could imagine them waving from the windows at the terminal as the plane taxied to the runway. I could imagine armed police escorting them away.

I got a call from Bob some hours later. I had already known about the hostage taking because the press had been able to file reports from Caracas. Bob's usually deep and self-assured voice sounded shaky.

"No, we'll be okay, it's just a matter of money," he said. "But look, here's Don Unferth's wife's number—call her and tell her he's okay."

The teams got back to Florida and it was evident that Bob and Don were going to be spending the night under house arrest in their hotel. Some people were making jokes about it, promoting me to PR director and so forth, but it was a nasty business, and we had no idea how it would work out.

Fortunately, it worked out fine the next day. Bob wrote a check for both clubs, and they were able to depart on the next flight home, receiving a hero's welcome at Miami airport, where I met them. Unferth was clearly shaken; Bob, by this point, had found humor in the situation.

The biggest story in baseball in 1971 was Vida Blue, the spectacular Oakland pitcher who was packing ballparks wherever he pitched.

All of the overnight phenomena of modern baseball have been pitchers—Blue, Mark Fidrych, Fernando Valenzuela, Doc Gooden. None have managed to maintain his drawing power, or go to the Hall of Fame, but in all cases the attendance value was a bit overrated anyway.

Say Valenzuela draws a crowd of 40,000 to a Friday night game, which otherwise might have drawn 26,000. Well, he's accounted for a lot of extra tickets, or so it would appear. But the real test is the attendance for the full weekend. A lot of people simply check the probable pitchers and, instead of going to a game on Saturday or Sunday, go Friday to see Fernando. Too much has always been made of the additional fans drawn by these box-office pitching heroes. In many cases, they just take away from other games and it all comes out even. Only a sensational everyday player can really tip the scales, and those have been few and far between.

Still, the Yankees were as happy as anyone to cash in, at a time when we were looking everywhere for excitement. And so the first time Blue came to pitch in New York, Fishel, Howard Berk, and I, along with the approval of MacPhail, had a Vida Blue Day, painted an entrance blue, and invited anyone named Blue in for free. (About 100 people named Blue took us up on the offer, as well as one woman named Violet, who did put up a pretty convincing argument.) We even flew Vida's parents in for the game. In fact, fearful that Blue could be knocked out in the first before the traffic jams thinned out and the fans got in, we even held up the start of the game for 20 minutes, making an appropriate public address announcement.

It was an exciting afternoon. Leroy Neiman was there to capture the sights on his sketchpad, and we got a lot of publicity out of it, but I have to admit to feeling let down when Stan Bahnsen, Blue's opponent, gently chided us after the game by saying, "Too bad my parents weren't flown in for the game." He was right.

Blue—one of the few breakthrough superstars to hit baseball in the early '70s—was changed from a delight to a bitter young man who was ready to quit baseball over miserable contract negotiations with Finley. He never again had a year like that first one, which was a great loss for baseball.

Fidrych burst on the scene in 1976 and really put himself on the map with a big nationally televised performance against us in Detroit. He talked to the ball, he manicured the mound, he looked like Big Bird, and he had an enthusiasm for the game that you used to find in Chip Hilton sports novels. He was, in short, the most fun player baseball has had since maybe Dizzy Dean, and what a loss for the game it was when injuries essentially ended his stardom after just one year.

These were tough years for baseball. Great players just weren't filing into the game. It was increasingly becoming a matter of promote, promote, promote.

Once we engaged George Plimpton to supervise a "George Plimpton's All Star Team," composed of people who wrote letters stating why they wanted to play at Yankee Stadium. In his best Walter Mitty–like style, George proved to be perfect to run this, and he plunged in with enormous enthusiasm, reading each letter and selecting a bunch of happy participants long before such things as fantasy camps were born.

Another early road trip I took had involved a major event—the final major league game played in Washington, D.C.

It was the end of the 1971 season, and Bob Short had announced that he was moving his team—along with Ted Williams, his manager—to Dallas–Ft. Worth to become the Texas Rangers. We knew the last game was going to be ugly as far as the fans were concerned, but we couldn't anticipate how ugly.

We had already become used to rowdy fan behavior. When the Mets won in 1969, their fans stormed the field and tore up the turf. I think that was the first evidence that we were entering an era of brash fan behavior, perhaps fueled by the turbulence of the '60s, and certainly fueled by the flow of Schaefer ("the one beer to have when you're having more than one") or "fine cold Rheingold, the extra dry beer," or whatever the local pour was.

Yankee Stadium would see its fair share of this when the fans hit the field during stormy rain delays. While the grounds crew battled to get the tarp on the field, they were fighting off intoxicated fans along the way.

(For a long time, the Yankees promoted their grounds crew as the best, setting "records" by covering the field in less than a minute. Then the crew got themselves a union, and the heart-attack-provoking stopwatch thing ended.)

Rowdy fan behavior was a sad thing to witness. Bob Sheppard, our PA announcer, could be the "Voice of God," imploring fans to return to their seats, but it was not an easy task. Our "Con Edison Good Kids" program, developed by the able Howard Berk, our vice president of administration, sent the right message and began to turn things around. But of course, when Chris Chambliss homered to win the '76 pennant, there wasn't a Con Edison Good Kid to be found, as the fans stormed the field and Chris was never able to touch home plate.

I missed the times when the fans could actually exit the stadium through the bullpen with no problem at all, a practice that went on into the mid-'60s. Everyone left, as they used to say in school, in an "orderly fashion." They could even pause to inspect the three monuments in center field if they wished.

(In answer to a most-asked question, no one is buried there; the monuments just happen to look like graves.)

(In answer to another question, no, we didn't permit loved ones' ashes to be spread at Yankee Stadium, and, yes, I did occasionally make an exception if the story was especially touching, the team was on the road, and no one would ever know).

The problem of crowd control finally began to ebb in the '80s, when the teams stopped selling beer after the seventh inning, and when the Philadelphia Phillies put mounted police on the field as they were about to win the World Series, keeping everyone at bay. And maybe the country became a little kinder and gentler as well.

But there was no kindness and gentleness in Washington as the '71 season came to a close.

This was a sad franchise. In '69, Ted Williams' first year as manager, positive things were happening for the team. Frank Howard was an enormous hero, a guy who could belt 10 homers in eight games in a pitching-dominated era. Mike Epstein found his stride. Things were going well for the Senators—a franchise that was forever awful, whether in the Griffith years or as an expansion team. But Bob Short, the owner, was a Minneapolis guy (we stayed in his hotel there), and he couldn't care less about the need to have a team in the nation's capital. Whatever positive had happened in '69, things were turning downward again. Texas, here we come.

I was in the Senators' dugout listening to Williams before the game. When Ted Williams speaks, you listen. He was John Wayne. He totally dominated any setting he was in. He was brash, opinionated, and had a presence unlike anyone's in the game. Short had lured him out of his glorious retirement, where he pursued his love of fishing each day, and put him in a Senators uniform. (A little heftier than he might have liked, he wore a jacket every day to hide his middle, even in the hottest weather the nation's capital could throw at him.)

"Let me tell you something," he barked, "Bob Short is as honorable a man as you're gonna meet! He's tried everything here! He's put his heart and his soul into this team, and backed it up with his wallet! Moving was a last option, but we're gonna have the best damn franchise in the league next year, and Texas is big time ready for major league baseball!"

Yes, sir!

Williams was fantastic to listen to. Almost 30 years later, I was with him in the lobby of the Otesaga Hotel in Cooperstown. It was induction weekend of 1997. A series of strokes had forced him into a wheelchair, but he was still a forceful presence.

"Mr. Williams?" said a voice as Ted was wheeled across the lobby. "May I introduce myself to you? I'm Dan Duquette, I'm the general manager of the Red Sox. I've always wanted to meet you."

"Well, Dan, I know who you are," said Teddy Ballgame. "And let me tell you, you're doing a helluva job, one helluva job. And let me tell you something else."

Now he was jabbing at Duquette with his index finger.

"That little infielder of yours, that Norman, or Nomar fellow, he is the best damn player I have EVER seen come out of the Red Sox organization. The best!"

Garciaparra had been a big leaguer for four months, and Ted would have seen him only on television. But that was Ted—opinionated and on the mark.

With the Senators, his patience had been tested. He was always praising players he knew to be frauds, but that was what managers did, and he went along with it. Now he was backing his owner and looking past this last day in D.C.

Short, whether in an act of courage or of foolishness, showed up at the game and let himself be seen. He actually sat next to the Senators' dugout. I couldn't believe it.

There may not have been a lot of Washington baseball fans, but those that went to that game sure were passionate. They hated what Short was doing. And they let him know it with obscene chants, curse-filled signs, and everything but thrown tomatoes.

Short sat there and took it. Frank Howard, in as fine a moment as

Washington ever had, hit the last home run for the team and blew kisses to the fans, who gave him a tremendous outpouring of love.

The Senators were actually going to beat us in the last game, and good for them; but in the ninth it was apparent that the fans were going to storm the field.

(The stadium was named after Bobby Kennedy following his assassination, by interior secretary Stewart Udall, a New Frontiersman. The decision, we later learned, so pissed off Lyndon Johnson that he had no use for the ballpark, the Senators, or the Redskins after that, and he never spoke to Udall again).

Jack Aker was on the mound for us in the ninth. Jack was a good guy, a side-arming relief specialist of Native American descent. I was watching him from the press box, and he was stalling for time, knowing that the fans were poised to pounce. He later said he was waving at them with his glove to come on the field. I didn't notice that, but here they came, by the thousands, sending our guys running for cover and forcing the umpires to forfeit the game to the Yankees. It was an ignoble finish for the Washington franchise, the only forfeit I ever saw, but a slice of history, to be sure. And it gave us an 82–80 record for the season, which should have been 81–81.

Try as it did in the '70s, Major League Baseball could never find new ownership in the nation's capital. The season-ticket base just wasn't there. There was no industry in Washington. There were no long-term residents. The government didn't have the ability to buy season boxes; it expected freebies by the wheelbarrow.

For a long time it seemed so wrong not to have a team in Washington. It would be like Moscow not having a team in a Russian league. But it's been more than a quarter of a century, and it appears the time has passed for a D.C. franchise, even with a more substantial business community having taken hold. And what a way it all ended.

If MacPhail's frugality was tested by the blank check he gave Bob Fishel in Venezuela, then his sense of decency was certainly breached when he learned that two of our lefthanded pitchers, Mike Kekich and Fritz Peterson, had swapped wives.

Kekich and Peterson, numbers 18 and 19 on the team, were bright, inquisitive, and personable. So were their wives, Susan Kekich and Marilyn Peterson, whom Fritz called Chip because her maiden name had been Monk. I got along well with both players; Fritz and I would occasionally slip out to the Bronx County Courthouse at lunchtime and take in a trial!

Mike and Fritz had grown close, and their wives had as well. When our sponsor, Schaefer, hosted a summer party in 1972 aboard a chartered yacht, the Petersons and the Kekichs had been photographed together enjoying the day's cruise.

Peterson had had the more successful career at the time, with the 20-win, All-Star season in 1970. He was the first person I ever knew who bought a pocket calculator, a 1971 Texas Instruments model for $200. I played with it endlessly on flights, and one day Fishel noted that you could figure batting averages and earned run averages much faster with this than using long division or unwieldy books published by *The Sporting News*. What a find! (With it came the official change in figuring earned run averages to include thirds of an inning, whereas previously the innings were always rounded off).

Kekich had grown up in the Dodgers organization, and had come to the Yanks in 1970 in a trade for Andy Kosco, an outfielder. So uninteresting were the Yankees in those days that when we traded Kosco, our phones didn't quit ringing all day. Andy Kosco, with his 15 homers and 59 RBIs, had become one of the more popular players on the team.

We gave Kekich a full page in color in the *Yearbook* the next year, and, as I was studying the final, absolutely final page proofs before we went to press, I noticed that he was throwing righthanded in his full-color photo. Oops. The negative had been flopped. The cost to correct and redo the color separations at this point was going to be almost $10,000, which was more than we were paying some of the players we had at Syracuse. I needed a lot of permissions to get this change made, but we would have looked foolish if we didn't make it.

Kekich had done well, battling periods of wildness, and was establishing himself as a big league pitcher you could depend on. Fritz, just flaky enough to let Jim Bouton interview him in spring training in front of all the other players, could be excused because, as Pete Sheehy's left-wrist snap would indicate, he was a southpaw too.

They were interesting guys in a lot of ways, just the sort of ballplayers Maury Allen liked to invite to his periodic house parties. Maury was a prolific author and influential columnist for the *New York Post*, and his friends were largely outside of baseball. He liked to mix his worlds when he and his wife, Janet, entertained. And so, in the dead of winter before the '73 season, the Petersons and the Kekiches drove to Dobbs Ferry and up the steep driveway to where the Allens lived.

Nothing at the party suggested that anything was amiss. There was lively conversation, plenty of good food and drink, and a homey environment with the Allens' two young children, a Christmas tree, bookcases full of fine literature, and some miscellaneous pictures from Maury's career.

Everyone said goodnight sometime after midnight. About an hour later, Maury heard talking in his driveway. Already retired for the night, he peered through the blinds and saw Mike and Fritz and Susan and Chip engaged in conversation.

"It's the Petersons and the Kekiches," he told Janet. "They're still here. Should I see if they're okay?"

"No," said Janet. "Obviously we got them into such a stimulating conversation that they can't turn it off. Let it be."

Only weeks later did the nature of that conversation emerge. They had decided right there—that night on that driveway—to trade lives. They had decided—confessed, as it were—that they loved each other's spouses more than their own. And it was further decided that they would switch wives, children, homes, and pets as part of the arrangement. And they would do it at once.

The roster page in the Yankee press guide had a column for "married" and a column for "children." It turned out we were the only team to have this, which was not something I had bothered to examine. A lot of the players didn't like it, because they'd wink at a pretty girl in the stands and then she'd look them up in the roster and check under the "married" column. But we still carried it.

We used M for married, S for single. There weren't many divorces among these young players (although a pitcher named Thad Tillotson had already been married three times when he got to us at age 26, so on a clubhouse sign-up sheet for a Bear Mountain picnic, under "wife" someone wrote "3" next to Tillotson's name instead of putting a check mark). We didn't have a designation for what our two crazy lefthanders were about to do.

Shortly before spring training, Kekich called MacPhail to let him know what was going on. It was not something they could keep from management. MacPhail must have fallen off his swivel chair. This was 1973, and wife swapping was going to be a fairly new concept for the conservative New York Yankees. Furthermore, the team had just been sold weeks before to a new owner, one George M. Steinbrenner III. This was going to be some sackful of news to deliver to the new boss.

Further complicating matters was the fact that Kekich would be in camp in a few days, as spring training always began early for pitchers and catchers, but Peterson was holding out on Florida's west coast and was engaged in a salary dispute. It was probably over $2,500 or so, but that was baseball before free agency.

We went to Fort Lauderdale, knowing that we had to, at some point, tell the press this story. Or, of course, we could say nothing and let it leak. The players would know in a nanosecond; nothing escaped that grapevine.

I was already scratching Family Day off our promotional calendar. There would be no father-son game at the Stadium in '73, and the page in the Yearbook with all the family pictures? Cut.

For a few days, we did nothing. Then, in St. Petersburg, Peterson heard that Kekich was going to call a press conference. Already, things were going badly with them. The bond wasn't holding; the friendship was failing. Kekich and Chip Peterson wanted out; Peterson and Susan Kekich were doing okay. Kekich thought that if it didn't work for everyone, all bets were off. Peterson didn't remember it that way.

There was no press conference by Kekich, but on the rumor that there was, Peterson ran into Milton Richman, the UPI baseball editor and columnist, and truly the last of the great "scoop" reporters.

"Milton," said Fritz, "I've got a story for you." And he proceeded to spell it out.

Richman called Bob Fishel looking for Kekich. We knew it was time to call the beat reporters in.

Here was one of the great PR blunders of my time with the Yankees. MacPhail, Houk, and Fishel decided that the beat reporters were our friends, they were part of the family, and, just like the old days, we would confide in them and ask them to keep it a private matter, and they would respect that.

The one wrinkle was that one of the beat reporters that spring was not one of the boys. Her name was Sheila Moran, and she was assigned by the *New York Post*—Maury Allen's paper—to cover the Yankees "from a woman's point of view," because Ike Gellis, the sports editor, figured the '73 Yanks had nothing interesting to sell in their first few weeks of training camp.

Houk, MacPhail, and Fishel made the decision to exclude Sheila from the news briefing. "She doesn't know Fritz and Mike, she wouldn't keep it quiet, and it is, after all, a personal matter," they concluded.

I was aware of all of this, although not part of the inner circle that would make the call. But I was present as the strategy was being discussed and it sounded okay to me. I voiced no objections.

And so Phil Pepe of the *News* and Murray Chass of the *Times* and Joe Donnelly of *Newsday* and Jim Ogle of the *Star-Ledger*, along with our announcer Frank Messer, huddled in Houk's small office by invitation only. And Houk and MacPhail gave them the play-by-play.

Ogle was the first to speak after the amazement expressed by everyone. "Well, it's what you say," he concluded. "It's a private matter. None of our business."

And as hard as it is to believe in today's age of "gotcha" journalism, agreement was reached in the room that it was indeed nobody's business.

The problem was, of course, over in St. Petersburg; Milt Richman was about to break Peterson's side of the story. And within minutes, the desks at the *Times*, the *News*, *Newsday*, the *Star-Ledger*, and the *Post* were frantically phoning their Ft. Lauderdale–based reporters, asking, "What the hell??"

Chass, Ogle, Donnelly, and Pepe could all say, "We've got the story, we're writing it now."

Sheila Moran, of course, was left completely in the dark. She was totally blindsided. It was a horrible lapse of judgment on our part, and it left her, predictably, fighting mad.

Sheila jumped into action and wound up with the best reporting of anyone on the story, getting interviews with the wives, with other players, wives of other players, church leaders, community leaders, even the prisoners who served on the grounds crew in Ft. Lauderdale. She needed little incentive to rise to the top with this story.

The *Daily News* found photographs from the Schaefer Beer yacht party with the Petersons and the Kekiches all together. Three straight days of front-page coverage.

I manned the phones late into the night. This was before the days of talk radio, but every newscaster in the country was calling to interview Kekich, Peterson, the wives, the teammates, and team management. I was all they got. I tried my best to call it a personal matter, not something the Yankees condoned, but of course fell short of confirming that we would be releasing or shooting the scoundrels by daybreak. Most did assume we would have to rid ourselves of at least one!

Peterson signed a few days later and reported to camp. Oh, was that awkward. Now Peterson and Kekich were at war, Mike seeking to call things off. Players normally have a sense of humor about the darkest of human frailties, but, in this case, everyone made wide circles around the pair. They had been close with the other pitchers, but now . . . well, no one really knew what to say. It was awful.

Steinbrenner, a team owner for barely seven weeks, was still an absentee owner whose league approval would not come until April. He was not heard from. Houk could only shrug and say, "I've got a camp to run."

Nobody was more offended by all of this than the *Daily News*' powerful columnist Dick Young. Young, the hardest-working journalist baseball had ever known, had moved from left to right politically over the years, befriending management as he grew older and feeling the generation gap with the nation's youth. He became the biggest flag-waver of the press corps, and, although outside the political mainstream compared to his colleagues, he was still the dean, still the most admired among them. When he railed against Peterson and Kekich, a lot of whispering kicked in over lapses in Young's own past, suggesting hypocrisy on his part. But he was the most important voice in town, and the offense he took over Fritz and Mike had a lot of the public nodding in agreement.

I observed a milestone in the passing-of-the-torch department that season when Young, leaving the Yankees in mid–road trip, was to brief a new *Daily News* writer on how to cover the team. This passing on of wisdom occurred in the seats immediately to my left in the Tiger Stadium press box. Over the course of an hour, Young, barechested and feisty, proceeded to lecture this newcomer on how you cover a team. It was fascinating to me—like listening to Beethoven explain how you write a symphony. Tony Kornheiser, also new to the beat for *The New York Times*, was listening in with me.

After a time, Young got up to get himself a hot dog. As soon as he left, the *Daily News* rookie turned to Kornheiser and said, exasperated, "What an asshole."

I could only shrug my shoulders. He had just received free career advice and coaching from the master, and this was how he saw it. It was clear that the next generation would not be following Young's preaching but would have no choice but to follow his hustle.

MacPhail urgently tried to move one of the players and finally sold Kekich to Cleveland, but not before June 12, ending a horribly frosty 12 weeks of agony, with the two barely coexisting as teammates. Fritz stayed with the club until the following April, but his good humor was gone, and his easy friendship with the other pitchers was gone. Nobody ever went so happily to play in dreadful Municipal Stadium in Cleveland.

Today, this would have been a *People* magazine cover, the *Star* and the *Enquirer* would have been on the case, the television tabloid shows would have had a field day, and there would certainly have been a TV movie. None of that happened in 1973. The story lasted a week, the pain lingered around us for a year or so, but, by the time Peterson was traded, it was old news.

The Petersons stayed together, found religion, and, as far as I know, are a happily married couple who have passed their 25th wedding anniversary. The Kekiches didn't make it, of course. Mike showed up in the spring of '76 as we were conducting a tour of new Yankee Stadium for the media. I just turned around and he was there. Like an old tenant, visiting his old home.

He went on to get a medical degree in Mexico, took off for points west on a Harley, and, I hope, is living happily ever after too.

DON'T MESS
WITH YANKEE
GHOSTS

The championship Yankee teams of the late '70s had their roots in the CBS years, despite a common feeling that those years were wholly unproductive.

As the franchise moved toward respectability, the holdover players were Mel Stottlemyre, Roy White, and Bobby Murcer. Then, with the exception of 1971, a key addition was made annually: Thurman Munson in 1970, Sparky Lyle in 1972, Graig Nettles in 1973, Lou Piniella and Chris Chambliss in 1974, Catfish Hunter in 1975, Willie Randolph, Ed Figueroa, and Mickey Rivers in 1976, Reggie Jackson in 1977, and Goose Gossage in 1978. It was quite a run to build quite a team, and of course, they weren't the only members.

Stottlemyre did not get to the promised land; he would have been our only player to span the dynasty years and the later successes, as he arrived in '64 and helped the team to its last pennant of that era.

I like Mel a lot. He was a leader, not just of the pitching staff, but of the team, and he filled the role with dignity. After we got Catfish Hunter, I casually asked our coach Dick Howser who he thought was the better pitcher—Hunter or Whitey Ford.

"Stottlemyre was better than both of them," he said, without hesitating. Both of them are in the Hall of Fame. Mel did not have the good fortune to be part of more than one pennant winner. But he hurled 40 shutouts, which is almost unthinkable today, and is near the top in most Yankee pitching categories.

The end of Mel's career was as shocking and sudden as his jump from Richmond to New York in August of '64.

He was pitching against the Angels in Shea Stadium in early June 1974. I had prepared the press notes that evening and noted that the greatest success in his career had in fact come against the Angels—a spectacular 19–4 record.

Early in the game, he delivered a pitch and reached for his shoulder. It wasn't a dramatic reach, just a passing motion. I noticed it from the press box, but I'm not sure others did.

He threw another pitch, touched his shoulder again, and called for Gene Monahan, our trainer, to come to the mound.

Mel had a beautiful delivery. I used to watch him warming up and admired the fluidity of his motion, how perfectly he would be set in a fielding position after he followed through. Now he knew at once that something was wrong.

Gino went to the mound. He and Mel talked, and the two of them walked to the dugout together.

Mel Stottlemyre never threw another pitch in a major league game. It was as though he had been granted only 40,000 pitches in his career, and that was number 40,001. Some say that every pitch is an act against nature, for the arm is intended to swing like a fulcrum, underhanded, and every over the shoulder pitch defies the law. Few pitchers ever retire without some injury shutting them down. Tom Seaver was one exception, Nolan Ryan another, but most can't fight nature forever.

It was a torn rotator cuff, and the ability to repair it was still a few years off.

Mel was determined to come back, and he worked hard to recondition his arm. In the spring of 1975, in an ugly moment of "he said, you said," he maintained that he was told to take his time reconditioning, he was under no timetable, he was a franchise player, and if he wasn't ready for Opening Day, no problem: he was to stay in Florida until he felt ready.

But in the final week of spring training, Gabe Paul, realizing that he would be obligated to pay a large chunk of Mel's salary if he wasn't released before Opening Day, sent Bill Kane off to give Mel his release papers. It was an off day, Mel was hard to find, but Killer caught up with him and Mel was absolutely stunned. It was, according to Mel, the dead opposite of what he had been told.

The story lost its edge somewhat when Mel's effort to come back with Detroit failed during a few days of work under manager Ralph Houk and pitching instructor Jim Turner in the Tiger camp. He was truly through, the unpleasantness of the release notwithstanding. It was a lesson that just like that—one pitch too many—a career could end.

We thought so much of Mel after he left, even if he ripped Gabe Paul and was sort of persona non grata for a time, that we unofficially put his uniform into retirement.

There were different kinds of uniform retirement on the Yankees. The formal kind was the ceremonial kind, commemorated in Monument Park in Yankee Stadium outfield once we inhabited the rebuilt ballpark and created that pasture.

Another kind was in the miscellaneous category. Number 33, for instance, was just a huge size, maybe a 52, that Pete would keep in case we got an oversized player or coach at the last minute. It was usually worn in spring training by an overweight instructor.

Or there was 56, Jim Bouton's old number, kept out of circulation by Pete because he couldn't bear the thought of anyone wearing this scarred reminder of a good kid gone bad.

The other kind was to keep a jersey out of circulation for a time, as a tribute to its wearer, knowing it would one day resurface without being retired. Pete didn't give out Ralph Houk's number 35 for a long time after Ralph resigned. Stottlemyre was another special case—his number 30 would just sit out a few years. Or so we thought.

When we got Willie Randolph from the Pirates before the 1976 season, Pete assigned him number 21. Seemed like a good enough number.

Willie, all of 21 years of age, showed up in spring training and asked for 30, the number he had worn during his few weeks with the Pirates the year before. (Maybe he had worn it in the minors too, I don't know.)

Well, we had already printed the rosters with Randolph as 21, he hadn't yet played his first game in New York, and we were sitting on Mel's uniform as a quiet tribute to the long-time team leader.

I went to Randolph, introduced myself, and explained, "Well, we'd sort of like to hold out 30 for now, in honor of Mel Stottlemyre."

"Who?" he asked.

"Mel Stottlemyre—he was released last year, three-time All-Star, one of the great Yankee pitchers in history."

"I don't give a shit about Mel Stottlemyre," he said. "I want 30. Nobody's using it."

He had a point, and even though he was 21, he was a Tilden High kid out of Brooklyn, and I wasn't going to argue with the guy being handed the second base job. I had too many other things to work with him on in the future.

"Pete, let him have 30," I said to Pete Sheehy. I think Pete liked the way Willie stood up for himself. He got his 30.

Mel and the Yankees were estranged for a long time. Billy Martin thought of bringing him back as a pitching coach, but there was bitterness there, and Gabe wouldn't have wanted Mel. (Billy, of course, always wanted his drinking buddy Art Fowler as coach, but he had to fight hard to get him, and always needed a backup plan. Stottlemyre, whom Gabe would veto, was a good step toward getting his way. He did the same thing another year with Camilo Pascual, knowing Gabe would give in and let him have Fowler.)

Mel went to the Mets in the '80s and coached those great pitching staffs of Gooden, Darling, Fernandez, Ojeda, and Cone before finally, finally, coming back to the Yankees under Joe Torre in 1996. The rift had lasted more than two decades.

Randolph and Stottlemyre were both coaches for Torre. Mel wore 34. Willie wore 30. Enough said.

Roy White was a bright, switch-hitting left fielder who batted cleanup and choked up. That said a lot about the Yankees of his time, which began in 1965, just a year too late to be part of the dynasty teams. He reached second place on the all-time Yankee stolen base list. One year, he set an AL record for the most sacrifice flies in a season. He hit .290 or better four times and was a terrific outfielder, lacking only a gun for a throwing arm, something the press tended to focus on a lot.

The fans appreciated his steady play and his ability to start rallies. Unlike Stottlemyre, Roy did make it to postseason play, and he was one player, more than anyone on the club, whom I rooted for to get an at bat in a World Series game. He had been at my wedding, we had shared all of those dismal seasons, and I had watched his children grow. When he was coaching at Vancouver in the Oakland organization years later and my son was working in that city during a college break, I called Roy to say, "keep an eye on him." I knew he would be there for me.

No player so willingly signed so many autographs, attended so many clinics, posed for so many photos, and spoke to so many fans as did Roy, and we had to do these things to promote the team. So personable was Roy that CBS trained him in sales one winter and wanted to offer him a full-time position, baseball be damned.

He was more than a holdover when the team came to life in the mid-'70s. He was still a strong contributor and an important building block. But when times were tough, he was always there, doing whatever it took to make the Yankees acceptable and marketable.

Roy once had a small part in a movie, something called *The Premonition*. He played a doctor, and his scene lasted about a minute, but we all went to the premiere and the postpremiere party and enjoyed Roy's night of stardom on the silver screen. He was just a good guy to be around, and in the days when we had little to show in terms of "Yankee class," we had Roy.

Bobby Murcer was our glamor guy. So much was expected of him that the success he managed to achieve was pretty remarkable under the circumstances. He was a teenager from Oklahoma City, who listed University of Oklahoma on his personal questionnaire one year. I said, "You went to Oklahoma?" And he said, "I was invited to a few frat parties."

Bobby had it all—he was handsome, personable, and talented, and his wife, Kay, was blessed with eternal Barbie doll looks. Bobby was signed by Tom Greenwade, the same scout who had discovered Mickey Mantle. He started as an infielder, like Mantle, before moving to the Yankee glamor position of center field. He was given Mantle's locker. He got Bobby Richardson's number 1. He came up in '65 for the first time, so he was able to be a teammate of Mantle and Maris and pose for pictures with them—the three M boys.

He may have had Okie roots, but he was a quick learner. He fit in well in New York without going the Joe Namath route. He was wholesome and down-home, and a fan favorite.

The Yankees (and the Giants) were the last teams to switch to double-knit uniforms (1973), and we needed a model to pose for us in the "sleek new look," late in '72. That was Bobby, and he posed like a professional model, no coaching necessary. He could do it all.

His popularity was tremendous, and, in 1970, after missing time for army duty, having his position switched to the outfield, and generally getting a later start on his career than was planned, he emerged as a genuine all-star, even finding a power stroke and taking advantage of the inviting right field stands of Yankee Stadium. He became a Gold Glove outfielder (which his teammates found amusing), but he had a good sense of humor about himself.

In Chicago one year, the White Sox erected signs showing the longest home runs ever hit in Comiskey Park, along with the name of the slugger. During batting practice, a teammate put a sign that said MURCER on the foul line, about halfway between first base and the right field fence. Bobby loved it.

It was never going to be Ruth-Gehrig-DiMaggio-Mantle-Murcer, but Bobby was our star, and, on his rocking chair in front of his locker, he would hold court and exude the easy-going self-confidence that is characteristic of most of the great ones. If we were going to be a contending team, it was hard to imagine that Bobby wouldn't be a big part of it.

I couldn't imagine Thurman Munson ever having doubts about

playing big league ball. Not only was he blessed with enormous self-confidence to complement his talent, but he was a winner. He could never accept second place as success, and every moment he spent on the field was all about finishing first. He was the piece of the puzzle that really started to restore the Yankees to greatness.

I met Thurman Munson for the first time when his Double-A team, the Binghamton Triplets, came to Yankee Stadium in the summer of 1968 for an exhibition game. It was a chance for us to get some publicity photos from a guy who had been our number one draft pick that summer and was clearly on the fast track to the majors. I remember his having that big league self-confidence about him that day—he seemed to know he would be in Yankee Stadium before long. A lot of rookies look like rookies in their early photographs. Rookie baseball cards often show players with the proverbial "deer caught in the headlights" look. Munson was all poise and confidence. He knew he belonged, and he knew he was coming.

He had been scouted the year before by affable Gene Woodling, our Ohio-based scout and a former Yankee outfielder during the five–straight–world championships era. A decade later, Woodling also played for Casey Stengel on the original Mets, and he liked to tell me about the special bond he and Casey had on that awful expansion team.

"Casey would walk up and down the Met dugout during those horrible losses," he would say, "and occasionally our eyes would meet. And Casey would wink at me and whisper, 'Ain't like the old days, is it?!'"

It didn't take a genius to scout Munson. He was the All-American catcher at Kent State and everyone knew about him. As Sparky Anderson, wearing a mike for the '76 World Series film would say during a mound conference, "He can flat-out hit, that Munson."

But he could do much more. He was a great defensive catcher who taught me a lot about what that meant. Until Munson, I thought great defense meant a strong arm, few passed balls, the ability to charge bunts, and so forth.

Early in Munson's career, however, he badly hurt his hand on a back-swing by a Mets outfielder named Dave Schneck during a spring exhibition game. His throwing hand was never the same, and he often hurled sidearm curveballs into center while trying to make a throw to second. It used to kill Rick Dempsey, one of his backups, that he would stay in there despite that, and that Dempsey—not a bad player himself—would never play.

But what I learned from Munson was that true defensive genius behind the plate was all about pitch calling and working with the pitcher. No one could call a game like Munson. The pitchers didn't care if he threw one or two into center field; it didn't matter. What mattered was the way he studied the batters, made his pitch selections, and goaded the pitchers into bearing down. When he walked halfway to the mound before throwing the ball back, his pitcher knew it was his "final warning."

It is the game within the game, the thing that fans can never see from the stands, nor can announcers from the broadcast booth. It is why catchers are often the smartest guys on the field and why so many become coaches and managers. And Munson seemed to have this all down before he even arrived.

The road to pro baseball wasn't all that smooth for Thurman. He was a high school basketball and football star, but he hated having a squatty body, and had to achieve all he did battling the package God had put him in. One of the reasons he hated Carlton Fisk, as the Yankee–Boston rivalry grew, was that Fisk seemed to have it all, including the perfect body. Thurman had to fight to achieve; it wasn't a natural blessing.

The other thing lurking in his past was a troubled father who grew increasingly jealous of Thurman's accomplishments. He was a long-distance truck driver, a man unable to give much emotionally, and tension always ran high between them.

When it was time to sign Thurman, the number four pick in the nation (behind Tim Foli of the Mets, Pete Broberg of the A's, and Marty Cott, who never made it to the majors), Lee MacPhail traveled to the Munson home in Canton for the signing. It was not done for the press. The Yankees were so high on Thurman and so anxious to return to glory behind him that Lee felt the trip was worthwhile to show the kind of confidence the team had in him. The general manager would handle the signing.

You would call this a big day in the Munson household, but Lee's story when he got back was puzzling.

"Woodling was there, I was there, his mother and his brother were there—we were all seated at the dining-room table. All except his father. His father was stretched out on the living-room sofa in his underwear. He never got up to shake hands. Never said a word at all, until at one point he called in and said, 'He ain't too good on pop fouls, ya know.'"

And that was the home Thurman was coming from. It was little wonder, and probably his greatest salvation, that Diana Dominick, who used to chase him on her bike when he delivered the *Canton Repository*, finally caught him and married him. And with that marriage, Thurman came to have a real family, for Diana's parents took to him as though he were their son. And because Diana's father had a build similar to Thurman's, many assumed he was Thurman's dad all along whenever he showed up.

After just 99 minor league games—a waste of time to Thurman—he arrived in 1969, in time to get in the team photo and to make his major league debut on August 8. In spring training of '70, we technically had three candidates for the catching job—Jake Gibbs, John Ellis, and Thurman. Gibbs, the incumbent, had done his best after converting from third base, but the former Ol' Miss quarterback was no Yogi and no Elston Howard back there—he was just the guy filling the position until someone better came along.

In fact, instead of a team photo for the 1970 Yearbook, we broke the team down by pitchers, catchers, infielders, and outfielders, and took group shots. There were our three catchers, Munson, Gibbs, and Ellis. We were going to set up one in the front, two behind. There was no question that Thurman was going to be our regular, but, out of respect for Gibbs, we put Jake up front. Even Jake knew it was silly, but he appreciated it.

Ellis, from Connecticut, was a tough guy handling Army Reserve duty, who once punched a young AP reporter, Frank Brown, for having long hair. John would be moved to first base for Opening Day of 1970 to make room for Munson, and would receive a letter from Eleanor Gehrig saying, "I've waited all of these years for a true successor for Lou, and I believe you are the one."

Aside from the insult to such fine players as Joe Collins, Moose Skowron, and Joe Pepitone, Eleanor was no scout. John was not a good first baseman.

John did win the James P. Dawson Award in spring training in 1970 as the best rookie in camp, for he did out-hit Munson, but no one had any doubt that Munson would be the catcher.

Thurman had a horrible start with the bat, but Houk told him to relax. "You'll win more games for me just concentrating on your catching than on worrying about your hitting," Houk told him. "You're out there every day, don't worry."

It relaxed Thurm a lot, and before long those line drives started to fall in. When he wanted to go deep, he could, but that wasn't his stroke. He would go with the pitch and you just couldn't defense him. He would be an incredible clutch hitter, the guy you would want up there with men on base. For three consecutive years, he drove in more than 100 runs—and did it without topping 18 home runs in any season. That's run production. In fact, in those three years (1975–77), he also hit above .300 each year, and no player in the league in a quarter century (since Al Rosen for Cleveland) had had three straight years of .300 and 100 RBIs.

Munson hit .302 in his rookie season, and won the Rookie of the

Year award. A very special day in my memory was a Sunday doubleheader in August when he was away for the weekend in south Jersey on Army Reserve duty.

In those days, a lot of players were in the Reserves, and weekend duty always forced teams to keep lineups fluid and to bring up players for weekend-only fill-in duty. Losing Munson for a weekend series was a big loss to our lineup. Ellis and Gibbs would catch, but the pitching staff missed their director.

Thurman finished his weekend duty about 5 P.M. He got in his car and raced up the Jersey Turnpike with his radio tuned to the Yankee game on WHN. He got to the Stadium in the late innings of the nightcap, rushed into his uniform, and slipped into the dugout.

In the ninth inning of a one-run game, the fans pretty much exhausted by now, suddenly number 15 emerged from the dugout. It was totally unexpected for the fans, who had simply scratched him from the day's lineup card.

It was the first time Munson ever got a standing ovation at Yankee Stadium. With that cocky swagger, he headed for home plate, having accomplished nothing but battle Sunday traffic up the turnpike. And the fans loved him that afternoon just for hustling his ass up to Yankee Stadium.

He didn't get a game-winning hit, but there would be plenty of those in the future. He had arrived on the scene in a big way, and he wasn't going to take losing as a matter of course. He was a winner, he demanded winning from his teammates, and his drive to excel began to penetrate the team's thinking. It was a big step for the dormant franchise.

He also supported his teammates—the talented and the weak. It was one of his great strengths. He knew as well as any observer that the Yankees could be stronger at second base. But when he saw the press repeatedly attack poor Horace Clarke, he cut off the press.

"The man does his best, he gets on base a lot, he plays every day, and because he doesn't fight back, they keep ripping him," he told me. "The hell with them."

And with that, he pretty much stopped having a relationship with the media.

As for Horace, the abuse was a killer. He did have the flaw of not looking very good on the double play pivot. Once it was noticed, he got the reputation of bailing out. And the reputation spread to all parts of his game until the press pretty much decided he had to go.

He finally went in '75. We were in our hotel in Minneapolis when I got a call from Gabe Paul informing me that Horace had been sold to San

Diego, and that Sandy Alomar would be our new second baseman.

By then it was a matter of "Good for Horace, talk about a guy who needs a fresh start."

But sitting in my hotel room, I thought about Clarke, thought about him packing and heading for the airport, off to a new team, a new league, after 17 years in the Yankee organization. Seventeen years! The man needed a handshake as he left.

I called his room, but he had checked out. I sped to the elevator and caught him waiting for a taxi. He was dressed as usual, in the worst combination of clothing you could throw together on short notice, including a little straw hat. This was the last Yankee to live in the Concourse Plaza Hotel on Grand Concourse in the Bronx, which was changing from a place where great Yankees resided in season into a welfare hotel. He looked dazed and carried a little suitcase that he might have picked up at a tourist stand in the Virgin Islands.

I extended my hand. I was the Yankees at this point.

"Horace, hey, seventeen years, mon," I laughed, imitating his West Indian accent. "You deserve a thank you. You did a lot."

We always got along well. I had used his son Jeffrey to pose for a Cap Day picture in the Yankee scorecard. His wife, Hilda, who used to cry about the bad newspaper stories, saw me as an ally in the fight to maintain his reputation.

The handshake was warm. I think he genuinely felt better that someone from the organization had seen to it that he didn't hop into a cab for the airport without some sendoff. This wasn't exactly Horace Clarke Day, but he deserved this much. And then off he went, finishing his career with a few weeks with the Padres, and then returning home to the Virgin Islands forever. No World Series rings for Horace.

After the 1971 season, our assistant clubhouse attendant, Nick Priore, a pretty smart baseball man, used to stop by my office and talk about trades that would really help the team. One that he had in mind that whole winter was getting Sparky Lyle from the Red Sox for our first baseman, Danny Cater. He had the whole deal figured out.

Lyle was enormously popular in Boston, and as likable a guy as I ever knew in baseball. And he had a lot of machismo, which gave him the presence of a matador without the sissy hat. Forget that he was really Albert Walter Lyle Jr.—he was one tough cookie.

By incredible coincidence, the Yankee roster going into spring training 1972 had every number accounted for from 1 to about 70, figuring in all of the retired numbers and all of the non-roster players.

The only vacancy was number 28, when Ron Hansen was released just before the spring. Twenty-eight was Lyle's number, but believe me when I say the last thing general managers pay attention to when they release a player is what uniform numbers are open.

Well, damned if Nick Priore didn't have it just right. Midway through the spring, the Red Sox dealt Lyle to us for Danny Cater. Our one-year announcer Bob Gamere used to say, "Danny Cater and see you later," and that was appropriate now, for off went the slow-drawling Cater, who, they said, was the only player in the league who could compute his batting average while running to first. (This spoke to his lack of speed, folks, not his quickness of mind.)

Well, it was mid–spring training of '72, and off went Cater to the Red Sox for Lyle, and because we were about two days away from printing the Yearbook, I rushed over to Winter Haven with a Yankee jersey (number 28, of course), to have Sparky photographed by the deadline. This mission made me the official welcoming party from the Yankees, and not only was Sparky thrilled with the trade but our friendship, which began that day, continued to grow. We would often talk about the makeup of the team, the relationship of Billy Martin to the players, and matters like that. Sparky had great baseball wisdom—but he was also such a fun-loving guy that it was rare to find him in a serious mood. If you ask me who—of all the players I ever knew—had the most easygoing personality, it was Lyle.

In Ft. Lauderdale, the bullpen is just outside the home clubhouse, underneath the bleachers. It was one of the few ballparks where you could stand behind the fence—not much farther back than where the umpire stood—and watch the pitchers warm up.

I won't ever forget watching Lyle's workouts. Oh, the sound of the ball hitting the catcher's mitt! The fire in that fastball!

This had been a pitching staff built on Stottlemyre's sinker, Peterson's screwball, Lindy McDaniel's forkball, and assorted breaking pitches from others, right down to Steve Hamilton's Folly Floater. I had never really experienced a power pitcher like Lyle. What a sight he was, and what a great addition, after all these years—a Yankee who could throw in the 90s. Lyle's first year was a smash hit. He was racking up the saves and blowing away opponents with "strike out the side" ninth innings, including one with the bases loaded against the Tigers in which he fired the final game ball into the stands and had Yankee Stadium rocking like it hadn't in years.

Lyle would enter the games in the bullpen car, a pinstripe-painted Datsun. When the car arrived at the Yankee dugout he would hurl open the door with enough force to almost tear it from its hinges. He would fire his jacket at the batboy, stomp to the mound, kick the dirt, fire his warm-ups and go to work. It was very theatrical, and it occurred to me that it could use a little music.

My friend Dave Carey's father was a studio musician who had played with everyone from Sinatra to the Four Seasons. I asked him to recommend a piece of music that would capture the moment. He suggested *Pomp and Circumstance*, better known to audiences as the music played at graduation ceremonies. In an empty stadium I had Toby Wright, our organist, play the music for me as I pictured Lyle's entrance.

"Slower," I said to Toby. "Needs to build. Get the crowd excited at the first note, and then make it a great processional, which culminates when he emerges from the car."

To this point, not a lot had been done with music and baseball. Organists played the familiar *dum-dum-dum-dum* to get the crowd clapping, or the *da-da-da-dum-da-dum—CHARGE!*, but the blend of familiar melodies with the field of play wasn't really happening. If a batter was from California, the organist might play *California Here I Come*, and no one was better than Nancy Faust in Chicago at picking tunes for players, but they always had to do with some fact about the player, usually his home state. We were finding music to match a personality.

My role, once we had the music down, was to watch the bullpen with binoculars from the press box, to make certain it was Lyle getting into the car, and to grab the direct phone line to Toby Wright and to say, "It's Lyle."

It worked very quickly. The writers noticed it the first time, and, by the third or fourth time, the fans were standing in their seats and screaming at the first note. By the time he blew out of the door, Yankee Stadium was shaking. What power at that moment! My only fear was that I would somehow misidentify Lyle getting into the car, and it would be Ron Klimkowski emerging from the Datsun. Fortunately, that never happened.

To my surprise, Sparky asked us to stop the music the following year.

"Who needs all the extra pressure?" he said. "You come in to the music, and one of these days I'm gonna get my brains blown out on the mound and the fans will sing it as I get yanked out of the game. I don't want that moment!"

So we killed it after only a year, but we made an impact.

About 20 years later I was with Sparky at a trading-card convention in Honolulu, long after he had left baseball. We had a quiet moment together, at which time I suggested to him that with all the glory that closers were now getting, he was really the start of it all, in the sense of having that theatrical majesty on the mound.

"Are you kidding?" he said. "*You're* the guy who invented the closer! It was the music, that damned *Pomp and Circumstance*! You invented the whole thing!"

It was at once the best compliment I ever got in baseball—and a total lie. The first guy to make drama of closing a game was Dick "The Monster" Radatz, Sparky's predecessor in Boston, who would raise his arms in the air after the final out and ignite the crowd. But it was still a great compliment. And today, with about a dozen closers using "theme" music to enter a game, I think I did, perhaps, start something.

I was able to work Sparky into two pieces of baseball research that I did on a freelance basis. Today, you can hardly come up with anything new, because Elias Sports Bureau, Stats Inc., Total Sports, and SABR seem to have uncovered everything there is to uncover. But in the mid-'70s I decided to try to trace baseball's longest-running trade lineage. I wondered whether there were any active players who, having been traded for so-and-so, who was traded for so-and-so, might have roots dating back 20, 30, even 40 years.

My research took me, coincidentally, to Lyle, who had been traded for Cater. Cater himself had been traded in 1964 for Ray Herbert, a White Sox pitcher. In '61 Herbert had been traded for Gerry Staley, and in '54 Staley had been traded for Al Smith. Now these were seldom one-for-one trades, and in some cases were out of sequence, although the same players were involved, but, basically, I tracked Lyle back to the debut of catcher Frankie Hayes of the Philadelphia Athletics in 1933.

Lyle himself was traded to Texas for Dave Righetti, and the GM of the Rangers who made the trade, Eddie Robinson, had actually been one of the players in the cycle, when he was traded for Early Wynn in 1948 and then for Ned Garver in 1956. I'm sure Eddie had no idea, nor did anybody else until I stumbled on all of this.

The whole thing went on to include Juan Beniquez, Ruppert Jones, Billy Hatcher, Wes Chamberlain, and Chris James, and finally ended with Chamberlain and James failing to see action in '96. The streak ran for 62 years after Hayes' debut. Of course, I was the only person in the universe who saw the significance of Chamberlain and James not getting re-signed in '96, including those two, plus any descendants of ol' Frankie Hayes.

I did manage to make a magazine story out of it all, which was reprinted in *The Fireside Book of Baseball* (fourth edition), a volume in which I was very proud to be included. And I also did a piece for *Baseball Digest* (it was unusual for them to run original pieces) in which I researched—page by page in the *Baseball Encyclopedia*—all relief pitchers who had never started a game. It happened that Bob Locker was first, but Sparky was seventh. The point of the story was the emergence of the true "relief specialist," a primitive idea in 1973. Today, there are many such pitchers—every team has them. Then, it was unique enough to be a cover story.

Sparky marched to the beat of his own drum and had his priorities in order. He was seated behind me on a West Coast flight on August 8, 1974. As we were flying over Prescott, Arizona, the pilot of our charter announced that he was giving us a radio frequency so we could listen to an announcement from the White House

I put on my headset and heard Richard Nixon deliver his resignation speech. I turned to Lyle (no headset) and said, "That's it, Nixon just resigned."

Sparky turned the hand of cards he was holding in my direction. "You think *he's* having a bad day?" he asked.

I don't think I ever knew an adult who enjoyed life more than did Sparky Lyle.

I never knew Roger Maris very well, but I knew Graig Nettles, and that was pretty close. Graig would be the Yankees' last acquisition under CBS ownership, and almost at once I spotted him as a Maris successor.

Maris was gone by the time I took my fan-mail job in 1968. He had become a victim of bad press in New York and was practically run out of town just five years after his 61-homer season. The Yankees, in fact, would likely have granted him an unconditional release had they not managed to extract a body—third baseman Charlie Smith—from the Cardinals for him. Maris for Smith. It seems almost impossible to fathom today. Roger went on to help the Cardinals win pennants in his final two seasons and then retired the same year as Mantle, 1968. He left with his dignity intact, but not without bitterness. He felt the Yankees had turned their backs on him when he injured his hand, masking the true nature of his injury and forcing him to play hurt. He hated what the Yankees did to him, what the New York media did to him, and the way the fans had started to boo him.

When I was charged with handling Old Timers Day invitations some years after he retired, he never responded. Some of the bitter players—and we had our share—would at least respond. Red Ruffing made it a point to argue that because we weren't paying for the wives' transportation, he wouldn't be coming, as a matter of principle. Bob Shawkey, who had started the first game in Yankee Stadium in 1923, was a kindly old gentleman with a neat gray crewcut, who would accept our invitations but would explain to me that he still held a grudge over being dropped as manager after one season when the Yankees went out and signed Joe McCarthy in 1931.

And Jackie Robinson, whom we often invited as a great New York opponent, would always phone me and say in his high, nasal voice, "Until such time as baseball can demonstrate a willingness to hire minorities for managing and front-office positions, I cannot support Old Timers Days and other such promotional events."

I explained to Jackie that we had met at my cousin Howie's bar mitzvah in 1959, when Jackie was available, for a fee, for such appearances. I told him that I had seen him speak in Oneonta in 1967, when I was in college and he was on a lecture tour. But the smalltalk didn't break the ice. He was going to be a no-show forever after.

But Maris, I guess, must have just laughed and thrown out his invitation. He was busy getting on with the rest of his life, running a lucrative beer distributorship in Gainesville, Florida.

Once or twice I followed up with a phone call, which I knew was a waste of time. And to my delight, he was very pleasant on the phone. He just said, "No, Marty, I don't need that; I don't need to fly fifteen hundred miles to get booed again."

I honestly didn't think he would be booed. To me, he had been a hero. My generation was coming back to the game. The older fans hadn't liked him. He was going after Babe Ruth's record and challenging Mantle in the process. Two Yankee legends about to be overtaken by this surly, second-year Yankee from North Dakota. At 26, who did he think he was?

But fans my age had been thrilled by the home run chase of 1961, and, Maris, in his own way, was one of the first "antiheroes" we were discovering. He had a beautiful swing, as only a lefthander can have, and he gave us some summer to remember.

The guys on the grounds crew loved Roger, which was usually good enough for me. They were salt-of-the-earth men, and they knew the good guys from the phonies. When they liked a player, I liked a player. They were my screening committee. Frankie Albohn, Jimmy Esposito, Danny Coletti, Moose (who hung the team pennants on the roof in order of the day's standings)—these were the guys who could see through the bullshit.

And so I never even met Roger Maris.

And then, one day in Washington in 1985, I was at a cocktail party during the Cracker Jack Old Timers Day events, and I found myself on the buffet line next to ol' number 9 himself. I usually didn't bother a player while he was holding plates of food in both hands, but I couldn't stop myself.

"Roger," I said, "You wouldn't remember me, but I'm Marty Appel, I was Bob Fishel's assistant on the Yankees after Bill Guilfoile, and then I became the PR Director, and I was the guy who used to call you and invite you to our Old Timers Games."

"Yeah, I remember you, Marty; I know who you are."

"Well," I continued, "I know I'm gonna sound like every fan you meet, but I just wanted to tell you that it's a kick to meet you after all these years. You're the only Yankee from my childhood I've not met. And I wanted you to know that if your memories of 1961 aren't the best, with the hair falling out and all of that—for me, it was the best summer of my life."

Maris put his plate down and extended his hand. He looked me right in the eye and, in an expressive voice, said, "Thanks, Marty—you'd be surprised that I *don't* hear that a lot—I still get a lot of crap over the record."

I *was* surprised. And I said, "Well, I was thirteen then, and, for my friends and me, it was all that mattered. And I think that you'd be surprised how much the fans of New York have come to respect you now."

It was a warm moment. He was fantastic.

He was also dying of cancer, which everyone knew, and he battled it courageously to the end, which came five months later. I went to the memorial service at St. Patrick's Cathedral in New York, sat behind Richard Nixon, in fact, and heard John Cardinal O'Connor lead a wonderful tribute to the man who had been, too late, a hero.

At the end of the service, he looked at Roger's grandchildren, who were seated in a front pew, and said, "At this time, in something somewhat unusual for this great cathedral, I am going to ask those in attendance to give us one last round of applause for your grandfather, so that you can get some understanding of how New York truly felt about him, and get some idea of the cheers that used to fill the great Yankee Stadium."

With that, everyone began to applaud, politely at first, and then quite loudly. Even Nixon. From the back of the church there even emerged cheers of "Ro-ger, Ro-ger," and I was in tears, as was everyone in St. Pat's. My God, I found myself shaking hands with Nixon!

So I had come to know Maris, a little. But in a way, I had already known him through Nettles.

Graig (it always looked misspelled until he became such a fixture that "Craig" now looks wrong) seemed to me to have the same red-ass personality, the same build, the same bearing as Maris. The circumstances of his arrival were also, to me, remarkably similar.

In 1959 Harry Craft, who had been Mantle's minor league manager, was managing Maris in Kansas City. Roger was enjoying a decent season by Kansas City standards—he would hit .273 with 16 homers in his first full season there. But Craft knew he was going to get fired at the end of the year, and when the Yankees were playing the A's late in the season, he said to Casey Stengel, "If you can get Maris, you've got yourself a helluva player."

This was at the time when the Yankees were treating the Athletics like a farm club. They were getting all sorts of good players from them, and the well hadn't run dry. On December 11 they traded Roger and two other bench players to the Yanks for Hank Bauer—who had long worn number 9—Norm Siebern, Marv Throneberry, and Mr. Perfect Game himself, Don Larsen. Roger got number 9, took Bauer's spot in right, won the MVP Award in 1960, and led the league with the 61 homers in '61, winning MVP again.

Nettles was on Cleveland in 1972—the team Maris had begun his career with. He was 28. He had batted .253 with 17 homers, but he had a beautiful swing from the left side, almost built for Yankee Stadium.

Gabe Paul was general manager of the Indians. Here things get a little tricky. It was around this time that CBS was quietly putting the Yankees up for sale. It was around this time that Mike Burke, through Gabe Paul, first met George Steinbrenner and began to talk about a sale of the club.

On November 27, 1972, Nettles was traded to the Yankees along with catcher Jerry Moses for four players—Charlie ("Sam") Spikes, Jerry Kenney, Rusty Torres, and John Ellis. All, coincidentally, had been winners of the James P. Dawson award as outstanding rookies in spring training. The award—a Longines watch—seemed to ensure that none of the four would ever be late for an Indians game.

I had liked Nettles and thought that this was not just good news—it was great news. I called Pete Sheehy, who used to hand out uniform numbers at his own discretion, and said, "Pete, you've got to give Nettles number 9. He just reminds me of all the circumstances of Maris coming to the Yankees."

Nine hadn't been very sacred after Maris left, partly due to the bitter split. Steve Whitaker wore it in '68. An outfielder named Dick Simpson wore it in '69. Ron Woods, a bald little outfielder whom we got in exchange for Tom Tresh, wore it in '70 and '71. Fred Frazier wore it in spring training of '72. Pete had managed to keep it out of circulation only the first year after Maris left. Today it is a sacred, retired number on the Yankees in Maris's honor.

My urging that Nettles get number 9 played out in Graig's fourth year with the Yankees. That was 1976, the year the Yanks returned to the newly refurbished Yankee Stadium and won a pennant. Nettles led the league in home runs, the first Yankee to accomplish this since Maris in '61.

Nettles was as good a fielder at third base as you could find—really up there with Brooks Robinson, for my money, and Brooks was one of the greatest of all time. But once you win a Gold Glove Award, you pretty much win it every year, as Brooks did. Nettles also had power, but he just didn't hit for a high enough average to put up Hall of Fame numbers.

I had my ups and downs with Graig. He could be surly like Maris, but he could be reasonable. He got mad at me one year for using a bad picture of him in the Yearbook—sort of a futile swing, really, not a wise choice at all. I apologized, he accepted it, and then he forgot about it. It was not the sort of thing he would dwell on.

He had a razor-sharp wit when it came to criticizing Steinbrenner, which sometimes went over the line, but he was flowering in an era when players could more freely knock management. The union was getting stronger, and what was management going to do but take it?

So we got Nettles on November 27, 1972. Five weeks later, Steinbrenner bought the team. A few days later, there was Gabe Paul, part of the new ownership. Had Paul dealt Nettles to the Yankees knowing he would himself soon be a Yankee?

The answer was probably yes. Gabe had been around long enough to know that deals sometimes go bad. There was always the chance that the Steinbrenner sale wouldn't happen, and that he'd still be in Cleveland. But what kind of chance was he taking? If he went to New York, he'd have Nettles, a nice improvement over Celerino Sanchez. If he stayed, he'd have a typical non-contending Cleveland team, and he wouldn't have Nettles. Big deal. It was a chance worth taking. And it paid off.

Recalling the ghosts of yesterday in old Yankee Stadium was, on occasion, closer to reality than one would expect.

One of my favorite responsibilities in my early years as Bob Fishel's assistant was programming the scoreboard messages.

Programming is a computer term; that was hardly the case then. The old Yankee scoreboard had been removed in 1959 and carted off to Connie Mack Stadium in Philadelphia as a hand-me-down. A new board emerged as the state of the art, the first to have a changeable message board.

The message board was eight characters wide and eight lines deep. It was the center of the perfectly arranged and rather elegant board that included, permanently, all the out-of-town scores, the lineups, and the score by innings. You hardly needed anything else, let alone hands clapping, fireworks exploding, or animated mascots hopping around.

Affable George Schmelzer was our stadium electrician. He repaired faulty wires, changed light bulbs, did whatever electricians did, and, during the games, he was in the scoreboard, changing the messages at my direction.

Ray Sanse sat to Fishel's left in the press box and through a squawk box, yelled "ball," "strike," and "out" to a Schmelzer assistant, who rapidly lit the appropriate bulbs to let the fans, players, and umpires know the count and the outs. He would also update the runs, hits, and errors. Ray always took pride in the ball-strike count changing so quickly on the board that fans looking up would not even see the switch. He never knew that George had a radio on in the scoreboard and was really doing it from the play-by-play.

George would handle the out-of-town scores when he had time, in between changing messages. It was my job to keep the uniform numbers of pitchers up-to-date in the scorecard so that if 41 appeared next to the Mets, you could check your scorecard and know Seaver was pitching. I took great pride in being as up-to-date as possible with those roster changes, and getting the uniform number right was important to me.

Usually the message board welcomed guests: CUB PACK 8, NUTLEY, NJ, or YANKEES WELCOME ELLIOT GOULD. Sometimes it would have announcements about the Yankee Yearbook, upcoming home games, or ticket-ordering information. Those were fairly standard, and seldom changed their style.

I enjoyed keeping things fresh and using noncommercial announcements. LYLE FIVE SHORT OF YANKEE SAVE RECORD might be an example.

One day we had a long rain delay. While organist Eddie Layton played *Raindrops Keep Falling on My Head* for the 40th time, I sensed that after 55 minutes the fans were getting a little restless. So I tried something new on the board.

"George," I said to Schmelzer, "look at page 16 of the press guide. You see we have those top 20 Yankees of all-time? Go to the home runs . . . punch them up there one at a time, letter by letter. That should kill some time, and it could be fun."

He punched up—one letter at a time—YANKEE HOME RUN LEADERS . . . 20. FRANK CROSETTI 98. Then he took that down and put up 19. GEORGE SELKIRK 108. Each stayed up for a couple of minutes. It didn't get much reaction.

But I realized that we were going to get to some serious names, and so did the fans. At 11. JOE PEPITONE 166, we had a mix of boos and cheers, but at least the rain-soaked fans were starting to get into it.

After we passed Lazzeri, Henrich, Keller, and Dickey came 6. ROGER MARIS 203. At the letters R-O-G the fans began to boo, and to sort of laugh as well. Now they had the spirit.

At 5. Y-O-G, huge cheers went up. Fans were almost dancing in the aisles (thanks also, I guess, to the beer)—huge applause for YOGI BERRA 358.

The ovations just grew tremendous for 4. JOE DiMAGGIO 361, and 3. LOU GEHRIG 493. At the first letter, of course, the fans knew what was coming and let loose. We had a rain delay going on? A ballgame? Fuhgeddaboutit, New York! We were putting on a show here. Even the people in the press box were laughing and enjoying it.

2. M . . . oh, now the place was going nuts; it was an ovation as big as on Old Timers Day when Mantle appeared in person. Talk about your standing O's, this was enough to wake up the folks at the Concourse Plaza. When 2. MICKEY MANTLE 536 came down, everyone knew what was coming next and was prepared for the biggest ovation of all, an ovation for a guy who had been dead for 22 years, who hadn't heard a cheer like this since his last goodbye.

Schmelzer punched up the number 1. Then the letter B. The crowd started to roar as if the Babe himself had just walked out of the dugout.

There was 1. BABE, and then suddenly, shockingly, a bolt of lightning from the darkness of the Bronx sky exploded over the very center of the scoreboard where these words were forming and, in an instant, silenced the entire board. Dead. The power was purged from the system; there would be no RUTH.

I hoped George Schmelzer was okay, and he was able to tell me that he was, with a startled "What happened!?" As for the fans, a collective gasp could be heard. I don't recall what our attendance was at that point in the rain delay—perhaps no more than 6,000 or so—but I would think everyone there at that moment remembers the event. It was as though the Babe himself had spoken to us. It was a night in which we truly felt the presence of the Yankee gods.

FOR SALE:
DYNASTY, SHAKEN

There was no warning that the Yankees were for sale.

This was amazing in that Gabe Paul, the man who introduced George Steinbrenner to Mike Burke, was one of the best news leakers in all of baseball. He was also a master at covering his own trail.

Once, Gabe demanded that I find out who leaked some piece of news to United Press International. Demanded! He was furious that his cloak-and-dagger transaction had been uncovered, and he swore that whoever had leaked the story was toast.

Charged with this mission, I went to the columnist who wrote the story. Choosing our friendship over journalistic ethics, he decided to sell out his source.

"It was Gabe!" he said.

When I never reported my findings to Gabe, the matter slipped away. I kind of thought it might.

The Christmas holidays had passed in 1972. We had had a nice employee Christmas party in the Stadium Club restaurant. Rob Franklin had put together a terrific slide show of old silent-movie stills, matched with appropriate captions to suit our current staff.

These parties were fun, and hardly massive events. Our front office staff was not much greater than 50, including the full-time ticket employees, and if you included the year-round grounds crew we were up to about 60. We would invite the scouts who lived nearby, all three of them, and call it a party.

In fact, the famous New York Yankees franchise was not really that big a business. Our logo was as well known as those of Exxon or Nabisco or GE, but we were really just a mom-and-pop business next to those guys. The team's revenues today—probably the tops in baseball—are around $175 million. Back when the team was sold in 1973, they were probably not much more than five percent of that. Broadcast revenues? There were years when nobody wanted us at all, and we had to buy our own time on the radio and hire someone to sell advertising, in the hope that we would break even. Television? From 135 games a year on WPIX in the early '60s, we were down to about 100 then, with no competition for the broadcast rights and very low ratings. In the real world of business, we were a small operation. It was nowhere near a *Fortune* 500 company and, in fact, really didn't generate enough income to get a line in *Fortune* at all.

The CEO, Mike Burke, knew everyone's name. You could memorize everyone's telephone extension. And I'm sure Bob Fishel remembered everyone's birthday, from Phyllis in the ticket office to Tracy the painter to Morris the elevator operator. We may have been known far and wide, but this was not much more than the tiniest division of CBS. And not a moneymaker, either.

CBS had bought the Yankees in 1964 at the height of the team's glory—another streak of five consecutive pennants. What CBS did not have among its fine programming and news staff was a baseball scout. There was no one to tell them—not Lucy, not Walter Cronkite, not Dick Van Dyke, not Allen Funt, not Ed Sullivan—that the well had run dry. There were no more pennant races in the future, because the stars had gotten old and the minor leagues were fallow. Dan Topping and Del Webb, perhaps with an eye toward selling, had let the farm system slip.

So CBS, imagining the fun of entertaining its big network sponsors at a Yankee Stadium World Series in 1965, put $14.4 million on the table and took over the franchise. Eight blah seasons later, they were looking for a buyer, happy to unload us and get out of the baseball business.

George Steinbrenner III of Cleveland had been trying to buy the Indians, but they were (in an unusual moment) not for sale. He asked Gabe Paul who might be for sale. With that in his ear, Gabe had a breakfast meeting with Mike Burke during the summer of '72. And the wheels started to turn. Slowly at first, then rapidly . . . but at all times, very quietly.

Steinbrenner was only 42 when these conversations were taking place. It was a very young age to get into a big negotiation like this, but there was nothing boylike about George. He had owned a pro basketball team in Cleveland—the Pipers—in his 30s. His father ran a shipbuilding and ship repair business on the Great Lakes. He learned business—and how to be a boss—from his dad. He tussled with unions and their muscled ship workers. He also learned discipline from serving as an assistant football coach at both Northwestern and Purdue for a year each.

He was a big man, but the size suited him. A skinny George Steinbrenner would not have worked. He was a capitalist and a leader and a man used to getting his way, and he needed the physical size to make it work.

Just before the New Year, an agreement was reached whereby a group headed by Steinbrenner would buy the Yankees from CBS for $10 million. It would be, I believe, the first and last time that a team had ever been sold at a loss.

CBS was happy to get out, embarrassing or not. It had come in at the tail end of a dynasty. Coupled with the new free agent draft that kept it from using the pinstripe prestige to sign every hot prospect, its reign could not have commenced at a worse moment.

The energy CBS thought it might bring to this entertainment property really never emerged.

CBS got a couple of Columbia Records in-house composers to put together a very catchy theme song, *Here Come the Yankees*, which is still played today to introduce broadcasts. (Some think this song is part of old-time Yankee history and should never be dropped; they are surprised to learn it only goes back to the '60s and the CBS days.)

They made Jerry Vale available to us to provide a recording of the National Anthem, which we alternated with Robert Merrill. Merrill would emerge as the performer of choice because he was truly a great Yankee fan and gave great enthusiasm to his live performances at the Stadium.

Some of our executives were CBS people, sent to run the team, and some of them were first rate, especially Howard Berk, our vice president of administration, who helped bring the team into the modern era of marketing.

Eddie Layton, who played the organ on many CBS soap operas, was enlisted to bring his talents to Yankee Stadium. He knew not a thing about baseball but became one of the best ballpark organ players in the country.

We employees had a stock-option plan, so we were able to purchase CBS stock through payroll deduction. In that last year, CBS spun off a new division to sell rerun rights for their properties—*Andy Griffith, I Love Lucy, The Beverly Hillbillies*, and so forth. The FCC had ruled that networks couldn't own programming, so CBS couldn't sell their shows into syndication. Thus was born a little company called Viacom. Twenty-six years later, Viacom bought CBS. None of the business coverage made note of the irony. The business world cares about "last year versus this year."

CBS had hoped there would be some broadcast synergy with the team, but there wasn't. The network was not involved in national telecasts, and local WPIX was more than capable of doing first-class broadcasts without them.

WPIX, in fact, had almost bought the Yankees from Topping and Webb in 1965. Lev Pope, the WPIX president, saw it—years before anyone else did—as a brilliant way to lock up broadcast rights. But WPIX was owned by the Tribune Company in Chicago (which later bought the Cubs, using Lev's logic), and in 1965 they told him to pull back; they were not interested in owning a team.

With Gabe Paul's intervention, Mike Burke saw an opportunity to become an owner—not just someone assigned by an owner to run a team. Steinbrenner and Burke would be the principal owners, and a group of limited partners would be assembled to handle about 70 percent of the financing. Burke wasn't putting up any money; he would just get his share for talking CBS's William Paley and Frank Stanton into doing it. Steinbrenner would put up about $2 or 3 million. And although that investment never catapulted him into the annual *Forbes* list of the wealthiest Americans, it did turn him into not only a very rich man but the American archetype of "the Boss," a nickname he came to enjoy.

So we hit the office early on the morning of January 3, 1973, cranked up the mimeograph machine, and began to prepare for a press conference that caught everyone by surprise.

I was on phone duty. Last-minute press conferences or rainouts were nightmares in the days of rotary telephones. I had my list of about 90 people to call—every sports desk, photo desk, television station, radio station, columnist at home, broadcaster at home, and the beat writers. Today there are more than 90—but the touch-tone telephone has made a world of difference. When we had rainouts, I had to make the same 90 calls, slowly, one by one, a job that took hours.

Fishel was nervous and agitated. He was pleased that the story hadn't leaked, but it hadn't even leaked to him until the day before. There was little time to prepare. We needed a general release; we needed a biography and a photo of Steinbrenner. There was no time for the photo to be mass-produced, but we cooked up the bio quickly with help from Marsh Samuel, a Cleveland associate of George's who had once been the Indians' PR director.

George came down to our office to read the release. We shook hands briefly, and he commented that he could certainly see what an efficient PR operation we had.

Bob's anxiety, even with his being the most respected public relations official in all of sports, was as natural as anyone's insecurities over new ownership. He had not only survived the transition from Topping and Webb to CBS but had thrived on it. Burke liked and respected him. He would tease Bob sometimes; Burke once called him to a breakfast meeting on the beach in Florida and, when Bob arrived in a shirt and tie, he made him strip down to his undershirt. Bob was a formal sort—in New York, he always threw on his jacket when Burke asked to see him.

Now we all faced the unknown. Burke would still be in charge, but what to make of this new fellow?

An answer was slipped to us a few hours later at the packed press conference in the Stadium Club. No one was there from CBS except Burke himself. No Paley, no Stanton, no one to deliver a eulogy for the dismal showing of the team and to explain why it was being sold at a loss.

Steinbrenner was engaging, showed some charm, spoke of his reverence for the Yankees, and finally delivered the line that would haunt him all the years he owned the club.

Asked about his role in running the club, he responded, "I'll leave that to Mike and Lee MacPhail. I'll stick to building ships."

In a way, it was unfair to throw that in his face every time he would later choose to get involved. Years pass, things change. But it went down in history, for better or worse, as a promise not kept. It was there with George Bush saying "Read my lips: no new taxes" or Gary Hart daring the press to follow him.

The press conference ended with a hastily prepared lunch. Burke and Steinbrenner retreated to a corner table, only to be joined, uninvited, by our diminutive Jackie Farrell, semi-retired head of the Speakers' Bureau, who no doubt told them of his Sally Rand letter and kept them from doing real business. It was an awkward moment, but, hey—it was the only seat left.

Getting a catered meal in January when the Stadium Club was closed was no easy task, but we came through. Both Burke and Steinbrenner had handled themselves well with the press, or so it seemed. Inside, Burke was seething.

Burke had stuck his neck out with William Paley—his mentor and a historic American figure whose friendship he treasured. Whatever happened, Paley did not want to be embarrassed by the sale. He did not want it viewed as a CBS failure, despite the diminished selling price.

Paley had instructed Burke to say, "CBS substantially recouped its investment." The wording was critical to Paley, and Burke delivered it verbatim.

What he failed to do, apparently, was impress upon Steinbrenner the importance of this, or perhaps the importance of his own promise to Paley. Caught up in the excitement of the purchase, Steinbrenner told the press, "It's the best buy in sports today. I think it's a bargain."

It was the last thing Paley wanted to read in the papers, and he never spoke to Burke again. Their trust was broken, and Burke was both heartsick over the matter and suddenly wary of his new business partner.

It would get worse. Fast.

Exactly one week later, a press conference was scheduled for the posh '21' Club on West 52nd Street. There, the limited partners would be introduced. For a week Fishel and I worked furiously to prepare biographies of each of the partners, all run off on Yankee letterhead and enclosed in a handsome Yankee media kit folder with Mickey Mantle's photo on the cover. Five-by-seven black-and-white photos of each partner were included in the kit.

"Helluva job," Steinbrenner told us.

But wait.

One of the photos was of Gabe Paul—the Indians' general manager, the man who had introduced Steinbrenner to Burke, the man who had traded Nettles to the Yankees weeks before.

The very morning of the '21' press conference, Steinbrenner informed Burke that Gabe was selling his interest in the Indians and purchasing a five percent interest in the Yanks.

Burke exploded. The entire press conference was suddenly in jeopardy. Not only was Gabe to have an interest in the team, but he would that very day be announced as president.

The infuriated Burke had been told that Gabe would be coming to New York to "close out his long career before retiring to his home in Tampa." According to Burke, Paul's team presidency was never mentioned until literally the 11th hour.

Fishel got wind of the furor but kept grinding out the press kits, trying his best to stay tuned to the prevailing winds. There was, for some time, the possibility of calling off the whole thing.

At noon, in a private, upstairs room at '21,' we seated the limited partners side by side on armless chairs from the dining tables. It was laughable, in its own way. These men were titans of American industry, pillars of the financial community, and now they looked like they were gathering for story time in the reading corner at nursery school.

On, Dancer; on, Dasher; on, Ginsberg and Greenberg (both named Edward). There was Tom Evans, partner of John Mitchell in Richard Nixon's old law firm, who had headed the finance committee of CREEP—the Committee to Re-Elect the President. There was Marvin Warner, soon to be appointed ambassador to Switzerland. Trucking magnate Francis O'Neill, cosmetics baron Jess Bell, theater producer James Nederlander, oil scion Nelson Bunker Hunt, and auto innovator John DeLorean. Magnate Lester Crown, horse baron Leslie Combs, Charlotte Witkind, and Sheldon Guren rounded out the crowd.

Many of this original cast would find themselves in varying degrees of hot water with the authorities over the coming years. I kept their page from the Yankee Yearbook in my desk—showing their photos in neat rows—and pasted little APPREHENDED or CONVICTED stickers across their faces as each went down. It may have been cruel, but it was remarkable how many fell.

And there was ol' Gabe, 63, sitting with the rest, our new limited partner, old enough to be Steinbrenner's father. Burke was roasting. But he had managed to put aside the issue of the presidency. In fact, Gabe was introduced as no more than "special projects," not even "director, special projects." There had been, for appearances' sake, a last-minute compromise.

The New York writers smelled a rat.

No way, they figured, was Gabe Paul going to have any special projects on his plate other than running the team. He ruled the Indians even without owning them. He had been hired to run the new Houston Colt .45s in 1961, but when Judge Roy Hofheinz wielded too much power, Gabe was gone. No way would Gabe now be in charge of deciding whether age 14 or 15 was the cutoff for Yankee Postcard Day.

Steinbrenner returned to Cleveland, and Burke to his Yankee Stadium office, his own contract as a partner still being crafted. As he received drafts of it, he didn't like what he was seeing. And his mistrust was growing by the day.

He confided this to Bob, who shared it with me. Bob was in a tight spot. If there was going to be a bloodbath, where was Bob to go? He was a very loyal man—but was his loyalty to Burke or to the Yankees? Or to himself and his career?

He had long talks with Howard Berk, who had become his close friend. Neither could forecast where this was going.

MacPhail and Ralph Houk—who had run the team on the field with no interference—could only imagine what changes might be coming, especially with Gabe Paul on the scene.

By spring training, in the midst of the Peterson–Kekich fiasco, tensions were building. We had to take a yearbook photo of Steinbrenner and Burke together. It was one of the most awkward photos you've ever seen. Michael Grossbardt, our photographer, said he could feel the tension through the lens.

Steinbrenner wore a navy sports jacket; Burke, an open denim shirt, his gray chest hairs blowing in the breeze. Steinbrenner told associates that Burke's appearance was a disgrace to the Yankees.

During training camp it was announced that Bobby Murcer was to receive a $100,000 salary for 1973. He would join DiMaggio and Mantle as $100,000 players. Steinbrenner was not consulted, and Burke had a nasty phone conversation defending the salary, and defending his position of not having to defend himself at all.

When Murcer went hitless on Opening Day back in New York, Steinbrenner, in the lobby, was overheard telling his friends, "There's your hundred-thousand-dollar player for you!" He had also made notes in his scorecard of all the players whose hair appeared too long as they lined up for the national anthem along the first base line. He had written "1, 17, 19, 25, 28" . . . and so on.

Before the end of the month, Burke was gone. When friends saw him at a Manhattan restaurant and asked how he was, he was heard to say, "I'll be fine when I get this knife out of my back."

He confronted George with the obvious—the two of them could not get along. George must have been relieved. It had to have been a very painful way to begin his reign as Yankee owner.

Mike Burke departed as Fishel and I handed out a simple, one-paragraph release in the press box during a game. Burke did not hang around to answer questions. He rode off into the sunset (he was a member of the Auxiliary Police Force of New York and got to ride horseback each morning in Central Park). He would emerge again as the head of the Knicks and the Rangers and of Madison Square Garden before retiring to Ireland as a gentleman farmer, and dying at 70 in 1987.

The liberal-minded New York sportswriters (which meant almost everyone but Dick Young) had always been taken with Mike Burke, even though he was not a winner. But he was not a phony either—he was a genuinely interesting man whose company was always sought. He was a bit highbrow for the baseball crowd sometimes, but it made him all the more fascinating, as he tried to be a "regular" guy, sitting in the stands and signing autographs with the little people.

And Fishel? How would he survive?

"Mike's not entirely blameless in this, you know," he said to me the day Burke resigned. Ah, ever the pragmatist. Bob was going to survive just fine. From Topping and Webb to CBS to Steinbrenner, he was always the loyalist. And of course, that was good news for me as well. Our PR team would continue onward.

One piece of business that carried over from one reign to the other was the little matter of rebuilding Yankee Stadium.

Those of us who worked there loved Yankee Stadium. Part of that love was in the knowledge that Ruth and Gehrig had played there, Ed Barrow had worked there, and that it was the most famous ballpark in the world. (I used to say it was the most famous sports arena in the world with the exception of the Coliseum in Rome, but it was a stretch to call lions eating Christians a sport.)

The PR office's bound copies of old baseball annuals had Barrow's name engraved on the covers. Everywhere you turned, there was some significant remembrance of the glory of this team's past.

No one appreciated the place more than I did, not even Fishel, who had grown up in Cleveland. I knew where the old, prewar Yankee club-house was. I prowled the dusty storage rooms and found buried treasure: old photographs and trophies. I was on the roof and in the scoreboard. I looked up old scouting reports on players in Johnny Johnson's files and sat across the picnic table in the clubhouse talking baseball with Big Pete.

At lunchtime employees would walk to River Avenue for a sandwich and bring it back to the Stadium. We'd sit in the sun in the empty ball-park, feeding squirrels, talking baseball, and watching the painters, the groundskeepers, and the maintenance people tend to the old place. I had George Schmelzer play *Sgt. Pepper's Lonely Hearts Club Band* on the PA system to hear the full power of the classic album.

But we as employees didn't have to fight traffic or sit behind a steel pole. We didn't have to climb 10 ramps to get to the upper deck.

We knew a little about these discomforts because we used to get free tickets to the Giants' football games (they were our tenants). From my seat in left field, with a pole partially blocking my view, I knew this wasn't right, because engineering had long ago enabled the building of ballparks without these obstructions.

And I totally gave up any thoughts of driving to the park on a foot-ball Sunday. Instead, I would park my car in the north Bronx and take the subway to the game, but it wasn't pleasant and it wasn't especially safe.

So, rationally, we did understand the need to consider a change. But emotionally, it was striking us hard, because we were so in love with Jacob

Ruppert's original structure, the first triple-decked stadium in the country—the first ballpark, in fact, to be called a stadium.

But then, when we started having Bat Day promotions, and the kids would rap their bats on the concrete floors to summon a Yankee rally, pieces of concrete would fall to the level below. Not good.

We had cursory inspections by independent engineers and they pronounced the building weakening as it approached its 50th anniversary.

Meanwhile, the Mets were drawing and the Yankees weren't, and the Mets went on to win another pennant in 1973. Our attendance was barely cracking a million and we were selling fewer than four thousand season tickets. Shea was ugly and had no charm—no one ever said, "Hey, when you're in New York, don't miss Shea Stadium." But it was livelier and it seemed safer, and its parking and access roads were far superior to ours.

In reality, police records showed that the parks were equally safe. But Shea had an openness, and the sunlight made it feel like a safe haven compared to the shadows cast by the decaying Bronx buildings along Jerome Avenue. And there was a prison three blocks away!

We obtained a pitcher one year at the old Yankee Stadium, Jim Hardin, from the Orioles. Jim drove up from Baltimore and parked his car outside the players' entrance to run inside and make sure the clubhouse was open. When he got back about 10 minutes later, his entire car had been looted—all his clothes and personal property were gone. The car itself was intact, doors properly locked. Welcome to the Bronx, Jim.

Quietly, in early 1972, Mike Burke began to meet with Mayor Lindsay about the situation. Lindsay, not a fan but a kindred spirit of Burke's, was a good listener. Both were antiwar, liberal-minded, and shared a common foundation for the small talk leading to the substance. The talks were going well.

In New Orleans, the Superdome was on the drawing boards, soon to be the nation's second indoor arena. Officials from New Orleans sent feelers to the Yankees, wondering if they might consider a move.

No move was ever seriously considered, but it gave Burke an option, one he gently presented to Lindsay. John may not have been a baseball fan, but he sure didn't want to be the mayor who lost the Yankees. Burke had gotten his attention.

Talks progressed, and Lindsay agreed to commit $24 million to a general refurbishing of Yankee Stadium in order to keep the team. This had been the cost of constructing Shea Stadium a decade earlier, and, given inflation, it seemed like a good number to use.

The city would condemn the ballpark (an ugly thing to do to our place, but simply a legal maneuver) and would take ownership from the incumbents—the Knights of Columbus and Rice University. (It had fallen to them after Ruppert's will had taken it out of family ownership.)

We announced the plans during our promotional caravan preceding the 1973 season. It was our last caravan, and Graig Nettles, our bright new face, was with us. It was also during the caravan that the American League announced adoption of the designated hitter rule, and one writer in New Jersey asked Ralph Houk, "Can you ever see yourself actually using this rule?"

But our big announcement at each stop was that 1973, the 50th anniversary of Yankee Stadium, would be the final year for the historic structure. Immediately after the season, the ballpark would be gutted and a new facility built. The concrete outer shell would remain. The project would take two seasons, during which we would be sharing Shea Stadium with the Mets.

There was a lot of public grumbling over the $24 million in public funds, but the plans were done, and it was time to hire architects. They would become part of our office environment throughout the year.

As for the 50th anniversary, we made the most of it. My good friend Tom Villante, the executive in charge of the Schaefer Beer account, took it upon himself to have a 50th anniversary logo designed, which was made into a sleeve patch for our first year of double-knit uniforms. Villante had brilliantly directed baseball's centennial celebration in 1969 and was a great addition to our marketing efforts. He had been a Yankee batboy in the mid-'40s, and his sharp mind, effervescent personality, and perpetual optimism provided a great boost for us all. Tom would go on to become one of the grand mentors of my career and would still counsel my children decades later on their career directions.

Tom was a terrific source of the most fascinatingly useless information—absolutely wonderful stuff. He could point to a Yankee team picture from his time there and say, "See this traveling secretary here, Rex Weyant? His sister was Jake Ruppert's mistress. That's how he got his job."

Our Old Timers Day in '73 was an all-Yankee affair, a very nostalgic sendoff for the old ballpark, which in some ways never looked better. CBS always kept it well maintained, freshly painted, and clean. A New York City problem with graffiti was hurting our exterior—a losing battle, it seemed—but otherwise we were sparkling in the south Bronx.

We had a helluva season and made a run at a pennant late in the summer, but then the team died and the fans started to get ugly, parading around with banners calling for Houk to be fired. We had been in first place from June 20 to July 31. We had picked up two veteran pitchers at the trading deadline—Pat Dobson and Sudden Sam McDowell, and we were rocking. With McDowell and Dobson, Murcer had all but guaranteed a pennant for Yankee fans. Murcer and Ron Blomberg had shared a *Sports Illustrated* cover, shot by the brilliant Neil Leifer in the umpire's dressing room across from my office. Blomberg, who on Opening Day had become baseball's first designated hitter (I had his bat sent to Cooperstown, a bat that produced . . . a walk!), was hitting over .400 as we went into July.

The team died in August. We went 20–34 from August 1 onward and faded quickly, finishing 17 games behind the great Orioles.

It was saddest on the final day of the season, the last game in old Yankee Stadium, when poor Ralph Houk had to go to the mound to make a pitching change. Fishel, a very emotional man about these things, was so hurt for Houk about this change being needed, because it exposed Houk to one last, loud barrage of boos from the discontented fans.

By this time, of course, the season had been a wipeout. Burke was gone, and Steinbrenner was becoming increasingly critical of MacPhail and Houk, particularly over Murcer's $100,000 contract. (Bobby did hit .304–22–95, but his home runs were down from 33 in '72.)

The final game was a rapid swirl of events, with a sad crowd of 32,000 in attendance. I had been asked to fill in for the UPI correspondent by filing a game story at the end of the afternoon. It was not uncommon for the PR man to do this, since it merely reported the facts in five or six paragraphs.

But around the fifth inning, Fishel got a phone call and whispered news to me that made me hurry to a phone and call UPI to tell them they better find somebody to get uptown.

Ralph Houk was resigning after the game. There was no way I was going to be a PR man for the team and a UPI reporter on that story.

Houk, still in uniform, came into the pressroom, about two hundred feet from the Yankee clubhouse. The room had a warmth to it that made it a pleasant retreat after games. Lou Napoli, behind the bar, was a throwback to Ebbets Field. There weren't a lot of baseball photos on the walls, but it had the feeling of a sports tavern.

Houk leaned on the bar and told everyone that he was quitting. "Time to move on, time to enter next phase of life, no plans now," and so forth. His voice was choking, and those of us who had worked with him and admired him were equally choked up.

This would be the first high-profile departure under Steinbrenner.

"Was it interference from George?" asked one writer.

Houk wouldn't bite. But to close friends, he said that was obviously the case. He had no respect for Steinbrenner's baseball pedigree and just couldn't take his criticisms and phone calls.

Many Yankee employees in the room had tears in their eyes.

Houk had a good thing under CBS. Burke may not have loved him, but he let him be, only confiding to close associates that he truly coveted Billy Martin. MacPhail was a friend and an ally, the best possible general manager that a manager could have. Houk was coasting. He was not prepared to take criticism, not prepared to have someone question his managing, and he did not adjust to it well. His resentment of Steinbrenner's interference was due largely to the cushy situation he had grown accustomed to. It was not unthinkable that an owner might question his manager—Houk had just never been forced to deal with it before.

Soon after his departure came news that Lee MacPhail would be succeeding Joe Cronin as president of the American League for the 1974 season. And that was that—Burke, MacPhail, and Houk, all gone in less than a year.

And with MacPhail leaving, there would be no doubt who would emerge as our de facto GM—none other than Gabe Paul.

Nothing would ever be tidy in the Yankee front office again.

Gabe Paul was as fascinating a figure as I ever encountered in baseball. His pedigree in the game was long, even if his list of successes wasn't. He was full of swagger and blarney and had a homily for every circumstance the game might throw at him.

What he had with the Yankees, for the first time in his long career, was a bankroll. He had never worked with a team where it was okay to order memo pads with your name on them without first consulting the balance in the checkbook. There was a sense that the baseball world was watching to see what he might do with the unthinkable—money to spend!

Gabe had long ago been the traveling secretary for the Cincinnati Reds, a team owned by Powell Crosley, the Ohio broadcasting pioneer. His days in those jobs had brought him his first—and only—taste of championship baseball. The Reds of 1939 and 1940 had been pennant winners.

What I liked most about Gabe was his resilience; he adapted to whatever the rule of the day was. He was no old fogy, locked into beliefs from his formative years. When free agency came along, for instance, it would have been very natural for Gabe to say, "This game has passed me by." Instead, he rolled up his sleeves, read over the new rules, and said, "Deal me in."

Gabe never lost his respect for the buck, however, and his interest in prudent fiscal management was always present. One tale we used to tell involved a long forgotten but horrific piece of baseball history from the summer of 1940. The Reds were on their way to a second pennant, but, playing in Braves Field on August 3, the team noticed that their catcher, Willard Hershberger, backup to Ernie Lombardi, was not at the park.

A ballplayer's absence, even due to injury or illness, is very unusual, and, after some time, manager Bill McKechnie told Gabe to call the Boston hotel. Hershberger, despondent over a personal matter, had told McKechnie the day before that he was contemplating suicide. The manager talked him into better humor, felt the crisis had passed, and retired to bed.

Now, concerned, he had Gabe call. Hershberger said he was sick. Gabe told him to just come out anyway and watch the game. Hershberger agreed.

But when he failed to show, Gabe returned to the hotel, got the hotel manager to open the door to Hershberger's room, and there they discovered Hershberger's body draped over the tub, his throat slashed with roommate Billy Werber's razor.

As our version of the story went, Gabe then went to a phone and called the team's owner.

"Powell? Gabe Paul. Listen, I have good news and I have bad news. The bad news is, Hershberger's dead. Yes, it was a suicide, very sad. The good news, though, is that I managed to get his meal money back from his wallet for the rest of the trip."

There weren't too many people in baseball that Gabe didn't have a history with. He had started as a batboy in his native Rochester when George Stallings managed the team. Stallings, manager of the 1914 miracle Braves, had roots in baseball that went back to 1890. One of Gabe's first jobs as batboy was to freeze the baseballs, and to see to it that the frozen ones were only used when the opponents were at bat.

Warren Giles took over the Rochester team when Gabe was a teenage correspondent for *The Sporting News*, and took Gabe under his wing. When Giles went to Cincinnati to become general manager, succeeding Larry MacPhail (Lee's father), he brought Gabe along, launching his long career in the big leagues. For years Gabe worked his way up the baseball ladder, his sharp baseball mind always ticking. He eventually had small ownership pieces of teams, and he ran the Reds and the Indians for years, with a brief stop in Houston in an ill-fated move to start up the original Colt .45s.

I liked Gabe when he was telling baseball tales or pontificating on life, but he could launch into tyrannical fits as well. All of us in the Yankee front office developed a dislike for his style—until he became a target of Steinbrenner. Then he was "one of us," and a much more sympathetic figure.

One year the matter of World Series tickets brought tears to his eyes. He had told George that he didn't need all of his allotment for Games 1 and 2, but, when the team returned for Games 6 and 7, he needed them back for his brother Sol, the publisher of a weekly broadcasting magazine.

"Screw you, Gabe, no tickets for you—you gave them back to me," said George (or words to that effect). They hollered at each other until Gabe retreated to his office, defeated. The general manager of the Yankees now had to tell his brother he couldn't get him tickets.

At that moment, Bob Fishel stuck his head into Gabe's office to say hello. Seeing tears streaming down Gabe's cheeks, and embarrassed to have walked in, Bob tried to leave, but Gabe motioned for him to sit, and told him what had happened.

Those were the times you could feel bad for Gabe.

One day, I was with him when we traded a player whom I liked.

"Oh," I said. "A shame—a nice guy."

"Marty," he roared, "I'll take you to church any Sunday you want, and introduce you to twenty-five of the nicest guys you'll ever meet, but they ain't gonna win us any ballgames."

The use of "church" was interesting, because he was Jewish, but he always made a good practice of hiding it. Some thought his adventure in Houston turned bad when his heritage was discovered and those invitations to country clubs and Texas civic organizations dried up.

When Gabe was caught in mid-bluster, the results could be hilarious. His office, when we played at Shea Stadium, was at the end of a long hallway, about the length of a football field. He had his own private entrance from the parking lot, and his own bathroom. And he never, never, left his office. Everyone went to see him.

One day, he misplaced some important papers. Whatever they were, he was very upset—almost panicky—over it.

He went to his secretary, Pearl Davis, and said, "Pearl, I've lost these papers; have you seen them?"

Pearl was a pretty, black woman, large and motherly, and city-smart as they came. We all loved her. She used to advise us, when we left work each day, to "always leave your typewriter on, leave a half-written page in it, and a sweater over your chair. That way, when you're late the next morning, it looks like you're here."

Anyway, Gabe, increasingly agitated, now left his office and began entering everyone else's office, asking if they'd seen his papers. This would have been his only visit to any of us. Naturally, I had my feet on my desk when he came into mine.

It didn't matter—he was totally focused on his papers. On he went, in and out of everyone's office, and he was nearly at the far end of the hall, some one hundred yards away, when Pearl called to him.

"Mr. Paul, Mr. Paul, I've got your papers!"

"Oh, thank God," he shouted, his voice carrying through every department. Then he made the mistake of adding "Where the hell were they!?"

Without missing a beat, Pearl gave him the news, her voice carrying down the hall like a John Elway touchdown pass:

"On the floor in your john, next to the toilet!"

In the summer of 1973, I was driving by Shea Stadium when I noticed buildings still standing in what had been the World's Fair park, just across Roosevelt Avenue from Shea. The Yankees still had no plan as to where to maintain our offices while we played at Shea, and veteran front-office people were fearing that we would be leasing space in Manhattan and commuting to the games each evening. There was no room for us at Shea.

I got back to my office in Yankee Stadium and wrote a memo to MacPhail, suggesting that the World's Fair grounds might have office space for us. For Lee, it was an epiphany. He immediately saw the word *free* in front of *office space*, since the City of New York owned that land, and they were the ones dispossessing us while they rebuilt the property that they would own.

In a matter of weeks, thanks in part to my memo, he had arranged for our offices to be moved to the Parks Administration Building, which was walking distance from Shea. The space was free, because the whole plan for rebuilding Yankee Stadium was now a city project. My little memo had saved the team a bunch of money.

The final game at old Yankee Stadium—the day of the Houk resignation—was ugly. Not enough preparation had gone into preserving the important artifacts of the place. And we had a rather hostile crowd on hand.

As a special treat for the fans, we had worked with a small record company in Boston to produce an LP, *Yankee Stadium: The 50th Anniversary*, which we gave away to all in attendance and then later inserted in our 1974 Yearbook as a soft vinyl version. The record, narrated by Mel Allen, was a compilation of actual broadcasts, recreations, and narratives of events over the past 50 years. It sold more than a quarter-million copies, qualifying as a Gold Record, which I received for my role as co-producer and writer, including the liner notes. (I tried to re-create Babe Ruth's 60th homer, complete with crowd noise. I decided it didn't sound real, and I threw it into a desk, unlabeled. Twenty-seven years later, I happened to hear it on a CD of great Yankee moments. Someone had found it and decided it was the real thing! I had to play it four times to make certain it was my voice.)

No film crews were recording the final days of the old park, so I took my 8mm home-movie camera (an Old Timers Day gift) and shot a few minutes of silent footage of the place, slowly panning the upper deck, the facade, the monuments, the press box, and the lower stands. It was an amateurish job, of course, and, with no lights, I couldn't shoot any interiors, but at least I had some color film of the place in its final days.

I had a special concern for one piece of history—the only thing in the whole park that dated back to the days of the New York Highlanders, the team's original name. The old Mosler safe in the Yankee clubhouse, where the players could deposit their valuables each day, had the names of the original 1903 Highlanders stenciled onto each drawer. There were Chesbro, Griffith, Fultz, Keeler, Conroy, Ganzel, Elberfeld ("The Tabasco Kid"), Long, Tannehill, and others. This heavy safe had been moved from Hilltop Park to the Polo Grounds in 1913, and then to Yankee Stadium in 1923. It was into these drawers that the wallets and watches and rings of Stottlemyre, Murcer, Munson, Blomberg, Swoboda, White, and Jim Ray Hart would go each day in that final season.

"Pete," I said to our clubhouse baron, about two weeks before the last game, "This safe—we've got to protect it—maybe we should move it out early."

Sheehy nodded, but then said, "Then we'll have no place for valuables in the last series."

He promised that he would watch out for it after the last game.

Bert Randolph Sugar, meanwhile, was about the only fellow with collectibles on his mind in the final month. In the years before the memorabilia business took off, Bert was a visionary. He asked for permission to scour the storage areas in the Stadium's basement, and, for an agreed-upon fee, he cleaned out all the old framed photos, trophies, file cabinets, and other dust collectors.

Manny Koeningsberg, of Manny's Baseball Land on River Avenue, bought some excess Yearbooks, programs, folders, and so on, and sold them for years.

I had my eyes on a souvenir as well—I wanted the padded panel at the right field foul pole that said "296," perhaps the most famous outfield measurement in the game.

We played the final game, the fans booed Houk, he resigned at the press conference, and then I returned to the field. It had become a war zone.

People had torn up the turf and ripped their seats out of the concrete, breaking off the iron legs in the process. All was chaos. Invirex-Cuyuga, the demolition contractor, was to start work the very next day, and its people were on the scene as observers. Yankee Stadium was being mauled, and it was a bad sight—although nothing we shouldn't have anticipated after the crowds had torn up Shea in '69.

My 296 panel was scooped up quickly.

The next morning, we had a little ceremony before the wrecking ball starting swinging. Mayor Lindsay was there, and he and Mike Burke presented home plate to Claire Ruth and first base to Eleanor Gehrig.

The department store E.J. Korvette's had acquired hundreds of seats and was selling them for $5.95 each. (Today they go for nearly a thousand dollars each.)

I went into the clubhouse. It too was in shambles, Pete trying to get things packed into trunks for storage.

"Pete, where's the safe?" I said.

We looked at the spot from which it hadn't moved in 50 years. It was gone.

Somehow, the 500-pound safe had been removed after everyone left. To this day, I have no idea where it went. It has never surfaced on the auction market. I have a suspicion, after all this time, that it somehow became an early casualty of the demolition people, perhaps that very morning. In any case, of all that was involved in the closing of Yankee Stadium, the loss of that last link to the franchise's very humble beginnings was the saddest thing of all.

CHEAP, BUT
FIRST CLASS

I made Casey Stengel yell at me. We had actually started off really well. He had ended a 10-year exile by agreeing to attend the 1970 Yankee Old Timers Day, convinced that it was time for bygones to be bygones. By 1970, there was no one left in the front office to hate anymore.

Casey and Edna came east, and the return was a triumph. He got a sensational hero's welcome, we retired his uniform number, we gave him his Old Timers Day gift (just like all the guests), and he signed a poster with his picture in a grand, sweeping autograph—a character trait of a man wholly at ease with his station in life.

On Monday morning, the phone on my desk rang. It was Stengel. He had no idea whom he was speaking with; he had just called the PR number on his instruction sheet, and he immediately began talking.

"I just wanted to say that Mrs. Stengel and I had a marrrrr-ve-lous time, and I wanted to say thank you to everybody who made it possible, and I also wanted to say thank you for my prize."

He had called his gift a prize. Perfect. *He* was the prize, and we were the recipients.

But now, five years and many Old Timers Day chats later, I was being a pest to him. He was much in demand as a living legend by 1975, and we were not always able to count on him. Sometimes he was able to attend, sometimes not. He was, in his golden years of retirement, both a sought-after personality and one who evoked moans from a dinner audience when he rambled on in Stengelese far too long. I loved the fact that I actually knew Casey Stengel, who broke into baseball in 1910, who played for John McGraw and managed Tug McGraw and caught fly balls hit by Tinker and Evers and Chance, and who hit the first World Series home run in Yankee Stadium and the first home run ever in Ebbets Field.

In '75 we hadn't heard back from him about Old Timers Day, and there was only a week to go before our annual gathering. I had written to him and he had said he was unable to commit. He didn't say no. A few weeks later I called him, and still, he couldn't say for sure. He was a busy man. It was a big trip from Glendale, California.

Then, the week before the game, I was in Texas with the Yankees and—what do you know?—there he is. Right in our own clubhouse, dressed in his uniform, participating in the Rangers' Old Timers Day.

So, naturally, I said, "So, Casey, will we be seeing you in New York next week?"

Oh, did he get mad.

"Now, damnit," he shouted at me, "I said I'd tell you when I knew, and I don't know yet!"

I had been put in my place. And he didn't make it the following week, which made me wonder if it was my fault for pushing him.

Nevertheless, I loved the old man, and I loved the history he represented, and, of course, he was the Yankee manager during all those great years in the '50s when I was growing up. And when he went to manage the Mets, I thought to myself, "Great, let him show them," because I didn't like the way the Yanks had treated him.

Show them, he did. He created something never since repeated in pro sports—loveable losers embraced by fans simply because the manager made them so entertaining.

Unlike so many Yankee fans, I could never hate the Mets, just as I never hated the Red Sox. In fact, I admired the Red Sox, with their loyal following, their beautiful ballpark, and their terrific city. Inwardly I had this feeling that despite the great rivalry, if we somehow ever went to war with, say, California, we sure would want Boston on our side. I think a lot of Yankee fans had this quiet respect.

With the Mets, my admiration had to do with Stengel, and then with Seaver, and later with Keith Hernandez, whom I loved to watch play the game. I had watched the Mets play at the Polo Grounds and sat there thinking about this being the site of Mathewson and the Merkle "boner" and of McGraw and Ott, and now Choo Choo Coleman. I loved how the Mets created the concept of bringing signs to the games ("placards," Stengel called them), and how the Yankees tried to confiscate them at the first Mayor's Trophy Game. I loved their "Let's Go Mets" chant and their *Meet the Mets* song and Kiner and Murphy and

Lindsey Nelson on the broadcasts, and of course, the '69 Mets—still, to my thinking, the greatest sports event of my life.

I loved ol' Jimmy Piersall circling the bases backwards on his 100th home run. (When I met Jimmy in Texas years later, he said to me, "Are you sane?" I smiled and said, "I think so." And he pulled out his release papers from the institution to which he had been remanded in the '50s and said, "Do you have the papers to prove it?")

One of my greatest personal athletic achievements came at Shea, when I participated in a media promotion run by Panasonic, which involved pitching to the Mets' catcher Duffy Dyer, under the judging of Tug McGraw. I always had good control, even if I only threw in the 60s, and I won the contest that day, throwing strikes and taking home a nice Panasonic television set. And this was while wearing street shoes and a tie!

I was good friends with a lot of the Mets' front-office people, and our spring training or Mayor's Trophy Games were always warm and happy gatherings. My counterpart on the Mets, Matt Winick, collaborated with me for five years on writing a paperback season preview book, he doing the National League and I the American.

A sad moment that brought our organizations together came on April 2, 1972, when Gil Hodges, the beloved Mets manager, died in West Palm Beach following a round of golf with his coaches. This came the day after the first baseball strike had begun, and, because we were flying back to New York on a charter, we stopped in West Palm to pick up Gil's body and fly it back to New York for burial. At such times, rivalries lost their meaning, and we were all part of the sports community, sharing a great loss together.

It was great for New York baseball when both teams did well. During many of my years with the Yankees, the Mets outdrew us, and people would say, "Well, it's a National League town," but I knew the town usually preferred winners (except in the case of the Stengel Mets), and I hoped for the day when we'd see a Subway Series, which made 2000 such a treat for me.

With the closing of Yankee Stadium for two years, we were to be the Mets' guests at Shea Stadium. As the first step in this process, Fishel and I drove to Shea for a meeting with Jim Thompson, the Mets' vice president and business manager. How sweet this meeting would be for Thompson. He had been the Yankees' stadium manager in the '50s but had been shown the door over what were called financial improprieties.

When George Weiss and Casey Stengel moved over to the newly formed Mets, bingo—Thompson was one of several Yankee office veterans who switched over.

Thompson was an imperial sort, and his office was set up so that guests—Fishel and I in this case—would sit in soft upholstered seats, facing his regal desk as our rear ends sunk deep into the plush seat cushions. We sat there like fourth graders in the principal's office as Thompson, elevated on the throne behind his desk, told us how it would be for us in the coming two years. Not only was he speaking from a position of power, but the Mets had won the pennant in '73 under Yogi Berra, further adding insult to injury.

We would have the Jets' clubhouse as our home clubhouse. We would not have any office space at Shea. All special requests would go through Thompson's office. Our game-day employees would be Mets employees, giving them the windfall of a double schedule. (Many ticket takers, ushers, and so forth worked for both teams anyway, as well as at Madison Square Garden in the winter.)

Bob and I were nodding yes, yes, yes, and Thompson was enjoying Fishel's humble position, because Bob had been part of the administration that had expelled him.

For two years we would work in our offices in the park across the street and then drive across Roosevelt Avenue for the games. If we needed something from the office—well, it would have to wait until the next day, because we weren't about to run to our cars during a game to look something up.

The deal would be a sweet one for the Mets, because any improvements, such as a new ticket office, would be left behind as freebies. But inwardly, the Mets lived with the fear that the Yankee Stadium project would somehow run out of money and they would be stuck with tenants for more than two seasons.

All things considered, the arrangement worked well. The Mets' scoreboard couldn't handle the letters DH in the lineups, so we settled on an awkward B (for "batter"), but, otherwise, a ballpark was a ballpark. It wasn't home, and Bobby Murcer lost his home run touch after we left Yankee Stadium, but we were going to make do while our stadium was gutted and rebuilt.

My favorite moment in Shea, in terms of our being good tenants, came when our promotion director, Barry Landers, scheduled a "salute to the military" night. General William Westmoreland was on hand, and the evening had a very patriotic flavor, including the presence of military cannons in center field that were prepared to fire off a 21-gun salute on cue. Compared to the noise of the jets from LaGuardia Airport next door, this was nothing.

But when Barry cued the cannons, we got a quick glimpse of why things hadn't gone so well in Vietnam. The very first shots blew down the center field fence at Shea. What a riot. Everyone came running out to dispel the smoke and prop up the fences, and the game was delayed 40 minutes.

The next day, we had to face Jim Thompson and explain why we had shot out his fences. It wasn't a very pleasant meeting, and he was prepared to slide the bill for the repair across his big desk toward us.

Barry was a remarkable promotion man, but things didn't always go according to plan for him. One year he engaged a fellow named Bill Press to pull off a very complicated promotion—a Photo Day—in which all the fans would line up along the aisles and each have their Polaroid photo taken with a Yankee as he or she reached the head of the line. Press set it up so that we photographed about twenty-two thousand people in an hour before the game, setting up stations throughout Shea to handle it as some thirty Polaroid SX-70s snapped away.

Barry got a call from Gabe Paul about ten days after the promotion. "Barry, have we paid Bill Press in full yet?" Gabe asked.

"Not in full," replied Barry. "About two-thirds."

"Good," said Gabe. "Did you see this morning's *Daily News?*"

It turned out Bill Press had been found packed into the trunk of a car at Kennedy Airport, his genitals stuffed in his mouth, Mafia shorthand for fooling around with a Mob woman. Not a smart move.

Barry concocted a great promotion one year: a genuine Glove Day. Not batting gloves, but real fielder's mitts. And not pancake mitts, either (like my first glove, my trusty Billy Goodman Hutch model). A real glove with a pocket.

Barry showed me a sample, and it was terrific. "The only thing is," he told me, "I have to go to Korea to sew up the deal."

I took a long look at him and said, "Do you mind if I go with you to Gabe's office when you tell him that?"

No Glove Day.

Barry eventually burned out with a heart attack and moved to Arizona with a new wife and the Babe Ruth autographed baseball from Fishel's old office that he said Bob had given him.

In his place came Dick King, a career minor league executive who was never comfortable in New York but had been one of Gabe's protégés. King never liked me, of which fact Gabe never hesitated to remind me. Brought in to handle promotions after Barry's exit, King told Gabe, with all modesty, that "executive director of promotions" sounded good to him as a title, because I was, at that point, director of public relations. I was never hung up on titles, but I knew when I was being elbowed aside by an old timer who didn't like the young upstart. It was one of the few times I stood up to Gabe over such nonsense as titles, and we wound up with equal titles, not many months before King packed it in for the quiet of Nebraska. That was a really unpleasant one.

Before we played our first game at Shea, there was the little business of selecting a manager for the '74 season. Houk had gone to Detroit, where his buddy Jim Campbell, the Tigers' general manager, was waiting, and it made me wonder whether his tears on that last day were real or he had made this deal with the Tigers before our finale. You never can be sure in baseball, because there is always the hidden game of old friendships and private phone conversations, and you never know, when trades are made between two old buddies who are general managers, whether one needs the other's help to try to keep his job. These things do happen, and friendships are usually stronger than loyalty to owners, because friendships are forever, and you never know when you'll need them. With owners, there aren't many happy endings.

With Houk in Detroit, the Yankees decided to go for the biggest and most glamorous name available—Dick Williams.

Williams had resigned from Charlie Finley's employ after the turbulent 1973 World Series, the one in which Finley had released second baseman Mike Andrews under fabricated medical excuses, right during the Series. The problem was, Williams might have resigned, but Finley still had a contract with him.

An offer was tendered to Williams by way of Nat Tarnopol, a record executive who was one of the most mesmerizing personalities I ever encountered. He was the middleman in this instance because Williams was a VP in his record company. Word came back that he would accept. This was huge. He was the manager of the world champions, had led the Red Sox to their impossible dream pennant in 1967, and now was coming to the Yankees. What a way to knock the Mets out of the news.

We scheduled a big-budget press conference at a catering hall in Queens called Terrace in the Park, a couple of miles from Shea.

As usual, I checked with Gabe about whether to order shrimp. As usual, he said, "Do it cheap, but make it first class!" This was my standard order for all events, whether it was a World Series party or a press dinner at the winter meetings. Cheap and first class. If only the world could really operate like that.

The Dick Williams press conference was a biggie. We were truly stealing back the headlines with this one, and the fans and the press loved it. After the press conference, Fishel and I took Williams over to

Shea, where he donned the pinstripes and posed for publicity pictures. He made a point of learning my name and, in the coming days, was often on the phone with me, clearing interview requests and as accommodating as could be.

For a time, he was the biggest thing we had to work with on the Yankees since Mickey Mantle. We all had a great feeling about this.

But there was a problem.

Finley, always representing trouble, was filing a protest, saying that Williams could not walk away from his Oakland contract and join the Yankees without some compensation for the A's. He was demanding two of our best prospects—pitcher Scott McGregor and outfielder Otto Velez. Finley always knew talent, and although Velez would never be a star, McGregor would be a fine pitcher for many years with the Orioles.

"McGregor and Velez?" said Gabe. "They're our crown jewels! No way will we trade them for a manager."

In Joe Cronin's final act as American League president, he ruled in favor of Finley and voided the Williams signing, thereby rendering our expensive press conference—shrimp and all—useless. Lee MacPhail, leaving us to replace Cronin, conceded that he would not have ruled the same way, but it was Joe's call and he would not overrule it upon taking office.

Now we were without a manager and heading for the winter meetings. Fishel had me prepare several biographical press releases before the meetings, in case we named one there, and he confided the names of those under consideration.

One was Frank Robinson, still an active player but already spoken of as a prime candidate to become the game's first black manager. A statement was written naming Frank as Yankee manager. It was never released.

As progressive as that sounded, another one was prepared with the name of Al Lopez, and another with the name of Birdie Tebbetts, Gabe's old crony. Lopez, 65, had last managed in 1969, and Tebbetts, 61, had last managed in 1966. Neither choice would have been well received.

Fishel and I hoped that Elston Howard would get consideration. He had been the first black Yankee player and the first black coach in the American League. But he was thought too gentle, too accommodating, and did not have the fiery image that was now capturing the imaginations of Gabe and George. Ellie would not make the short list.

Now we added another body to our front office. Calling a "major press conference" at our office in the Parks Administration Building, we were announcing that Tal Smith was joining us to succeed Lee MacPhail as general manager.

Tal was one of the most able minds in all of baseball. He had been a protégé of Gabe's in Cincinnati and then had become a senior VP with the Houston Astros. He had integrity and he knew talent. He was a terrific addition to our front office, and Gabe introduced him as our new GM and "in the upper echelon in salary" when that question was raised at the press conference.

Sadly, it was one of the last times Tal's name would be heard in public, because, although Gabe had now elevated himself to president (so much for quietly retiring to Florida after two years), he was, in effect, our general manager, too. Tal would really be Gabe's assistant, and a buffer for all of us who reported to Gabe.

So gifted was he that, when Bowie Kuhn was leaving the commissioner's office in the mid-'80s, *The Sporting News* editorialized that Tal was the best possible successor in the game. By then he had won Executive of the Year with Houston and had moved on to his own consulting business, specializing in salary arbitration on behalf of many teams. He was enjoying that greatly and making too good a living to put up with the politics of the commissioner's job, and ruled himself out immediately. He would have been a great choice.

With Tal part of the team to find a new manager, the Yankees settled on Bill Virdon. Virdon had been a Yankee farmhand in the early '50s before going on to a distinguished career as a Pittsburgh center fielder. He had managed the Pirates until the final weeks of the '73 season, when he was unceremoniously dumped in a late bid by the Bucs to bring back Danny Murtaugh and try to knock off the Mets. It didn't work, and Virdon was unemployed.

Tal and Virdon would become great friends, and Tal would bring him to Houston some years later as manager. For now, Gabe liked what he saw in Virdon. He had done fairly well in Pittsburgh, he would listen to management, and he would work for much less than Williams, thereby helping to pay off the Terrace in the Park press conference.

No big press conference awaited Virdon, which was a signal that he was not only a second choice but somehow second rate. He should have had an unveiling equal to Williams'. Instead, we had a modest press conference at the Parks Administration Building, complete with plenty of Coke and Tab and potato chips, and . . . well, we had our manager. Many in the room thought the term *interim manager* was more appropriate—the manager until Dick Williams was truly available.

As the press conference was concluding, Fishel told me that he wanted to talk to me privately after everyone had dispersed.

Some months earlier, Bob had promoted me to publicity director. He had been named vice president. Although our job responsibilities did not appreciably change, it was a great honor for me and a terrific compliment.

"You deserve it," he said. "You work hard, the press likes you, and you know the job. And you're traveling more than I am—the team should be represented by a director, not an assistant, on the road."

Bob explained that his model for having a VP and a publicity director came from the Dodgers. Although the Yankees and Dodgers were always great rivals, Bob considered the Dodger front office to be the model for all of baseball—the most efficient, the most effective. He saw no shame in copying their organization chart.

Now, just months later, he had another bombshell for me.

"I'm leaving," he said. "Lee has asked me to go with him to the American League as their publicity director. I'm going to do it. I can get a pension there, which I've never had here, and, frankly, all I've been doing here is sitting and listening to Gabe's stories. I can contribute more than being a good listener."

This was huge. I had no idea how it would affect me, whether I would be forced out when a new VP was named or what my fate would be. But at that moment, I could think only of Bob leaving the Yankees. He was an institution! He was the best publicity man baseball had ever seen, and it did the Yankees such credit that he was part of them.

But Bob belonged with Lee. Once Gabe took travel away from him and dispatched me with the team, the joy of it was gone for Bob. He needed to feel a part of the wins and losses. The league wouldn't provide that for him, but his relationship with Lee was a deep and faithful one, and when the opportunity presented itself, he jumped.

A few days after he informed George of his decision, I was invited to have coffee with the Boss.

My dealings with George up to this point were few. He was, frankly, not on the scene a lot. I tended to see him more on the road than at home. I noticed some of his special gestures with admiration, such as the way he would be waiting for us at LaGuardia or Newark at four in the morning after a road trip, handing everyone $20 cab fare so we wouldn't have to first take the bus to Yankee Stadium.

"Do you feel you would be up to the job as PR director?" he asked me.

I told him, "I think the job requires the ability to represent management professionally, the ability to establish credibility and friendship with the media, the ability to have a trust with the players and the manager, a working knowledge of this franchise and all that it stands for, and first-rate public relations skills."

I had rehearsed that answer more than a few times in my head.

If I had to rank those abilities, knowledge of the franchise would come first. That stemmed from my early years as a fan and my insatiable interest in learning all I could about the game's history and the team's legacy. In most businesses, a keen knowledge of the history of your company means little. In baseball, this mattered a lot.

I hadn't been trained in public relations in college, but I had spent six seasons studying under Bob Fishel. He was the best. A compass of integrity and honesty guided him, and I could do no worse than to learn from the best PR man baseball ever had.

The media liked and trusted me. I was the first to go out of my way to treat the suburban papers as equal to the city papers, including them in dinners on road trips, reserving seats for them in press boxes, calling them early with stories. I had been a product of a suburban paper in Rockland County myself.

Also, I was a contemporary of many of the new writers on the beat. Some of those friendships have lasted more than a quarter century. They became my guys, just as Fishel had deep friendships with the older writers who were now moving on to retirement.

I was also a contemporary of the players, and although I did not socialize with them on the road, they kidded me, confided in me, and trusted me. One of my favorite compliments came when I was having lunch one day with pitcher Pat Dobson and his girlfriend. He had invited me to the table and said to her, "He's cool; he's not one of *them!*" I counted Lyle, Murcer, Blomberg, Swoboda, Peterson, Steve Kline, Doc Medich, Clarke, Munson, White, Howard, and Howser as friends. That was half the roster and half the coaching staff.

Representing management would only have to be proven as we went along. I knew this was where Bob felt he and the Yankees needed to part ways. He did not have the highest regard for Gabe's business practices.

But as for personal poise and maturity in the position, I was there. I felt very much like a colleague of the other PR directors. I had become an accomplished public speaker on behalf of the club and was a frequent guest for television and radio interviews.

I would never have another job in which I could sit behind my desk with such total confidence that nothing could cross that desk and throw me. If there was ever a job I was born for, it was this one.

Steinbrenner told me that he considered me the man for the job. As a student of baseball, the enormity of this was not lost on me.

Aside from replacing Fishel, a legend, I would be only the third PR director in the history of the Yankees, Red Patterson having preceded Bob. But more to the point, I would be the first of my generation to assume a major league PR directorship—and with the high-profile New York Yankees, no less. I was 25. Most PR directors had been twice as old when they got the job, perhaps veteran newspapermen making career changes or longtime assistants advancing to the top. To turn the Yankees over to a 25-year-old was a remarkable move by Steinbrenner, one for which I will be forever grateful.

This promotion could not have happened had Steinbrenner not bought the club. If Mike Burke and CBS were still there, aside from the fact that MacPhail and Fishel would probably not have left, I would not have been considered for the top spot. When you begin in an organization as the fan-mail clerk, or as a mailroom attendant, you will always be "the kid" in the eyes of management. You could be there for a decade, you could marry and have a family, but, in the eyes of management, "the kid" will always be "the kid."

I was not a kid when Steinbrenner bought the club. I was Fishel's assistant; an executive in my own right. I worked side-by-side with him during the sale by CBS, during the Peterson–Kekich scandal, during the closing of Yankee Stadium, during the Dick Williams hiring. I handled the team's PR on road trips, I had taken over the staging of the Old Timers Days and the writing of the Yearbook and the program. I had been involved with the team's broadcasters and its station executives. Fishel, to his credit, had given me chances to grow.

Still, despite my love of the Yankees and the kick I got out of going to work each day at Yankee Stadium and in traveling the country with the team, I was not advancing, my salary was too low, and I had been thinking the unthinkable—of moving on. When it seemed that the San Diego Padres were going to move to Washington, a number of close friends in baseball put forth my name to head PR for the new team in D.C. Indications were that I was a serious candidate, but, in the end, the team didn't move. For a time I was seriously considering an offer from Madison Square Garden to move downtown to "the world's most famous arena" in a public relations capacity there.

But the timing of Fishel's departure worked for me. Bob was nearing 60, but he was a robust 60. He looked as he had 20 years before, and I'd figured he could go another 10 years with the Yankees. He was a much-loved figure throughout baseball and throughout the organization. (Only the batboys didn't like him—he would tell them to stay out of the picture when a home run–hitting Yankee met his teammates at home plate.)

And suddenly, he was leaving.

I will always be indebted to George Steinbrenner for his confidence in me and for trusting me with this enormous responsibility. He took a chance on a young man who had come to the team six years earlier as the fan-mail clerk, practically a fan off the streets. He observed enough and, I assume, spoke to enough people to know that I had developed a good reputation in the game, knew the Yankees, knew PR, and knew him. And he must have asked Fishel his opinion, and Bob supported my promotion.

With a handshake from George, a pat on the back from Bob, and a warning from Gabe to always "leave tracks," I was now the Yankees' PR director.

Who could forecast what a job it was about to become?

For Bob Fishel's retirement from the Yankees, the Baseball Writers Association of America's New York chapter honored him at their 1974 "pre-dinner dinner," an annual affair. His favorite parting gift was a Yankee uniform bearing the number 20, representative of his 20 years with the Yankees, and the number worn by Horace Clarke, the workmanlike but unappreciated second baseman for the last seven of those years. Bob loved it.

We remained close. He was my mentor, and we had what some might call a father-son relationship, which served us both well. For his 65th birthday in 1979, I got his closest friends to chip in for a 1958 World Series ring. Front-office people never got rings in those days, and it was his favorite World Series, the Yankees having come back, down 3–1, to beat the Braves after losing to them in '57. At the party we organized at Gallagher's Steak House, he got a 36-by-48 photo of Eddie Gaedel batting for the Browns (Bob had been the guy who signed him in the back seat of his Packard).

He spent 14 years with the American League and was hurt when he was demoted to a smaller office and less responsibility when the league moved its offices late in his career. But he never complained; it wasn't his style.

Plagued by asthma and chronic bronchitis, Bob died in 1988. He was 74. His AL assistant, Phyllis Merhige, who was my baseball "sister" in that she was the daughter he never had, called me in tears, and I knew at once what the call meant.

I was very lucky to have written my letter to Bob Fishel in 1967 and to have been called in for an interview. I was trained by a man whose integrity and honor would have translated nobly to any path in life.

Lou Piniella was our big offseason acquisition before the '74 campaign. The problem was, when the Yankees and Royals made the trade during the winter meetings, Dean Vogelaar, the Royals' PR director, was having dinner with me—and neither of us could be found to make the announcement. This was what Gabe had meant by "leaving tracks." How much easier life would have been in those days had we had cell phones or beepers! There was seldom any time away from the hotel when you could truly relax without the fear that George or Gabe would come looking for you. I remember playing six holes of golf in Dallas one afternoon, and then I couldn't stand my own anxiety any longer and just picked up and went home.

Piniella, with his handsome Latin looks (many fans thought he was Italian), great smile, ferocious will to win, and good humor, was an immediate favorite of everyone who met him. He had a voice much too high for his physique, and, for that matter, where was the power on his 6´2˝, 200-pound frame? He had yet to hit more than 11 home runs in a season. With the Royals, at last, he became a .300 hitter and an All-Star. But when he slipped to .250 in 1973, the Yankees were able to grab him for Lindy McDaniel, who had become expendable with the addition of Lyle. So slim were Lindy's significant appearances after Sparky arrived that in his final year, his only "save" was the soul of a wandering batboy who became a subscriber to Lindy's periodic religious tract, *Pitching for the Master*.

Piniella was an immediate hit in New York and would remain a fan favorite for years, on into his tenure as Yankee manager.

But we were to make much bigger news in center field that spring training.

Gabe had made a number of small trades to bolster the club, including the purchase of Elliott Maddox from the Texas Rangers on March 23. Although barely noted when it was announced, it would have a profound effect on the team's fortunes—and morale.

Virdon, a former center fielder, had long appreciated the value of a good glove out there. He had played next to Clemente in Pittsburgh and knew that if he could get a Gold Glove in center, the man could bat .260 and still win a lot of games. Murcer had in fact won a Gold Glove, but no one took that seriously. He was good, but not great. Virdon decided he wanted Maddox in center, Murcer in right. Few realized when we bought Elliott that the intention was to get a regular center fielder.

This was a huge move, because center field for the Yankees had been covered by a succession of Hall of Famers—Earle Combs, Joe DiMaggio, and Mickey Mantle. Murcer had been groomed to be the successor and had in fact become an All-Star and a 30-homer man.

Maddox, 25, was a prelaw graduate of Michigan, and a New Jersey native. An African-American who was studying Judaism, he was soft spoken, professional, and a brilliant defensive player, well equipped to take over the task. The better baseball minds in Florida immediately saw what Virdon was doing and applauded the move.

However, there were a number of loyalists who did not like this at all. The move had racial overtones—the grand, exalted position of Yankee center fielder had been a "white" position since 1903. Who did Virdon, this National Leaguer, think he was?

Murcer was very unhappy, as were his closest friends on the team. Maddox was not well accepted by the veterans. It was, from a baseball standpoint, a good move. It was also, in true Gabe Paul style, a move without any thought of team chemistry. It was probably the right move to make with the team, but Gabe's "I don't care what they think" attitude upset the team's preparation for the season.

And he wasn't through yet. A bombshell hit the Yankee clubhouse on Friday evening, April 26, three weeks into the season. Right after the game, I announced that we had traded four of our eight pitchers—Fritz Peterson, Steve Kline, Fred Beene, and Tom Buskey—to the Indians (Gabe's old understudy Phil Seghi made the deal on their end) for Chris Chambliss, Dick Tidrow, and Cecil Upshaw.

You would have thought our franchise had folded. Munson stormed around the clubhouse shouting at anyone who would listen, "Beeney! How could they trade Fred Beene?" Murcer, sitting in his rocking chair in front of his locker, tried to be the wise team leader, but he kept shaking his head and saying, "I can't believe this, I just can't believe this."

In the midst of this whining, Gabe came strutting into the clubhouse, his chest puffed out, ready to talk to the press in front of the stewing players. It was his moment to preen and remind everyone who was in charge. It was a grand Gabe moment.

And it was a helluva deal. In Chambliss and Tidrow came two key contributors to our future success. The four pitchers we traded didn't do much with the remainder of their careers, winning 53 games among them. But the clubhouse had been rocked, the welcome mat was not extended to Maddox, or Chambliss, or Tidrow, or Upshaw, and, when we added pitcher Rudy May a few weeks later, you couldn't identify the team without a scorecard. You could tell only that this was no longer a MacPhail–Houk team; this roster had its very own Gabe Paul look.

The club, meanwhile, was starting to win. Maddox was a big reason, and things were going well. Elliott played brilliantly in center and was putting up a .300 season, far above expectations. Murcer, stewing in right, was totally psyched out by Shea Stadium, and went nearly the whole season without homering there.

Whitey Ford was our pitching coach. This was, for me, one of the great memories of the '74 season. Virdon turned over the pitching staff to Whitey, and the ol' Chairman of the Board proved to be a great teacher, as well as an engaging presence in a new Yankee ballclub. Whitey wasn't the sort of guy who looked around wondering where his great teammates had gone. He could kid and jab with any rookie who showed up for a week and had no problem fitting in with a team of strangers, all a generation younger than he.

During the Yankees' occasional midsummer pennant races in the late '60s and early '70s, Fishel and MacPhail would sit around the lunch table in the pressroom and fantasize about a wonderful "what if." Whitey had retired in 1967. But "what if" he came back, in his early 40s, to use his wisdom and skill as a short-relief man down a pennant stretch? Would that be a great story, or what?! It was the stuff of fantasy, like trading DiMaggio for Williams, and it never made it to the newspapers—but it was a tantalizing thought.

Now Whitey was the pitching coach, and I got to spend a lot of time with him discussing pitching. The public relations director always had to compile a list of the upcoming pitchers for each series and trade it with the opposing team's PR director. That's how "probable pitchers" made their way into the newspapers. Usually you get the names from the manager, but Virdon had totally turned pitching over to Ford, so I was forever getting the probables from Whitey. And we would talk about pitching and conditioning (he was not a fan of running at all), and I loved the enthusiasm he would show over the progress of young pitchers, such as a Mike Wallace or Larry Gura.

He had one of the greatest senses of humor I ever encountered: razor sharp, timely, playful. Years later, when baseball selected its 100 best players of the century, he and I talked about whether he would make it. I told him of course he would; he was the best pitcher in Yankee history.

"I'll bet they pick Billy Short instead," he said. Billy Short was a Whitey lookalike who had a shot with the team in the early '60s but never made it. That was Ford humor.

Everyone loved Whitey Ford. He had class and that New York swagger that made Mickey Mantle call him Slick, but he never acted as if he were better than anybody else, nor as if he might be somehow "above" things just because this wasn't the Casey-Yogi-Mickey era.

On Old Timers Day, he would dutifully submit his expenses to me before heading home for Lake Success—his 50-cent toll, each way, on the Whitestone Bridge.

When he pitched batting practice, I would stare endlessly at the classic, fluid motion that made him the Hall of Famer he was. Even when he put on some weight after he retired, the style was there—the way he would swing his arms back in unison and then lean back to the side and deliver those impossible pitches.

I got to taste them one day, which was one of my great thrills. It was early morning in Ft. Lauderdale, and he was preparing to pitch BP. I was standing by the cage in slacks and a polo shirt and he said, "Get in there, kid; show me what you've got."

Had Virdon been around, I probably wouldn't have done it; it wasn't very professional. I had had the thrill of playing in sportswriters' games on the field at Yankee Stadium—an awesome experience—but those were against the breaking balls of Phil Pepe. Now, a chance to hit off Whitey Ford? I grabbed a bat—a Horace Clarke "U1" model. I liked that style a lot—it had no knob, a thick handle, and great weight distribution.

I thought about wearing a helmet but decided against it. Bad decision. Whitey threw me a "purpose pitch," behind my head. He laughed and assumed he had scared the hell out of me. He had.

By now a couple of players were watching, including Roy White, so I dug my spikeless shoes in and took a couple of pitches. Now it was evident that he was going to let me hit the ball. I stood there thinking that I was watching the classic delivery that I'd grown up with but watching it with a bat in my hand from 60 feet, 6 inches away.

He pitched, I swung—and punched a soft liner just onto the outfield grass over second base. It was a base hit, in my book.

He pitched again, and I swung a little harder. Same result. Three more pitches, and three more base hits to short right, each a little farther out. I was five-for-five, unless, of course, a tall second baseman were standing out there.

The next pitch was a classic Whitey Ford breaking ball, which broke toward me and dropped down. His laugh told me he might have thrown me an illegal pitch. I had the good sense to drop my bat, bow, and get the hell out of there while I had my 1.000 average intact.

Whitey began to develop a heart problem while he was our pitching coach, and that effectively took him off the road and ended his coaching days. He continued to come to spring training as a guest instructor, and he worked at it; he never considered himself there for show. He always learned the names of every player and team employee in camp.

Whitey continued to have health problems, but he always maintained his sharp wit and good humor. He saw the passing of his great buddy, Mickey Mantle, a few years after they had had a rare falling out over the business of their fantasy baseball camp. But they were like brothers, and Mickey's death was a great loss for Whitey.

From time to time I would call Whitey, sometimes just to say hello, sometimes with some appearance or media request. I helped him with his speech for Whitey Ford Day in 2000. He always liked to chat; he never was quick to get off the phone. His son Eddie, a shortstop under Bobby Richardson's coaching at South Carolina, had been drafted by the Red Sox but never reached the big leagues. Tommy, another son, worked as a cameraman at Yankee Stadium shortly before I joined WPIX. Like any good father, Whitey asked me to see if I could get him back on the Stadium crew—there had been a personnel change. I wasn't able to, and I felt bad that I couldn't do that for him.

Tommy died from a tick bite in the summer of 1999 at 42, a fluke thing. Whitey and I spoke a few weeks after the funeral, and, his voice breaking, he told me how awful it is to outlive one's child. I felt so helpless, not being able to say something that might lift his spirits. He was always able to make others laugh or smile.

It was Elston Howard who nicknamed him Chairman of the Board, which was absolutely perfect. He and Ellie were coaches on the '74 Yankees, and it was a delight to share their company.

We had a sub on the team in '74 named Bill Sudakis, and it was on his boom box that I used to hear Band on the Run by Paul McCartney and Wings repeatedly. I had our organist, Eddie Layton, play the chorus during rallies because it was a great theme for this overachieving team, which was moving from city to city, winning two of three here, three of four there, and suddenly finding itself in a race. The newspapers and the fans picked up on it, and we had ourselves a theme song. The only problem was, George Steinbrenner never recognized the song, even though it was being written about in the papers, and when Eddie would start playing it after a game, my phone would ring and George would say, "What's that!?" And he made me stop it. So Band on the Run was never the hit I had had with Pomp and Circumstance.

On September 9, still in the race, we picked up Alex Johnson from Texas. His brother, Ron, was a star running back for the Giants and, by all accounts, a terrific guy. Alex, however, had a very surly reputation and, despite having won a batting title for the Angels four years earlier, was known to march to his own drummer and had not always run out ground balls, as a big leaguer is supposed to do.

This was another typical Gabe Paul move. He never really cared about a man's reputation or character and didn't value team chemistry at all.

Alex flew to Boston to join us on the second day of a critical road trip. The Yankees–Red Sox rivalry was just heating up—so much so that we had a police escort to accompany our bus from the hotel to Fenway, and private security guards to ride with us. We had a large contingent of media along, because this team was absolutely in the hunt. The suburban papers that normally didn't send writers on the road sent them on this trip. I thought we were all being treated to a slice of 19th century baseball, when visiting teams often had to slip in and out of town unnoticed for fear of being pelted with vegetables by partisan fans.

I told Gabe that we ought to have a small press conference in our hotel with Alex before we went to Fenway, something like two in the afternoon. He said he'd get Alex to do it, and, sure enough, "AJ" showed up in the suite with about a dozen writers. I introduced myself to him, and then I introduced him to the press, highlighting his batting championship of 1970.

I immediately felt tension in the room. And I immediately kicked myself for not making sure that Bill White, our broadcaster, was there, so that there would at least be one black face in the room. Instead, as was immediately clear, Alex was being interrogated by a dozen white writers. It made me uncomfortable, and I can only imagine how it made him feel.

Henry Hecht, a likeable and unkempt writer from the *New York Post*, asked the first question. Henry was Woody Allen with a notepad, and a second cousin of future vice presidential candidate Joe Lieberman. He had a pleasant manner, but he could also ask the tough questions—and not always in the most respectful way.

"What are your plans about running out ground balls?" he said.

Hoo-boy, what an opener for the press conference.

"You ever see me not run out a ground ball?" snapped AJ.

Henry stood his ground.

"Yes, many times!" he said.

Alex muttered something under his breath that seemed to have four syllables and began with an *m*.

On to the next question.

"Do you think you can fit in with this team, what with them playing so well and all?"

Suddenly, I realized that this press conference, held to satisfy the needs of the press for their early stories, was ill conceived. I learned my lesson: Just because the press has a need, it doesn't mean it absolutely has to be accommodated. The conference was a bad idea, and we wrapped it up in a hurry.

Wouldn't you know it, Alex played that night and hit a game-winning homer in the 12th inning off Diego Segui. It broke a 1–1 tie in a masterpiece of a pitching duel between Pat Dobson and Luis Tiant and put the Yankees in first place on September 10. This was huge, an enormous event—a September pennant race in Fenway, an extra-inning home run to win it—and the press raced down to the clubhouse for more from Alex.

But AJ was gone. Never big on postgame showers, he had run in from the field and dressed and was out of the ballpark within minutes. No AJ, no postgame interview.

Alex stayed with us for another year. He was mostly a DH and was certainly not the player he had been when he won the batting crown. There were times he didn't hustle, but he was actually a more likeable figure than advertised. Bill Kane and I were his front-office buddies. He was apparently also preparing for his post-baseball career by carrying that book about auto repair with him all season. Either he was using it as a prop or he had found a fascinating chapter on transmission fluid, but the bookmark—a Yankee schedule—never moved from the page it was on when I first noticed him with the book.

Another character on the team that year was Walt "No Neck" Williams, who had been a popular player with the White Sox. Walt (no one actually called him No Neck, although it was an apt nickname) was a slippery fellow, and I mean this literally. He had been told, or he read, that it was a good idea to coat your entire body, top to bottom, with Vaseline. Something about it being good for the skin. So Walt would perform this ritual before and after each game, going through gallons of the stuff.

We got a middle infielder early in '74 from Kansas City named Fernando Gonzalez. He was a 23-year-old Puerto Rican with a reputation as a good fielder, weak hitter. He was not blessed with an athlete's body but was instead rather stumpy and not very muscular.

When he arrived at our clubhouse, Nettles thought he was a clubhouse attendant and gave him a few bucks to run an errand. A few minutes later, there he was, buttoning his Yankee uniform.

Tal Smith had made the deal for us. In Fernando's first few weeks, he was making a lot of errors and misplays but was hitting a ton.

Tal was sitting next to me in the press box one day when Fernando got his third hit of the game. He looked at me and said, "You know, how do we really know this is Fernando Gonzalez? He's nothing like the scouting report. Technically, they could have sent us a different guy and told us it was Fernando Gonzalez."

What a concept. Except, it was unlikely they would send us a guy who hit this well. But Tal's fears were soon cast aside. Fernando began to field as he was expected to, and he wound up hitting .215 with seven RBIs in 121 at bats. That was more like it.

George "Doc" Medich emerged as a 19-game winner for us in '74, and what an interesting guy he was. Like Bobby Brown, the Yankee third baseman of a generation earlier, Medich was studying medicine while playing ball and would go on to become an MD. He was always carrying medical textbooks with him (in his case, the bookmark moved), and he would occasionally work with the team doctor, Ed Crane, to minister to a teammate.

One day in Oakland, George got hit in the thumb by a line drive while running in the outfield during BP. It hurt like hell, and he decided he should have it x-rayed.

I accompanied him by cab to the nearest hospital, where he made himself quite at home. When the film was developed, rather than waiting for it to be examined, Doc just reached behind the counter and took his x-ray, held it up to the light, and pronounced it fine. "No break," he said. "Let's go."

And we got in a cab and were back at the ballpark before the first pitch.

While we were winning, a rather remarkable thing was going on down on the field. Many of the veteran players in the club were feeling that Virdon was not providing the leadership that the team needed. They were beyond pep talks, but they felt that his manner was far too reclusive.

Bill was reserved in a strong-silent-type way. He flexed his muscles a lot when he stood by the batting cage. He could raise his voice when he was so moved but found it hard to do it naturally.

One day we had a lunatic bus driver taking us to the airport at a speed far in excess of common sense. Virdon, in the manager's seat up front, told him to slow down.

"I'm driving for the Lord," said the bus driver.

Bill couldn't believe what he had heard. He stood up and said, "You're driving for the New York Yankees and you are to slow this bus down immediately!" That outburst came quite naturally.

Bill could be tough if necessary. I watched him grab a drunken Sam McDowell in a hotel lobby and forcibly throw him into an elevator and march him to his room. McDowell was a big man and it was a bold move by Virdon, but there was more than a small chance that Sudden Sam was going to embarrass us big time in a major hotel's lobby in front of families looking for player autographs.

Sam once showed up at Yankee Stadium just before game time, only to find me at the top of the stairs leading to the clubhouse. He looked like he hadn't slept in two days. He was with a woman who had a similar look. He tossed the woman at me and said with a wink, "Here, find her a seat."

It should be noted that Sam took control of his life after his career ended and became a model citizen. But those were rough days for one of the hardest throwers in American League history. He wore monogrammed shirts that said "SS" for "Sudden Sam," but told me it really meant "Seldom Sudden."

Virdon, meanwhile, was increasingly removed from his players. Munson told me that he hadn't exchanged two words with Virdon in more than six weeks when Bill suddenly called him into his office. On his desk were a bunch of baseball cards, mailed in by a fan. The fan had asked Bill if he could get them signed, and that was what prompted the invitation.

Munson didn't even have mound conferences with Virdon. Bill was sending Ford to the mound to remove pitchers, and Dick Howser to home plate to bring up the lineups. Fans weren't paying to see Virdon manage, but we hardly ever saw him emerge from the dugout at all.

Then, through one of the players, I became aware that some of the veterans had begun to use their own signs to play the game. They took to ignoring whatever came from the dugout and were flashing signs among themselves.

And the signs were working. They were bunting and hitting-and-running and stealing on their own, and the strategy was paying off.

Virdon could say nothing, because it was undermining him, because it was working, and because to confront it would have only acknowledged the growing mutiny. It never exploded because the team kept winning, but, in the end, Virdon was named Manager of the Year by *The Sporting News*, which, to say the least, was quite amusing to a number of the players. (Other managers do the voting.)

The '74 season came to a close in Milwaukee. This was a dizzying time for me, because I was feverishly working on LCS and World Series logistics in New York—credentials, media buses, box lunches, press-box seating, postseason media guides, press pins, and scores of other details—while traveling to Milwaukee with a large press contingent for these big games.

Unfortunately, we fell short. The most memorable moment was an ugly fight in the lobby of the Pfister Hotel in Milwaukee between Rick Dempsey, our backup catcher, and Bill "Band on the Run" Sudakis, our third-stringer.

Dempsey, a very entertaining guy who was distantly related to heavy-weight champ Jack Dempsey, was Munson's backup but seldom played. The pitchers respected Munson's pitch calling much more, and Rick usually sat in the bullpen. (His father was a Broadway actor, and Rick himself did memorable Carlton Fisk and Babe Ruth impressions on the wet tarpaulin of Fenway Park one year, entertaining fans for years on blooper videos.)

Sudakis, also a catcher, really moaned about not playing. When Munson was hurt one week, Sudakis got two starts, which produced two hitless games against Jim Palmer and Luis Tiant. That pretty much shut him up for the season, at least until this trip to Milwaukee.

This was a case of too much beer on a long and delayed flight that had a stopover in Cleveland. Some players smuggled extra beer onto the bus. Sudakis had been on Dempsey's case about not playing—the last thing the team needed at this point. When we got to the Pfister, Virdon, first off the bus, disappeared into the hotel to meet his wife, Shirley.

With no principal around to calm the class, tempers got hot. Sudakis and Dempsey found themselves jammed into a single compartment of the revolving door, and by the time they emerged together, Rick had had enough and punched Sudakis.

In an instant, the two of them were brawling in the hotel lobby, in front of the guests. Lamps were flying, tables were overturned, and we had an impossible scene on our hands.

Out of nowhere, Bobby Murcer—all 175 pounds of him—decided he needed to be the peacemaker and got into it. He emerged with an injured hand—and was unable to play in the final games.

Lou Piniella played right for the first time all season. Doc Medich had a 2–0 lead when a liner to right got Lou tangled up and he misplayed it into a triple. The Brewers beat us 3–2 in 10 innings and put us out of the race on the next-to-last day of the season, with Murcer on the bench. An ugly finish, to say the least.

Steinbrenner and Gabe Paul came into the clubhouse the next day, and George told everyone what a great year it had been, which was a nice gesture. And Baltimore was just unbeatable down the stretch, winning almost every day. So we had a team of overachievers, and we had a lot of fun under unusual circumstances, what with the oddity of playing home games at Shea, the players flashing their own signals, the "Friday Night Massacre" trade at the start of the year, and the fistfight in the Pfister to end it.

When I went in to commiserate with Gabe the next day, I found him jovial and more upbeat than usual. I would even describe him as happy.

A longtime baseball official who had worked for Gabe told me he wasn't surprised.

"Oh, Gabe would have hated to win," he said. "A good, solid second place sells a lot of tickets for next year and doesn't overdo expectations. It's all business with him. To win would mean to spend all that money entertaining, being the host, instead of being the guest, working the room, glad-handing people. That's why he was pretty happy in Cleveland—no expectations, no pressure, just show up at the other guy's parties and work a trade here or there. And no big raises for next season."

As for PR people, we drown our tears by going off and helping the winners get through the post-season. I remember being at the '75 World Series, assigned to the auxiliary press box in Fenway Park, an unpleasant place for the overflow who didn't qualify for the main press box. I was seated at the end of a row, which was enhanced by a long plank of wood for a desk. If you weren't seated on the end, you had to make everyone get out in order to exit. No place for someone with a weak bladder.

It was with a touch of sadness that I greeted the journalist seated next to me. He was on assignment from a local television station, but those guys didn't get into the main press box, no matter who they were.

He was Tony Conigliaro.   .

Tony had actually begun the '75 season with Boston, his final attempt at a comeback from the awful eye injury that had essentially ended his promising career. He couldn't go the distance, couldn't qualify for the Series roster. With his enormous popularity in Boston, it was no wonder that he got a TV job. But now that the game was beginning, and he was seated way up here with a box lunch and a plank of wood in front of him, I couldn't help but wonder what in the world he must have been thinking as he watched his former teammates below.

As Vin Scully once said so poignantly, "It's just a moment in time between Opening Day and Old Timers Day."

THE KLUTTZ AND
THE CATFISH

While the excitement of the 1974 pennant race was building, so too were events that would find me serving as a spokesman on Watergate-related matters.

And if Richard Nixon had famously shoved his press secretary Ron Ziegler in anger one day, I could only imagine what my boss might do to me.

In April of '74, Steinbrenner had been indicted on five counts of violating campaign-contribution laws. The ugliest instance involved his paying phony bonuses to eight of his employees at American Ship Building Company, which they had to in turn contribute to the Committee to Re-elect the President. It was a way of getting around the campaign-contribution laws.

Had it just been a matter of making excessive contributions, and had we not suddenly entered an era of widespread political corruption, this might have passed. But by 1974 we were in full "get the bastards" mode, and the Steinbrenner matter made its way to the special prosecutor, Leon Jaworski. Steinbrenner became the first corporate executive to be nailed for political contributions, and with this came charges of obstruction of justice, obstructing a criminal investigation, aiding and abetting false statements to the FBI, and conspiracy.

This was not only a major legal problem for Steinbrenner but a politically embarrassing one. He was, in fact, a big contributor to the Democrats and counted Ted Kennedy as a "close friend." This claim had merit, because when I met Kennedy in the Fenway Park pressroom one day and was introduced as the Yankees' public relations director, I got a big handshake and smile, and, in that unmistakable accent, a "give my best to Jawge."

Now, however, because he was taking care of AmShip business as he thought best—reliant on government repair contracts, as it were—he would be forever linked to the Republicans and the whole Watergate gang.

He hired Edward Bennett Williams as his attorney—that's when you know things are serious in Washington—and proceeded to slug it out as best as he could while our pennant race heated up.

George loved celebrity lawyers, and during my time with him I was introduced to Louis Nizer, Roy Cohn, Bill Shea, and Williams.

On August 23, Steinbrenner pled guilty before a federal judge in Washington. He could have been sentenced to six years in prison but was fined $15,000. AmShip was fined $20,000, and Steinbrenner had to reimburse the company $42,325 for the false bonuses. The proceeding, with its relatively small fines, nevertheless made him a convicted felon— a horrible tag to carry and one that writers (and, in one memorable moment, Billy Martin) used when it suited them.

Most damaging, I thought, was that a core group of writers, led by Murray Chass of the *Times*, was so appalled by the details of what had transpired that they could never be charmed by "good George" again. And any time a feature story on George mentioned the Watergate conviction, the writer was off the favored list and banished from George's good graces. The matter cut both ways and forever tainted his important relationship with the media. Needless to say, this affected me, as his PR man. There were many ways in which George could be a positive force in selling our club. But any time a major interview opportunity opened, I always held my breath, waiting for the "convicted felon" sentence. Frequently, it would appear, and I would be blamed for poor judgment in arranging the interview. Finally, I had to refuse most such requests, and we lost what could have been an important selling asset.

As he saw it, he was taking care of business as it had played out over decades; it was his bad timing to get nailed during the Watergate frenzy.

The one thing, of course, that really cast him in a bad light was his passing the bribes through AmShip employees and essentially forcing them to lie about it, for obvious fear of their jobs. This was "bad George," the intimidating George, and the one who would rise up from time to time and incur the ire of the media. I put myself in the place of his AmShip people and thought of how easily it could have been in our laps. The Yankees didn't have a need for government repair contracts at the time—but as history would show, the government held a lot of cards when it came to stadium leases.

The act of corporate contributions to campaigns as a business practice was not unlike a situation I would become familiar with many years later, when the Atlanta Organizing Committee, seeking to host the 1996 Olympics, overspent on gifts to IOC members. This was common practice, but time had run out on authorities looking the other way.

If we thought the Watergate matter was over, we were wrong. It turned out that Bowie Kuhn, the commissioner, had been following the events from his office, and on September 6 he ordered Steinbrenner to have no contact with the team pending his own investigation of the matter.

The question of a convicted felon owning a major league team disturbed Kuhn's sense of propriety. Had Steinbrenner known that to be the case, he might not have pled guilty, and might have decided to slug it out and take his chances. This was a whole new twist.

True to his word that he would abide by the commissioner's ruling, he dropped out of sight for a month. He appeared outside the clubhouse in Cleveland in late September, seemingly just to gawk at his young heroes as they stayed in the race, and he sent a personal "inspiration" tape recording into the clubhouse in Milwaukee, dutifully played at a team meeting by Virdon.

In Cleveland, as always, he picked up the tab at the Theatrical Grill near our hotel for the whole traveling party, and at Kennedy Airport we all got $20 bills from Bill Kane for cabs home, courtesy of George, after our road trip.

When we got knocked out of the race in Milwaukee after the Dempsey-Sudakis-Murcer fiasco, George did come into the clubhouse and shake hands with everyone. "I don't care what they do to me; I want to be with these guys."

Just before Thanksgiving, Gabe Paul summoned me into his office. He told me the commissioner was going to suspend George from baseball for two years, and that I would be getting a call from George to prepare a statement.

I was pretty shocked at the severity of this, and I asked Gabe if he was too. By this point, his relationship with George had cooled. Used to having his own way and telling his owners how to proceed, he was getting tired of taking orders from a man young enough to be his son, someone who he thought showed little respect for Gabe's four decades in baseball. There was a part of Gabe that was going to welcome this respite, especially if the power to run the team fell cleanly into his lap.

Gabe shrugged his shoulders and said, "You've got to just listen to what the commissioner says."

I felt bad for Steinbrenner. He had treated me well. Although he could be bombastic, would call me up and tell me to fire the organist in the middle of a game, would take me away from the press box to dictate long press releases on the poor quality of umpiring, he had never really unloaded on me. Occasionally, upset if I didn't get his point in the first draft of a release, he might say, "Now look, I'm not going to put you out in the street over this, but . . ."

When we first moved into the Parks Administration Building in Queens, after MacPhail and Fishel were gone, George had called the full staff into the large group-ticket-sales office for a talk. It was the only "all hands" meeting we ever had while I was there.

He sat on a desk in the corner, facing the 40 or so of us who constituted our front office. I was standing with Jimmy Esposito, our head groundskeeper, and Dave Weidler, our chief accountant.

"I know there's a lot of talk out there about changes," he told us. "It's natural when you have new ownership. But from what I can see, this is a terrific staff, a great operation, and, I'm told, one of the best in baseball. I just wanted to tell you all that if you keep up the good jobs you've been doing, you have no reason to worry about losing your jobs, or massive changes in the office."

A lot of people did need that reassurance, which is natural after a management change. We still had Topping and Webb people, and we had a number of CBS people who chose to leave CBS and stay with the Yankees. Weidler was one of them. And although change was inevitable, and there would always be normal attrition, mass turnover had not hit the staff in '74, and the pennant race had made us all feel pretty good about the new ownership. Plus, everyone liked what a genuine fan George had become. The man liked to win.

So I was sad when I picked up the phone in the late afternoon and took George's call. He was clearly shaken by the ruling, in which Kuhn said, "Attempting to influence employees to behave dishonestly is the kind of misconduct, which, if ignored by baseball, would undermine the public's confidence in our game. I have decided to place Mr. Steinbrenner on the ineligible list for a period of two years. In accordance, he is declared ineligible and incompetent to manage or advise in the management of the affairs of the New York Yankees."

"How could he call me incompetent?" George said to me. "Is Buddy Selig competent? He's a car dealer in Milwaukee! How do you do that?"

I offered that it was probably a legal term, not a reflection of his ability. But he wanted to stay with it. He wanted to focus on that word, as though it were personal, as though it were a judgment—and a bad one—by Kuhn.

So he began to dictate a statement to me. I was seated at my desk, in the large office I had inherited from Fishel. Babe and Casey were on the wall, watching my every move. I wrote as fast as I could, because dictation from George always meant creatively inventing new forms of shorthand. I always used the symbols from team caps to indicate cities, even knowing the difference between a Cleveland C, a Cincinnati C, and a Chicago Cubs C in my own shorthand.

His statement began sarcastically. "It is certainly a wonderful Thanksgiving present." I asked if he really wanted that to be part of the statement, and he said, "Absolutely; you don't do this to a man just before Thanksgiving." (Twenty-two years later, he dismissed his PR director at Christmas because he wouldn't cut short his vacation plans to be present for David Cone's free-agent-signing announcement.)

He continued: "It's impossible to understand how the commissioner of baseball could call me incompetent."

Again, I suggested it was only a legal term. George didn't want to hear it. He was going for public support now, the populist approach. Thanksgiving, incompetent—it was playing out. Now to get conciliatory.

"Let me be perfectly frank. I don't agree with the commissioner's decision. I felt it was too harsh in view of the facts, the federal bench's decision, and in view of action, or lack of action he took in other cases which I considered far more injurious to baseball. I feel that Bowie believed that what he was doing he had to do, and I respect him for that. I probably think more of him as a commissioner than he does of me as an owner. There will not be any lawsuit. The only thing that really matters is that the Yankees win a pennant and hopefully a World Series for the people of New York. To involve myself, the Yankees, and baseball in a lawsuit would detract from that goal."

I typed it out on my trusty Royal typewriter and read it back to him. He tinkered with some of the words. I didn't think he should call the commissioner Bowie, and he thought about it and stayed with it. He wanted somehow to make this seem as though they were partners in this grand design that was making victims of them both. Kuhn was doing what he had to do; he couldn't help it.

We didn't have fax machines, let alone e-mail, in those days, so, one by one, I called each news outlet and dictated the statement. The *Times*, the *News*, the *Post*, *Newsday*, the *Star-Ledger*, the *Long Island Press*, the Westchester papers, the *Bergen Record*, AP, UPI, the news radio stations, and Sportsphone. Each one stopped to question the sentence on "incompetent."

"Isn't that just a legal term?" they'd ask.

"Just take the statement," I'd say.

I did not, incidentally, have an assistant, as Fishel had had in me. Not only were they saving money by replacing Bob with me, but no one was named to replace me. Sometimes Anne Mileo, my very capable secretary, would help, and sometimes Mickey Morabito would assist me, although that was practically voluntary.

Mickey had been the kid in the red blazer who sat by the dugout and gave the lineup changes to Bob Sheppard in the PA booth. He had begun to accompany players on speaking engagements, was well liked, and showed genuine promise and interest in moving up. Another Marty, so to speak.

One day he asked if he could possibly get business cards to give out when he went with the players to their banquets. Just his name, no title. Gabe said no.

Mickey continued to assist me without a title. He was paid by the hour, and Gabe never told him to stay home, but he wouldn't make him assistant PR director, and he wouldn't give him business cards, even with only his name and no title. We were just about the only team without an assistant PR man, and we were the Yankees. But that was Gabe.

I finished the calls, pretty much exhausted. Today, with the click of a button, I could send a mass fax or e-mail. Back then we had "telecopier" machines, into which you would put a sheet of paper around a cylinder, and it would transmit over a phone line to another telecopier, taking four to six minutes per page. A writer sending his story to his paper after a game gave his copy to a service that handled the transmission, because Western Union was being phased out of the business. (I told my father about this and he said, "We had that machine in the thirties when I worked at Jacobs Shoe Factory in Brooklyn. We would send written messages over phone lines to our plant in Pennsylvania. Not a new thing.")

The offices were deserted now; it was the day before Thanksgiving. My conversation with Steinbrenner would be the last time I would speak to him until almost eight months later, when he met with sportswriters in Texas to talk about Kuhn's upcoming re-election vote. He then turned up at my bachelor party at Shea Stadium's Diamond Club in October 1975. When people would later say to me, "How could you put in four years under him?!" I would smile and say, "Well, he was suspended for the middle two; I get an asterisk."

But the George Steinbrenner I had said goodbye to that day in 1974 had been a good boss and, of course, had been the guy who promoted me. I felt bad for him on a personal level and bad for the team as well. We had come so close in '74, and it was clear that this guy wanted to win, wanted to do what it took. I hoped this wasn't going to be a major setback.

So, during the remainder of his suspension, I had to be conversant with the facts of his case, with names like Maurice Stans and John Mitchell, Archibald Cox and Leon Jaworski. I frequently did radio or print interviews explaining the suspension and its impact on our operation. Fortunately, having been a political science major, I was not without some measure of credibility when speaking on these issues.

A month before George's "Thanksgiving present," Gabe called me down to his office at the end of the hall in our new headquarters.

It had once been the office of Robert Moses, the legendary "power broker" who had planned New York's highways and numerous public works projects and who had used this very office during the World's Fair of 1964–65. In this big office, Gabe sat behind his desk and motioned for me to sit on a sofa facing him. Gabe was well unpacked by now, about three weeks after our move. He never had any photos in his office recalling his long career in the game, but always had his little overnight kit there at the ready should he have reason to fly somewhere quickly.

He smiled at me.

"I want you to hear this phone call," he said. "Pearl! Get me Bobby Murcer."

It was about 8 A.M. in Oklahoma City, and I was picturing Bobby getting up to play golf or to meet someone to talk about some new business scheme. He always had interesting business friends and always had something cooking.

I could hear Pearl in the outer office. "Bobby? Hi, it's Pearl Davis; how you doin', sweetie? Just a second; Mr. Paul wants to speak with you."

"Mr. Paul, he's on the phone."

"Bobby? Good morning; Gabe Paul."

Gabe winked at me.

"You were? Well, Bobby, let me remind you that there's an old saying—'Only whores make money in bed.'"

I think Bobby had a rejoinder on his end, but I couldn't make out what he was saying.

"Listen," continued Gabe, "I've got some news for you this morning. I think you'll like it, or at least if you don't at first, I think you'll come to like it; it can be a terrific opportunity for you."

Another brief pause for Bobby's response.

"Well, we've traded you to the San Francisco Giants."

This time I could hear Bobby's familiar voice on the other end.

"You *what??*"

Gabe covered the mouthpiece and said to me, "What's his wife's name?"

"Kay," I responded.

"Yes, we've traded you to the Giants, Bobby; it's a terrific organization, you're going to love the city, they have great restaurants out there, Kay will love it, and it will be a fantastic opportunity for you with a whole new league. Great cities in that league, you know. Ever been to San Diego?"

I think there was silence on Bobby's end. Total, utter silence.

"Well, Bobby, I can tell from your reaction that this has caught you by surprise, but let me assure you that everyone feels that way the first time they're traded, and I can assure you that very few players with long careers don't get traded, so give it some time, it will settle in, and you know we wish you all the best.

"Please give my regards to Kay and the children, and let me know if there's anything we can do for you. Take care.

"Oh, what's that? Oh, yes, Bobby Bonds. Take care."

Click.

It was only as an afterthought that Murcer had decided to ask. And only then did Gabe tell him what the trade had been.

Gabe looked at me with a glow of satisfaction. "What do you think of that?"

"Wow," was about the best I could muster. "What a deal. Of course, we're losing a nice guy . . ."

"Marty," he bellowed, "I'll take you to church any Sunday . . ." You know the rest.

And with that, I was off to make the announcement to the press, coordinating it with the Giants' public relations department.

This was a blockbuster, all right. Not long before, Steinbrenner had told Bobby that he was a franchise player, never leaving the team. He had forgiven him his $100,000 contract. But Bobby's first year at Shea had been disappointing; he hadn't hit a home run at Shea until September and had just 10 for the full season and a .274 average. Not the kind of production you needed from the number three hitter.

Bonds was also coming off a disappointing season with a .256 average and just 21 homers. But he had been the Player of the Year in the National League in 1973, and he and Willie Mays were the only two men in baseball history to twice record 30-30 seasons—30 homers, 30 stolen bases. His 263 career steals were more than any Yankee in history, although he had only played six and a half seasons in the majors. He had missed the first 40-40 season by one homer, with 39-43 in '73.

He had the grace of an antelope, and, as Tal Smith said to me, "Any time you can get one of the five best players in the game—you just do it."

Any baseball man would tell you that Bonds was one of the best players in the league at age 28. You would have to be nuts not to want him. It was not unlike the reaction 25 years later when the Yanks dealt the popular David Wells to Toronto for Roger Clemens. The fans loved Wells and cried over losing him, but at the end of the day they realized that they'd landed the defending Cy Young Award winner and a future Hall of Famer. Never mind that '99 didn't go that well for Roger—by the time the fans came to their senses, they realized this was a spectacular deal.

It was my style to always seek links to historical events when I had an announcement to make, because baseball lent itself to that so easily. My angle on this trade was that it was "the biggest one-for-one deal in baseball history." The only thing that came close, in my research, was Rogers Hornsby for Frankie Frisch in 1926, but, in the end, the Giants included pitcher Jimmy Ring with Frisch. So it was two for one. Homer champ Rocky Colavito for batting champ Harvey Kuenn in 1960 was up there too.

As a courtesy, before I began calling the press, I called Bob Fishel at his American League office. He had always liked Bobby and Kay—we all did—and he appreciated the heads-up and the chance to call them before the media did.

Bob later told me, "You and I really made that trade, Marty. It was one of the few times I can ever say that the public relations department engineered a trade."

I asked him what he meant, and he said, "There is really no way Murcer equals Bonds. The tools just aren't there; Bonds is a far superior player. Even Murcer would admit that when the shock passes. But the way we built Bobby up over the years, as Mantle's successor and all of that—we made him shine far beyond what his capabilities are. We created a following for Bobby Murcer like the old Hollywood press agents did at MGM and Warner Brothers. The Giants, 3,000 miles away, bought into this too. They needed a big star, and Bobby sounded like one to them. One-for-one for Bonds? They grabbed at it. It was a PR deal all the way."

Bob took a lot of pride in that, but he kept it between us, of course. Not many people in baseball would have been happy to hear that theory.

Murcer, like others before him, left his heart in New York City. He was not a happy National Leaguer. He broke the unwritten rules in San

Francisco by complaining about the wind and the cold, something only visiting players were supposed to do. The home team was supposed to make the best of it and let the visitors suffer. Bobby was the first Giant to bad-mouth the ill winds at Candlestick.

Then the Giants traded him to the Cubs, where he actually complained about all the day games. "It's like having a real job," he told me. "You have to wake up early every morning and go to work. No golf!"

Bobby finally returned from his five-year exile in 1979. He was no longer a great star, just a good designated hitter, and in some years the 25th man on the roster. But he managed to get into the '81 World Series, so he had a brief, if ineffective, taste of the Yankee glory that he had missed just before and just after his significant Yankee tenure. And years later, when I was producing Yankee telecasts, I was able to bring him back as a broadcaster.

I took an immediate liking to Bobby Bonds. We flew him into New York for a press conference, and I picked him up at LaGuardia in my new, sporty Oldsmobile Starfire, one of the worst cars ever invented at GM. What was Olds thinking when it made a sports car? That they would find me out there?

Bobby stuffed himself into the front seat, and there was something I liked about him at once. I took it upon myself, as I usually did, to welcome him with an overview of the Yankee organization, who did what, how Yankee Stadium was being rebuilt, where our offices were, where the players lived, who else we had on the team that he might have played with. I told him funny stories about his old teammate, Jim Ray Hart—our DH in 1973, and a fishing (and drinking) buddy of his. Jim Ray Hart was our immediate connection. We both liked him.

There had been whispers about Bobby having a drinking problem, and, in truth, he had been in the papers once or twice for offseason problems related to alcohol. But, as Gabe would say, that was the off-season, and 25 of the nicest guys . . . and so on. The fact was, Bobby liked his beer, but he was a hardworking, magnificently built athlete who never got out of shape and who had a dignity and stature that were instantly recognizable.

Bobby and I had dinner that first night, and I took him for a drive through my neighborhood in Riverdale, where Ron Blomberg and Willie Mays both lived. Mays had been his teammate and friend, and godfather to his son Barry. Riverdale was not the ideal location while we were at Shea—Long Island made more sense—but on that very trip, Bobby put down a deposit on a sparkling new apartment in the neighborhood and felt good that he could get that done right off the bat.

He told me about his family and how they would all look forward to his first spring training in Florida. His oldest son, Barry, was 10 "and a helluva player," I recall him saying. There were also Ricky, nine, and Bobby, five. His wife's name was Pat. I told him about the homes that players rented in Ft. Lauderdale, and he was genuinely excited to be joining the Yankees.

Bobby would hang around in baseball long enough to become a millionaire, which, to my thinking, might have made his son Barry the first ballplayer who was ever the son of a millionaire. I could be wrong—you never know these things for sure—but when Barry reached the big leagues, the possibility did occur to me.

"Well, we have one helluva baseball player here," I thought. Way to go, Gabe.

Just when I was all set to use Bobby Bonds as my cover boy for the Yearbook and the press guide, along came the story of Jim "Catfish" Hunter.

Hunter was another one you liked right away, especially if he was polite enough to miss your shoes while spitting tobacco juice. One of the great things about working for the Yankees was meeting people from all over, like Ron Guidry of Louisiana or James Augustus Hunter, the peanut farmer from Hertford, North Carolina. It was like having a free subscription to *National Geographic*.

Hunter was the youngest of nine children, and I give his parents a tremendous amount of credit for raising their youngest to emerge with such self-confidence, self-assurance, and decency. No doubt his older siblings helped, and it was of interest to me that Nolan Ryan, a Hall of Fame contemporary with equal dignity, was the youngest of six. Tom Seaver was the youngest of four, Kirby Puckett the youngest of six.

Jimmy was raised to farm, and he hunted and fished, and his career almost ended before it started. His brother Pete accidentally misfired a shotgun while hunting and loaded his right foot with buckshot.

"You shot my damned foot off!" Jimmy yelled. They got him to a hospital, where he lost his small right toe and the use of the adjoining ones. Many thought his hopes for playing pro ball were dashed. (It was very much like Joe DiMaggio, a hot prospect in San Francisco 40 years earlier, badly injuring his knee. Everyone lost interest in him except the Yankees.)

But the Kansas City Athletics gave Jimmy a contract, and their owner, Charles O. Finley, gave him a nickname. Having signed a Blue Moon Odom and a Jumbo Jim Nash and a Mudcat Grant, he was now bent on having a team with colorful nicknames. He told Jimmy, "You're now 'Catfish' Hunter. You got the name when you ran away from home and came back with catfish for dinner."

The scout who signed Hunter for the A's was another southern gentleman, with the unlikely name of Clyde Kluttz. Clyde had been an average ballplayer, a catcher, but, like Hunter, he was a man of his word, an honorable presence in baseball, and, in his long scouting and player-development career, everyone respected him.

We had the good fortune to have Clyde in our employ at the time. Lee MacPhail had brought him to the organization in 1971 to run our scouting operation. Aside from his unusual name (and he signed a center fielder named Mickey Klutts for us while he was there), he was a delightful man with a terrific wife named Wayne. Clyde and Wayne Kluttz. At work, Clyde shared an office with our farm-system administrator—a former Dodger catcher and Rickey disciple named George Pfister. So it was Pfister and Kluttz. Great baseball names.

Pfister had, interestingly, been an illegal player in his only major league appearance. He started a game at the end of the '41 season for Brooklyn when he had not yet signed a contract. Later on, after he left the Yankees, he was in charge of enforcing these details in the commissioner's office.

Details, details, details. Finley did not like to be bothered by them, but, as an insurance man, he should have been used to them. The whole insurance world was based on details. Actuarial tables, premium schedules, assigned-risk auto policies.

So it was odd that ol' Charlie simply "forgot" to make the final payment on Catfish's 1974 contract in time. And when Cat got himself an agent, Jerry Kapstein, to announce that he was considering himself a free agent because of the delay, Finley was sure he would set things right by just making the payment. It would be late, but it would be paid.

Charlie, for all of his rascally behavior, would lend players money, give them nice bonuses, and treat them to big parties at his ranch. But he could also cheap out on World Series rings, hotel selection, and so forth. You never knew which Charlie you were getting. My pal Jimmy Bank, his traveling secretary, was a great source for these stories.

It was during the World Series of '74 that Kapstein was telling everyone that Hunter's contract had been voided. It wasn't really a distraction, because the A's themselves were controversial, and something was always going on with them. The '73 Series had been an embarrassment, with the Mike Andrews affair, and here they were, back for more. The Kapstein–Hunter story was just another sidebar.

But things had been going on in the labor movement since Curt Flood had challenged the reserve clause and gone all the way to the Supreme Court with it. Marvin Miller had coaxed the players into a more cohesive union, making them realize that there were more than pensions to be negotiated. The players had come to trust Miller, to appreciate the uncondescending style with which he addressed them, and the depth of his sincerity. Owners would call him an old-fashioned and dangerous zealot, but the players were uniting behind him because he shot straight from the hip and, with just the right touch, connected with them over their common enemy—baseball's reserve clause and those who administered it.

The brilliant Leonard Koppett of the *Times*, a Russian-born Jew, had been in Washington to hear arguments in the Flood case, and he returned to the press box in Sarasota, where we were playing the White Sox in an exhibition game. Koppett reported that Arthur Goldberg, Flood's lawyer, was "the second stupidest Jew I've ever seen," leaving out who his number one might be, but clearly telling us that Goldberg had blown the oral arguments. Koppett, like most writers (mostly union men themselves, and mostly labor-supporting), was very sympathetic to Flood. But he felt that he could have argued the case far better than Goldberg, who, it turned out, was not well prepared for the case.

Koppett was right: Flood lost. In 1973 our own Sparky Lyle, the Cardinals' Ted Simmons, and Cincinnati's Bobby Tolan held out virtually all season, with the thought that if they didn't sign, they would have played out their option year and could be free agents. A lot of people saw the tidal wave coming. First Flood—close call. Then Lyle, Simmons, and Tolan—but they all signed in the end. The fort was beginning to feel the siege.

Now Hunter was saying he was free. What might this mean?

In 1967 Ken "Hawk" Harrelson had been released in midseason by Finley over a disciplinary dispute. Finley just cut him loose in the middle of the year. He was hitting .305, and, in an era of pitching dominance, he was one of the league's better hitters and more colorful characters.

Suddenly on the open market, he was able to turn himself into a $100,000 player, as the Red Sox picked him up and made him part of their "Impossible Dream" stretch run. The following year, the "Year of the Pitcher," he led the league with 109 RBIs while belting 35 homers with his $100,000 contract. That was what free agency was worth then for an everyday position player.

What would it mean now?

It didn't seem to matter; most people thought that there was no way Finley would really lose the guy over just a late payment.

But Miller had managed to negotiate a system of arbitration when a grievance was filed, and, as a result, this would not be a case of the commissioner fining Finley and sending Hunter back home. This time, the arbitrator, Peter Seitz, ruled that Hunter and Kapstein were correct—he was a free agent.

Chaos!

Kuhn quickly instituted a cooling-down period of a few days to let teams decide what to do, but early indications were that the Harrelson days were long gone. We were about to be talking much bigger bucks here.

People looked at the Yankees and wondered whether the now-suspended Steinbrenner could authorize Gabe Paul to bid for Hunter.

Kuhn later said he had no doubt that Steinbrenner would be involved, and it was foolish to prohibit him from decision making after he'd spent $10 million (with his partners) on the whole franchise. So long as he wasn't publicly seen doing the negotiating, Kuhn let it be.

I was sitting with Gabe Paul and talking about our plans.

"Do you think," I asked, "that this could go over a million dollars?"

"Hell, yes!" he roared, "This is war! It's going to be a lot *more* than a million dollars!"

Good ol' Gabe. He was playing with someone else's money, and he was loving it.

One by one, teams flew to Ahoskie, North Carolina, to visit with Catfish's law firm, and the wizened old J. Carlton Cherry Sr. Almost every team made an appearance—sometimes an owner, sometimes a pitching coach (San Diego's Bill Posedel, Hunter's old Oakland pitching coach), sometimes a player (Cleveland sent fellow Carolinian Gaylord Perry), and once even Finley went himself, not too embarrassed to try and re-sign his ace. For the Yankees, it was all in the hands of our director of player procurement and scouting, Clyde Kluttz.

This qualified as player procurement. And boy, did we have the right man on the case.

By today's standards, the numbers are small, but, in the context of 1974, this was an unqualified extravaganza. Baseball had barely made its way to the $200,000 annual salary at this point, with Hank Aaron achieving it. Six digits was still reserved for the elite. Many young players were earning in the $25,000 to $40,000 range. Murcer had been our only $100,000 player since Mantle. Signing bonuses? Forget it. Multiyear contracts? We knew of one—Earl Wilson with Boston, through his agent, Bob Woolf.

Now the talk was millions.

The bidding war dominated the sports news for weeks. Hunter would take a break from farming or fishing to wander down to Ahoskie to greet visitors at his attorney's office. The media was, miserably, camped out at whatever cheap lodging they could get in Ahoskie, no hotspot for Marriotts, Sheratons, or Hiltons.

I am positive that at no time did Catfish close the door to his house, look at his wife, Helen, jump up and down, and yell, "We're gonna be rich! We're gonna be rich!" Jimmy Hunter took life as it came. Excitement for him might be a pennant, but that was the competitive juices flowing—the real rush of a great athlete.

He was a big kid, picked off the peanut farm, having some fun, playing some ball. If he'd been assigned to grounds crew duty, he'd have loved it—working the soil, having a beer with the guys after work. He could have dragged that infield and pumped his million-dollar arm to YMCA with the best of them.

One of my favorite Catfish stories involved him and a teammate, Nelson Mathews, traveling with the Kansas City Athletics when they were just breaking in. The team found themselves killing time in the railroad depot in Cleveland. Wearing raincoats over their sport jackets, Mathews and Hunter fished out some quarters and had their pictures taken in one of those "four pictures for a quarter" booths. They turned up their collars and posed face-forward and in profile, trying to look as sinister as they could.

When they got their strips of pictures, they headed back into the big waiting room and came upon a little old lady, minding her own business. With Mathews looking to the side and standing a few feet away, Hunter went to the woman and, rapidly popping open his wallet, said, "Excuse me, ma'am, Cleveland Police, undercover division. Can you tell me if you've seen this man?"

He flashed the strip of Mathews' photos. The woman studied them and then looked up to see Mathews standing a few feet behind Hunter, glancing nervously around the station.

The woman nearly fainted as she silently pointed over Hunter's shoulder, her eyes bulging. Cat turned around, recognized the suspect, and began chasing him all around the station as the woman yelled. It was one of the greatest moments in killing-time-in-a-railroad-station history.

Now this big kid–turned–Cy Young winner was gonna be rich.

Showing absolutely no restraint, as though giving no thought to the consequences, the owners practically trampled each other with wheelbarrows full of money. What they were doing was not only making Catfish Hunter rich but sending a very clear message to Marvin Miller and the Players' Association: "Hey, this is what you guys are really worth without the reserve clause. This is what you could get on the open market if you were free agents."

The owners still blame the players today, or the arbitrator, but it was their own actions that got the ball rolling. Whatever had happened in baseball between Finley firing Hawk Harrelson in '67 and Finley breaching Catfish Hunter's contract seven years later, it was obvious that it was a call to arms for Miller. And his musket was ready.

I was going to be at a New Year's Eve party in New Jersey with Ron and Mara Blomberg, a date, and Ron's lawyer and his wife. But the plans began to unravel when my phone rang in Riverdale at 10 a.m.

"Better get in here," said Gabe. "We may be signing Hunter today."

I headed for our offices on the final day of 1974 and realized when I arrived that the trip might be for nothing. Clyde Kluttz had persuaded Hunter to fly to New York to meet with Gabe. They boarded George Steinbrenner's private jet and headed for LaGuardia. In the plane was Ed Greenwald, one of Steinbrenner's partners, and it was Greenwald who was writing out the details of an elaborate contract for Hunter and Paul to negotiate. Hunter's three lawyers were aboard as well.

The Padres, Expos, and Angels all offered more money to Catfish, but it was his trust in Clyde Kluttz, almost a father figure to him, that was winning the day for the Yankees.

In Gabe's office, our little elite team of commandos had gathered. Tal Smith, Elliot Wahle (the bright young minor league administrator), and Mickey Morabito, my unofficial assistant without business cards, were present for history. Dave Weidler was there—someone had to be able to cut a check.

"We'll meet with him right here, and if he signs, we'll announce it immediately," Gabe told me. "No delay. As soon as he signs, I'll call you, and you call the press. You might as well start preparing a release, just in case."

We had entered the era of photocopying machines, so that in most places of business you would prepare the release and then run off however many you needed. Indeed, when I traveled with the Yankees, even to cheap Oakland, I would show up with my press notes on letterhead, and they would "Xerox" a hundred or so for me. It was standard procedure now, except at the Yankees.

Gabe had decided that the cost of photocopying was too high.

"Call A.B. Dick," he told me, "and tell them you're with the Yankees and you want their finest mimeograph machine. With a supply of stencils."

This had happened a few weeks before, and the machine had been delivered this very week. If Catfish wasn't jumping up and down when he was ruled a free agent, I am sure that the people at A.B. Dick were dancing when I called. It had to be their first sale in a year, and maybe their last ever.

So, on top of all the responsibility of assembling the sports world's biggest news conference on New Year's Eve, as snow was falling over New York, there I was, reading the instruction manual for the new mimeograph machine, and trying my best to type a stencil without making a mistake so that we might look "first class." All while we were about to pour millions onto Hunter.

The Hunter party arrived around two. Catfish was wearing a pullover shirt and carrying a cup to spit his tobacco juice into. He said "hi" to me, knowing me through our mutual buddy Jimmy Bank. I smiled back and gave him the thumbs-up, as in, "Make it happen, Catfish."

At four, Gabe called me and said, "Start calling the press."

"We have a deal?" I asked.

"No, but if we don't, we'll give them a statement anyway."

So I began calling the press. By this time, at least, we had moved on to touch-tone telephones, and I didn't have to deal with the rotary dial any longer. And Mickey helped with the calls, as well as with the mimeographing.

No one was happy to receive my call. Everyone had New Year's Eve plans, and this was right smack in the middle of preparation. I heard groans and sighs and the voices of irate wives in the background. In addition, the snow was falling harder and travel was difficult. If we didn't have a signing to announce, this was going to be very embarrassing, and we were really going to piss people off.

The press began arriving around six. Still no signing. They knew that Hunter was down the hall in Gabe's corner office. We only had coffee to offer them.

My phone rang. It was Gabe. "Come on down," he said.

I went in, and there was Catfish, wearing a Yankee cap. There were about nine of us in the room, and Gabe had popped open some New Year's Eve champagne (cheap, but first class). The deal was done, and the Yankees were making baseball history, as this great franchise had once been accustomed to doing.

The nine of us walked down the hall to the group-ticket-sales office, the biggest room we had, the one in which Steinbrenner had addressed the entire staff, the one in which we had introduced Tal Smith and then Bill Virdon to the press.

I spoke first.

"Gentlemen, I give you Gabe Paul for a very special announcement, on a very special New Year's Eve for the New York Yankees."

Gabe took center stage and proceeded to say that Catfish had signed literally 15 minutes before. He could think of no other transaction that had been announced so quickly. But this story could hardly keep, and, for tax reasons, they wanted the contract and some of the payments made in calendar year 1974.

The deal was said to be between $2.8 million and $3.5 million. It was still an age when such things were kept quiet. It was revealed years later that the package was actually worth $2,931,000, and that because part of it was deferred and part of it was insurance annuities for his two children, as well as college scholarships, it cost the Yankees only $1,762,836. The actual salary was, surprisingly, only $100,000 a year, plus a $50,000 annual signing bonus for five years, deferred. For all the talk of millions, Catfish was not about to move to a bigger house or buy everyone a new car. (He did get a new Buick for himself for each of the five years as part of the deal.)

Catfish was calm and poised throughout the press conference. He continued to spit tobacco juice into his cup. Neil Walsh, director of special events for New York City, presented him with a fishing pole on behalf of the City. Aside from the Yankee cap, it was the only prop we had for still photographers.

The six New York television stations each got their filmed interviews, the written press got what they needed, and, by eight, everyone was departing. Catfish? He was getting right back on the plane for Hertford. He was going hunting in the morning; had to be up early.

I found myself alone with Gabe in his office, the last two left. I said, "This was a proud day for us. This is where the Yankees should be. This can be a real turnaround day for this team."

Gabe agreed. We actually had a nice conversation. He even asked me what the ink was on my sleeve. I asked him if he'd ever been part of anything quite like this before, and he paused for a long time and couldn't think of a thing. That's when I knew we had truly written history.

"Which pen did he use to sign the contract?" I asked.

"Well, this one right here," said Gabe.

It was a 19-cent Bic pen.

"Mind if I take it?" I asked. "I think I might like to give it to Cooperstown."

"No, be my guest," he said.

A few weeks later, at a winter sports banquet in Oneonta, I presented the pen to Kenny Smith, the old New York newspaperman who was now the public relations director at the Hall of Fame. And that little pen that started it all is still on display there.

Exhausted, I said good night to Gabe and wished him a happy New Year.

"Where are you going?" he asked. He was mellow; he wanted to sit around and talk baseball some more. Under other circumstances, finding him in a warm mood, I would have enjoyed it. His stories could be great.

"Jersey. A party."

"Well, drive carefully," he warned me. "And be here early on Tuesday. Things are going to get mighty interesting around here."

As I made my way across the snowy George Washington Bridge, I had a sense that the franchise was back.

BILLY'S OLD TIMERS INVITATION

The presence of Catfish Hunter on our roster overwhelmed the sports news as 1975 began. He was, for weeks, a household name, the biggest story in America. We decided to bring him back to New York early in January to do a round of media, making up for the haste with which we had hauled out a press conference on New Year's Eve.

Cat would have rather been hunting, but he was accommodating, and, in a way, I think he was enjoying it despite himself.

Roger Kahn, who had written *The Boys of Summer* not too many years before, was assigned to follow him around for the day and do a magazine piece on him. Richard Avedon, the celebrated photographer, set up a temporary studio at Shea to take stark black-and-white portraits of him to accompany the article.

We booked him on *Good Morning America*, and, when we arrived, we found the Reverend Jesse Jackson in the green room, waiting his turn.

"You related to Reggie Jackson?" said Hunter. "You guys look alike."

I cringed.

Jesse just laughed and said something about wishing he could play ball like Reggie. And then he got Hunter's autograph. It was going to be a good day.

At midday we retreated to the Americana Hotel on Seventh Avenue for a rest and then an informal press luncheon over pastrami sandwiches from the Stage Deli. The New York beat writers who hadn't celebrated with us on New Year's Eve sat around on sofas and chairs and pummeled Catfish with good-natured questions. He took a few pops at Finley but mostly thanked him for the screwup that had allowed him to be a free agent. And he remembered to thank him for past favors, for indeed, cheap as he was, Finley was not beyond reaching into his pocket to help a player in need.

Someone asked him about his salary. In those days, salaries were still pretty personal and not automatically reported through the Players' Association so that everyone knew what everyone made. Hunter surprised everyone in the room by saying, "Well, it will come out eventually; it's $150,000 a year."

After all the talk of millions, that was a surprise.

Hunter took it upon himself that day to start lobbying the Yankees to sign his buddy Dick Green, the departing Oakland second baseman, but he couldn't quite pull it off. That night the two of us had dinner at Top of the Sixes, atop 666 Fifth Avenue, where we traded Finley and Steinbrenner stories. We drank beer, and he was just a great companion, as everyone had said. He was funny, he was wily, and he had the bearing of a winner. He didn't wear any of his championship rings ("I hang them on the antlers of a stuffed deer head in my den"), but he was clearly a champion. He was taking us to a new level.

Bill Virdon was not a part of any of this. The Manager of the Year had not been brought in for New Year's Eve, or for this round of media. It didn't seem like he was being embraced as a long-term manager. I knew that Steinbrenner seethed when Dick Howser brought out the lineups and Whitey Ford made the pitching changes, and that there was little visibility for the manager.

I hired a fine illustrator named Jack Havey, whose *Sporting News* covers I had admired, to paint the faces of Hunter and Bonds for the cover of our media guide and program in 1975. Working from an Oakland photo and just putting a Yankee cap on Catfish, Havey gave us the right representation of the Oakland Hunter, including very long hair. I would be hearing about that subject.

The day of Hunter's arrival in Ft. Lauderdale was not going to be ordinary. Every New York television station flew a crew down, but the biggest event was the arrival of Howard Cosell. ABC Sports had arranged for a Brinks armored car to deliver Hunter to the ballpark, and Catfish laughed and thought it was great and said he'd go along with it.

Cosell was an enormous celebrity in his own right by now. He was at the top of everyone's list of most hated broadcasters but was also the most respected. He had accomplished what everyone in show business hopes to—develop a unique style that translates to celebrity and acceptance. He was one of the few media types in sports who would get players whispering when he arrived. More than a few asked to have their pictures taken with him.

Monday Night Football and boxing had made him famous; his baseball broadcasting would not be heard for another year. Everyone imitated his delivery, and those especially skilled could do "a Cosell," complete with showing off a vocabulary far beyond anyone's normal speech.

This being an event for national broadcast, I personally went to Ft. Lauderdale Airport to pick Howard up. His relationship with the Yankees was important in his past. He had arrived in the '50s with a heavy reel-to-reel tape recorder, assigned to interview Mantle and Ford and Berra and Stengel and the rest of the great Yankees.

No one would give him the time of day until he pleaded with Bob Fishel for help, and Fishel coaxed them all into talking to him. He was able to complete his assignment, and many thought this was a breakthrough moment for him. His first time out of the studio, and he would have fallen on his face if not for Fishel.

Then, of course, he grew in stature, and did remarkable programs with Jackie Robinson and Mickey Mantle, actually getting Mantle to reveal that he feared an early death because his father and grandfather had both died before they were 40.

Now Cosell was all bravado and swagger, and his act was great fun. He got into my car and said something like this: "Marty Appel, the stylish young righthander from Brooklyn, New York, in the unenviable position of succeeding the legendary Robert O. Fishel, not unlike the task faced by the now forgotten George 'Twinkletoes' Selkirk, successor to the Bambino, the Sultan of Swat, George Herman Ruth, who, despite a career of .300 seasons, has faded into oblivion, certainly an ominous role model for the gifted but beleaguered Appel."

He noticed a book in the back of my car, They Call Me Gump by hockey goalie Gump Worsley, and he picked it up and said, "Look at this drivel that so-called major publishers continue to foist on an unsuspecting public. They Call Me Gump, indeed."

Howard had me laughing out loud now, but the show wasn't over. Which writers were in camp? he wanted to know.

"Well, there's Jim Ogle from the Star-Ledger—"

"Jim Ogle! That inane drone! Does he still sit there in the corner of the press box wearing his Yankee cap under the pretense of being anything less than a Yankee fan?! Has he yet been formally placed on the team payroll?"

I was so entertained by Howard that I couldn't resist having my picture taken with him when we got to camp.

What a swagger he had as he strolled around with his yellow ABC

A baseball card pose at seven with my trusty Yankees shirt and cap.

High school graduation, 1966, with Mom, Dad, and my brother, Norm.

I love this photo—the upper deck is the new Yankee Stadium, but the old posts in the lower boxes and mezzanine are still standing. This shot was taken on December 17, 1974, sixteen months before reconstruction concluded. LOUIS REQUENA

Mike Burke greets Casey Stengel during his return to Yankee Stadium in 1970. I'm on the left. ERNIE SISTO

New Year's Eve, 1974—
the night we signed Catfish Hunter.
LOUIS REQUENA

Fritz Peterson and Mike Kekich take
turns conking me on the head
(before they got into more serious
swapping) at spring training in 1970.
MICHAEL GROSSBARDT

Conferring with Thurman Munson about his autobiography in 1977. In his honor,
that locker remains unused to this day.   LOUIS REQUENA

A night on the town, and Billy Martin already looks like he's over the edge. Bottom row, left to right: batting practice pitcher Tony Ferrara, Yogi Berra, Elston Howard, George Steinbrenner. Top row, left to right: Gabe Paul, Billy, me, and the restaurateur, who has probably been wondering all these years who the guy next to him is.

It would be hard to root against the Mets after this kind gesture in 1975. DENNIS BURKE

My man King Kelly. His biography was my favorite research and writing project. MILO STEWART JR.

Billie Jean King and me during my World Team Tennis days, 1978. JOHN WOODWARD

Managing the National League old timers team in Buffalo in 1990, with my ace reliever, Tom Seaver.

A press event with Derek Jeter and artist Peter Max in 1997. JIM SULLEY

Running a press conference for the Boys & Girls Clubs of America with
Ken Griffey Jr. in 1999.

With Bob Fishel in Ft. Lauderdale—my first spring training, 1970.
MICHAEL GROSSBARDT

Watching from the Yankee Stadium press box in 1972, I'm upset at the call. Bob Fishel is on the phone telling Lee MacPhail how it looked on the replay. MICHAEL GROSSBARDT

As a consultant on the HBO film *61**, about the home run race between Roger Maris and Mickey Mantle, with director Billy Crystal, left, and executive producer Ross Greenburg.

My best projects have been Brian and Debbie Appel, seen here with my Dad.

jacket and his cigar and his wisecracks. Underneath all of this, we would come to learn, was a very insecure man who went crazy over the slightest criticism from even the most rural columnists, at a time when it was fashionable to take him on. It was, in fact, part of the *Monday Night Football* act, for he was bigger than the game itself. Tuesdays were generally spent critiquing Cosell from coast to coast.

I wouldn't say that I ever grew close to Howard, but he would call from time to time with some request or other, and, on at least a couple of occasions, I learned, spoke glowingly of my work to prospective employers.

Late in his life his insecurities got the better of him, and his distrust of people spilled over into a book that effectively ended his career. He found himself friendless, and, when his beloved wife, Emmy, passed away, he had an emptiness in life no man should ever face. I used to have lunch with a friend at the Friar's Club and see Howard seated at a corner table, dining alone, beginning to look frail, and certainly looking depressed about his fate. If any man had ever deliberately brought about this fate, it was Howard. But it was no less sad to see.

Well, ABC pulled off their Brinks truck feature, and, every day, demands were made on Hunter for interviews far beyond reasonable expectations. But Catfish was great; he did them all, and when he saw me approaching with my scraps of paper containing such requests, he would laugh and tell me to "get organized," but he would accommodate everyone.

The enormous focus on Hunter took all the pressure off Bonds and everyone else and created an easy camp. We had abandoned our beautiful beachfront hotel under the guise of economy, and were now residing in a second-rate motel on Federal Highway, but there was a feeling of great optimism in camp. The team had just missed winning in '74, and now we had added Hunter and Bonds. We were the favorites to win it all in '75.

Bonds was a terrific guy. If he expected more attention and found himself overshadowed by Hunter, he didn't complain. Compared to the Giants' camps, there was a much higher level of media interest than he had ever experienced, anyway.

One day Bonds lost his sunglasses. I didn't know if they were expensive, but he was unusually upset over it, so I drove to a nearby Eckerd Drug Store and bought a seven-dollar pair that looked like what I remembered he had. He was so appreciative that he bought me dinner and always brought up what a nice gesture I had made over the lost sunglasses.

One evening Blomberg got tipsy on his occasional one vodka gimlet, and Bonds literally carried him back to our dumpy motel and got him to bed. He had a nice way about him; he didn't make a big deal out of these little acts of team leadership, but it seemed we certainly had gotten our-selves a quality star.

Whitey and Mickey were our matinee-idol spring coaches. They had gone into the Hall of Fame together the summer before. Ed Arrigoni, who owned New York Bus Service, gave them a luxury bus to get them and their friends up to Cooperstown, and, from what I heard, it was the bus trip to end all bus trips. I was invited, but, because it was in midsea-son, I couldn't go. I helped Mick with his speech a little, reminding him to mention that he was named for a Hall of Famer—Mickey Cochrane, his dad's favorite player.

Whitey was still our regular-season pitching coach and worked hard with the young pitchers. We had our regular spring routines. Because he had a lot of friends in the harness-racing world, he would give us tips for the evening's races at Pompano Race Track, and, sure enough, he was usually right.

We would always take the "On the Way Up" instructional photos for the Yearbook and would always pose pitching prospects with Whitey—the master showing the students how it's done. Just as Michael Grossbardt would get ready to snap the photo, Whitey would spit on the baseball he was holding. The joke never seemed to get old.

Part of the reason for the easy camp was that there was no owner on the scene. George was still under suspension, and Gabe was running the show. Tyrant though Gabe was, he still liked his evenings free for dinner with his old baseball friends, so we were usually done by five. In the early weeks before the games, we might be done as early as two.

We still had our Gabe moments. I was seated in his office one day when a ticket taker came in to say that they had run out of tickets for the right field bleachers, with hundreds more fans still seeking admission. Our attendance had soared with the Hunter and Bonds arrivals.

"You ran out of tickets?" said Gabe. "What did you do?"

"We just let everyone in," said the daily hire, a local retiree who was delivering the news.

Gabe exploded. This had violated every tenet of ballpark operation he had ever held. In a rush of fury, he grabbed the stapler from his desk and flung it—at me! It hit my shoulder and crashed to the floor.

"What the hell?!" I said, but Gabe was on to the ticket taker, totally berating this poor old buzzard who had been hired for the day to work the bleacher gate. His bluster went on long enough that by the time he was through, my moment to protest had passed. All I said was, "You want your stapler back? Some other innocent victim may need his shoulder whacked before the end of the day."

He didn't appreciate the sarcasm, and he didn't apologize either.

I went back to my trailer and told Anne Mileo about the stapler incident. Poor Anne, our great PR secretary, who had had so many personal tragedies in her life . . . a stapler to the shoulder would not have made her top 200. She looked at me and listened to my tale of woe and my railing about Gabe and said, "Well, he's very clean, you know; I never knew someone who was as well scrubbed as Gabe is."

That pretty much ended the stapler story until I heard from Dave Weidler, our chief financial officer, that he too had been "stapled" in the shoulder over a similar incident during a spring training visit. Gabe, it turned out, was a serial staple hurler.

Gabe had little use for the accountants, anyway. One employee thought he had racked up enough years to qualify for a better raise. So he made an appointment to discuss it with Gabe.

Gabe heard him out and then said, "Vic, pencil pushers like you are a dime a dozen. Be thankful for what you've got."

You would have expected Catfish Hunter to be our Opening Day pitcher, but we opened in Cleveland, so Hunter was held back for our home opener. This was just as well, because that particular Opening Day in Cleveland was historic and would have far overshadowed anything we were doing.

It was the debut of Frank Robinson, the new player-manager of the Indians and, at long last, the first black manager in the major leagues.

Frank had been the logical candidate for this honor for some years. He had done all you had to do, even as a player, such as managing winter ball in Puerto Rico. He was testy, not the easiest guy to get along with, but he was a smart baseball man and, of course, a great player. Respect did not automatically come with that—a number of his players never accepted him—but the time for a black manager was long overdue, and, to the credit of Cleveland owner Ted Bonda, the time had finally come.

Bowie Kuhn played a big role in finally bringing this about. Jackie Robinson had pushed Kuhn hard on the issue. Jackie had sat with Kuhn in Cincinnati at the 1972 World Series, nearly blind, agreeing to participate in a 25th anniversary salute to his breaking the color line, as long as Kuhn pledged to lobby hard for blacks in management. And true to his word, Kuhn did just that.

Bonda was finally the guy who made it happen. Kuhn was present, along with Rachel Robinson, Jackie's beautiful and gracious widow, lending her blessing and, in a way, Jackie's. Jackie had died of diabetes just days after the '72 Series.

There was a press conference before the game, with Frank, Rachel, Kuhn, and Bonda all present, and one writer asked Bonda if Kuhn had played any role in bringing this about. If so, this would be one of the finest hours of the Kuhn administration.

"No, not at all," said Bonda.

Kuhn went to him later and said, "Frankly, Ted, I was a little surprised by your answer, after all the conversations we have had."

"Oh, commissioner," he replied, "I just didn't want to embarrass you."

The rain was falling hard on this day in miserable Municipal Stadium, but 56,715 fans were on hand for history. I was really glad that the Yankees were—by the luck of the draw—the opposing team, so that I could witness it.

Cleveland was the last ballpark in which photographers were allowed on the field while the game was going on, and, when Robinson came to bat in the first inning, the scene was utter madness. There were 20 photographers hovering within 20 feet of the batter's box, like a scene from some old Babe Ruth newsreel. In most parks, this practice had ended with the advent of long camera lenses, "Big Berthas," but they went back some 25 years!

Robinson was the designated hitter that afternoon, because he was one of the last playing managers baseball would see (Joe Torre with the '77 Mets and Pete Rose with the Reds until his banishment in '85 were the last).

Robinson was batting against our Doc Medich, and, on a 2-2 pitch, damned if he didn't line a home run to left that absolutely turned the place into bedlam. Of all of the emotional events I have witnessed in person, this had to rank among the greatest. It was absolutely perfect that he would do that at that moment, and, a year later, when Cleveland fans joined others around the country in selecting the "greatest moment in team history," Robinson's home run was the winner.

We lost the game 5–3, and it seemed only right and proper for it to end that way.

We had only 26,000 on hand for our Catfish opener, and a huge press corps turned out to see him lose 5–3 to Mickey Lolich. He then lost his next two starts, and suddenly he was 0–3 and everyone was wondering if we had made the blunder of the century, pouring millions into a has-been.

And in truth, because pitchers are human, and humans are fallible, it was certainly possible that he was not going to have a season like the one he had had in Oakland when he won the Cy Young Award in '74. (The

Yankees would relive this anxiety with Roger Clemens in 1999.)

But Catfish was never worried, not for a second. He knew that losses were part of baseball, and they didn't bother him a bit. He was famous for being a home run pitcher, and he had a way of admiring them and then moving on to the next batter.

In spring training of '75, in fact, he gave up a home run to Dave Kingman that those of us who were there in Ft. Lauderdale still talk about. There is no way of knowing how far it went; Kingman sent it high and deep into the black sky and no one ever saw it come down. We guessed that it went over 500 feet—Catfish thought 600—but the important thing was, he could tip his cap to Kingman and get the next guy to ground out.

Catfish didn't win his first game until April 27, when he beat the Brewers 10–1 before 42,000 at Shea. Johnny Carson had already started telling Hunter jokes at 0–3, but this win not only ended that, it set him up for a remarkable season in which he went 23–14 (23–11 after the bad start), hurling 328 innings and 30 complete games in 39 starts. By today's standards, these read like stats from the turn of the century. Some thought the Yankees were trying too hard to get their money's worth in the first year of his five-year deal. But Hunter knew his arm better than anyone, and people trusted his ability to say "enough" if he had to leave a game.

Of greater concern, at least to me, was a deal Gabe made in April when he decided we should all have matching luggage. He made a deal to get everyone a "Yankee trunk"—not a suitcase, but a hard-sided, heavily reinforced foot locker like the kind you send kids to camp with. It was about 14 inches wide and weighed about 20 pounds empty. When I would see Hunter carrying this awkward piece of luggage with his right arm, even from his car to the stadium, I wanted to call security. This was nuts. But we went through the whole season with these monsters, even when the handles would break and they had to be carried by barely holding on to the broken handle in the most awkward of positions. Gabe apparently had found a bargain.

The season was not going well on the field. We were 12–20 and in sixth place, despite all the expectations, when the disabled list came calling. And it was calling me.

I had been fighting a toothache that wouldn't go away, and there were days I would lie out in the training room with ice on my cheek, almost doubled over in pain. On Patriot's Day in Boston, Gene Monahan managed to find a dentist for me to help relieve the suffering, but it wasn't really going away.

Finally, I found a dentist with a panoramic x-ray machine that could view the entire mandible. And sure enough, he found a tumor the size of a quarter in my lower-right jaw. He thought it had been "years in the making." It had eaten through the jawbone until the bone itself was barely a quarter-inch thick.

When this hits you, when words like *cancer* and *biopsy* and *tumor* start getting thrown at you, the subsequent events become a blur. You turn your fate over to the professionals and hope for the best.

The first thing was a biopsy in the dentist's office. He said that to save time I could bring the specimen to the lab myself, rather than having it mailed. So, there I was, driving along the Long Island Expressway with a little tube containing my tissue sample in the passenger seat, knowing that life or death might be in that little package. A very odd feeling.

The tumor, fortunately, was benign. I had what is called a giant cell lesion, but I needed surgery, in which they would break what was left of my jaw to remove the tumor. Then, in a procedure so unusual at the time that it was written up in medical journals, bone marrow would be taken from my own hip and grafted into my jaw to rebuild it.

Although I was not facing cancer, a lot could have gone wrong with this surgery. They might have had to reach the tumor from the outside, leaving me with a badly scarred face. I might have lost motor neurons, which could have caused the right side of my face to permanently droop. The procedure on my hip could have left me with a permanent limp.

But, because of the skilled work of my surgeons, Dr. Bert Blum and Dr. David Schwartz, none of that happened. All it left me with was a loss of sensory nerves in one section of my jaw, so that if I cut myself shaving, I don't feel it. Otherwise, it was a brilliant piece of surgery.

David Schwartz was more than repaid when I took him as my guest to Shea Stadium for the sixth game of the 1986 World Series. You may have heard of Bill Buckner. We were there.

I was in the hospital for a week, then sent home to my parents for recovery, because I was in need of assistance. It was like being a kid again, sitting there watching *I Love Lucy* reruns. My jaw was wired shut; a tooth had been pulled simply to create a space for a straw to deliver liquids to me. I lost 20 pounds over the next six weeks, but slowly began to recover. I learned to speak with my jaw wired and could have had an alternative career in ventriloquism had the Yankees not taken me back.

As it was, however, the Yankees were great. I was flooded with cards and flowers and get-well wishes from players, employees, other teams, and even from George Steinbrenner. The Mets put good wishes up on their Shea scoreboard and sent me the photo. I even discovered that there were fans that cared about the Yankees' PR director, and I got messages from them! In fact, I was considered something of a minor celebrity while I was hospitalized, and one older doctor came into my room one day and gave me an autographed baseball from the 1933 Yankees, which had been in his family for years. I wanted to protest and tell him, "No, don't do this, it's too valuable," but I couldn't speak, and he patted me on the head and left.

I went back to work after three weeks, still wired but at least able to drive. Catfish immediately began imitating my speech and was doing a great Lou Gehrig impression of "Today . . . today . . . I consider myself . . . self . . . the luckiest sonofabitch . . ." with his teeth clenched together. Mickey Morabito, my assistant without business cards, had carried on brilliantly in my absence.

Doc Medich was interested in every aspect of the surgery, of course, but his need for graphic description required more than I wanted to relive. (When Whitey Ford had heart problems, Doc calmly described for him how, in heart surgery, they saw open your rib cage to get to the heart . . . just what Whitey needed to hear.)

My very first day back, Gabe called me. Not to welcome me back, but to say he expected me to be at a luncheon in Queens at which Mrs. Babe Ruth was being honored. I thought he was kidding, but he wasn't. It was too much for the first day, but off I went, unable to eat, of course, but, dutiful employee that I was, representing the Yankees proudly.

The wires were finally cut in late June, and I couldn't wait to bite into a Quarter Pounder at McDonald's. I went with Bill Kane and Mickey Morabito for this grand event, only to discover that my muscles had atrophied during the past six weeks, and I couldn't open my jaw wide enough to get a Quarter Pounder in. It would take time, but eventually I healed completely.

The summer wasn't going well. Expectations had been raised, and we weren't delivering. Bonds was playing hard but frequently getting hurt. Just when he got into a groove and was carrying the team, *bang*, he ran into a wall at Comiskey Park and we lost him. Bobby Bonds was a helluva player, and his reputation was only enhanced in New York because he played hurt and still put up numbers. He was going to have a 30-30 season for us despite being hurt, but losing him effectively killed what little momentum was building.

In early July I sent out invitations to our Old Timers Day on August 2. Gabe had left the guest list pretty much up to me but told me not to invite guys who were playing or coaching on other teams.

"There are too many of these games now; too many requests to give guys days off. Don't invite these people."

That made sense, and I abided by it. Then, on July 7, the Texas Rangers came to town, and Mickey Rendine, our visiting clubhouse attendant, sent word that Billy Martin wanted to see me.

Billy was the Rangers' manager, but, even now, 18 years removed from his Yankee playing days, he was a Yankee at heart. One spring he was off on a day of fishing with his boss, Bob Short, as well as with Bob Fishel and some Yankee people. And right in front of his Texas Ranger boss, he said to Fishel, "I'll always be a Yankee; I wear the team on my sleeve."

His annual invitations to Old Timers Days—to wear the uniform again, to be with Mickey and Whitey and the guys—were important to his summer. Now he had heard that he wasn't invited, and he was told that Appel made up the guest list.

It was our first conversation in years; the last time we'd spoken he had a radio job after being fired by Minnesota, and showed up in spring training looking very out of place with his tape recorder.

"Is this true?" he asked. "I'm not invited to Old Timers Day?"

I explained that it was Gabe's feeling that we were asking too many people to leave their clubs, and that there were so many Old Timers Days now, and . . .

"But, Marty," he interrupted, "you don't know how much this means to me; I've got to be there."

I was surprised by his passion, and I agreed to discuss it with Gabe. I was about to shake hands and leave when Billy said, "And how about Charlie Silvera here?"

His coach, Silvera, had been Yogi's backup in the early '50s. We wouldn't sell one extra ticket with Silvera on the bill, but Billy was always loyal to his friends, and he got in the request for Charlie. I said I'd mention that to Gabe, too.

Gabe wanted as little to do with these old-timers matters as possible. In his first year as our team president, he had followed the tradition that went back to Topping and Webb and to Mike Burke and had stood on the field to greet each returning player.

Wouldn't you know it, that first year, the very first player was Ralph Terry. You always introduced the younger players in good shape first, because they could stand out there in the sun longer. Terry, now a pro golfer, was first, and he shook Gabe's hand and lined up on the baseline.

That would be Gabe's last year on the field. It turned out that he had once really screwed Terry when he had him in Cleveland. If Ralph made so many starts, he would get a bonus. He was having a good year, but when he was one start short of the bonus, he didn't start again for the final month of the season. Gabe had pulled the plug on him to save money. It was a good thing that Terry didn't slug Gabe.

It turned out that there were just too many old timers with stories like this, so Gabe realized he was better off watching the festivities from his office.

I told him about Martin, and he just sort of waved me off, saying, "I told you no!"

So I went back to the visitors' clubhouse and told Billy that he—and Charlie Silvera—should not plan on being with us on August 2. He was pissed, but he knew it didn't come from me.

On July 21, the Rangers fired him. He had been fired in Minnesota and Detroit before, so these things could hardly catch him by surprise anymore. This time he'd punched out Burt Hawkins, the Rangers' traveling secretary.

With the Yankees foundering, with Martin free, and with the assumption that Bill Virdon was not going to be Joe McCarthy, the media immediately began a "Billy Watch."

This was very painful for those of us who liked Virdon. The team refused to catch fire, and, with each loss, even if it were followed by a win, the speculation had it that Virdon was cooked.

In late July, Gabe gathered up his little overnight kit, complete with miniature English Leather shaving cream canisters he had made me find for him, and prepared for a trip.

Jimmy Hoffa had disappeared that week, and Gabe said to me, "If anyone notices that I'm gone, tell them I went fishing with Jimmy Hoffa." Then he realized that Hoffa might be dead, so he said, "No, never mind—don't say that; don't say anything."

He was going to Colorado, where, he was told, Billy had retreated after his firing to go hunting with his current in-laws. Gabe's job was to find him. We can only imagine who gave the orders.

Gabe would not like Billy Martin as manager. Gabe liked his managers subservient, and "subservient" was not one of the qualities listed on the back of Billy's baseball card.

We played an exhibition game at Syracuse on Thursday evening, July 31, and then came home to open a weekend series with the Indians, with Saturday being Old Timers Day.

Friday afternoon, Gabe called me in and told me that Virdon was going to be fired after the game that night and that we would announce Billy Martin as manager the next morning.

He told me matter-of-factly and without much pleasure.

My first thought was the overwhelming work ahead of me—running the old-timers program as well as a major press conference. I asked Gabe if he'd mind if I took a hotel room across the street from LaGuardia (five minutes from Shea) on Friday night, and, to my surprise, he said I could.

On Friday before the game, the press was abuzz with rumors, and film crews from the New York TV stations filled Virdon's office to ask him, with no delicacy, "Are you being fired?"

And poor Bill would answer, "If I am, no one has said anything to me." Which is the way it always works in baseball.

Hunter beat the Indians on Friday night for his 13th win, and Virdon returned to his small office that was filled with media. Phil Pepe took me aside and said, "Oh, this is terrible; how can they do this to the man?", referring to his journalism colleagues.

Then, in front of everyone, Virdon's phone rang. He answered it and then said to the press, "Will you excuse me?"

He dressed and walked across the street, under the train tracks that ran above Roosevelt Ave., to Gabe's office. And there, Gabe fired him.

Bill came into Shea early Saturday, cleaned out his things, and left before 9 A.M. No one really said goodbye, not even his players.

Back at the office, I went to see Gabe around 9:30, and there was Billy, smoking a pipe, dressed in western wear. He greeted me by saying, "I told you I'd be here for Old Timers Day!"

This had to be one of the greatest days of Billy's life. Unceremoniously traded by the Yankees in 1957 after a fight at the Copa during his birthday celebration, he had been labeled a "bad influence" on Mantle and others and was sent packing. He was never as good a player for the rest of his career. The Yankees inspired him to stretch his abilities. He wore a Yankee uniform the way a frat brother wears his frat jacket—with utmost pride. For 18 years he had been wandering in baseball exile, waiting to come home.

He was not going to come home under Topping and Webb and Weiss, and then the CBS and MacPhail years had locked Ralph Houk up, so the exile continued. Now Steinbrenner, free of any of 1957's baggage, could hire a guy that he felt was the missing ingredient in a promising but underachieving team.

My press release written, arrangements for the press conference made, I now raced over to Shea to handle Old Timers Day. I greeted DiMaggio nice and early. He was, as always, impeccably dressed in an expensive suit; more handsome, it seemed, with each succeeding year.

I walked with Joe from the office entrance to the Yankee clubhouse.

"I guess you've heard what's happening here today," I said to him.

"If the morning papers are right, you're going to have a new manager?" he said.

"Yes," I answered, "Billy Martin."

Joe rolled his eyes. I saw at once that the announcement did not have his blessing. Joe, I had been told, was never really a Martin fan, although Billy presented himself as one of Joe's buddies. It seems that when Joe was around to do pre- and postgame shows at Yankee Stadium shortly after he retired as a player, brash Billy had hung a nude photo of Marilyn Monroe in his locker and would bump and grind toward the photo as Joe passed. Billy must have thought it was ballplayer humor, the kind of thing that went on all the time. He, of course, misread Joe on this issue; Joe's sensitivity about Marilyn became legendary. This episode, taking place when they were first dating, was unacceptable to Joe, and he would remain fairly aloof toward Martin. It wasn't a major feud, and he might pose with him for photos, but it became clear that day that Billy had crossed the line.

"Strange things are happening," DiMaggio said to me as we took our walk.

We got through Old Timers Day and we got through the press conference, and then Billy began his tenure with a 5–3 win. In fact, we won four of our first five games, and a new style was evident at once. It was "Billy Ball," something that wasn't named until he later managed Oakland, but here it was, with veteran slowpokes like Graig Nettles suddenly stealing bases, with a little more daring in our offense.

It was clear at once that Billy liked some guys and hated others. There weren't many in between. He hated Larry Gura, our quiet left-hander, because he used to see Gura going off with a tennis racket, and, to Billy, tennis was a sissy sport that real men didn't play. Our broadcaster Bill White, whom no one ever mistook for a sissy, was a tennis player too. He got on Billy's list.

Rich Coggins, a reserve outfielder we had picked up from the Orioles, wore an odd outer garment that wasn't quite a dress but, on the other hand, didn't have pant legs either. It was some form of African garb, but, to Billy, he was a major leaguer in a dress, and Coggins immediately went on the "get rid of this guy" list.

Billy pumped me about the writers: Who was covering the team? Were they "rippers?" Could he win favor with them if he gave them a cigar?

I asked Billy how he felt about my calling the dugout to ask about a lineup change that seemed confusing.

"Marty, call anytime. I know you have a job to do, just like we all do.

Don't hesitate to call, even during the game."

A few weeks later we did have a moment that required just such a call. Gene Monahan answered the phone and handed it to Billy.

"Who's this?" he kept repeating.

"It's Marty, Marty Appel, in the press box . . . did Nettles leave because he was injured?"

"Don't ever call me during a game again! Can't you see we're busy down here?!"

He later apologized and said, Forget about it, call again. But it was clear that the man was so intense during a game that anything could make him snap. I never called and asked for him again. I got all my questions answered by Monahan.

New managers often bring a brief spurt of success to a team, but, in the end, this was a doomed season. We were going to finish third with or without Billy, and all he could do was lay the groundwork for '76. "Wait until you see this team after I have them for a spring training," he told me.

We won 30 and lost 26 under Billy and finished the year six games over .500. We were 12 behind the Red Sox, who were headed for their incredible World Series against Cincinnati.

A lot of people came to think that baseball's popularity began to grow again in the wake of the excitement of the '75 Series, which included the famous Carlton Fisk home run and the play of the great Big Red Machine.

While this may have been true, the resurgence of the game would also coincide with the return to championship form of the 1976 Yankees. Baseball has always been strongest with a strong Yankee team, and that is what we were about to put together during a remarkable offseason.

When Joe DiMaggio joined the Yankees in the '30s, as a teammate of Lou Gehrig, he was quite assimilated but still quite ethnic, a first-generation Italian American and happy to pose for photographers hoisting a huge forkful of spaghetti to his mouth.

He became a handsome, well-dressed, classy fellow, who did not especially fit in with his more rough-and-tumble teammates. Tommy Henrich, who played alongside him in the outfield for years, claimed to have never had dinner with him. Henrich—an easy, happy, wonderful guy—used to have trouble just shaking hands with Joe at Old Timers Day. "Oh, you can't just walk up to him," Tommy said. "You have to *approach* him!" And Tommy would do an impression of a man of great hauteur receiving a lesser.

Phil Rizzuto was like his ward, totally in awe throughout his career. Rizzuto says he used to find himself just watching DiMaggio shave! (Rizzuto also met his wife, Cora, through the happy coincidence of filling in for DiMaggio at an appearance.)

For many years, Joe enjoyed the friendship and hospitality of the noted memorabilia collector Barry Halper. Barry and his wife, Sharon, were sensational hosts in a beautiful home in New Jersey. Joe felt comfortable there; he could relax, he could avoid Manhattan street gawkers, he didn't have to order room service. He accommodated Barry's thirst for autographs and storytelling and did genuinely like Barry, which is not hard to do.

Barry also owned a piece of a trading-card company, Score, which was ultimately absorbed into a larger company, Pinnacle Brands. One year, Pinnacle offered as a contest prize a tour of Barry's collection. What's more, the tour would be hosted by not only Barry but DiMaggio. Yes, Barry had talked Joe into participating.

Pinnacle, not one to miss a great PR opportunity, naturally arranged for a photographer to capture the lucky winners on their grand tour. The photos would run in hobby magazines and enhance its image. But, when the photographer arrived, Joe was startled.

"You didn't say anything about press," he said to Barry.

"But, Joe, this isn't really press, this isn't an interview; it's just some photographs with the winners," explained a mortified Halper.

DiMaggio never again visited the Halper home and went years without speaking to Barry. And like so many before him, Barry was crushed. He had seen Joe at his worst but would, of course, do anything to have his friendship back.

In my early fan-mail days with the Yankees, I was given "dugout duty" on Old Timers Day, and so, there I was in '68, right in the Yankee dugout next to Joe as he awaited his introduction. It had been 17 years since he retired, but he was still an athlete, still in wonderful condition, and still able to swing a bat and look great doing it. Within a few years, though, he knew he didn't look quite as good, so he retired from taking swings. And a few years after that, he abandoned donning a uniform. Just as he had walked away in 1951 when he felt his game slipping, he always knew when the time was right to shed the next layer of his public persona. Perhaps no one has ever had such a good eye for his own image. (Or, with only 369 strikeouts in 13 years, such a good eye, period!)

With all the esteem in which he was held, no one held him in higher esteem than Italian Americans did. My Yankee secretary, Anne Mileo, would blush like a schoolgirl in his presence and would always make sure she was at the door when he was due. One of our salesmen at the time, Vince Natrella, was active in an organization called the Sons of Italy. He told a story about approaching Joe (he, unlike Henrich, would just walk right up) and saying, "Joe, we'd like the Sons of Italy to have a DiMaggio Day here—we'll sell a lot of tickets." According to Natrella, Joe's response was, "They're not big enough."

When I became PR director at the Yankees, my name was on the Old Timers Day invitation and instructions sent to all guests. DiMaggio, it happened, would then become a regular caller as the day approached.

"Marty?" he'd say, as I picked up the phone. "It's Joe. Say, any chance you could leave a couple of tickets for this cab driver I had today—if it's a problem, just say so!"

"Problem? For you? Don't be ridiculous," I'd say, and write up the order. My hand shook a little. "Call anytime, Joe."

Because DiMaggio didn't get paid for coming to Old Timers Day, and because he accounted for a lot of the tickets we sold, yes, we could handle some freebies for him.

A few hours later the phone would ring again, and Anne would say excitedly, "Marty, it's *him*!"

"Hi, Joe."

"Marty, how are you, buddy? Any chance you could help me out here? I sort of promised a pair of tickets for the doorman here at the Americana, and . . . well, you know, if it's a problem, I understand."

Bang, two more. Problem? For an excuse to talk to my buddy Joe?

Now it was Old Timers Day itself. Saturday. Joe had been in town about four days, and we had done a brisk free-ticket business, probably about 12 pairs. That was 12 conversations, though, and well worth it. It had become the Joe and Marty Show.

In old Yankee Stadium, the players entered on the first base side, walking past Mahoney, the old doorman, and through an interior passage, where we would set up a table to check them in and handle special needs. Two of us sat at the table while other Yankee employees came and went, many timing their walk-bys to when DiMaggio might be expected.

After a week of phone chats, I was particularly looking forward to his arrival. Perhaps some last-minute ticket needs? Perhaps he needed to cash a check? Speed up his expense account? Perhaps he wanted to take me out to Toots Shor after the game?

It was 11 A.M. He was here. Perfect business suit, perfect stride, all business. I rose from my seat. "Joe," I said, extending my hand, smiling broadly. "It's me, Marty Appel."

He just kept walking. No smile, no handshake, no recognition.

His needs were satisfied.

It was time to suit up and be Joe DiMaggio, to give it that smart, double-handed wave as he emerged from the dugout, to dress, and to leave. Appel was part of the Tuesday-through-Friday "things to do today." This was Saturday.

Was I shattered? For a moment, maybe. But I smiled anyway. I would still hope he would remember my name the next time. I was as bad as the rest of them.

11

OSCAR'S
HAIRCUT

The start of what would prove to be a whirlwind period in my life—and in the life of the Yankee franchise—occurred in the summer of 1975, when Bowie Kuhn was re-elected commissioner for a second term. It was thought that one vote he could hardly count on would be the Yankees' vote, since their principal owner had been chucked out of the game by you-know-who.

But at the Major League Baseball meeting in Milwaukee to decide Kuhn's future, Patrick Cunningham, a Bronx politician designated to represent the Yankees, voted yes under Steinbrenner's directive, and that proved to be a key vote in securing Kuhn's return.

The next day, in the hotel restaurant at Inn of the Six Flags in Arlington, Texas, I was having lunch with a group of sportswriters when none other than George Steinbrenner himself pulled up a chair.

George loved the Inn of the Six Flags; loved to host Texas-sized barbecues on the patio outside the main house. This was, however, one tough hotel in the summer. It had a multi-building layout, and, with temperatures well into the hundreds each day, the walk from our rooms to the restaurant was a killer. I walked with Whitey Ford one day to a late breakfast; when we got to the restaurant, he announced that he would be right back—he was going to return to his room for a shower and then try again.

Having George sidle up to our table was a bit of a shock. I hadn't had any direct contact with him since the winter. I was sure he spoke with Gabe, but, as for the rest of us, he seemed to be following the law of the suspension by the book.

Murray Chass of the *Times* seized the moment.

"Why did you vote to retain Bowie?" he asked. He had predicted that the Yankee vote would be a goner.

George leaned forward to bring us all into his confidence.

"You're gonna see some changes over in that office," he said. "Big changes. You know how the American League has always been treated as second fiddle by the commissioner's office? Well, all that is over. We were assured those days are gone."

What an odd announcement. It was true that at Major League Baseball meetings, the American League was considered the league with the oddball owners—the Finleys, the Veecks, the Bob Shorts, the Steinbrenners. The National League, the older league, would never put those sorts into their company. They were the league of Wrigley and O'Malley and Busch and Payson—rock-solid citizens, no lunacy, no dancing on the roof of the dugout after a World Series win. (Somehow, Ted Turner had shown up in the wrong league.) But as for the commissioner's office somehow treating one league differently than another—well, that was a stretch. Kuhn did listen to Walter O'Malley more than to any other owner, but he unabashedly attributed that to O'Malley's genius, not to any prejudice favoring the "senior circuit," for which he had once been legal counsel.

Did we ever truly see George's prophecy materialize? Not really. But, for him, it was enough to move the Yankees into the "yes" column.

Or had there been a deal?

That was immediately on Chass's mind.

"Watch," he told me. "That suspension is going to be lifted early."

Soon after the '75 season ended, Joe Garagiola Jr., our in-house lawyer, was told to accompany me to a law office in Manhattan to "begin working on the necessary briefs to apply for early return from the suspension."

Joe could have been making three times his salary starting out at a major law firm, but baseball was in his blood, and he loved this opportunity. He was, of course, the son of Joe Garagiola, former catcher–turned–American wit and one of America's most beloved television personalities, on the NBC baseball telecasts and the *Today* show.

Joe Jr. and I had quickly become very close friends. We were born two years apart—he on August 6, 1950, me on August 7, 1948. As a Notre Dame undergraduate, he had worked as my intern in the summer of '72, helping out in the PR department. After graduating from Georgetown law school, he was hired to be the first in-house counsel the Yankees ever employed. He was assigned to share an office in Flushing with Jimmy Esposito, our head groundskeeper. There was one desk. If you asked Joe for a recent deposition to review, he might have to rummage among Jimmy's hammers and screwdrivers to find it. Because he was blessed with his father's sense of humor, matters like this brought no outrage from Joe; it only gave him great material to work with when we drove to work together from our homes near each other in Westchester. We both loved Bob and Ray on the radio, we both hid Hydrox cookies in our desks, and we didn't think it at all odd to spend a wintry weekend running all the World Series highlight movies from 1943 to the present during a big baseball film fest in his father's Scarsdale basement.

So, here we were, headed down to Park Avenue for after-hours meetings with the lawyers, drafting all sorts of good-citizen reports to help bring George back early.

"You know," Joe offered one day during the ride, "here we are, helping on this, and this may hardly be in our own best interests."

We both laughed at life's ironies. The George Steinbrenner who had left in '74 gave a lot of indications that he was going to be one tough cookie whenever he returned. But, here we were, dutifully helping to speed that return.

Just before we left for the winter meetings, we made a truly joyous announcement regarding our coaching staff.

Yogi Berra was coming home. Fired by the Mets as their manager the previous summer, he was now returning to the team that had unceremoniously canned him after he won the '64 pennant. It was beautiful, really, to think that this wonderful man could have a job with either one of the New York teams, with only a scant different in his commute from Montclair, New Jersey.

"Two tolls to get to Shea," he noted. "This is better."

Everybody liked Yogi, whether they thought he was a good manager or not. No one doubted that he had an IQ of 200 when it came to baseball—he was born to excel at the game. According to Yogi, his older brothers were better players, but they had to work during the Depression. It was they who convinced their father to let "Lawdie" try pro baseball.

All that resulted in was a Hall of Fame career with more World Series records than anyone. Yogi won three MVP Awards, earned an incredible 39 rings as player, coach, and manager for All-Star Games and World Series, and was Casey Stengel's unofficial "assistant manager" during Stengel's full run at the helm.

And although some laughed at Yogi's twists of the language, everyone who knew him knew that (1) somewhere in there he always made sense, and (2) he was always right. He was also a warm, honorable, decent human being with strong moral convictions. It was truly a great day when we welcomed him back to Yankee pinstripes.

"What's your phone number?" he asked me after his press conference ended. "You know, the one where you pick up yourself."

"271-2818," I told him. "Call anytime."

And he did. Every day, that whole winter.

Anne would buzz me.

"Yogi on eighteen," she'd say.

"Hey, I thought you answered this yourself."

"Only if I'm not on another call, Yogi. And if I am, I hang up and talk to you."

Then he would get to the point.

"So, what's new? Whadya hear? Any rumors? Any gossip?"

So the Yogster liked rumors and gossip! And I made a point of jotting down all that I heard, big and small, so that I'd have stuff to share with him when he made his daily call.

It was my own form of public service to keep this great American treasure entertained.

The winter meetings were days away when a big cocktail party was scheduled in Manhattan by our broadcast-rights holders to woo prospective advertisers for the coming season. They asked for our help in providing a ballplayer for the event, and Gabe wasted no time in asking Bobby Bonds to attend.

Bobby was a class act and would be perfect in this setting. He had given us a great season in '75, despite playing hurt, and was still very much the most threatening member of our offense.

True to his word, Bobby showed up early, posed for photos with everyone, signed autographs long after things had broken up, and was just a great ambassador for the team. He had really come to like the Yankees after his shock at being traded by the Giants. He was looking forward to the return to Yankee Stadium.

We were now off for the winter meetings, which in those days were hotbeds of trades and created a flurry of excitement for baseball. The '75 winter meetings were in Hollywood, Florida, a welcome change from New Orleans the year before, where my hotel was directly across from a department store that played *Silver Bells* over and over and over until I thought I would jump off the roof.

Monday, Tuesday, and Wednesday passed, and not a single trade was announced. The press was hungry for news, and the lack of any was very unusual.

On Thursday, Gabe called me to his room. "We have a trade," he said. We'd break the ice.

We were trading Bonds.

I had given up showing shock or surprise with Gabe, although this one tested that principle. He had just made Bonds appear before our advertisers—for free—a few days before! He had to have been shopping him around!

"Who did we get?" I inquired, my pen now scribbling notes to myself. I made a mental note not to say what a good guy I thought Bonds was.

"We got Mickey Rivers and Ed Figueroa from the Angels," he told me. "It's a steal."

I have to admit that I didn't think so at first, and, as usual, I was more focused on my personal regard for Bonds and the shock this would give him.

I went to the pressroom with Tom Seeberg, the Angels' PR man, and we rounded up the writers and headed for the mike.

I spoke first.

"The New York Yankees have today obtained outfielder Mickey Rivers and pitcher Ed Figueroa from the California Angels for outfielder Bobby Bonds."

A gasp went up from the room. Bonds and Hunter were still our poster boys. One year and out. Bonds would be the greatest Yankee to never play in Yankee Stadium. It was a shock.

It was also a helluva deal. In Rivers, we got the quintessential leadoff man—a base stealer the likes of which the Yankee franchise had never known. He was a perfect player for Billy Martin, and, like Oscar Gamble, a wonderfully likeable guy, if just a bit eccentric. Mickey was not going to make them forget Mickey Mantle, but he was going to be an impact player for this team.

Figueroa, a righthander who spoke little English, had spent eight years toiling in the minors before getting his break, and before he was through with the Yankees he would become the first Puerto Rican to ever win 20 games in a season in the big leagues. Eddie proved popular with fans, but the language barrier kept those of us in management from getting closer to him. I wish I had learned Spanish along the way, particularly with the ascent of Latin players into the big leagues.

Years after his retirement, Ed wrote a book called *Yankee Stranger*, detailing the separation he felt from the organization despite being a 20-game winner.

The writers all hurried back to the pressroom to file their Bonds stories, with Gabe holding court and explaining the deal, as he had so many times over the years at winter meetings. But then he uncharacteristically excused himself and summoned me upstairs with a serious wave.

Gabe's gestures were always dramatic. No one was better at getting a cab in New York than he was. No cab driver could ever ignore his whistle or dare run him over as he stepped into traffic. He could poke you in the chest when he was making a point—hard enough that Bill Kane once threatened to punch him if he didn't knock it off.

The two of us retreated to his suite and were joined by Billy Martin.

"We've got another one," he said. "Get this written up and let's announce it in an hour. We're sending Doc Medich to the Pirates for Dock Ellis, Ken Brett, and one of their kid infielders, Willie Randolph."

Well, for winter meetings that had been moving slowly, the Yankees were grabbing all the headlines now. And what was going on here, besides making some great trades, was that we were stealing the back pages away from the Mets.

I always hated the trite nickname of "Doc" for George Medich, our med student in pinstripes. In Dock Ellis, however, we were getting a real Dock—for that was his given name. He was a controversial righthander who had been in the Pirates' rotation for eight years and had talked himself into starting the 1971 All-Star Game by announcing, "No way are they going to let me start; no way they let two brothers start," the other being Vida Blue. He liked to cause outrage, but, when you got to know him, you knew there was a good heart and a sharp mind at work in there.

Dock had a daughter named Shangaleza Talwange Ellis, wore dashikis, and was living the Afrocentric experience to the hilt. These were absolutely not the Yankees of the Ed Barrow and George Weiss days.

On television that night, back in New York, we were hammered over this deal. Tom McDonald on channel 5 said, "And can you believe this? The Yankees give up Doc Medich for Dock Ellis and Ken Brett? What were they thinking?"

What they—or Gabe Paul—were thinking was about the throw-in infielder, Willie Randolph. This was the real key to the deal and a credit to our scouting department and to Gabe's wily trading skills. He had positioned this as Medich for Ellis and Brett, but he got Randolph thrown in, when that was what he wanted all the time. Had he made the deal even up, Medich for Randolph, it would have proven to be a sensational deal.

Willie was a Brooklyn guy, Tilden High, only 21 years of age. The Yanks and Pirates had played six games in spring training in '75, and our guys had made note of this youngster with good range and, like all Pirates prospects, a good bat. In a late-season trial with the Pirates, he had batted only .164 in 30 games, making Pittsburgh less certain about retaining him despite a .339 season in Triple A. This was truly one of the great scouting jobs of the last quarter century in baseball. Although we'd had a Hall of Famer named Tony Lazzeri, an MVP named Joe Gordon, a World Series MVP named Billy Martin, and another named Bobby Richardson, you could make a good argument that Randolph turned out to be the best sec-ond baseman in Yankee history.

So, in a matter of hours, the look of our team had changed signifi-cantly. We had dealt Bonds and Medich and were coming home with five players, four of whom would be impact performers for us in '76. It was, in fact, one of the great wheeling-and-dealing days in Gabe Paul's life. And in front of the baseball community, as team spokesman, I was suddenly one of the high-profile figures of this suddenly erupting franchise.

Two days before Christmas, arbitrator Peter Seitz set Andy Messersmith and Dave McNally (who had retired anyway) free. It was the end of the reserve clause as we knew it. No longer would a contract tie you to a team for life.

If you don't think that the teams took this seriously, I had in my office a regular list of all our retired players.

That meant, in effect, that should Joe DiMaggio or Gil McDougald or Jerry Coleman or Mickey Mantle or Whitey Ford ever choose to make a comeback, it would have to be with the Yankees. We owned them for life.

It was not a long list. Few players retire. Often you hear that a player "retired after the 1988 season . . ." but, in all likelihood, he was released after one last spring training attempt. Most players, in fact, end their careers by being released, which would make them free agents. But occa-sionally a player retired, and, if he did, on that list he went, bound for life. Technically, Seitz's ruling ended my need for that list, and made free agents out of those guys too.

The Messersmith and McNally decision was not wholly unexpected, Peter Seitz having shown with Catfish Hunter that he could set a player free simply over a late payment. There were many in baseball, including the lawyers in the commissioner's office, who felt they had made a compelling argument to keep the reserve clause intact. But, by this time, a lot of us were beginning to get the message—there were not going to be many decisions favoring management in the future. You could almost count on losing every time you went before an arbitrator or a judge.

I talked with a lot of players that winter, and, to a man, they were all eager to try free agency, because "look at Catfish—you don't think I'm half as good?" Players began to grab agents to help them evaluate their options, with Jerry Kapstein, Hunter's guy, being the most prominent.

In mid-January 1976, as though signaling to us that the return of George Steinbrenner was imminent, the commissioner permitted him to host a two-day planning session at the posh Carlyle Hotel, where he lived when he was in town. (Now viewed as the quintessential New Yorker, George has never really had a residence in New York other than a hotel, save for a brief period in which he rented an Upper East Side townhouse.)

This was to be an all-purpose, get-ready-for-a-new-stadium planning session. We had a private conference room, and a court reporter on hand to create transcripts.

On the first day, there were 19 of us in the room. George had his limited partner Dan McCarthy present, along with various department heads, architectural and design people connected with the stadium, our trainer, our ticket manager, our head groundskeeper, our lawyer, and a few others.

I looked around the table and marveled at how, at 27, I was embarking on my ninth season with the team and was one of the senior people in the room. I was one of the few there who spanned the CBS and Steinbrenner eras and probably the one best schooled in Yankee history.

George had an enormous agenda, and he ran the meeting efficiently. It was clear—and surprising—that he needed to be filled in a lot on what was going on with the new Stadium. This had been, after all, a Mike Burke–John Lindsay project, and he had inherited it. He would be subject to a lot of barbs over its cost, and there would be, no doubt, flaws and growing pains associated with it.

We would cover such things as ticket pricing, public access, hospitality, employee courtesy, luxury suites, the logistics of moving back, and even training facilities.

I liked what I was hearing. George was placing an emphasis on common courtesy among ticket takers and ushers and parking lot attendants, urging that they greet fans with friendliness and make their experience a positive one from the moment they arrived.

"You see this in Anaheim all the time," he said. "It can be done. Don't tell me about hard-boiled New Yorkers. Make it clear—if they can't say, "Welcome to Yankee Stadium," we'll get others who can."

The ticket situation was tricky. In an effort to increase revenues, a decision was made to virtually eliminate general-admission seating. There would be either box or reserved seats in Yankee Stadium, and what had been general admission—formerly the last few rows—would now be bleacher tickets.

Part of this was done because revenue projections, even with the new Stadium, were not strong. Around the table that day, the number 30,000 was thrown out as the likely Opening Day attendance. No one was projecting a sellout, which was just as well, because the traffic was projected to be a horror show. Certain roadways and parking lots would not be complete, and the end of the game would coincide with evening rush hour, putting everyone into a bad state of mind by the time they got home.

Barry Landers brought up the pace of luxury-suite sales, a new experience for us. "We only have one sample suite to show customers," he said, "and there's no heat in it. It's freezing. You can't spend more than five minutes there. Even the paintings on the walls are cracking."

"The paintings are cracking?" said George. "That's my suite! I paid for it! Get that fixed!"

When our in-house architect, Perry Green, gave us the move-back schedule, he used January 15 as the day the ticket department would start returning from Shea.

"January 15?" said Mike Rendine, the crusty ticket manager. "Why hasn't anyone told me about this? Does anyone happen to know when January 15 is?"

It was, in fact, that day. Clearly some lines of communication were not as open as they should be.

Perry Green was not a sports fan, but he was enjoying the Yankee Stadium project, unfurling his giant blueprints for anyone to see and lecturing long and hard about the cookie-cutter parks that had long been the architectural style in baseball. I liked Perry, because it was interesting to me to have an architect on staff, to learn what they do and see the detail and precision of his drawings.

But he also took advantage of me one day. An artist named Ralph Fasanella specialized in folk art street scenes, often with a baseball theme. He had done a primitive of Yankee Stadium and its environs, and I had helped him with reference material. It was not an unusual request. I remember helping a sculptress named Rhoda Sherbell with likenesses of Casey and Yogi. We did that sort of thing a lot.

Fasanella was very appreciative, and some weeks later he delivered a massive signed lithograph to me of Yankee Stadium, perhaps five feet high and seven feet wide. I was not an art student; I couldn't judge its worth as fine art, but I liked it. One day Perry came by and saw it in my office, sticking out from behind a couch until I could figure out where to hang it.

"This is nice," he said.

"Perry, it's so big, I can't figure out what to do with it," I answered.

"Let me try?" he inquired.

"Take it, it's yours."

Well, he did. He took it home. And it turned out that Fasanella was more than a little bit prominent, although his greater fame was still to come. His works became quite valuable, and he was one of those rare artists whose death rated a lengthy New York Times obit. I thought I had been had by Perry, and don't anybody tell me what it's worth today; I'd rather not know.

On the second day we were joined by Billy Martin, and I was embarrassed and uncomfortable for him. George had decided to talk about the roster, and Billy found himself talking up, or down, the merits of his players in front of a lot of people who had no business hearing it. I would include myself in that group, in fact. It was awkward to watch Billy perform in a business meeting like this, telling his boss who he was intending to drop from the roster while the architect, the ticket manager, the team attorney, the interior designers of the luxury suites, and, yes, even the PR director, were there.

When Billy happened to mention Thurman Munson's name, George interrupted to say that the players were going to have to be more courteous to the fans. They were going to have to be more accommodating with autographs, and that meant Munson, who was developing an especially grumpy reputation.

"Speaking of Munson," said George, "that brings up something that I want you to give some thought to, not necessarily speaking in terms of Thurman Munson. But Billy—and this should be your decision, your decision strictly—we have never had a leader per se on the ballclub. We've never had a captain. If you've got the guy that can be a leader—I don't know how you feel about this, but that's something I want you to wrestle with and make up your mind whether you want to appoint a captain to the ballclub. I hear pros and cons. I've seen it be great and I've seen it when it was a nothing. So that's something that I want you to address yourself to, okay?"

I jumped in.

"Lou Gehrig was a captain of the Yankees. When he became ill and subsequently died, Joe McCarthy said something about 'Lou will always remain the Yankee captain and there'll never be another one.' And for that reason DiMaggio and Mantle were never officially called captain or anything like that, so it's always been a practice that existed."

Steinbrenner brushed it off. "Well, I think that's fine. But I'm not . . .

you know, as much as I respect him, and I don't think anybody's done any more to try to preserve the memory of those guys than we have since we took this team over—CBS certainly didn't—I'm out for what's best for this ballclub.

"And the minute we win a pennant and win the World Series, you know, that's . . . that's why I say it's your problem to wrestle with. If you decide not to, that's fine. And I don't say it should always be the Mantle, the DiMaggio, the Gehrig, or the Ruth that's going to be your best leader out there. That sometimes can cause you more problems. Maybe it's got to be some other guy. But that's something for the manager.

"I appreciate the history on it, Marty, and I'm not saying we have to do it. I'm just saying I wish you'd wrestle with that problem and give it some thought."

We went on to talk about making Yankee Stadium more of a show, using music more, using the scoreboard, enhancing the fans' experience.

Gabe spoke up. "The Mets are less public relations conscious than we are, because they've been high and mighty."

"Well, that's what killed the Yankees," said George. "After that era ended when the Yankees were on top, then the management of the Yankees wouldn't listen to the fans and then that's when the Mets came up. And we want to do the same thing; except when we get up, we want to stay up this time."

Those two-day meetings at the Carlyle set the pace for the next quarter century at the new Yankee Stadium. True, the parking lot people and the ticket takers weren't always fan friendly. But George's outline for bringing the Yankees back, for making the Stadium experience a positive one, took hold. Personally, I found the music too loud and missed the more pastoral days of baseball. But I also recognized that kids needed to be brought back to the game, and if creating a show was the master plan, I was willing to go along with it.

Yankee Stadium today, with its very slick, synchronized scoreboard-and-music presentation, is a great experience, unless you happen to be seated among rowdies. That can happen. But cutting off beer sales after seven innings has helped that, and a lot about the stadium has been carefully honed to enhance fan enjoyment.

Walk into a lot of parks, and you will find garbage cans overflowing after two innings and never emptied. Yankee Stadium is constantly maintained during a game.

For years, in the final CBS days, graffiti was a major problem. Kids from Bronx street gangs would spray-paint their names on the outer walls of Yankee Stadium. Steinbrenner said, "Paint over it, every day. Don't ever miss a day. They'll get tired of it. We'll outlast them."

Eventually, the New York City graffiti problem went away. But it went away first at Yankee Stadium, because George willed it away. He could buy more paint—and charge it to the city—than the kids ever could.

As we were packing our Queens office, half for spring training and half for Yankee Stadium, I got a call from Don Carney, the director of Yankee telecasts on WPIX.

"We're going to do a special on the new Stadium," he said. "Mel Allen will narrate it. Do you think you could write it? Nobody knows that stuff like you do."

It would be my first attempt at a television script. But I was anxious to give it a whirl. Don showed me the footage they had, and I suggested what they should shoot at the new ballpark.

Mel Allen's cadence and style was always in my head. I could hear Mel's voice, I knew the material we were working from, and I had watched enough television in my life to know the pacing and the look of such a program.

So, armed with some notes on what tape and film existed, I went home and set up my typewriter. It was 7:30 in the evening.

At 8:15 I was done. In one take, I had written my first television script, and they never changed a word. Forty-five minutes for a half-hour special.

As Mel would say, "How about that!"

Baseball had its Messersmith and McNally decision, but it was operating in a wilderness. There was no plan to work with. Under the decision, all players could be free agents every year if they didn't sign their contracts. Even Marvin Miller saw the folly in that. By flooding the market with available players, demand would be lessened, and the salaries might not change. There had to be a structure created after a century of the reserve clause.

On February 23, the owners voted to shut down the spring training camps until an agreement was reached. Seizing what they saw as their best negotiating ploy—no spring training—they hoped to force the Players' Association into reaching an agreement on their terms.

It was during this period when the camps were closed (and I remained in New York) that Kuhn formally lifted Steinbrenner's suspension. He had come to feel that George had paid his price, and that it was unfair to our organization to continue to have the owner absent from decision making while the game was embarking on a new era.

Not all of us knew, in 1976, what the effects of the Seitz decision would be, and there was genuine concern that the rich clubs would forever sign all the best players and win every year, but, clearly, change was coming to the game as we knew it.

The March days in New York were cold and gloomy. This was supposed to be spring training, and we had no idea whether there would even be a 1976 season. Pat Gillick, our scouting director, took me outside and we practiced throwing snowballs for a new toy he'd picked up—a Juggs Gun, to measure the speed of pitches. That was how we passed the time—trying to top 30 with snowballs on the Juggs Gun.

Bowie Kuhn, defying the owners, ordered the camps to open on March 17. A lot of the owners were furious with him, and his reputation for being "their guy" was certainly contradicted by this move. In a flash, we headed for Ft. Lauderdale and the promise that every spring provides—a fresh start. It had been 12 years since our last pennant. Suddenly, we were the favorites to win.

Billy Martin had said all winter that what he really needed to get a "Billy Martin kind of team" off and running was a full spring. Now that had been taken away from him. Decisions on roster moves were going to have to be made quickly. He felt cheated. He didn't have a full six weeks to create a team in his image.

George's presence on the scene was immediately felt. There was a special urgency to everything. There was a tension when he was present. I, for one, developed a nervous cough that lasted all spring. I thought it was allergies, but it may well have been the tension everyone was feeling.

Beautiful Ft. Lauderdale might just as well have been Waterbury, Connecticut. We had changed our schedule to play almost all night games, effectively wiping out all opportunities to experience the good restaurants and nightlife in town. We would be at our trailer in the parking lot at 8:30 in the morning and fall into bed around midnight, day after day. It was grueling.

The day before our first workout was a Sunday. Gabe called me.

"Now, Marty," he said, "I had a look at Oscar Gamble from my window when he pulled in this morning. His hair is still all bushied up. We have a hair policy on this team that forbids it—and if he shows up like that tomorrow, we're not going to let him dress."

I appreciated the warning. That would be big news on the first day, and it was important for the PR man to know what might be coming.

"So," he continued, "you have to get him to cut it today. Otherwise, he'll file a grievance, and he'll win it, and we'll have a bad situation on our hands."

I was silent for a moment and then said, "I understand everything you've said, except for the part about me having to get his hair cut. Why me?"

"Now, damnit," said Gabe, "just get it done. I'm making it your responsibility, that's all there is to it."

Well, this was going to be interesting.

In the first place, Oscar barely knew me. It seemed highly unlikely that he would shed the signature Afro he was so proud of at my suggestion. In the second, more practical place, it was Sunday. There were no barbershops open.

I called Elston Howard, our coach, the first black Yankee, and a genuinely good guy. Ellie was often the poor sap who was called upon to be the go-between. Once Billy Martin had sent him to the back of a plane to tell Munson to turn down his loud tape player.

"What are you, the music coach?" said Thurman.

Such was Ellie's lot.

"Ellie, I'm in a spot. Do you know any barbers in town who might cut Oscar's hair?"

"You gotta be shitting me," he said. "He's not going to get his hair cut. And no way will you find anyone on a Sunday to do it, anyway."

I went to the weekend hotel manager at our run-down Ft. Lauderdale Inn. There was a barbershop in the lobby—could he possibly call the barber at home and see if he would be available to come in?

"Tell him I'll make it worth his while," I said. "I'll give him thirty dollars."

To my good fortune—or rather, to his—he agreed to come in. If, of course, Gamble would go through with it. I hadn't even called him yet.

"Hello, Oscar? It's Marty Appel, the Yankees' PR director. We met when you came in with your agent a few weeks ago, remember? We took some pictures?

"Anyway, Oscar, here's the thing. You know the Yankees have this short-hair policy for players, and, um . . . well, if I could arrange for a barber this afternoon to come here to the hotel, do you think you'd have some time to get yours cut?"

There followed a silence from both of us.

"What time?" he said.

It sounded like a breakthrough to me.

"I think I can have the barber here in an hour; would that work for you?"

"Yeah, that's cool."

This must have fallen under the "good things" column in the Act of God clause in my PR contract. No argument, no debate, just "Yeah, that's cool." I couldn't believe it.

I called the barber and told him to come in. I called Ellie and asked if he'd sit in with us, sort of moral support in case there was a last-minute change of heart.

When the barber arrived, I gave him $30 in advance and said, "By the way, have you ever cut a black man's hair before?"

"Nope, this will be a first for me," he said.

"Well, don't mention that to Oscar, whatever you do," I responded.

Ellie came in with Oscar. If he was there for moral support, I had miscalculated, because all he did was say, "I've never seen anything like this before." And he was laughing and enjoying the whole thing.

Oscar was a perfect gentleman. He shook hands with the barber and watched the *snip, snip, snip* as his treasured 'fro fell to the floor.

When we were done, he looked like a completely different person. He looked at himself in the mirror and smiled. He liked it!

The next day, photographers couldn't get enough of Oscar, and the Associated Press moved a "before and after" picture that made every sports section in the country.

And my expense account for the week had a line that read, "Haircut, Oscar Gamble, $30."

"You handled that well," said Gabe. "We could have had a real mess there with the grievance process and all. We never could have won that. I don't know what you said to him, but good job."

Oscar and I became good friends that day, forever linked in haircut history.

Ed Brinkman, the slightly built veteran shortstop, was one of those guys that Billy tried to bring to every team he managed. He was a Billy-ball kind of player. Billy had brought him to New York at the end of the '75 season, but, now, as was evident to everyone, there was no room for him on the '76 roster.

On a three-day road trip to St. Petersburg, Bill Kane and I were standing with Billy when he began to tear up. I knew Billy could be emotional, but I didn't know what this was about.

"We've got to release Eddie Brinkman," he said. "I love the guy; I can't do it. You guys will have to tell him, okay?"

Well, no, I didn't think it was okay at all. Getting Oscar's haircut was one thing. To me, releasing à player was strictly a manager's or general manager's responsibility. I even thought Billy owed him that—to look him in the eye, give him the news. Brinkman was a veteran; he could see the writing on the wall. He hit .175 for us in 1975. Now we had Sandy Alomar, Jim Mason, Willie Randolph, Graig Nettles, and Fred Stanley all on the roster in the infield. Brinkman didn't fit. It's baseball, it happens.

Bill Kane said we'd do it. When Billy left, I told Killer that I was disappointed that he had given in so easily. It was cowardly of Billy—not that I would say that to him.

"Aw, look at the guy, he was starting to cry," said Kane. "We can do this for him."

"He didn't cry when his daughter was arrested in South America with drugs," I reminded Kane. "His priorities are all out of whack."

And so, we called Brinkman, who was in his hotel room. We said we needed to talk to him.

I let Kane do most of the talking, and, I have to say, he handled it well. Better than Brinkman, anyway. Brinkman was angry and shocked.

"Released? You gotta be kidding! Where's Billy, why are you doing this? What's going on here?"

I wanted to be someplace else really bad.

"Billy has so much respect for you, Eddie, that he just couldn't bring himself to have this talk with you," I said. "He felt very personally hurt by this development."

"Bullshit," he said. "This is bullshit. Gimme that phone."

He called Billy's room and Gabe Paul's room and got no answer. Killer had some papers for Brinkman to sign, but he thought better of shoving them in his face. We excused ourselves and left.

We went for a drink.

"Yeah, that was tough," said Kane. "Guys never know when they're through, even the smartest of them." Brinkman would never play another game for anyone.

Monte Irvin, the Hall of Famer from the Giants and the Negro Leagues, had once shared a theory on this with me.

"Power hitters see their game ending," he said. "They hit the ball as good as they used to, and suddenly they're hitting long flyouts. It's the singles hitters who never see those signs—they're still hitting those singles—those guys never know when it's over."

Spring training had barely begun when Ron Blomberg crashed into the wall in Winter Haven and so badly wrecked his shoulder that for all intents and purposes, his career ended that day. He had spent most of '75 on the disabled list, had rehabbed long and hard to get back, and now this.

Blomberg, my friend and neighbor, an usher at my wedding, and one helluva hitter against righthanders, would bat only two times for us late that September. He missed all of '77 and then, seeking a change of scenery, went to the White Sox in '78 as a free agent. Gabe thought that was very ungrateful of him after the team had paid his salary and medical expenses for three years in which he'd played 35 games. But he did need a change, and Bill Veeck told him he'd be a big hit in Chicago.

It was his bad timing that he joined a White Sox team just getting into the born-again spirit that was making its way into baseball and left this Jewish slugger on the outside looking in, both at Sunday chapel service and in the lineup. The Boomer called it quits at age 30, a lifetime .293 hitter.

Billy called Munson into his office a few days into camp.

"I want to make you captain," he said. "I've discussed it with George and the coaches, and you're a natural leader on this team, and I want you to be the captain."

"What does it mean?" he asked. "Like, I take the lineup out every game?"

"No," said Billy, "I'll do that. I need to do that. It gives me time to talk to the umps, ask about their kids, get on their good side if we need a close call."

"Then what am I supposed to do?"

"Just be a leader by example. You already are. But, with the title, even a new player will know that you're the guy carrying on Yankee tradition. It's a good idea, the more I think about it."

Munson shrugged his shoulders. He didn't know what it really meant, but it sounded okay to him.

Only Phil Pepe, among the press corps, remembered the Joe McCarthy and Lou Gehrig pledge.

George was ready with an answer and it was a beauty.

"If Joe McCarthy could meet Thurman Munson, he'd agree that this is the right guy."

Actually McCarthy was still alive and living in Tonawanda, New York, up near Buffalo. Nobody bothered to get his reaction.

He was never seen in public much, and had long ago stopped attending baseball functions. But we decided to honor him in the new Stadium with a plaque in what would be called Monument Park. It would be the first new plaque in the newly designed area, off beyond the playing field. I had the pleasure of calling him and telling him what we were doing and of recording a greeting from him to the fans on the day we would unveil it, because he would not be able to attend. That would be

April 20, the eve of his 89th birthday. He was very moved by this, and I credited Gabe with making it happen "while he was alive and could still enjoy it." We had planned on a plaque for Casey Stengel, who had died the previous September, and Gabe said, "Do McCarthy while you're at it."

Casey had died the day after the '75 season ended, making it possible for his protégé, Billy Martin, to attend his funeral. Billy not only attended but slept in Casey's bed that night at his Glendale home. And he alone would wear a black armband on his sleeve throughout the '76 season in Casey's honor.

I always liked what I hoped were actually Casey's last words: "There comes a time in every man's life, and I've had plenty of them."

12

MICKEY, GET BACK TO YOUR SPOT!

A s an indicator of what lay ahead for the Yankees, the newly returned George Steinbrenner jumped feet-first into the battle to sign Andy Messersmith.

Returned to power only days earlier, George wasted no time in going after the 30-year-old righthander who had won 39 games for the Dodgers during the past two seasons.

Gabe was dispatched to bring Messersmith into the fold, armed with suitcases of cash. Having been through the Catfish pursuit the previous year, he was becoming skilled at this. But, somewhere along the line, a dispute emerged with Messersmith's agent, Herb Osmond, over the matter of interest accrual of deferred payments. It was the first indication that no Yankee signings were going to be without complications, and we as PR people were going to have to brush up on our glossary of economic terms.

The issue, to Osmond and Messersmith at least, was unresolved when we announced the signing on March 31. This ran counter to Gabe's long-standing practice of never announcing anything before a contract was signed. It seemed as though he was following a bargaining strategy from a higher team official.

Osmond said, "Signing? We didn't sign."

Climenko was a shrewd lawyer with a kindly appearance, and much of what he would be handling for us in the coming years seemed to puzzle him as much as entertain him.

An example of poor Climenko's fate when the Yankees became his client involved a time when a friend of mine, who supported himself with freelance magazine assignments, called to say he needed a credential to interview Catfish Hunter for a story he was doing for a publication called *High Society*.

I gave him the credential and he wrote a straight baseball story, which could just as well have appeared in *Esquire* or *Sport*.

A few days later, I was summoned into George's office. Jess Climenko, looking very concerned, was present.

"Did you give a credential to the guy who wrote this story?" asked George. Across his big round captain's desk he hurled the latest copy of *High Society*, which turned out to be a T&A magazine. The Hunter story was pure baseball, but the cover read, "Catfish Hunter—The Life and Loves of the Yankee Superstar." (The loves were hunting and fishing.)

Some of the skin magazines would run one legit story per issue to get some newsstand distribution they might otherwise be shut out from.

I gave it my best Ralph Kramden "humaduh, humaduh, humaduh" and proceeded to talk Climenko through the process, swearing (truthfully) that I did not know *High Society* was a soft-porn magazine. Catfish was understandably upset, and George was threatening to sue. (When George threatened to sue, which was about twice a day, he would turn to Joe Garagiola Jr. and say, "Now, Joe, get your papers together," which was a sign we were headed for court.)

Well, here was Climenko in a more serious hearing, with Bowie Kuhn, Marvin Miller, and poor Gabe being grilled by everyone involved in the Messersmith "signing." In the end, Bowie agreed that the deal had not really been consummated and ruled that Messersmith was still a free agent. I think, within himself, Gabe Paul enjoyed the defeat. He had been vindicated by his "don't announce until it's a deal" rule and had embarrassed George.

Back in Florida, we couldn't just let it be. I had to draft a press release and walk it back and forth to George's trailer about nine times before he was satisfied.

George wanted to clear up some points made by various parties. So the release said, in part, ". . . contrary to a direct quote attributed to the worthy legal counsel for the Players Association, Mr. Richard Moss, in a New York paper, a story which was circulated widely across the nation to the effect that the Yankees during their negotiations with Herb Osmond did ply him with drinks in order to get him to sign an agreement for his client—that this alleged statement was totally false and was most damaging to the Yankees, and personally to Mr. Paul and myself if allowed to stand unchallenged. Mr. Osmond's own testimony under oath stated that in the seven hours he was with Yankee personnel in negotiations, that he had only a total of one and a half bottles of beer. If that could by any stretch of the imagination be considered as 'plying him with drinks,'—then the liquor stores are in trouble. The Yankees just don't operate that way."

Accepting Kuhn's judgment and sending Messersmith on his way, George's statement said, "I have stated that there really can be no place in the Yankee organization for any player who cannot find it in himself to understand and feel this. I bear them no malice, but I feel that it is essential to what I am trying to build here—to borrow the title of a great movie, *The Pride of the Yankees*."

There was one subtle parting shot at Andy before the statement ended, when he said, "This is in no way a criticism of Andy, whom I found in these proceedings to be a very fine young man . . ." Andy was 30, not a young man by baseball standards, and the use of the term was somehow demeaning. George could craft the use of "young" or "little" to demean an adversary. When Buck Showalter left the team after the 1995 season, George went out of his way to compliment Buck and his "nice little family."

"Someday," the statement concluded, "Andy may feel differently about representing the New York Yankees and if that day should come, we would certainly be willing to meet with Andy and pursue that possibility, but for now I consider the Messersmith matter closed."

Andy quickly signed a "lifetime contract" with the new owner of the Atlanta Braves, one Ted Turner, a guy who owned a local TV station— channel 17—in Atlanta. Turner quickly assigned Andy the nickname Channel and made him number 17, so that the back of his uniform became a billboard for his station (Ted's father owned a billboard company).

Messersmith was 16–15 in two lackluster seasons for Atlanta, and then went to the Yankees after all in '78, a world championship season. Injured, he was winless in six appearances and then wrapped up his career in '79 with the Dodgers. Lifetime record in his five seasons after free agency: 18–22. He should have been the first free agent we would be lucky to lose—except, of course, George couldn't resist bringing him back in '78 when all signs pointed to his being through.

I felt as though we'd been through a season and a half, and it wasn't even Opening Day yet. The team headed to Milwaukee to launch the season on April 8, but I returned to New York to prepare for the opening of Yankee Stadium.

The question of whether the PR director needed to be with the team was one that George often wrestled with. Teams were always looking to reduce travel costs. Many owners viewed the PR job as just typing up the stats and the press notes and being available for questions in the press box.

A defining moment on this subject would come early in the season, and I look back at it now and admire my quick thinking, which may have saved road trips for generations of public relations directors.

The team was in Texas for the first game of a road trip, and I was scheduled to fly out on a noon flight to be there by game time.

We found ourselves in a meeting of some importance in George's office when I interrupted to say that I would have to leave shortly if I were to catch my flight.

"When's the next flight?" George asked.

"I think around two, it would still get me there by game time."

"After that?"

"Probably about four, but I would miss three innings or so."

George was quiet for a moment and then said, "Is it essential that you be there?"

In one of my better moments of quick thinking, I said, "Absolutely. This is the New York Yankees. Things are happening around this club every day. We have seven writers traveling with us. You can't *not* have a club representative there with the press."

It was all true, but I could have just as easily said, "Oh, I suppose they could play a few innings without me." And had I said that, he would have quickly translated it to, "A few innings? I'll bet they can play a whole game without you. I'll bet we could do a whole road trip without you. I'll bet we could do a whole season without you. Gabe, how much money does it cost to travel a PR guy?"

Gabe would have said, "About seven thousand a year," and George would have said, "Well, I have a way we can save seven thousand a year, then."

But I was quick.

And so, George said, "How about then if we put Morabito on that noon flight, and you take the four and relieve him in the third inning?" I guess I had made my case well.

"Get Morabito in here."

Mickey strolled in, and George said, "Now, Mickey, I want you leaving the office right now and taking a noon flight to Texas. Marty will get in later and relieve you around the third inning. Can you handle this?"

Mickey was flabbergasted, but I gave him a quick nod as if to say, "Don't ask questions, just do it."

And so, off he went to Dallas on a moment's notice, and, sure enough, I got to Arlington Stadium in the third inning, just as planned, and he got the last flight out that evening back to New York. It was ridiculous, but at the moment it seemed essential to keep the PR man on the road. Any hesitation and I am sure the media would have traveled PR-less from that point on. And with the Yankees setting such an example, and with all teams looking to save money as player salaries were about to soar, I may well have saved everyone's travel in that brief second I had to think.

It was ironic that Texas would be the focus of this story, for it was not too many years later that Billy Martin found himself battered and bloodied outside a strip club and tried to slip back unnoticed to the hotel in the early morning, one ear dangling. His bad luck was that as he entered around four in the morning, the hotel lobby was filling with evacuating guests. A fire alarm had gone off, and bloody Billy marched in, with his entire team and press corps seemingly awaiting his arrival. It was a good thing that a PR man was with the team that night, hustling Billy off and returning with a statement for the press that would keep them—at least for several hours—from doing their own investigation. Better to get the club's statement and go back to bed.

Now Billy Martin had his club as ready as it could be for Opening Day of the '76 season in Milwaukee.

Hank Aaron was on the Brewers, marking the final Opening Day of his illustrious career. I had always admired Aaron; I liked the dignity with which he played the game, how understated he was in the on-deck circle, how unlikely a curtain call would have been for the Hammer or that he would stand there and admire his homers. He was the ultimate professional.

When he broke Babe Ruth's career record, amid racial threats and hate mail, I took it upon myself to create a plaque, FROM THE NEW YORK YANKEES, to honor him and sent it to Donald Davidson, the Braves' diminutive road secretary. It was not a big deal, but I didn't want him to think that the Yankees were snubbing him after he broke a Ruth record.

Besides, Aaron's accomplishment came against overwhelming odds. Odds of more than 15,000 to 1, in fact. What were the chances that baseball's all-time home run leader would also be first among the more than 15,000 big leaguers in alphabetical order! Now, that's a remarkable press note to me.

Jim Slaton beat Catfish on Opening Day before a full house in County Stadium, but it was the second game, two days later, that gave us an indication that it was going to be a wild year.

The Yanks had a 9–7 lead in the ninth, having come from behind, with Dave Pagan on the mound for us and Don Money at bat for the Brewers. The bases were loaded.

For a major league ballplayer, Pagan (pronounced "PAY-gan," not the Spanish pronunciation) was a very timid-looking, 6´2´´, 176-pounder. He threw hard but was pale with wide eyes and a bewildered look. Only 25, he was not Billy Martin's idea of a tough guy you took to battle with you.

Pagan was from a small town in Saskatchewan called Nipawin. When we sent questionnaires to the players over the winter for press guide and Yearbook information, one of the standard, top-of-form blanks was "telephone number." I'm not saying that Nipawin was a small town, but, on that blank, Pagan wrote "8."

Now, here he was, facing Money with the bases loaded in a 9–7 game, the team looking for its first win.

Pagan took his sign from Munson and delivered. Money connected and sent the ball soaring out over the left field wall for a grand slam to finish us off.

In a flash, Billy Martin came racing onto the field, filled with anger. Pagan took one look, turned toward third base, and started running away. He must have thought Billy was going to kill him.

But no, it wasn't that at all. Over at first base, Chris Chambliss had called timeout before the pitch to Money. The first base umpire had granted it—the pitch didn't count! No home run! Still a 9–7 Yankee lead!

Pagan lives! The Yankees won the game 9–7, and I think he changed his phone number to 9 so that Billy wouldn't find him.

I have seen a lot of funny things on the ballfield over the years, but never anything as funny as watching Pagan run for his life when Billy came dashing out of that dugout.

We worked all weekend making plans for the big home opener. *Time* magazine even put the event on its cover that week. George was absolutely furious that our new high-tech scoreboard, developed by a company called Conrac, was not going to be ready. He wanted a press release issued saying that it had failed to make its deadline, and giving its phone number for angry fans. I talked him into just a one-sentence press note stating that "Conrac Corp. has informed the Yankees that the Telscreen portion of the board will not be functioning today due to technical difficulties."

Actually, the scoreboard matter was a huge fiasco. Designed to show animation, as well as to keep the lineups current, it was constructed in dead center field, right in the batter's field of vision. After careful review and testing during batting practice prior to the opener, it was determined that it couldn't be lit at all when a batter was up, for it might distract him. This enormous project, one of the centerpieces of the whole rebuild, was, in effect, worthless, except between innings. How we could blow this one with all of our skilled baseball people overseeing the project remains a mystery to me to this day.

The scoreboard would also have the capability of showing instant replay, the first in America to offer that (sacred Fenway Park, of all places, followed later that year). Naturally, we abused it early on, when Steinbrenner insisted on replaying what he thought were bad umpiring calls. That only served to incite the fans and embarrass the umpires, and we were quickly told to cease that usage and only use it to show great catches and home runs. That edict remains in force, wisely, to this day.

As Opening Day approached, George got involved in every last detail. The parking list for the media lot was going to have to be approved by him—and he wouldn't review it until the morning of Opening Day. Obviously, when Opening Day came, he had so much on his mind that the parking list had a lower priority. And downstairs, the lot remained shut until he signed off on it. A policeman found me to say that Dick Young was not being allowed to park his car and had left his car parked in the middle of the street, causing an enormous backup to the Major Deegan and up toward the Washington Bridge.

As traffic mounted for what turned out to be a sellout event, we had another problem. One of our unions was threatening a strike, and, as a result, the gates were being kept closed until the matter was resolved. Gabe was negotiating with the union chief, and thousands of early arriv- ing fans were being crushed along the gates as noon became 12:30 and still the park was shut.

The temperature was in the 80s, a remarkably hot spring day, as tempers were rising and paperwork was accumulating on Steinbrenner's desk, awaiting approval.

To my dismay, our press box would be overflowing, and thus very uncomfortable for the media gathered that day. I was concerned that it would leave a bad impression on everyone. Poor Red Smith had to stand in the back of the press box because two beat reporters had the only seats I could give to the *Times*. Beat reporters always got priority, but I had hoped one of them would yield his seat to the aging but brilliant and wonderful Red.

The field ceremony was elaborate, and it was my baby. I was to be on the field to orchestrate it, assisted only by two security people for crowd control. I had to run the program while photographers and reporters approached me with questions and requests. I had assigned Mickey Morabito to stay in the press box and deal with that crowd and to focus on the lineups and the actual game.

Suddenly, I looked around and couldn't find my two security guys. They had been called away by Steinbrenner, who needed additional help with his special guests for the day. He was hosting a big party in his large office for many city officials and celebrities, and he was being overrun. So he pulled my two helpers. I was now totally alone on the field.

We had put together one helluva ceremony, I must say. I brought my old hero, Bobby Richardson, up to deliver an invocation. Terrance Cardinal Cooke delivered a blessing. My buddy and neighbor, Robert Merrill, performed the national anthem in his usual soaring and rapid style—which made him a fan favorite.

To commemorate the great moments from old Yankee Stadium, we had DiMaggio, Mantle, Howard, Martin, Ford, Berra, and Larsen stand on the field. Claire Ruth and Eleanor Gehrig were there. The great boxing immortal Joe Louis was present. Save for DiMaggio, Louis always received the biggest hand from sports fans whenever he was present at an event.

From the '58 Giants–Colts championship game came Frank Gifford, Kyle Rote, Jim Parker, and Weeb Ewbank. College football was represented by Johnny Lujack and Arnold Tucker.

Six members of the 1923 Yankees were on hand, men who were there for the first opener. They were Bob Shawkey, the Opening Day pitcher; Whitey Witt, who had been the first Yankee hitter; Waite Hoyt; Joe Dugan; Hinkey Haines; and Oscar Roettger. I wish I'd known that Little Ray Kelly was living in the area—he had been Babe Ruth's five-year-old mascot and posed for a lot of pictures with the Babe that day. I didn't know that Little Ray was a Rockland County resident until almost 20 years later, when I ran into him at a Ruth symposium at Hofstra University. We quickly became friends, and I helped make a mini-celebrity out of him at that time. But had I known he was around back in the '70s, he would have been a fixture at these gatherings. I loved stuff like that.

George himself had decided that four special guests would stand on the pitcher's mound when Shawkey delivered the ceremonial first pitch. These were his personal choices.

The first would be Mel Allen, the voice of the Yankees, who was now, 12 years after his departure, not only welcomed back, but honored in this grand style.

The second was Pete Sheehy, our clubhouse man since 1927, and, on this day, a plaque went on the door (at my suggestion), naming the club-house in his honor.

The third was James Farley, the longest-running season-ticket holder at Yankee Stadium, the one-time postmaster general in the Roosevelt administration, and head of the National Democratic Party. Farley, once a potential buyer for the team after Ruppert died, was tall and thin like Connie Mack. He wore a straw hat beginning with the first day of spring each year and was truly a throwback to the golden age of sports.

The fourth guest was Toots Shor, the restauranteur and friend to so many sports figures over the years. Toots was now in failing health, had lost his restaurant, and was going through rough times. Steinbrenner, the Cleveland native, knew little of Shor but, when educated about him, extended this wonderful gesture to the old saloonkeeper who called everyone a "crumb bum."

Alone on the field, I waved at Bob Sheppard in the PA booth to begin the program. Given the heat and the long walk, I took it upon myself to escort Mrs. Ruth, Mrs. Gehrig, Toots, Farley, and a few of the '23 Yankees onto the field. I deposited each where he needed to stand and raced back for the next one. I was wringing wet, with no help in sight. I was walking arm-in-arm with Claire Ruth when the *New York Times* photographer ran up to me and asked if he could get two tickets for his son for Saturday's game.

As I was placing the four special guests around the pitcher's mound, Mantle left his spot and walked about 60 feet right to me. With every-thing going on and my mind racing, completely out of nowhere he said, "Marty, y'all know a girl name-a Angel?"

I looked at him in wonder.

"Um . . . from Shreveport?"

"Yeah!" he broke into a big smile. "That's her. I was with her in Tahoe last month, and all she did was talk about you!"

I think they saw me blush in section 58, out there near the Jerome Cafeteria. It was at once my all-time Yankee highlight—me and the Mick, bonding like this—and so totally off the wall that I didn't know what in the world to say. I was just glad that Bobby Richardson wasn't lis-tening. I had dated Angel (her last name) one spring training when she was in Ft. Lauderdale.

"Mick, get back to your spot; we've got a stadium to open here," I said good-naturedly. I think he enjoyed that he had totally thrown me right there.

I stood by as Shawkey, in street clothes, made the first pitch, with Witt standing in the batter's box. A nice moment. As I shook Shawkey's hand, he said to me, "I should still be managing this team."

Once before, he had walked me through that. He had been fired after one season as manager, in 1930, after finishing third as Miller Huggins' successor. The Yankees replaced him with Joe McCarthy. He felt screwed, and obviously believed that all of the success McCarthy enjoyed—and perhaps Stengel after that—should have been his. Despite these feelings, he was a kindly old man with a white crewcut, and having him throw out the first ball 53 years after he pitched the first game in old Yankee Stadium was a wonderful moment.

"You know who did the national anthem when we opened here in twenty-three?" he asked me. In fact, I did. He was very impressed when I said, "John Philip Sousa!"

The stadium still had a ways to go. A giant smokestack outside gate 4 was, at Joe Garagiola Jr.'s suggestion, offered to Louisville Slugger for advertising purposes and made to look like a Babe Ruth bat. "Meet me at the bat" would become a frequent message for New Yorkers.

Despite the problems, we were going to be a hit. The team was going to be the first American League team since the 1950 Yankees to draw two million fans. The traffic was terrible, the lots took hours to exit, but I felt that the stadium was an architectural triumph. The grandeur was intact, down to the facade design that now spanned the bleacher advertising panels (Mike Burke had insisted on this touch, even threatening to call off the deal if the design wasn't maintained). The poles had been removed. Our Opening Day attendance was the biggest for a Yankee opener since 1946, although we'd lost 11,000 seats during the rebuild.

I got to the press box in the second inning. Disco Dan Ford of the Twins had already hit the first home run in the new ballpark (Ruth had christened it in '23). Morabito had held the fort well while I was being put through my paces on the field. Now we just settled back and watched Rudy May and Dick Tidrow stop the Twins, and we had an Opening Day victory.

My phone, however, rang in the eighth inning. It was George, and he wanted to see me. Not after the game—now.

I walked into his office, which was littered with party material and champagne bottles. He said, "You're responsible for this?"

He threw a Yankee Yearbook at me. It had been ready, as always, for Opening Day.

"It's my responsibility, yes; what's wrong?"

"Look at this!" he demanded as he furiously turned the pages. "Hair's too long, hair's too long, hair's too long, hair's too long, hair's too long, I can count twenty players with their hair too long in the photos you chose. Now, I'm not saying that I'm putting you out on the street over this, but I am saying you better get it fixed."

Well, he was right that the hair in the photos did not meet his specifications. What he didn't understand was that because spring training had opened so late, I'd had no choice but to use photos taken in 1975, when, while he was under suspension, the hair did get long. In the case of our newer players—Figueroa, Ellis, Randolph, Rivers, Brett, Gamble—I hired Charlie McGill, one of my favorite sports artists, to draw the new guys in Yankee uniforms, using photos from the previous year. Naturally, their hair was too long as well.

George was right that the hair was too long for his new team rules—but wrong to throw the Yearbook at me and call it, as he did, a piece of crap. My explanation was appropriate. To take new photos in spring training would have made it impossible to have the Yearbook ready for Opening Day. And we would have missed a sales opportunity for the entire opening week, when huge crowds were expected.

But he was right that this showcase for his team did not present the players as he wanted them presented. I should have gone over this with him during the planning stages and explained the reason for using 1975 photos. Frankly, in his absence, the hair issue had gone away (as the '75 photos evidenced), and it was not at the forefront of my mind as I was editing the book.

I had shown the Yearbook to Cedric Tallis—our vice president whose primary responsibility had been overseeing the Stadium modernization—and Gabe Paul and they had approved it, but I didn't bring that up because I didn't want them called on the carpet on Opening Day with all that was going on. I took my lumps, defended myself appropriately, and went back to my office a beaten man.

I made a decision to redo the "bad" pages. I would replace color with black-and-white and go back to press in time for the second homestand, which began May 11. In the meantime, I would quietly sell what we had for the remaining seven games on this homestand, because the sales dollars eventually reflected my management of the Yearbook project. I would destroy the unsold Yearbooks after the April 25 game.

All my enthusiasm for Opening Day, and the classy way in which we had staged it, was diminished by the stupid Yearbook. Late that night, my phone rang at home. It was Cedric, whose own hands were full with the logistics he was responsible for in the new Stadium.

"I heard about the Yearbook and the way George spoke to you," he said.

"Well, thanks, yeah, it was rough. A lot of extenuating circumstances, but maybe he had a point."

Cedric cut me off. "He had no point; it was a terrible thing to do to you today. It could have waited. He has to get mad; he can't let a day go by without getting mad. It went from the parking lot to the seating arrangements to the union situation to the scoreboard not working to Rudy May giving up that homer to Ford to the traffic outside and to you having two people assigned to you on the field. He was out of control all day. Don't take it personally. We're all starting to learn that this is the way life is going to be around here now. Gabe was almost in tears at one point. You have no idea how awful it was."

I was silent.

"The Yearbook was terrific; I just went through it again. I already signed off on it last week. Don't let this stuff get to you. We've got a long season ahead of us."

What a great call for Cedric to have made. It put things in perspective, and I went to bed knowing that it wasn't the end of the world. Close to it, but not the very end.

Anyone holding a 1976 Yankee Yearbook today either has the long-hair version, in much scarcer supply, or the short-hair version, with lots of black-and-white. Believe me, I know which one is which at a glance.

Steinbrenner was a tough boss; this is not a news flash. He could be exasperating. But he happened to be a tough boss in a high-profile industry. I am quite certain there are many CEOs in America, titans of industry, with a similar lack of patience, more explosive tempers, and a style of rule by intimidation. George Steinbrenner would exemplify the breed—and be asked to host *Saturday Night Live*—because . . . well, because he ran the New York Yankees. You can be sure there are many like him in industries far less interesting to the public. Does anyone out there really care about the management style in the flavor and fragrance industry? Paper mills? Meat packing? Corrugated boxes? Glassware?

George would be the first to say that the close inspection of his style came with the territory. Yes, he was tough. But it wasn't for lack of caring about his franchise. If there had to be some bodies strewn along the roadside on the way to restoring the dynasty, so be it.

We played well in those first few months of the season, so well that it appeared the prophets were correct and that the Yankees would indeed win. This was remarkable because the season was unfolding quite easily, barely reminding you that it had been 12 years since we had finished first.

Billy was proving to be a great strategist, and, in a close game, you tended to think he would find a way to outmanage the other guy. His explanations in the clubhouse were always logical and well thought out.

He would sit behind his desk, with a picture of Casey on the wall, with his Sherlock Holmes–style pipe, with some Civil War books at the front. During the good times, he was charming, funny, and great to be with.

Still, there were times when he was drinking where he would be sarcastic, insulting, and belligerent. You never knew which Billy you were getting. We never had a bad word between us, and I thought he liked me, but I often had a feeling that as I turned my back to exit his office, he might be smiling at someone else in the room and mouthing "what an idiot" or something less flattering to his guest.

Still, we were getting along fine. He liked the fact that I knew his history and all about Casey and that I could talk with him on plane rides about the '53 World Series. He felt he could confide in me about his dis-agreements with George or Gabe.

I told him about a book I had read on him when I was a kid, and I remembered that it captured him thinking, "Please, don't hit it to me" when Don Larsen stood on the mound for the final inning of his perfect game.

"Was that true?" I asked. "Did you really feel that way?"

He got angry about the story and demanded to know who had writ-ten it. It was impossible, he said; he'd never felt like that in his life. This was almost 20 years after the book had been written, a Billy biography, and I had a feeling it was the first time he had ever heard of the book.

Once, we were doing so well together that I said, "Billy, for all the famous fights you've been in over the years, how many have you had that nobody ever heard about?"

He laughed and leaned across me and repeated the question for Yogi, who was seated across the aisle to my left. Then he thought for a moment and said, "Probably twelve to one. Twelve you never heard of for every one you heard of."

That would come out to more than 100 fights as I figured it, and, yes, that was entirely possible. People did pick on him in barrooms; I witnessed it. He was just never very good at walking away from it.

I always thought that one of Billy's problems was that his hair never turned gray. If he could see himself aging in the mirror, he might have stepped up his responsibility and his maturity and avoided the brawls associated with his youth. But he would still see himself as Billy the Kid, the underdog, the victim, Peck's Bad Boy.

I also felt that beneath the bravado, beneath the Yankee jacket that he wore like a frat jacket, was a fairly insecure man. He had been fired enough times in his life to make anyone humble. He was traded by the Yankees, A's, Tigers, Indians, Reds, Braves, and Twins. Then he was fired as manager of the Twins, Tigers, and Rangers, with five more Yankee firings and one by Oakland still to come. It would make any man insecure, you would think.

I always suspected—and this is purely amateur psychology, which everyone seemed to do with Billy—that on some level he was jealous of Whitey Ford's friendship with Mickey Mantle. Billy and Mickey were great friends—there was no need to prove it and no reason to doubt it. But Mickey and Whitey were also great friends, and they were both Hall of Famers and teammates forever. I saw little indicators along the way that Billy was insecure about his place in Mantle's world, as if there weren't room for two best friends. No one ever expressed that to me, and I may well be dead wrong, because I sure never discussed it with any of them, but it was just a hunch I had based on a few small observations over the years.

The other thing that was baffling to me about Billy was his identification crisis with this western gunslinger image. He wore western clothing all the time, opened a western-wear store on Madison Avenue, and enjoyed Frederick Remington cowboy sculptures.

But Billy was from Berkeley, California, and had never lived in Texas until he managed the Rangers in 1973. This was, to me, either an attempt to more closely identify with Mantle, who was from Oklahoma and Texas, or to embrace an image that he felt was really him—the lonesome cowboy.

We met Billy's mother out in Berkeley that summer, and what a character she turned out to be. It was easy to see where the feistiness came from when you looked at this frail, hard-swearing septuagenarian with her sweater full of dirty-joke buttons.

We also got to know Billy's daughter a bit. She was busted and imprisoned in South America on drug charges during the summer. Billy was long estranged from her, and the last thing he needed was this distraction. But he knew the world would be watching because her arrest got wide publicity, and he met with George, who put him on the phone with the State Department to do all he could to spring her.

In mid-May the Yankees recalled Ron Guidry from the minors. Because spring training had been so brief, I never had a chance to introduce myself to him in Florida, as I always tried to do with rookies. Taking one look at this wiry lightweight would tell most people "Don't bother; he won't be around long."

I never made that my rule—I tried to welcome everyone. I knew that any man in that clubhouse was going to get his name in the baseball encyclopedia someday, and what an accomplishment that was—whether he played one game or went on to the Hall of Fame. It was certainly more than I could ever claim.

Guidry's arrival came at a busy time. I was spending less and less time in the clubhouse before home games because there was always some crisis to deal with in George's office. If we weren't putting out a press release about lousy umpiring, we were threatening the city with some action over some overlooked detail at the stadium.

So my "hi, hello" to Guidry was as quick as I'd ever done it. We passed in the tunnel leading to the dugout and I introduced myself in a flash but was in a hurry to get upstairs. He was not, to my thinking, going to be a very significant guy to get to know.

By May, George had grown frustrated with the telephone system at the stadium. If my extension rang twice and I got a dial tone when I picked up, I knew it was him. He had no patience for a second ring. Finally, he succumbed to his obsession and ordered "hot line" red phones for many of us. I had one on my desk in my office and one in the press box. I was glad I didn't have one at home.

My office looked very much like the one designed for George Costanza on *Seinfeld*. I had an end-to-end window that overlooked the field, with a door to the press box. I had a credenza behind my desk, and on that credenza was the Steinbrenner phone.

Riiing.

I got it on the first bounce.

"What do you think about Carlos May?" he asked me.

It was the first time he'd ever asked my opinion of a player. I suppose he was on the fence and was polling everybody he could think of.

"Good RBI guy, professional hitter," I said. "Not much power, but terrific story, coming back from blowing off his thumb during Army Reserve duty."

"The guy's missing a thumb?" said George.

"It's pretty well known," I answered, wondering whether that was insulting to the Boss. "A lot of people thought he was through, but he came back, pretty much as good as before."

That evening we got him. We traded Rich Coggins and Ken Brett—neither favorites of Billy's. The day before we had traded Larry Gura to the Royals for Fran Healy. You couldn't respect a guy who wore little shorts and played tennis if you were a gunslinger from Texas.

As the season moved forward, it was obvious that Thurman Munson was having an MVP kind of year. He was living up to the captaincy that he claimed to misunderstand by offering leadership by example. Although his throwing was scattered since the hand injury received during an exhibition game, he was calling pitches so well that the staff cringed when he would get a rare day off.

Munson was cocky and confident and full of self-assurance, but he was not without his own insecurities. It aggravated him terribly that Carlton Fisk, who was always getting hurt, seemed to get more attention.

"It's that [Curt] Gowdy on NBC," Munson told me. "He's from Boston. He can't stop talking about Fisk on national telecasts."

I accidentally pushed a Munson button one day in June when I put some fielding stats in the daily press notes. In those days, fielding stats were only published monthly in *The Sporting News*. I would cull some interesting ones and make a small note of them.

So one day I showed "Catcher, Assist Leaders: Fisk 48, Munson 46, Sundberg 40."

Not a real big deal.

In the clubhouse before the game, Munson was in my face.

"What the hell is this?" he said. "This is a bullshit statistic. How could you print this?"

That evening, a batter struck out in the first inning and Munson dropped the ball. He had to throw to first to retire him. Joe Garagiola Jr. tapped me on the shoulder and told me to look down.

Munson was pointing a finger at me, as though to say, "That was for you."

Twice more in that game, he dropped third strikes and threw to first. Each time he looked up at me. Three assists. He had passed Fisk. And he was right, at least as far as that was concerned; it was a bullshit statistic.

"Did you drop those on purpose because of that press note?" I asked him after the game. He ignored me. He was strolling from the shower to his locker, toweling himself off and singing "America loves burgers, and we're America's Burger King!"

God, he could be exasperating. But he was taking this team to heights none of them had been to before, and we were all having a good time.

Gene Michael, as personable a ballplayer as you'd want to meet, had finally run out of time after a month with Boston, and got his last release. He had gone as far as he could on a .229 lifetime average but had squeezed 10 seasons out of it, hitting 15 homers and never playing in a World Series.

And he made a pretty good living at it too, being a very able negotiator.

When I read that he was released, I brought his name up with Steinbrenner.

"You know, he's a very classy guy and always represented this team well," I said. "I've been with him a lot of times on speaking engagements around the area, and he's just terrific. It would be good if we found a place for him back here."

George didn't really know him. He had once put him on his bad list when someone stuffed a piece of frankfurter in his glove and he jumped around the infield like a maniac with Steinbrenner watching. I once got mad at him when he told me he was going to manage in winter ball—which he wasn't—and I used it as a pretty important press note. But you couldn't stay mad at Stick.

"Have him call me," said George.

I phoned Stick at his New Jersey home and told him what I had done.

On June 14 he was added to our coaching staff as an "eye in the sky" observer from the press box. It wasn't exactly what I had in mind, but, as the years rolled on, and he went from coach to manager to general manager to superscout—it was really a matter of "Look what I've started!" I'm sure there were many days in which he wished I'd never gone to George at all, such as the day in Comiskey Park when Bill Veeck made him sit next to the clown while on his walkie-talkie assignment. But I consider him very much responsible for Joe Torre's great Yankee teams. And I'm proud.

The June draft was held on the eighth of the month. Your scouts all send in reports, you collect reports from a joint scouting bureau, you have additional notes from college coaches and bird dogs, and then your player-development people meet and plan the selection process, based on the best high school and college prospects in the country. The Yankees may not have had the best scouting department in baseball, but we were pretty near the top. And we had a great history in this area, going back to Paul Krichell (who signed players from Lou Gehrig to Whitey Ford), Bill Essick, Joe Devine (who found Joe DiMaggio and Billy Martin), and Tom Greenwade (Mickey Mantle and Bobby Murcer).

But scouting, like public relations, is an inexact science, and there are no sure successes. Maybe that was why I liked the scouts so much.

That day we drafted Pat Tabler number one and then 23 other players. Tabler had a 12-year career, playing 1,202 games—none for the Yankees. He had been sold to the Cubs in 1981. Not one other player we drafted that year ever played a single game in the big leagues except for Chris Welsh, who pitched 23 games for the Padres and Expos. We didn't get a single inning or a single at bat from any of the 24 players we drafted. Go figure.

For years the Yankees had a profit sharing plan, which did well in the Topping-Webb years but dried up along with the profits during the CBS years.

I, of course, had nothing. There was no profit in any of the years I had been there. We had no pension. And my salary, fast approaching the big $15,000 mark, hardly reflected the responsibility I was carrying by being the spokesman for a team that was on the back page of the *News* and the *Post* on a daily basis.

The one good thing was that we were, at last, making a profit in 1976. Our attendance was soaring, postseason games appeared likely, we had a favorable lease, and we were making some broadcast revenues.

So when a note landed on our desks saying that the profit-sharing plan was being canceled, I immediately marched right into Steinbrenner's office without a phone call.

I didn't scream, but I was pretty firm.

"This is terrible," I said. "A lot of people have waited twelve years for a profit. I've been here nine. How can you do this?"

"I've got a first obligation to my partners," he said.

"Well, I don't know. Here, we weren't eligible for these new IRA plans because we had a profit-sharing plan, even if we had no profit. Now, we don't even have the plan."

"So that's good news," he said. "Now you can start an IRA!"

My tail between my legs, I went back to my office. I wasn't prepared to win an economics debate with our managing general partner.

The legendary rivalry between the Yankees and Red Sox really took on new life in '76, when both teams were strong. Games between the two really stirred up the fans, and the action was intense—for the players as well as the fans.

In May the players had an on-field brawl that was pretty ugly. It began with Piniella—who always played his heart out—colliding with Fisk in a bang-bang play at the plate. As soon as they hit I said "uh-oh" to myself, because you could feel tension on the field during the whole game. Some of it was due to Billy's provocative style of play, no doubt.

Instantly, both benches emptied and the bullpen crews came charging in. Sparky Lyle led the charge for our side.

Fists were flying. Mickey Rivers, Graig Nettles, Munson, and battlin' Billy were all getting in shots for the pinstripers. Bill Lee, the loony left-hander on the Sox who took to calling Steinbrenner a Nazi, was on the receiving end of a lot of it. The battle left Lee with a shoulder separation and two months on the disabled list, giving him plenty of time for his Steinbrenner comments.

George reacted to Lee's "Nazi" comments by having me issue a statement that called for a lifetime suspension for Lee, "not to run concurrent with his immediate suspension." Wouldn't want that.

Tempers were high, and, sure enough, we went to Boston the very next week.

I have to admit that there was something enjoyable about this—this heightened interest, this magnificent rivalry coming alive again. And as Yogi pointed out, "Hell, we've been playing these guys for seventy years—they can't beat us."

It was a little less enjoyable when Chris Chambliss hit a triple and, while leading off third, looked down to find a dart in his right arm. Someone in the stands had thrown a dart as he rounded the bases! Chris, a bear of a man with a gentle nature and a navy chaplain for a dad, just removed the dart and showed it to everyone after the game. It could have hit him in the eye. But he just shook his head about how nasty things had turned.

At midnight on the June 15 trading deadline, Charlie Finley, seeing a grim future, took his fate into his own hands. With free agency at his doorstep, he knew he would be unable to sign his great players, the men who had led his A's to three straight world championships in 1972, 1973, and 1974. He didn't win in '75, because we had Catfish. But he knew that most of his stars would walk after the '76 season because he couldn't pay them what they would get on the open market. And, of course, they hated him.

So he did the only thing he felt he could do, and that was to sell Joe Rudi and Rollie Fingers to the Red Sox for $1 million each and Vida Blue to us. We were to pay $1.5 million for Blue, still one of the glamor players in the game since his sensational debut season of '71.

My phone rang shortly after midnight. I was now used to these middle-of-the-night calls, and they were often nothing more than "I want to see you first thing in the morning!" Very conducive to getting back to sleep.

This time, there was plenty of substance to it. What a blockbuster. I splashed some water on my face, pulled out my press list, and began making my calls.

"The Yankees have announced that they have purchased the contract of Vida Blue from the Oakland A's, and that he in turn has agreed to a new, three-year contract, signed just before the transaction was completed."

It never occurred to me—or to anyone else in baseball—that this wasn't going to happen.

But that wasn't all.

On the same day, we pulled off a monster trade with the Baltimore Orioles, a team we had battled unsuccessfully for years.

We were sending them Scott McGregor, Tippy Martinez, Dave Pagan, Rudy May, and Rick Dempsey, for Ken Holtzman, Doyle Alexander, Elrod Hendricks, Grant Jackson, and a minor league pitcher. A nine-player deal—the biggest trade since the Yankees and Browns had done a 17-player deal in 1954, the Browns having been the Orioles' direct ancestors.

I went to work a few hours later and rushed to press with an insert page on all the new guys for our press guide. Blue would wear number 20 and would start Monday against Cleveland.

I was glad to see some of our guys go because they would have a chance to blossom as big leaguers. McGregor was a quality pitcher who never did make it to the Yankees, but he was a friend from a number of spring training camps. Martinez, a Colorado-born relief pitcher, sat next to me on a bus going to Anaheim Stadium the first night he was ever in the majors. "Tell me, Tippy," I said, "do you ever think about managing when your career is over?" I stayed on his Christmas card list for years.

Tippy, like Tino Martinez later, was always encountering people who would speak slowly and loudly and gesture a lot with their hands so that he might understand English. Both laughed about it; English was their first language. I am not sure Tippy knew a word of Spanish.

McGregor, Martinez, and Dempsey would become stars for Baltimore. But, for the here and now, the Yankees were going for the '76 pennant, and Holtzman, Jackson, and Alexander could play key roles. It was a trade intended for the present, not for the future.

The next day, we found out that Bowie Kuhn had decided to hold up the sales of the Oakland players.

It was pretty much unprecedented, uncharted waters, and almost surely would guarantee a lawsuit by Finley.

Finley would claim that he could not sign the players and would use the $3.5 million to get new players, which he was good at doing. Unfortunately, his credibility was nil with Kuhn, who had spent much of his time in office disciplining the maverick owner. Kuhn just wasn't buying it—he was sure that Finley was prepared to pocket the money and run his franchise into the ground. And he wasn't going to stand for it.

He visited Finley the very night of the trades (both were in Chicago) and did not come out convinced that Finley meant what he said. What a surprise.

He held up the sales for three days and then on the 18th announced that they would not be honored. Rudi and Fingers, who had actually reported to Boston and posed for pictures in Red Sox uniforms, were going back to Oakland. And Blue, who never did make it to New York, was likewise going back, except that he had a three-year contract that he wouldn't have signed had he not been sold. What a mess.

It was one gutsy move by Kuhn. It infuriated a number of owners, who thought he had no business getting into this. Finley said he would climb to the top of the Sears Tower in downtown Chicago and hoist a flag calling Kuhn the village idiot.

Village idiot or not, Kuhn felt he had the power to do anything in the best interests of baseball, and that included not standing by while an owner dismantled his team. He wanted to see players returned to the A's, not just cash, and they had to be players of some value.

Surprisingly, George was not very vocal over Kuhn's decision. At another time, in another place, over another player, he might have really kicked up a fuss. We could have had dueling press-release wars, not an atypical development.

On the day of the ruling, we merely announced that we had no comment at that time and would hold a press conference early the following week to announce our reaction.

And then, well . . . we said very little. We sort of agreed with Finley, sort of would like to have Blue, but we didn't attack Kuhn and we didn't make much noise about lawsuits, injunctions, Yankee honor, fine young men, and all of that. George was actually being a good citizen on this one.

In the end, no Vida for us. Kuhn would prevail in court, Finley would sulk for years, and my Vida Blue press-guide insert would become a collector's item. On we went to the second half of the season. We were Blue-less, but we were rolling.

ANOTHER WEEK
OF THIS!!

John Milton Rivers was not named after a poet, but "Mickey" Rivers was a poet of the baseball diamond, creating a legend among his peers as his career unfolded. The fans loved Mick the Quick for his entertaining play and the catalytic effect he was having on the club. His teammates loved him because he was just an innocently funny guy.

As great a player as Bobby Bonds had been, Rivers was doing more to win games for us. Rickey Henderson would later define the leadoff spot in the lineup and bring it to new levels, including power, but Rivers was a rally-starter unlike anything the Yankees had known before in their glorious history.

He came to the team having stolen 100 bases in his two previous years with the Angels. At that point, after 73 seasons, the Yankee franchise's all-time leader was still Hal Chase, the game-fixing first baseman of pre-1920 baseball, with 248. Ninety-six steals would get you into the top 20. Rivers was going to be a Yankee the likes of which the franchise had never known.

One thing we would learn about Mickey was that he absolutely marched to his own drummer. He was invariably a few days late for spring training, and, although we were accustomed to the visa problems of Latin American players, Mickey was only commuting up I-95 from Miami. It was a 45-minute drive and he'd be three days late.

His philosophy in life was, "Ain't no sense worrying about things you got control over, 'cause if you got control over them, ain't no sense worrying. And there ain't no sense worrying about things you got no control over, 'cause if you got no control over them, ain't no sense worrying."

Mickey walked like an elderly man on aching bunions. But on the field he was a blur. His acceleration off a base was amazing, and it was a thing of beauty to see him go from first to third on singles to center. Sometimes our bus would pass an old wino on the street and someone would invariably point him out and say, "Mickey, that's you in six years." And Mickey would laugh and return the volley with something funny of his own.

He liked to pick on Reggie Jackson, and everyone would be quiet when that happened, because it became a great battle of "last words." Mick would philosophize about something and Reggie would say, "What can you possibly know about this, how can you possibly disagree with me? I've got an IQ of one-seventy."

And Mickey would say, "Out of what, a thousand?"

Asked one year about his goals for the season, he said, "I want to hit .300 and stay injury prone."

Kids loved to watch Mickey play. When he swung and missed, he'd twirl his bat like a baton, and Little Leaguers all over New York started to imitate him (Jim Leyritz later did it on every pitch). If you asked Mick why he did it, he'd say, "Always done it."

He liked to go to the track, and he had not the slightest sense of money. It would kill Bill Kane to give him his full road trip's worth of meal money on the first day—as was common—because he would run out of money by the second or third day, depending on whether there was time to visit a track. He had terrible luck with the horses but was always studying the *Daily Racing Form* in hopes of finding the ultimate underdog.

Mick and I got along terrifically, but I was never really sure that he knew my name. I was shocked one day—years after we had both left the Yankees—when we bumped into each other on the street in Manhattan and he hugged me and called me by my name at once. I didn't even have to re-introduce myself. I always suspected there was a lot more going on upstairs there than met the eye.

I had to ask him about the rumor I had heard.

"I heard that you are now a jai alai player under the name of Miguel Rivera," I said. "Is this true?"

"Where'd you hear that?" he said.

"Well, you know, you bump into people, stories spread. I think Sparky told me that."

"Yeah, well, nothing is amazing to me anymore. You never know."

So we embraced and walked on, and I still didn't know if he was in fact Miguel Rivera.

Easy going as Mickey was, he also seemed to have a propensity for getting married without all the legal paperwork necessary to dissolve previously existing marriages. Mickey just wasn't a paperwork kind of guy. There may have been times in his life when he just managed to exceed the legal limit on marriages.

The first year we had him, his New York–based wife was a beautiful woman named Mary. Mary was high maintenance and liked Mickey a lot more at the start of a road trip, when he had all that money, than at the end, when he was broke. One day, when Mickey met Mary after the game, a dispute arose as they walked to the players' parking lot past auto-graph-seeking fans. Ignoring the fans, they walked and yelled and then got into their separate cars. They were, as you would expect, late-model, expensive cars—nothing that would embarrass the players' parking lot.

The dispute continued without words, but with vehicles. *Crash.* Mickey and Mary proceeded to stage a demolition derby in the lot as spectators looked on, banging into each other's cars and leaving it to insurance adjusters to handle the paperwork later that week.

On the field, his 43 stolen bases in 1976 were the most by a Yankee in 32 years; he made the All-Star team, scored 95 runs in 137 games, batted .312, and was third in MVP voting. The only thing that drove Billy Martin crazy was that he had no patience at the plate and walked only 12 times in more than 600 at bats.

Complimenting Rivers was Willie Randolph with 37 steals, and Roy White with 31. The top of our lineup was very daring, typifying Billy Martin's style. It was a lineup that was hard to pitch to, and we were coasting along to the division title.

Billy was staying trouble free too. We were always expecting a fight to be lurking just around the corner, because he was still the short-fused Martin—sarcastic, insecure, and always feeling challenged.

There were those late nights that forced him to wear sunglasses in the dugout to camouflage his bloodshot eyes, and, occasionally, he would just make it to the dugout by the first pitch after snoozing on the couch in his office. But, generally speaking, he was having a good season, winning over the fans, and staying out of trouble.

We had, since the season opened, been under fire from various community groups who remained enraged that more than $100 million had been spent on Yankee Stadium, with nothing for the surrounding parks and sandlots. At the start of the project, all that was supposed to have been included, creating a "Yankeeland" around the ballpark. All that had happened, in fact, had been new paint jobs for the Macombs Dam Bridge and the subway station near the park and new costly exit ramps off the Major Deegan Expressway. Nothing had happened at the city parks.

I liked the parks. I used to disappear at lunchtime on occasion and watch the basketball games or the softball games across the street while munching on a hot dog from a local pushcart. On a balmy spring after-noon, nothing was as nice as the smell of a New York hot dog, my trusty *New York Times*, and the sounds of a good softball game in front of me. It was a great way to spend a lunch hour.

But the parks were neglected, and what should have been a beautiful adjunct to the professional game across the street was instead becoming an eyesore.

Finally, succumbing to community pressure, we held a press confer-ence in early July to announce that we would throw in some money to help spruce up the parks. Part of the money went into big signs that said, WE DO CARE—NEW YORK YANKEES, which were attached to the fences.

Our grounds crew, to its dismay, was dispatched across the street to help get the fields in shape. Improvements were made and the protests quieted, although, like a lot of well-intentioned ideas, phase 1 took a long time getting to phase 2 once the community activists were silenced.

The protests over the cost of Yankee Stadium never really died out. Steinbrenner was always taking abuse for that, even though it had not been his project. And as for the $24 million the rebuild was supposed to have cost, that had been the price only of building Shea Stadium, proposed with no real knowledge at that time of what the Yankee Stadium upgrade would cost in 1976 dollars.

On July 7, we announced that our Con Edison Yankee Program, through which underprivileged kids had been attending games for free since 1968, was being recognized by the Baseball Hall of Fame through its acceptance of a plaque on which Mayor Abe Beame declared "Con Edison–Yankee Baseball Day." (I have never really seen this plaque in Cooperstown, by the way.)

Four days later, we suspended the program.

Talk about your public relations nightmares.

I stood in the pressroom before a game, the lone Yankee official, and announced that "increasing disturbances in the Con Edison section and throughout the park involving Con Edison Kids, bordering on serious incidents" had forced us to suspend the program.

Russ Holt, a Con Ed official, said that we were suspending the program because our attendance was increasing and we could now sell those free tickets.

We answered in a press release, "If the high-salaried Con Edison executives spent more time trying to reduce skyrocketing electric rates for New Yorkers, and less time inventing false accusations, they would be better off."

It was a bad statement by Holt, a cheap shot. We did have serious security issues. It was hard to keep 11-year-old kids, seated 500 feet from home plate, interested in a baseball game. Kids get into trouble. You could only ask Earl Battey, the former catcher and "Con Edison Answer Man," so many questions in one afternoon.

In many, many meetings with Steinbrenner, I had never heard him utter one racial epithet, never heard him tell an ethnic joke, and always felt that he supported these kids. He had the 1950s sports ethic that seemed to come from Bob Richards, who did all of those uplifting Wheaties TV commercials then. His heroes tended to be guys like Otto Graham, the wholesome Cleveland Browns Hall of Famer. He funded college and prep athletic facilities around the country and reached out generously to provide scholarships for needy kids. He liked it when these facts were included in long feature stories about him, but he didn't do it for the publicity. In these areas, he was generous and color blind.

The Con Ed shutdown was nevertheless a PR nightmare. YANKS CUT OFF NEEDY KIDS was now the tabloid headline, and it was hard to get people to listen to the facts when you were dealing with that. Whoever gets the first headline in a PR battle will usually hold the advantage, particularly as the stories get smaller, the responses less interesting, and the public's attention span fades.

We provided lists of incidents, including robberies, use of weapons, hurling of objects onto the field, muggings, arson, and even a case of a seven-year-old boy's head being held in a toilet until he surrendered his baseball glove. All of these acts occurred in the Con Edison section.

This PR battle played out for days. Local sportscasters would say to us, "Yeah, we know what those kids can be like, it must have been terrible for you to cancel the program," but then they would go on the air and interview the mothers of honor students who had counted on going to the games as a reward for their hard work.

The battle finally ended with an agreement that Con Edison would provide greater adult supervision, and the program was restored. We had another big pregame press conference with the mayor and the Con Ed officials, including Russ Holt, and everything was back in place. For the first time (in what was private property), New York City police were assigned to patrol within Yankee Stadium.

Gabe was the negotiator, as was his skill. He could wheel out the charm when he had to, but he could be firm when needed.

One year we had a problem because non-union printers had printed our Yearbook. We had subcontracted the production, and the subcontractor was free to use anyone he wanted. But New York was a big union town, and that didn't play well. The printers' union in New York threatened to throw a picket line around the stadium. As the team's spokesman, my response to this, while not disrespectful, managed to anger them further, and Gabe had to take them all to lunch at the Stadium Club to convince them to call off the picket line.

"I should charge you for the lunch," he said sternly. "You made me have lunch with them because of what you said. Did you see those guys?"

Gabe was no longer the intimidating figure he had been during George's suspension. He was now one of us. He had his red phone, he was frequently summoned down the hall, and he would be berated over some detail in front of the rest of us during staff meetings. We never thought we could feel sorry for Gabe; he was hardly an object of sympathy. But, as the year moved forward, he was taking his lumps just like the rest of us. Getting a chance to pounce on me once in a while probably did him good.

The second half of the season seemed like a tune-up for the postseason. After 12 years in the wilderness with no titles to show for it, we were coasting. And yet, because we were favored, there was no amazement to this; no upset in the making. We were, in fact, back where we belonged, as though it had only been yesterday that we were a dynasty.

The '76 Yankees were the start, in fact, of a new mini-dynasty. Gabe had spun masterful trades, the farm system had delivered a few key players, and we had made the best of the beginning of free agency by signing Hunter, a real leader who was showing us how to win.

Munson was brilliant as captain; leading by example, playing on guts and determination, and never letting a little thing like a concussion slow him down. One season he made only one error all year, and that one came when he was knocked unconscious on a play at the plate.

Instead of worrying about a collapse or about the day-to-day on-field triumphs, as a front office we were now dealing with a boss's style we were wholly unfamiliar with.

Under Topping, Webb, and Weiss, or under Burke and MacPhail, there was a relaxed pace to the playing of the season. Now it was all frenzy, played at breakneck speed. We were on our way to breaking two million in attendance, but it had to be more. There were always battles to fight, early in the morning, late at night.

We had a 30-minute rule. None of us could leave the ballpark for 30 minutes after a game in case a meeting was called. This would get us home well past midnight, with the requirement that we still be back at nine the next morning, day after day. I violated this one day after a Sunday doubleheader, having promised my wife I would take her to dinner. When I got home there was a message to call George, and he told me to get back. It wasn't easy to say no, but I did, and I told him I would see him in the morning.

We never had that morning meeting, fortunately, or I might have been out in the street at last.

The need for a break grew. I looked forward to road trips, when you could sleep a little later, only one phone line could ring in the room, and you could actually spend time with the writers and the players without sitting in meetings. At home, I was growing increasingly removed from the players. I was forever in meetings and was dispatching Mickey Morabito to the clubhouse to see players about different requests. I'd get on a plane with the team, and the guys would say, "Where have you been?"

This frenzied year also coincided with the first year of my marriage, and what a strain that was! When the team was on the road, that would be one thing, but when we were home—I was never home either! And this pace continued from the day we went to spring training in March until the World Series ended in late October. I was now living in Tarrytown (we had rented a garden apartment in historic Sleepy Hollow that had been previously occupied by Olympic star Bruce Jenner and his family), but there were nights when I came home feeling very much like the Headless Horseman of Washington Irving's novel.

It hurt Joe Garagiola Jr. and me to now find ourselves picking on Lee MacPhail on a fairly regular basis. George had never liked Lee and really beat him up in public over the quality of umpiring. We had an incident in July where Hal McRae of the Royals took too many warm-up throws when he went into the game as a defensive replacement in the outfield. Under Joe's name, we released a statement calling for Lee to either enforce these rules or change them, as we put the game under protest. Joe fought hard to tone down the inflammatory language in the release—and won. But such battles took a lot out of him—and me.

We both took great pains to privately assure MacPhail that these increasing attacks were not at all personal, and he, of course, totally understood. He just never understood why George seemed to hate him so much.

The ultimate rift between the two would come a few years later, when MacPhail overruled his umpires in the famous "Pine Tar Game" and allowed George Brett's home run to stand. Steinbrenner responded with a statement suggesting that MacPhail ought to go house hunting in Kansas City, implying that fans in New York might somehow cause him harm. George came very close to being suspended again by Kuhn over this one, and he promptly paid a big fine to avoid that.

We clinched the Eastern Division title in Detroit on September 25. We didn't have a clubhouse celebration because the clinching didn't come until hours later, when the Orioles lost.

On October 1, 1976, the 15th anniversary of Maris's 61st home run, I invited Sal Durante to Yankee Stadium to throw out the first ball. Sal, as a teenager, had come to the game 15 years ago with his girlfriend and caught the ball. He looked like a guy out of the cast of *Grease*, the sort of guy who would have a pack of Camels rolled up in the sleeve of his T-shirt, snapping his fingers to Dion and the Belmonts. He was a great kid, and the photos of him and Maris after the game were terrific. Maris told him to keep the ball and "Get what you can for it." It wasn't the $3 million that went to the guy who caught Mark McGwire's 70th, but it was a few thousand that Sal could use. He was about to marry his girl-friend, and they needed the money.

I had kept in touch with Sal over the years, feeling he was an impor-tant part of Yankee history; on October 1, 1976, I sent him out to the right field stands to throw out the first ball from approximately the same spot where he had caught number 61. Because I just sent him out there, unaccompanied, I didn't realize that he would be hassled by stadium security because his ticket was not for that section. But hey—he was a Brooklyn guy; he'd get the job done.

I didn't just have Sal throw out the first ball from right field. I had him throw it to Nettles. I took Nettles out to right so that that big number nine on his back would be facing in, and I had Bob Sheppard set the stage by saying (1) this was the 15th anniversary, (2) Sal Durante would throw out the first ball from right field, and (3) the first Yankee home run champion since Maris, also wearing number nine, would catch the ball. It was a beautiful ceremony. I only wish Maris had been there.

The next days were spent frantically preparing for our first World Series since 1964. To increase stadium capacity, benches of bleacher seats were installed in deep left center, beyond the bullpens. The area was considered too far away for seating when the stadium was constructed, but, since the '76 Series, these seats have been regularly filled with "bleacher bums" with good eyesight.

All the details fell on me. Press credentials. First-pitch ceremonies. National anthem singers. Where Mrs. Ruth and Mrs. Gehrig would sit. Whether Cary Grant would be coming to the games. What if President Ford attended? Barry Landers, our promotion director, took on some of this burden. Mickey Morabito was a great help.

Anne Mileo, our beloved and efficient PR secretary, had by now had enough of the pressure. She announced that she was checking into the hospital for elective ear surgery and would miss the playoffs and the World Series. Her role was critical, especially because we were now also in the ticket business, handling media requests and physically apportioning the tickets based on the total allotment provided by the ticket office. I tried to talk her into postponing the surgery, but it was clear that she needed it—to break away from the stress. I was going to have a temp during these critical weeks, answering phone calls and parceling out tickets and credentials. Argh!

Things would have worked well if we had all been trusted to do our jobs. But, as feared, every minute detail had to be cleared with the Boss. The process, which needed to run as rapidly as it did efficiently, was now delayed by 24 to 48 hours on all requests.

We did site surveys with ABC, which was doing its first playoff, and NBC, the experienced World Series provider. The ABC people were no novices in big-time sports, but baseball was new to them. NBC, under Harry Coyle's direction, had some novel camera locations in mind and begged us not to tell ABC their plans.

ABC hired Reggie Jackson as a commentator, and that got off to a bad start when Reggie, sitting in my office, overheard Howard Cosell ridiculing him from the press box to production assistants. Now, these two guys had to work side by side for the games, and it was to Reggie's credit that he did a professional job.

Cosell was a critic of baseball, and his participation in ABC's new baseball package had been opposed by Kuhn. But the '76 season had softened him. Mark Fidrych had been a delight, and his performance (talking to the ball, manicuring the mound) on an ABC Monday-night telecast of a Yanks–Tigers game had put ABC on the map. It was one of the biggest days of the year, a great night for baseball. Cosell was smart enough to see that the game was coming back and that he could ride its coattails and be perceived as one of the reasons the national pastime was heating up.

My office was overrun by visitors looking for things big and small. I was told that the broadcast area assigned to the Venezuelan television crew was "the greatest insult ever perpetrated upon the Latin American people."

Everyone who got a press pin needed two. Everyone who got two needed three. In the midst of this, my black phone was ringing, with callers in bars asking, "Who wore number three after Babe Ruth?" And the red phone was ringing to say, "Get down here right now for a meeting."

I truly needed a staff of eight or ten. Instead, it was Mickey, the temp secretary, and me. I checked into the Midtown hotel that would serve as postseason headquarters for hospitality and ate my meals across the street at the Stage Deli. I pretty much told my wife that I would see her "whenever this is over."

Joe Garagiola Jr., whose father would broadcast the World Series for NBC, was a help. When he wasn't issuing threatening statements demanding better umpiring for these crucial games, he would come in and say, "Need anything done?" That was great. Also high on the "great" list was the appearance of other PR directors from the league. It was customary for them to pitch in when the games began, monitoring the auxiliary press boxes and helping in the interview rooms, the clubhouses, the field, and the hospitality areas. When Bob Brown of the Orioles arrived, sleeves rolled up and ready to go, it was as though the cavalry had come to save the day. Bob had been in the postseason almost every year since '66 with Baltimore. If ever a friendly face walked into my office, it was his. When the whole postseason ended, I personally bought custom-made Cross pen sets with the Yankee logo on them, as gifts for all the PR guys who helped.

The League Champion Series opened in Kansas City. I stayed in New York to prepare for the days when the party would move to our place.

Yankee Stadium never looked grander. This would be the first postseason played in the remodeled ballpark, which had been host to 27 previous World Series. There is nothing in all of sports quite like the look of Yankee Stadium in October, bedecked with bunting and fresh paint and added seats for dignitaries.

The team got new uniforms for the postseason. We took studio portraits of each member for the World Series program, in case we made it. The Yankee pinstripe jerseys over long-sleeve navy-blue sweatshirts was the classic look of October baseball. It doesn't get any better.

If we had brought Catfish Hunter to New York to "show us how to win," that's what he did in Game 1 in Kansas City. He beat the Royals 4–1 on a five-hitter, with five strikeouts and no walks, a 2 hour, 6 minute performance. Larry Gura was the loser, to Billy's delight.

The Royals won Game 2, and then it was back to New York for the final three games of the best-of-five series. Somehow, we got everyone credentialed, parked, and seated and let the games take over.

We split Games 3 and 4, setting up a climactic Game 5, which would be one for the history books. It was Thursday night, October 14. This was the Royals' first postseason appearance—the Yankees' 30th. But these two teams were beginning a great rivalry that would last some six years, and this game would be the biggest of them all.

I sat in the press box with Dean Vogelaar, the Royals' PR man, on my left, Joe Garagiola Jr. on my right. Almost 57,000 people were in the stands, on a very chilly night. My black phone only rang if the switchboard cleared it with me first. My red phone would (I hoped) be silent.

The Yankees fans were very loud and exuberant. It wasn't as many had forecast—a quiet crowd made up of well-connected businesspeople who somehow "knew how to get tickets." The real fans were there, many of them having stuck with us during the lean years.

Ed Figueroa would start for us against Dennis Leonard, who had been knocked out early on Sunday in Game 2 at Royals Stadium.

Both pitchers allowed two runs in the first, with Leonard knocked out without retiring a hitter.

Now we had to face Paul Splittorff, who had also relieved Leonard on Sunday and had won the game.

After seven tough innings, we had a 6–3 lead. It was Pete Sheehy's job to get the champagne on ice for the clubhouse, which had to have been a tricky assignment for a very superstitious guy. He had, of course, handled this before. Even during Prohibition.

We were six outs away in the eighth when the Royals got two runners on. Grant Jackson, who had come over in that big trade with the Orioles, relieved Figueroa, who left to a great Yankee Stadium ovation, the fans chanting "ED-die, Ed-die" as they did at Madison Square Garden for goalie Ed Giacomin.

Jackson was facing George Brett, one tough out. And sure enough, Brett, who would positively kill us over the years, launched a game-tying home run to make it 6–6, and absolutely silenced everyone.

Dean Vogelaar, seated to my left, tried to be professionally quiet, but one couldn't help but feel his excitement. The momentum had shifted back to Kansas City, even though the home team always has an edge in a tie game. I smiled at him, patted him on the back, and said, "Keep your seat belt on; this is one hell of a game."

Mark Littell retired us in the eighth. I could see Munson urging his teammates on, thumping his glove as he took Tidrow's warm-up throws in the ninth. Thurman had come too far to lose this game. Seven seasons of battling for just this moment, a full season of inspired baseball. I could read Thurman's mind: "No way are we going to lose this game."

Tidrow, our scruffy spot starter and long reliever who went by the nickname "Dirt," set the Royals down in the ninth.

Last of the ninth, 6–6. The place was going crazy. In the press box, we were all standing between innings, and we remained so as play resumed, with Chris Chambliss our leadoff hitter.

Chambliss had come to the Yankees the year before in that "Friday Night Massacre" engineered by Gabe. He had not been well received, because we had traded half our pitching staff and he was replacing "one of the boys," the slick-fielding Mike Hegan. But Chris was a quality player and a great person, who bore leadership skills on his broad back and a tough, competitive nature inside.

Sandy Alomar was on deck; Nettles would follow.

There was a long delay while debris was cleared from the field. The crowd was restless, and the new, ugly New York tradition of running on the field and tearing up the turf had developed in recent years. There were signs that a Yankee win would result in just that.

The field was cleared, but toilet paper streamers kept sailing down. Play resumed.

Littell looked in for the sign. He delivered his first pitch.

Chambliss put everything he had into his swing. He was going for the money. He'd been 10-for-20 in this series and was on a tear. The ball left his bat in a high arc and, to me, seemed to stay aloft for minutes. It was headed for right-center. McRae, the right fielder, was in pursuit.

It began its downward arc, and you could tell from McRae's body-language that he was not going to get it. The noise of the crowd grew with the realization of what was about to happen. Finally, it disappeared over the wall.

A home run! One of the great home runs in baseball history. The Yankees were in the World Series! Bedlam!

The security guards were no match for the determined fans, who stormed the field as though that in itself were a sporting event. By the time Chambliss was approaching second base, we had a riot on hand.

At the moment the ball had crossed the fence, Chris had raised his arms in triumph. Alomar, on deck, and Munson, emerging from the dugout, were euphoric in photos we would later see.

In the press box, I had just witnessed my most historic moment after nine years with the team. Joe grabbed me as if I were a tackling dummy and hugged the stuffing out of me. This was what the hard work was all about.

As energized as I was by the blast, as empowered as I felt from the rush of excitement, there was a voice within me that said, "Damn! Another week of this!"

I tried to block it out and savor the moment. But it was strong. We had been put through so much in the preceding days that a part of me wanted it to be over right now. I fought those voices off—I was in baseball; baseball was about moments like this. But it was there, it was reality. And I hated that feeling.

Chambliss never did touch home plate, except for hours later, when the place had finally cleared and he went back outside, just for history's sake. Twenty-three years later, when he was miked while coaching the '99 Yankees, he was overheard in this exchange with trainer Gene Monahan.

Chris: Did you hear what happened in the Mets game? Robin Ventura hit a grand slam to win it, and he only got credit for a single because he never rounded the bases.
Gene: Those are the rules.
Chris: Well, I never touched home.

The police were overwhelmed, and, as years passed, security would be beefed up by the presence of mounted police (Wade Boggs would ride one of those horses after the '96 world championship). But, in 1976, there was no controlling the mobs, and it was not a pretty sight. The fans tore up $100,000 worth of turf and embarrassed New York on national television. It was as if the home run wasn't the story; their excessive behavior was the story. It wasn't a proud moment.

I threw on my raincoat and headed for the clubhouse, which was a madhouse. But it was just what I had always wanted to experience—a pennant-winning clubhouse, complete with champagne. Everyone was hugging each other, oblivious to the fans destroying the field. Catfish was the first to grab me, and he said, "Where you been all week?" With that, he poured a full bottle over my head. It burned my eyes but it felt fantastic, and I couldn't have picked a better guy to christen me.

I especially enjoyed embracing the guys who had been there during the losing years. White, Munson, Nettles, Lyle, Piniella, Stanley. I found Billy, too. He'd said he'd win. He'd said, "Watch me after I have this team for a spring training." And his first full year out, he won it. Billy had tasted Yankee champagne many times before, but not since 1956. He said, "I wish Casey could see me now."

We celebrated there for a good hour, and then I made my way back to my office. The quiet felt so odd. The field was finally cleared and the damage was horrid to see. The work that would need to be done in time for the third game of the World Series was enormous. Joe and I and Morabito sat quietly for a bit in the office, talked about the upcoming Series, and covered some additional details we would need to review, and then I headed back downtown to my hotel. It was almost impossible to think about the fact that we would be in the World Series in Cincinnati in about 36 hours.

I got to the stadium early Friday and the big buses were already outside, revving their engines for the trip to the airport. Bill Kane had risen to the occasion, taking care of every detail that a traveling secretary must. The wives would be going, the media would be going, and Billy Martin even grabbed three regular stadium plainclothes policemen, threw them on the bus, and said, "You're going with us."

They did.

We did not have a downtown hotel; we stayed, instead, about 40 miles outside of Cincinnati. We checked in and got right back on a bus to Riverfront Stadium for a late-afternoon workout.

Make no mistake: The Reds were heavily favored to win. Not only had they finished on Tuesday, sweeping the Phillies, but they were the Big Red Machine, one of the great assemblies of baseball talent of the century. With Johnny Bench, Pete Rose, Joe Morgan, Tony Perez, George Foster, Ken Griffey, Dan Driessen, and Dave Concepcion, this was an incredible lineup. The pitchers were not spectacular, but, like the great Yankee teams of the past, the Reds were good enough to know how to win with that lineup behind them. The Yankees never had a Mathewson or a Grove or a Feller or a Koufax, but their great ones—Ford, Ruffing, Gomez, Hoyt—were money pitchers.

It was unusual being Yankees and being underdogs, but the Reds were defending champions, had swept their LCS, and were appreciated in their time as sensational.

On the other hand, we were exhausted. The five-game series with the Royals had taken a lot out of us, our rotation was shot, and, man for man, we just didn't measure up. I think most of the players felt that way. It seemed that only Munson was loose, ready to have some fun and play in a World Series.

We got to Riverfront in a fun mood, though. Dock Ellis's autobiography had recently been published, and he sat on the bus reading aloud selections from it about big games against the Reds and how he'd "whupped them." He had a lot of Ali in him—he was fun to be around if you didn't take him too seriously.

Pulling up to Riverfront, our driver couldn't negotiate the tough turns and we hit the concrete sidings. A bad omen, perhaps.

Finally, I sat in the training room with Chambliss, talking about his big home run. I thought this was a good time to tell him about all the big homers in baseball history, so, with Gene Monahan and a few players listening, I walked him through Gabby Hartnett, Bobby Thomson, Bill Mazeroski, and, of course, Carlton Fisk from the year before. While I was talking, Monahan came by with a pair of surgical scissors and cut my necktie in half, leaving me in a bit of a fix for the Series. I had to borrow one from Bob Lemon, our pitching coach, who always came prepared. "We lemons and apples have to stick together," he said, intentionally mispronouncing my name. Lem was one of the game's beautiful people. It gave me great pleasure when he eventually led the Yankees to a world championship, for which, strangely, he became better known than for his brilliance as a pitcher in the '50s.

At the workout, Billy had to name his starting pitcher for Saturday. Figueroa, Ellis, and Hunter weren't ready. Holtzman had been our fourth starter and had World Series experience, but there was something about Ken Holtzman that just rubbed Billy the wrong way. He would not use Holtzman at all in the postseason.

Instead, he named Doyle Alexander, who had made 19 starts for us but hadn't pitched since the pennant clincher in Detroit 21 days earlier. It was a shocking announcement, with most people having assumed that Holtzman would get the ball.

I had to scramble to write my press notes that evening. Doyle had a history against Cincinnati, because he had been with the Dodgers early in his career. And the press notes demanded that I show his career mark against the Reds. Damn! I hadn't expected this at all.

Back in my hotel room, I called the Elias Sports Bureau, but it had closed for the day. I sat and considered my options.

I picked up the phone and called the *Los Angeles Times*. It was still early on the West Coast, and I got someone from the sports staff on the phone. I told him who I was and that I needed him to go to the microfilm for 1971, look up Dodger games against the Reds, and write down what Alexander had done. To my relief, he was able to help me, and I had that important paragraph in my notes. If I hadn't found it, I would have looked bad.

Now it was Saturday, the only day game of the Series. It was cold— our players on the bench wore towels around their necks in addition to jackets—but it was festive. It was the World Series.

Sad to say, we totally screwed up the first game. Not only did we lose

5–1, with Don Gullett pitching beautifully for the Reds, but we just looked outclassed, as if we didn't belong on the same field. Whether it was fatigue, the partying on Thursday night, or whatever, this was the Big Red Machine, and we weren't really the Bronx Bombers.

To make matters worse, we were embarrassed by an incident early in the game. Gene Michael had been our "eye in the sky" during the season. For the Series, George added two additional "eyes" in Clyde King and Karl Kuehl, who had recently managed in Montreal. Now we had three men at press level directing our defense from above.

Sparky Anderson, notified of this by Reds officials, stopped the game and complained to the home plate umpire. Play was stopped while he conferred with Commissioner Kuhn. After some delay, Kuhn ruled that we could have one, but not three.

The game over, the Yanks down 1–0, Steinbrenner went into fury mode. All the joy of the LCS was history. We had not only played poorly but had embarrassed him by getting caught with too many walkie-talkies, allowing Kuhn to win a round.

Someone among us asked George if he would be going to the World Series party that night.

"No one is going," he announced. "Parties are for winners. You guys are a bunch of losers. You're all confined to your rooms."

By "all," he made it clear that he meant not only Bill Kane, Gene Michael, and Marty Appel, but also Cedric Tallis, the scouts, old Birdie Tebbetts, poor Karl Kuehl and Clyde King, and even Gabe Paul.

"The hell with that," said Gabe. Gabe was not one to miss a party in his old town.

On the other hand, my colleagues and I did not need to get fired during the World Series and be stranded in Cincinnati, hitchhiking home with Birdie Tebbetts. I took George seriously.

So we all went back to our little motel 40 miles out of town, where I put on the TV, wrote my press notes, and then worked on a freelance project: compiling the stats for the backs of 3-D baseball cards included in Kellogg's cereal. A fine thing this was on the first night of my first World Series.

We lost the second game 4–3 on Sunday night, despite a gallant effort by Catfish, the Reds winning in the last of the ninth on a Tony Perez single.

So, we had been on top of the world Thursday night. And now, 72 hours later, we were already down 2–0 in the World Series and headed back to New York with our tails between our legs.

The party at the Americana the night before Game 3 was festive and even had shrimp cocktail. First class, and not cheap. This was a party I did attend, both because I was somewhat of a host and because I was living in that hotel for the week. The whole baseball community was there—other managers, scouts, front-office people, league officials, old timers, the Cooperstown crowd. It was really a great gathering. Baseball parties today are filled with sponsors and licensees and advertising executives, most of whom change every year. You can wander for hours without seeing a familiar face. Peter Ueberroth brought that change to the parties at the All-Star Game and the World Series, and, although it is probably good business, there remains today only one pure-baseball event each year—the party in Cooperstown the night before the Hall of Fame inductions. Pure baseball.

I was summoned to the field prior to the start of Game 3. Yankee Stadium looked great, especially from field level, as I looked up at its grandeur.

I was called to the field because Dick Young was in a snit. An area behind the batting cage had been roped off to give the hitters some peace as they waited to hit during batting practice. Young was outraged that the press had been moved back and was personally pulling up the stakes in the ground to remove that partition. Young won that battle; baseball backed down. Young knocking the World Series arrangements was not something baseball needed.

I stood by the batting cage as Morgan hit. He was the best second baseman of his time, and how they managed to pass him by on the final All-Century team escapes me. I don't know how anyone else could have ever played that position and hit and run as well as he did.

Bench stood in and hit some rockets. The ball zoomed off Rose's bat. I was surprised by how muscular and broad Rose was. Foster hit some out of sight. So did Griffey. For a moment, I recalled the story of the Yankees' "Murderers' Row" team taking batting practice against Pittsburgh in 1927 and scaring them to death before the game even started.

We had our "first" team on hand for the festivities—Joe DiMaggio to throw out the first ball, Robert Merrill to sing the national anthem. It was freezing, and Bowie Kuhn was getting blasted for the night-game concept for the World Series, particularly because he wasn't even wearing an overcoat, as though oblivious to the chill.

I wish we had put on a better show, but the Reds had a 4–0 lead before we crossed the plate, and they won the game 6–2. One of our runs came on our only home run of the Series, hit by the least likely of our players, backup shortstop Jim Mason. When Mason connected, I turned to Jim Ferguson, the Reds' PR director, and shook my head as if to say, "This is surreal."

All that was left was the final nail in the coffin, the fourth game on October 21. The crowd was mostly silent throughout. Johnny Bench hit two tremendous home runs; righthanded hitters had managed about six all season where he parked them. We went down quietly, 7–2, managing only eight runs and 30 hits for the four games. I waited for my own little highlight, hearing Joe Garagiola Sr. say my name on NBC when he thanked people with the Reds and the Yankees for their assistance.

After such a high the week before on the Chambliss homer, the season ended with a whimper.

There was one spark left, and that was Sparky Anderson, the Reds' manager, in his postgame press conference. I had brought Munson into the room to represent us. Billy was in no condition to speak to the press. He had, in fact, been ejected from that final game when he let his frustration boil over and rolled a baseball hard at the home plate umpire in disgust.

Anderson didn't see me standing with Munson, off to the side in the interview room. He was asked to compare the two catchers, Bench and Munson. Johnny had hit the two homers and was named the Series MVP.

"Don't never ask me to compare nobody to Johnny Bench," he said. "There's nobody that can play the game like he can; nobody."

Thurman took this as a personal insult. I could hardly restrain him from rushing the stage. It coincided with Sparky's rapid departure, so Sparky never heard Munson furiously saying, "After what I've done [he hit .529], to have to listen to this is the ultimate insult."

I didn't see it the way Munson did. I thought Sparky was avoiding any names by just proclaiming his player the best in the world, but Munson took it to heart after the tough four-game sweep and unloaded. Everyone leaving the interview room that night was confused.

We had come far, but we clearly were not as good as the Reds. We didn't have that big thumper in the lineup to get us back into games. I know George had to be thinking that as he saw our guys go down weakly. I remembered an owners' meeting in the summer when old Joe Iglehart, a former director with CBS and the Baltimore Orioles and a consulting partner with the Yankees, stood to speak. He lived in Baltimore, where Reggie Jackson was spending the 1976 season.

"Gentlemen," he said, "I only want to tell you that I have observed Reggie Jackson this year, and I most definitely say to you, do not bring this man to New York. He is a poison on a team, an egomaniac who bats .260, and he will bring with him nothing but trouble and unrest."

And Joe sat down. George thanked him for expressing that view.

And now, I was certain that George would go after Reggie, seeing him as the missing ingredient.

I returned upstairs to the mess that was my office. It would take a week to get it back in order. It had become Mission Control; it was now, oddly, a quiet and reflective place.

I went to the clubhouse to shake hands with the guys and wish them a good winter. As befits a clubhouse after a loss, it was quiet, somber. It's a shame a pennant-winning season has to end like that for the World Series losers. There was nothing to be ashamed of in the '76 Yankees. I looked at that proud man at his locker outside the manager's office, the one they called Yogi. He had been the manager in '64; then he was fired. As if cursed, the Yankees would never win again. At least until he came home, in 1976.

I was just about the only one in at nine the next morning. My phone rang. Someone wanted to know who held the record for consecutive scoreless innings pitched in the World Series before Whitey Ford. Having all that important knowledge stored in my brain could be valuable at times like this. It prevented me from (1) having to politely look it up, or (2) asking the guy to please call back another time. It was much easier to know the answer, say "Babe Ruth," and hang up.

I started to clean up the mess, okay some bills, and catch up on life. I even contemplated taking the weekend off.

14

I ALMOST LOSE
REGGIE FOR THE
YANKEES

Just a few days after the World Series ended, Claire Ruth passed away. Because I had been the person at the Yankees she was in touch with most often, I was asked to be an honorary pallbearer at her funeral.

The funeral was sad not only because of her passing but because of its low attendance. There were representatives of Babe Ruth League Baseball and the Hall of Fame, but her daughter and stepdaughter, who barely spoke to each other, were pretty much it for relatives.

Dorothy lived until 1988. She was the daughter of the Babe and a woman named Juanita Jennings. She didn't learn this until late in her life. She was brought up believing that her mother was Helen, Babe's first wife, who died in a fire some years after they had separated.

I remained friendly with Claire's daughter, Julia Ruth Stevens, a fine lady, whose son Tom was an international bridge engineer. Julia was Claire's daughter from a previous marriage, born when Claire was just 16. She adored the Babe, and I loved talking to her about him. We even came to be e-mail buddies. She represented him proudly at ceremonial events, such as film premieres or the *Sports Illustrated* "Athletes of the Century" event in 1999. She called him daddy, which was sweet. I would see her and Tom in Cooperstown for induction weekend if Tom was in the States and could accompany her from her home in New Hampshire. I liked to kid Tom about what it must have been like to play Little League ball and be Babe Ruth's "grandson." He'd been fortunate to have the last name Stevens, but he admitted that he let his friends know the truth.

Roy White was at the stadium as I was preparing to go downtown to

Claire's funeral, so I asked if he wanted to go with me.

Claire and Eleanor Gehrig didn't care for each other very much, but they had much in common. Both remained professional-ballplayer widows for a long time—Claire for 28 years and Eleanor for 45. Both remained in New York, where they would occasionally be recognized, and would annually troop out to Yankee Stadium for the cheers of the crowd. Sometimes Claire would come just for an ordinary midweek game. She still lived in the same apartment on Riverside Drive she had shared with the Babe. Eleanor and Lou had lived first in New Rochelle, then at 21 North Chatsworth Avenue in Larchmont, about a half-mile from my future home. It was a nice apartment building, which still stands across the street from my train station, while Ed Barrow lived a half-mile away in a beautiful house on Howard Street. After Lou became ill, he was given a job on the New York City parole board by Mayor LaGuardia and moved to the Riverdale section of the Bronx to meet residency requirements. After he died there, Eleanor moved to East 53rd Street in Manhattan, where she lived until her death in 1986.

Both of the widows drank too much. It was a consequence of the loneliness of their lives, I suppose. They should have been friends, but I suppose that little rivalry that simmered between them never faded. They didn't sit with each other at Yankee Stadium. So we always had the "Mrs. Ruth here, Mrs. Gehrig there, Babe's daughter Dorothy here, his daughter Julia there" thing going on.

My buddy Barry Halper got to know Eleanor when he drove her home from the stadium one day after an Old Timers Game. Barry was not yet the world's best-known memorabilia collector, but he was getting there. After he dropped her off, Eleanor suggested that she might just have a little something for Barry if he would be good enough to bring her some "hooch."

Barry said he would and asked her doorman what she meant by "hooch."

"Oh, just scotch," he said. "Bring her some Johnnie Walker."

So Barry went down the street and came back with a case of Johnnie Walker Black. And Eleanor was so pleased that she gave Barry the actual jersey that Lou had worn when he delivered his "luckiest man on the face of the earth" speech in 1939. What a treasure!

I always wondered, though, whether she had a few dozen of those jerseys in the closet and was just waiting to trade them for a good supply of hooch.

Years later, doing the PR for Leland's Auctions, I was involved in the auction of that jersey. It went for nearly $400,000.

We always laughed when people said, "Do you work all year, or are you off during the winter?" With the coming of free agency, and with the whirlwind that was now the Yankees, there was no safe way to plan for a few days off. With the exception of five days off for my honeymoon in 1975, I never took a full week off during any offseason and never missed a game in all the years I was there.

Oh, wait—I missed one. I missed a day game with the Brewers when I was still Bob Fishel's assistant, to see John Lennon play a charity concert at Madison Square Garden. And I felt such guilt as I sat there that it spoiled the whole experience. I never missed another game.

On November 4 and 5 at the Plaza Hotel, consecutive drafts were held; first to apportion signing rights for the first "free agent class" following the Messersmith decision, and then, on the second day, to stock the new Toronto Blue Jays and Seattle Mariners. It made sense to do it on consecutive days to save travel costs for all of the general managers and team officials who had to come to New York.

The free agency draft, on day 1, found Charlie Finley strutting into the room, aware that the days of the mighty Oakland A's were officially over. All of his remaining stars were taking a hike as soon as they could. It was sad to see that dynasty collapse; they did a lot for baseball. For one thing, while they were hot, they sold a lot of green-and-gold baseball caps, which marked the beginning of baseball's large-scale marketing efforts. I believe that until the colorful A's, people bought their own team's cap, or they didn't buy anything. With the A's, it seemed as if whoever was the hot team had its cap in demand. The colors were suddenly cool. We would see hundreds of Oakland caps at our games. Kids liked them. It was part of what the marketing of baseball was all about.

Credit Finley. He was a scoundrel, and he probably got what was coming to him, but he had vision, and a lot of his ideas for the game took hold. It took guts for him to show up at the free agent draft, but he was there.

Of course, he could hardly delegate authority. His front-office staff numbered fewer than a dozen people. Your local Burger King probably has more employees. His cousin Carl handled pretty much everything. I was surprised that Finley didn't have his accountants use the back of the adding-machine paper when they ran out. It was a very stingy operation, hardly befitting Major League Baseball.

Charlie could pick 'em, though. He had a kid in the press box who ran errands and did small chores, and, as if to stick it to the other owners, he made the kid a vice president. The kid's name was Stanley Burrell, but everyone called him Hammer because he looked like Hank Aaron. I used to say, "Hi, Hammer," and not much else when we were in Oakland, because, frankly, he was a bit too self-important for my taste and seemed determined to exercise some authority in that press box.

Hammer would become MC Hammer, one of the nation's first main-stream rap recording artists.

Charlie liked to have pretty ballgirls down the foul lines. One of them was named Debbie. She was gorgeous, with sort of a Shania Twain look. All she did was become Mrs. Fields of cookie fame.

We lost Doyle Alexander in that first free agent draft, but we drafted the rights to Don Baylor, Bert Campaneris, Bobby Grich, Reggie Jackson, Don Gullett, Dave Cash, Wayne Garland, Gary Matthews, and Billy Smith. You were allowed to sign two. Grich, Jackson, and Gullett were our most desired, despite Joe Iglehart's warnings, and when Grich expressed intentions to sign with the Angels, we were focused first on Gullett and then on Reggie, almost as an afterthought.

We had a press conference at the Americana on November 18 to announce the Gullett signing. He was to get $2 million over six years, but arm injuries would see to it that he never filled out the term, and it wasn't a good signing, as classy a guy as Don was. It was a shame, but it wasn't as if he was a picture of fitness before we got him, having spent long stretches on the disabled list.

That brought us to Reggeroo, as Howard Cosell called him. And the matter of luring Reggie Jackson was personally in the hands of George Steinbrenner. Although not a New York resident, George could sell the sizzle of the town like no one else. He walked the streets of New York with Reggie, had the cabbies and the construction workers call out to him, and really moved like he owned the city.

He seduced Reggie. They wanted each other. Montreal, of all teams, offered Reggie more money, but New York had glamor, and that was Reggie. "If I played in New York, they'd name a candy bar after me," he said. And he was right. Standard Brands did make a candy bar, a Reggie Bar, during his first season, and it got more publicity than it could dream of when fans pelted the field with them on a giveaway day, forcing a long postponement while the field was cleared.

This was not an easy signing. Reggie had very bright attorneys work-ing for him. The contract would be long and detailed. For several days and evenings in a row, Joe Garagiola Jr. and I were summoned to the townhouse that George was renting on the Upper East Side to review its terms and plan for his signing. Joe was our point man here; George trusted him. And Joe was very, very smart on all of the rules and regula-tions of baseball, codified in both the new Basic Agreement with the

Players Association, and spelled out in the *Blue Book* as the Major League Agreement.

On our first visit to George's house, he graciously offered us coffee. Joe passed, but I said okay. George sort of grunted with displeasure and I politely withdrew my request, but he said, "No, it's okay."

He went into the kitchen and began fumbling with the coffee machine. He asked how I wanted it. I was in too deep now.

"Light with sugar," I said, wishing the whole thing would go away.

He took out a two-pound bag of sugar and tried to get it open, to no avail. Suddenly he reached into a drawer, pulled out a steak knife, and began stabbing the bag to break it open. Somehow, I saw myself as the two-pound bag and wished I had never asked for the coffee.

"Thank you" hardly seemed to begin to tell the story when I got my cup. Joe looked at me as if to say, "Don't ever do this again."

I was there because George knew this was a huge PR thing as well as a matter of working out a contract. And I knew it, too. We were American League champions, but we had a missing cog, and that would be the big boomer in the middle of the lineup. George wanted to make Reggie as big as any star on Broadway, any Hollywood legend. The Yankees would be his stage. George was then dabbling in Broadway production with the Nederlander family, co-producing *No, No Nanette*, among others. *No, No Nanette* was originally produced by Harry Frazee, the Red Sox owner, who lost his shirt on it and had to sell Babe Ruth to the Yankees to cover his losses. What an irony that the Yankees' owner, having inherited all of those pennants, was, as a final blow, now producing Frazee's play.

After each meeting, Joe and I would cross the street to P.J. Bernstein's deli for a good pastrami fix. We would talk about the deal, talk about how baseball was changing, and talk about the year we had just been through.

On the last of these nights we came out of a particularly rough session. Reggie's lawyers had been there, and there was a lot of difficult give and take over wording. Joe was not especially pleased with the direction things were going.

"Everybody in that room is getting rich except us," we jointly noted at P.J. Bernstein's that night. "Maybe there is more out there than we realize."

Letting it rest with just those general thoughts, we proceeded with plans for the press conference. On the night of November 28, I was entrusted with getting Reggie a room at the Americana so that we could have a press conference there the next morning.

My phone rang at 1:30 A.M. It was George.

"You've screwed up. Get your ass into the city. Reggie is upset with his room and he's threatening to not sign and to go back to Oakland. Go straighten this out, right now."

I dialed the night manager at the Americana.

"What is going on?" I asked.

"Mr. Jackson arrived here around one with a lady friend. The suite we gave him was the same one used by President-elect Carter during the Democratic Convention. But it only has twin beds. And Mr. Jackson was very upset and has threatened to leave."

"Twin beds? In a suite? Can you put him in a room with a queen or a king?"

"I'm sorry, Mr. Appel, all of our rooms are twins."

I couldn't believe this. Twin beds in a first-class hotel?

"Can you put Reggie on with me?"

"He is at the front door now with his suitcases, Mr. Appel. I'll try to catch him."

Reggie got on.

"Reggie, I didn't know about the bed thing; isn't this the hotel the A's stay in when they're in New York?"

"Yeah, but I didn't remember the single-bed thing."

"Reggie, give me fifteen minutes; I'll get you a room at the Plaza or the Sherry-Netherland. Don't go away."

I called and got him a room at the Plaza. I called back the Americana and they told me they had somehow found a room with a foldout double bed and that he'd taken it. I should go to sleep.

Right.

Now came the morning of the big press conference. We met in a private room at the Americana—Joe, me, George, Gabe, and Reggie's team of lawyers. I had already alerted the media to an 11 A.M. press conference. They had a pretty good idea of the subject matter. I also invited Roy White, Elston Howard, and Thurman Munson to attend, to welcome their new teammate.

Thurman had just been named American League MVP. Although the baseball writers usually announced it, they had asked me to handle the announcement. Eyebrows were raised when Munson, accepting his honor, with George in the room, spoke about renegotiating his contract so that he would keep pace with whoever the new free agents would be. He thought this was understood. What should have been an easy, joyous press conference had grown difficult, and, the next day, I was playing serve and volley in the papers, with George and Thurman trading barbs.

But now, as captain, he would attend this conference.

At around 10 it was suggested that I go to Reggie's room to brief him on the press conference, with the contract still unsigned.

I called from the lobby to say I was coming up.

I knocked on the door. A naked woman answered.

I suppose I gulped.

"Ummm . . . I'm Marty; Reggie here?"

He walked in as if this was no big deal. The woman disappeared into the bathroom.

"Very nice suit," I said to Reggie.

"You like this?" he said. "Geoffrey Beene. I endorse their clothing. You want some? I'll get 'em for you."

I smiled. What could you say? "Put me down for a dozen"?

We went over the press who were likely to be there and who the Yankee beat reporters were these days. He knew them all. We went downstairs, he signed his five-year deal, worth $3 million, and then headed for the press conference.

I never saw anyone handle himself better. He called everyone by name. He was funny, bright, respectful, perfect.

He held up number 42 and said he was going to wear this number in honor of Jackie Robinson. (By spring training, however, he changed his mind and went to 44, the number worn by Aaron and McCovey. His number 9, which he wore in Oakland and Baltimore, was worn by Nettles.)

He was something else. Masterful. He could have been running for office, and, in a sense, he was. I was very, very impressed.

The expansion draft to stock Toronto and Seattle took place November 5. No one in the room was very happy about Seattle getting a team; it was the only way the league could get out of a huge damage suit still lingering in Seattle over their loss of the Pilots after one season. As for Toronto, this was considered a golden market—better than Montreal—and both leagues had wanted this city badly. It was a rare American League triumph.

I sat at the Yankee table with George, Gabe, Billy Martin, Cedric Tallis, and Pat Nugent, our young farm director. Teams had until minutes before the actual draft to submit their list of protected players.

We were, as usual, going to wait until the very last minute to submit.

"I want to protect Grant Jackson," said George, overlooking the big homer he had given up to Brett in the final LCS game. "The guy was 6–0 for us, he goes long relief, he can finish, and you can use him as an occasional starter. I like the guy."

"It's not a good move," argued Gabe from his four decades in the game. "We can replace Grant Jackson. I feel we need to protect Guidry."

Billy sided with Gabe, but not so much as to seem as if he were opposing George's viewpoint.

I listened with great interest. This was a classic debate between the owner with the bucks and the general manager with the experience.

"Guidry hasn't shown me anything," said George. "Billy wouldn't even put him into the Series except as a pinch runner. Look at him; look how thin he is. He'll break down on you. He looks like a runner, not a pitcher."

"We only had four games," said Billy. "But I wasn't sure where I could pitch him even if we went seven."

"George, I know your feelings, and I respect them," said Gabe. "But there comes a time when you have to listen to your scouts. That's what they're paid for. You hire scouts because you trust their abilities. And our scouts tell me that Guidry can be a great pitcher. I admit I haven't seen it any more than you have, but you have to go with your scouts."

It was Jackson or Guidry.

What made this all the more interesting was that Pat Gillick, who had been our scouting director, had jumped to Toronto, taking with him full knowledge of our players. This had infuriated George. And when Gillick hired Elliot Wahle, his assistant in New York, to assist him in Toronto, George had gone ballistic. He practically threw Elliot out of the stadium and wouldn't let him back into his office to clear out his stuff.

If Gabe was right about the scouts, then Gillick would probably be on Guidry with his first pick. That would really exacerbate the Gillick–Steinbrenner feud.

Imagine if George had known that I had been in touch with Peter Bavasi, the new president of the Blue Jays. I had made an inquiry right after the World Series to see about their PR job. I wasn't sure I wanted to leave the Yankees, but I thought I might test the waters. Peter, a friend to this day, essentially hired me, happy to check off a key spot on his front-office roster with an experienced guy.

But then he called about 48 hours later to say, "Oh, bad news. We have to hire a Canadian citizen for the job. We can only get waivers on certain positions, and that's not one of them."

So he hired Howard Starkman, who is still on the job as this is written, 24 years later. I guess I'm sort of a former Blue Jay.

I sat and listened as Gabe and George debated over Guidry and Jackson. George took a deep breath and said, "Okay, Gabe, we'll protect Guidry. But this is on your head. Just remember that."

"I can only tell you that you have to go with your scouts, or what's the point of having them?" said Gabe.

I was handed our protected list and I delivered it to Lee MacPhail, the league president, presiding over the draft.

The Jays wound up taking Otto Velez (our one-time "crown jewel"), Jim Mason, and Garth Iorg from us, and we lost Grant Jackson to the Mariners.

The saga didn't quite end there. Gillick had taken Bill Singer, a one-time 20-game winner, and was intending to trade him to the Yankees for Guidry. Unable to draft the Louisiana lefty, Pat was trying another approach. He actually worked out a deal, Singer for Guidry, a few weeks into the new year.

But Bavasi killed the deal.

"We had made Singer into a marquee player," he said. "He was a known veteran, and, along with Bob Bailor, he had emerged as one of our poster boys for sponsors and season tickets. We couldn't trade him now for an unknown."

So that was how Guidry remained a Yankee. And he would, of course, go on to become one of the greatest and most popular Yankee pitchers in history.

It had been an incredible 12 months.

We had been through storms and crises and highs and lows and tension and tumult and headlines. It was quite clear that the return of George Steinbrenner was going to have a profound effect on the New York sports pages and on the Yankee franchise. So much for absentee ownership, and so much for the power of the general manager to run the team. What had been established in 1976 was activism in ownership. No longer would the MacPhails and the Rickeys and the Bavasis and the Pauls be the high-profile club executives. Now, if you were going to buy a team, you were going to have a big say in it.

That's not to say it was a bad idea. You just needed to be lucky and have an owner who knew what he was doing.

Steinbrenner, interestingly, would spend his entire Yankee career hearing the repeated barbs of those who remembered his "I'll stick to building ships" remark. But, although the media liked to ridicule him with it, he worked hard at learning the machinations of baseball and the skills of athletes. He could get carried away in criticizing players, but he was learning the game as well as most GMs. Scouts could talk to him and he could speak their language. He was no fool in judging talent—only too quick to make a decision and too eager to get rid of prospects for a win-now program. Still, it was a style, and not necessarily a flawed one.

His teams would win three pennants in the '70s, win more regular-season games than any other team in the '80s, and become the team of the decade in the '90s. His fans got their money's worth. With few exceptions, the team was generally in contention, or at least put on a good performance on the field. Having the threat of a good Mets team in town was like having a good pony chasing one of his racehorses. It kept him going.

I liked the guy despite his rule-by-intimidation style. For me, it was certainly an unnecessary approach. I was going to love the Yankees and do my best whether I was under the threat of being fired or whether I was completely left alone. I enjoyed my job, enjoyed the company of the baseball community, and felt good about my abilities every day I went to work.

I saw George at his best moments, reaching out with an act of charity, charming someone he admired on the phone, or making you proud to be a New Yorker.

I saw him at his less than charming moments too.

But where was it written that your boss had to be a great guy? I had been spoiled by having Mike Burke, Lee MacPhail, and Bob Fishel as bosses. And although there were days when I was exasperated by George's intimidating manner, I would still say to myself, "Maybe this is how it is sometimes in the real world."

I was seeing new things in myself I didn't like. I was growing increasingly tense. If I was away from the red phone, I could never relax. I thought he was looking for me. There were times that I would think I'd done a good job, and it wasn't appreciated. We all need a pat on the back. Especially when I was putting in 80-hour workweeks for what averaged out to less than minimum wage.

Joe and I had a lot of talks about this. He had a more easy-going personality and, like his father, could laugh things off more easily than I could. But he was increasingly disappointed in the way we were doing business and how it might come to reflect on him. His personal honor was important to him, as was his professional reputation as an attorney.

Those chats at B.J. Bernstein's Deli after the Reggie meetings were taking us down a road I had never thought I'd be on. We were talking about there being other opportunities out there.

All along, I had felt that I was the luckiest man on the face of the earth. I had the perfect job for Marty Appel. And I hoped that I'd have it forever. I had become the Yankees' PR director at age 24 and could conceivably have that job for 40 years or more! Think of the baseball history I would witness.

But I had also gotten married in October 1975, and what a stress I put on my marriage in those first 12 months! I would work 80 hours a week in New York and then leave for a 10-day road trip. I wanted to start a family one day; this hardly seemed like the right formula.

Forces were coming together. I knew that I should have been happier with the team's success. Instead, it was creating more tension for me. A person with a different type of personality might roll with it better. I began to think I didn't have the right stuff for the long haul.

My inquiry—and near-hire—with the Blue Jays had caught even me by surprise. Leave the Yankees and move to Canada? What was I thinking?

I would have done it. And to me that meant I was ready to consider leaving. But as with many decisions in my life, I needed some coaxing.

Joe would be my support in that. We began to think about forming our own business. We got along so well as friends and colleagues that we had no worries about working together. A sports management company seemed right for us because of our contacts, our reputations, the different strengths each of us would bring, and because we could offer credible service. And when we realized the revenue possibilities, it was a lure.

We talked about it quietly with some trusted friends. Roy White told us he would have hired us in a minute if he'd known but had just signed with Jerry Kapstein. Whitey Ford was dead serious when he said he was so sure of our success that he wanted to invest in our business. And Joe's father, preparing to move from Westchester to Arizona, offered to back us if times got bad. I could never imagine taking him up on the offer, but it was a generous one.

Barry Landers, our promotion director, came into my office one day and said, "I got George to approve World Series rings for all the department heads. You think we should get them on Opening Day like the players?"

I looked at him and said, "See if you can get him to make them a Christmas present." I had a feeling I might not see mine if I waited for Opening Day.

By Christmas, we knew we were going to leave. It was a sad holiday for me. In my heart, I didn't want to leave. But I knew that all the factors favoring departure were there. We would do well financially, I would be better able to begin a family and spend time raising children, and the pressure and tension that was not fitting well with my particular personality would be lifted.

Naturally, I ran the whole thing by Bob Fishel. He understood perfectly and thought that under the circumstances, I had to do it. But it saddened him that his protégé was leaving the Yankees and, in fact, stepping back from baseball. He offered to check on what else was opening up in the American League. Nothing was.

As with many life decisions, I had one final consultation: with Tom Villante.

Tom thought the idea was "terrific." Tom loved the word *terrific*.

"Are you kidding?" he said. "You'll be great. With the people you and Joe know? What an opportunity! This is the perfect time in your life to do this."

Joe needed little convincing. He didn't feel the pull of 20 years of being a Yankee fan or of nine years of working with them. His father had played for the Cardinals, Pirates, Cubs, and Giants and had broadcast for the Cards and Yankees, and he knew about shifting gears. I was more the sort of person who liked thinking about a "job for life."

Right after the New Year, we shook hands on what would be Garagiola & Appel Enterprises, Inc. There was no doubt that I wanted Joe's name to come first because of its wide recognition. We would seek out individual players needing personal representation, largely in the commercial and marketing end. I was selected president by the flip of a coin. We would work out of our homes, seven miles apart, and frequently drive to the city together for meetings.

I hurried on with my Yankee chores, completing the Yearbook and the media guide for 1977 because I wanted to do that one last thing and not burden a successor with the responsibility. The Yearbook included a 50th anniversary "Yearbook within a Yearbook"—a 1927 Yearbook honoring the legendary Murderers' Row team, assembled by my friend Bill Madden. I would miss those sorts of projects a lot.

I had one last trade to announce: Elliott Maddox to the Orioles for Paul Blair. My first, back in '68, had been Bill Monbouquette for Lindy McDaniel. My team had come a long way. We had come from second-class citizenship in our own city—happy to announce that we had drawn a million fans, dealing with irate fans because we had traded Andy Kosco—to a championship, with a 2 million gate, and the team of Jackson and Hunter and Munson, Chambliss and Randolph and Nettles, Guidry, Lyle, Piniella . . . almost an All-Star at every position.

We needed to plan our resignations. We talked for many days about how to handle it. We knew we wanted to do it in person, face to face with the Boss. And we imagined all sorts of wild scenarios about how George might react and what our responses should be.

We called his secretary and said we needed to see him together.

Joe began.

"We've been giving a lot of thought to our futures," he said, "and, to tell you the truth, taking a page out of your own book, there came a time when you were an assistant football coach and you decided to go out on your own. You made a good choice, you've been a tremendous success—we think the time is right in our lives to take that chance as well."

Just as rehearsed.

I explained our plan.

George blinked rapidly a few times and sort of craned his neck as though relieving a momentary muscle spasm. He pursed his lips.

"I think you guys are making a big mistake," he said. "This field is already saturated out there. You are getting into something that you think is big, and it may not be."

"Well," Joe said, "that may well be true, and we'll learn that soon enough. But you should know we haven't done a thing to line up clients yet. We are starting cold and never gave a minute of Yankee time toward getting this jump-started."

George pondered the situation. He would be losing his in-house lawyer and his public relations man. It was six weeks to spring training.

"This is a bad time to be doing this, you know," he said. "It leaves me in a tough spot with those two positions at once."

"There really isn't one time that's better than another," I said. "This has become a twelve-months-a-year business. And we have both made certain that there will be no loose ends. All our spring-training and season publications are ahead of schedule."

"You ought to know that my policy is that you can never come back. It's not personal; it's just my policy. Once you leave, that's it; you're gone."

It hurt to hear that, even though I hadn't given it a thought. And as events would play out in later years, I was offered opportunities to return three times—twice as PR director and once, oddly, as farm director. Each time, it was tempting, but each time, I moved on with my life and remembered the reasons I had left in the first place.

We shook hands all around. I wish it had been warmer, but he was very businesslike about it all. Joe and I were tremendously relieved that the conversation was over. Doing it in person was the right thing to do, but it wasn't easy.

I went back to my office and called Anne Mileo in. I gave her a hug, which surprised her, and told her what had just happened. Within minutes, everyone was coming in and congratulating me, all saying things like "Take me with you."

I reached Mickey Morabito, who was on vacation in Puerto Rico.

"Mickey, I just resigned. I don't know if he's going to offer you the job, but you ought to stay available and be ready to come home."

George had asked if I thought Mickey was up to the job, and I said that he was. The best thing he had going for him was a terrific relationship with Billy. George hired him, and he finally got his business cards.

During my remaining two weeks, I helped Mickey prepare for the job, helped him hire a new assistant, Larry Wahl, and introduced him to the media at the writer's "pre-dinner dinner." I wrote out pages of instructions and assured him he could call me at any time. I really wanted him to, and I'm pleased to say that not only did he call, but most of *his* successors—Wahl, Dave Szen, Irv Kaze, Ken Nigro, Joe Safety, Harvey Greene, Jeff Idelson, Rob Butcher, and Rick Cerrone—called as well. I always kidded them that I was the best of them all because I had been trained by Fishel, and the others had only inherited advice from me.

I had been so proud of having been only the third PR director in the franchise's great history. It saddened me to see how quickly burnout would occur as the years went on, although it did reinforce my own feelings to an extent. More than 20 years after I left, when Cerrone would call me and ask where a certain photo was, and I could tell him which file cabinet it was in and how it was captioned—that felt great to me.

My last day there was January 20, 1977. I remember it because I brought a portable television in with me to watch the Jimmy Carter inauguration. There was a little farewell party for Joe and me—we received leather monogrammed briefcases—and then we departed. I probably should have loaded my car with Yankee Yearbooks, press pins, original photos, game-used equipment, autographed correspondence, and so forth, but I took nothing other than one copy of each Yearbook and media guide that I had helped to prepare and the good wishes and friendship of a lot of fine people in that front office.

It wasn't as if I would never see these people again or work with them again. But baseball as an industry is very insular. You're in or you're out. If you are on the outside, no matter whom you know and how close you remain to the scene, there is always a transparent wall that separates you from it. Players feel it a lot more than front office people do. The day after a player is released, when no one knows quite what to say to him as he cleans out his locker, can be the loneliest day of his life.

I had called Yankee Stadium home for nearly a third of my life. In many ways, it was my dream job, although it was my first job out of college. The association one feels with an organization like this, when you leave on good terms, is very strong. I knew that for many people, no matter what I did for the remainder of my life, I would forever be the "former PR director of the Yankees." What else could have led to my name being rhymed with Pete Rozelle's in Red Smith's annual *New York Times* Christmas poem?

I gathered up my remaining items and stuffed them into my new car. I had purchased the pinstriped Toyota the Yankees had used in '76, with 89 miles on it. Most of them had been rung up by Sparky Lyle, who, knowing I bought the car, stayed in the bullpen and protected it while the fans stormed the field during the Chambliss homer. It was guys like that I would miss the most.

I was told that once I lost my ability to provide free tickets, a lot of people I had thought were my friends would disappear. I was pleased to discover that that wasn't the case at all. I have always worked at maintaining friendships, and many from those days continued for decades, even without the occasional free tickets.

Likewise, although I cut my attendance at Yankee games from 150 a year to about 10, I was always warmly received by old colleagues whenever I went to the stadium and was treated well by new employees. I continued as a contributor to *Yankees Magazine*, and would usually sit in the press box with my successors when I was there. I always went to the Yankees box score in the newspaper before any other and found myself to be just as much a fan of the team as I had been before and during my employment there.

Leaving for the final time was one of the saddest moments of my professional career, but I was going to have to look forward now. I had a business to build and bills to pay.

OF SCOOTERS AND
ROSES, KINGS
AND KUHNS

Well, we weren't a great success after all. Somewhere along the line we came to realize that for all the skills each of us brought to the table, neither of us was especially comfortable with working the hotel lobbies, courting the players, and hustling for business in that fashion.

But we had some good times and adventures in the process of finding this out.

Just a month into the business, we headed for Florida to meet with players who had responded to a mailing introducing our services. Joe's godfather, no less than Stan Musial, had fixed us up at a nice motel in Clearwater, which became our base of operations.

We met with a number of good players for whom we promised to make the best effort to secure increased marketing and commercial opportunities. We particularly liked Bob Watson, Joe Torre, Bob Boone, and Al Oliver in our meetings. Among others we worked with were Larry Bowa, Tim Foli, and Lee Mazzilli.

We had one player whom we tried to help get a new job after the Rangers released him. His name was Joe Lahoud, and he had had a stormy ride in Boston some years earlier after he had criticized management over playing time and dared invoke the name of Conigliaro in his remarks, albeit Tony's brother Billy. In truth, Joe must have been considered to be in the lower tier of marketable players, but he was still a big leaguer with a measure of ability. And he was a good guy—he even invited us to his wedding.

When he was released, we decided that Oakland, now dismantled, would be the perfect club for him. That would require a phone call to Charles O. Finley himself. We flipped a coin to see who got to talk to Charlie. It was heads—me.

I called him at his Michigan Avenue insurance office in Chicago, and I wasn't surprised when that gravelly voice answered the phone himself. No secretary.

I cleared my throat.

"Mr. Finley?"

"Who wants him?"

"My name is Marty Appel; I have a sports management company in association with Joe Garagiola Jr., and we would like to talk about a ballplayer who is now a free agent."

"Well, start talking and I'll see if he's in," he replied.

I glanced up at Joe, signifying, "I've got him; this is our shot."

"Our player is Joe Lahoud, the lefthanded-hitting outfielder who has been with Boston, Milwaukee, California, and Texas. He's got a great arm, and in every season he's played in over a hundred games, he's had double digits in home runs. He could be a regular for you, or a very strong fourth outfielder. He'll be thirty next month and is in perfect health."

I could hear pages turning as Finley muttered, "Lahoud, Lahoud. Do you mean Pete LaCock?"

"No, Lahoud, Joe Lahoud."

"How do you spell that?"

I spelled it. More pages turning.

"Nope, not interested; I'll tell him that you called, though." Click.

We managed to get him a spring training walk-on with Kansas City but then fell upon an opportunity to sell his contract to Japan. We were instant international agents on this one, exchanging calls with the Japanese and trying to persuade John Schuerholz, the Royals' general manager, that this sale could benefit everyone. But Schuerholz liked having Lahoud as a reserve outfielder, and we were never able to execute the sale. It was a shame, because Joe played only 34 games for the Royals that year and wasn't needed at all. We did pass the Royals team bus as it approached Yankee Stadium for the '77 ALCS, and there was Joe in the window, waving at us on the street, a member of the Western Division champions.

Certainly the great adventure of our spring, though, had to be our dinner with Pete Rose.

Pete was at the absolute top of his game in 1977, on his way to being the player of the decade. When he sent back his little reply card from our mailing, we were stunned. Pete Rose, interested in us?

No sooner did we check into our Clearwater motel than we called Rose and made arrangements to have dinner with him at Bern's Steak House in Tampa on Friday night.

This was Pete's 17th spring training in Tampa, and Bern's was perhaps the most famous restaurant on Florida's Gulf coast. "Art in Steaks," the menu read, and the menu was a virtual encyclopedia of steak preparation. We figured that if we were going to blow our entertainment budget on anyone, it would be Pete Rose.

"Where's Bern's?" he asked.

We realized we were talking to a fast-food kinda guy. Seventeen years in Tampa and he hadn't heard of Bern's.

We gave him the address and said, "Bring Karolyn," his wife.

We called Bern's, dropped Pete's name, and asked if a private room was possible. The owner set aside a dining room with a table for four. We set the time for eight.

It was eight. 8:15. 8:30. No Pete. This was not unusual for a ballplayer, but we had confirmed earlier in the day with Karolyn. "Oh yes," she said, "it's on the calendar; he'll be there." As we sat there by ourselves, loading up on dinner rolls, we knew a no-show was a possibility.

At about 8:40, Pete burst into the room. Instead of Karolyn, he had the Reds' young second baseman, Doug Flynn, with him.

We shook hands and introduced ourselves as the sommelier approached with a napkin over his forearm and a very thick book in his hand.

"May I show you the wine list?" he asked.

Pete took charge.

"No time for that; we're on our way to the dog track. Just bring me out a slab of beef as soon as you can. Rare."

"Yes, sir," said the sommelier.

"So, what do you guys do again?" said Pete.

We barely finished explaining, when Pete's slab arrived. By 9:15, he and Doug were on their way to the dog track. Pete's parting words were "Hey, great, whatever you guys can dig up for me, that's fine."

Doug was a little more interested and asked for our cards. (My best business-card story was the time Jerry Holtzman, the legendary Chicago sportswriter, expressed interest in what I was doing and asked for a card. He proceeded to pick his teeth with it and left it on the table.)

We had a feeling that Pete had a map on the wall in his kitchen with little pins indicating where he had agents. We were gonna be his New York guys. That was all right.

We did get Pete some endorsements, and, as it turned out, we also helped

Doug Flynn get settled when he came to New York in the big Tom Seaver trade that June. We spent a whole day apartment hunting with Doug and then suggested that we might call the Mets on his behalf to see if we could negotiate a long-term contract for him.

"Well, they already offered me triple my pay for next year, and I told them okay," he said. "So I'll sure call you guys when that contract runs out."

We contacted Pittsburgh Steeler star Rocky Bleier, who did some motivational-speaking appearances for us. Tony Kubek engaged us to represent his broadcast negotiations with the CBC, where he was going to be the Blue Jays' broadcaster. Tony was a no-nonsense businessman; he had his price, and that was it. If they paid it, he'd be there; if not, he'd stay home.

A special client for me was a very close friend named Lee Arthur, who was a pioneer among women sportscasters. She worked briefly at WCBS-TV in New York, where we met, and then had longer and very successful stints in Pittsburgh and Miami. For no particular reason, I taught her the names of the World Series MVPs, in order, going back to 1955. She had a propensity for marrying wealthy guys, the first of whom, coincidentally, was named Appel. We dated in the early '70s, and I thought I was doing fine with her, until we walked by a yacht on Ft. Lauderdale's intracoastal waterway and she pointed out that the name of the yacht was *Lee*. It was a present from another guy she was seeing.

She was bright and fun and pretty and talented, and she should be better remembered for her pioneering work as a woman in sportscasting as early as 1971. Sadly, she died of cancer at a very young age, and she called me a few days before she passed away to say goodbye. You don't forget things like that.

The biggest thing Joe and I did during our time together was to negotiate a deal under which Phil Rizzuto would leave the Yankees to become a broadcaster for the Kansas City Royals. It never happened, but we did make the deal.

Joe and I met with Phil for lunch one day, and Phil went through a list of reasons for his unhappiness with his Yankee job. First among them was his pay, but there was a general sense of underappreciation as well. Like most of us, he needed stroking, not only by his adoring fans, but also by the television, radio, and team officials.

This was a bombshell to us, and we emphasized, "Are you absolutely sure you would leave?"

He was 59 years old, had been with the Yankees for 36 years, and had long ago settled into his home and a comfortable lifestyle in New Jersey. But, yes, he assured us that he was serious—he was very unhappy—and asked us to quietly look around for other opportunities.

"We're not just testing the waters here, Phil, right? You would go for the right offer?"

"Oh, yes," he said. We both had our doubts but proceeded with caution.

We were very quiet and discreet about it, and in fact it never reached the press at all. But, with a series of phone calls, we identified the Royals as a team that would be thrilled to have him, on wonderful terms. He had played minor league ball in Kansas City and, with his good-natured kidding, had always made friends wherever he went.

Step by step, we put together a multiyear deal, with more money and less travel than the Yankees offered. So anxious were the Royals to have him that membership in a prestigious country club was included. At each stage of the negotiations, we kept Phil informed, and kept doing "reality checks" to be sure he could still make a move like this.

We knew the Yankees might make a counteroffer, and we wanted his commitment that he wasn't just using the Royals to get a better deal from the Yankees. We couldn't shake hands and then let him be talked out of it. It was tricky for everyone, and we all lost more than a few nights' sleep over it. Even our contacts at the Royals kept saying, "You're sure he's serious, right?"

Finally, the day came when it was time to shake hands. This deal was made; Rizzuto was to leave New York and go to Kansas City, taking his huckleberries with him. It would be enormous news.

I called Scooter.

"Phil, we are prepared today to agree to this deal if you are. We all know the mixed feelings that must be going on with you. Before I make the call, are we all together on this?"

He paused. It was my own "uh-oh" moment. I looked at Joe and raised my eyebrows.

"You know," Phil said, "I've been thinking about how hot it gets there in the summer. I played there, you know; you wouldn't believe the heat. Cora hates the heat."

I wanted to say that he'd played there before they invented air conditioning. But if he was suddenly going to bail on this and use the fact that Cora hated the heat—we knew we were going to have to cut bait at that moment. We all knew that his heart wasn't in it. He was a Yankee and would always be a Yankee.

It was a broken mission. Our hearts weren't in it either, because we knew he might very well be unhappy. But we were following his directives.

We called the Royals, they understood, and the opportunity passed, without anyone the wiser. We had put a lot of hours into this and now would receive no fee. But we felt it had turned out as it should have.

Still, it was another setback for the business. We weren't getting any big scores. And we were running into bad luck. We were often on the verge of a big opportunity when something would come along and sweep it away. Lahoud to Japan, Flynn with the Mets, or Rizzuto to Kansas City: things that could have made our first year a financial success.

We worked well together; there were no problems there. The friendship was intact, and the work effort was unquestioned. But we needed a big client, and it wasn't kicking in.

Just after our first anniversary, Larry Gura, the Royals' star left-hander, called. We had been friends when he pitched for the Yankees, and he had tracked me down. He was interested in our representation.

It was, for me, too little, too late. I had already decided that this wasn't going to work for me. I wasn't about to ask Joe Sr. for financial support, even though he had offered it. I called Joe Jr. and said, "Here's Larry Gura for you, but I need to find something else. I'm sorry, I really am. I wanted this to work so much."

He understood, and we parted as friends and remain so to this day. He kept the business going for a time with Gura and Kubek and then later added Mike Morgan and took to publishing an interesting monthly newsletter on sports law.

He moved to Phoenix, where, as part of a large law firm, he became one of the lead attorneys helping to bring an expansion franchise to the area. And when Jerry Colangelo was awarded the franchise, he named Joe his first general manager. When the announcement was made in West Palm Beach that Arizona had been awarded a franchise, I was there with Joe. And in the team's second season, 1999, Joe finished third in Executive of the Year voting through my client, *The Sporting News*, and I made sure to pack his name high into the press release.

World Team Tennis was a league of professional tennis stars with a franchise in New York called the Sets. This was an attempt to rhyme with "Mets" and "Jets" and "Nets," but it hadn't caught on, and the franchise was faltering despite the presence of two entertaining stars, Billie Jean King and Long Island's own Vitas Gerulaitis.

A decision was made to dump the Sets and move to Madison Square Garden as the reborn New York Apples. What better move than to have the Apples engage Appel as their PR director?

I enjoyed doing their PR. The matches—team oriented, with an ongoing point system in the 1-2-3-4 style of scoring (VASSS system)—

had men's and women's singles, men's and women's doubles, and mixed doubles. Five matches an evening. A colorful court and a mix of the old, aristocratic tennis crowd and a more vocal, youthful crowd that didn't mind shouting during points. The old guard hated it, but this was show biz.

The aristocratic crowd was well represented by players like Virginia Wade, who had been with the Sets the year before, even if playing in this contrived setting seemed beneath her dignity.

After the Sets won the 1977 championship, Howard Freeman, the bright young promotion manager of the team, arranged for a champagne celebration. Virginia, however, had other plans and was anxious to leave.

"Virginia," he said, "won't you even stay for the champagne?"

"What kind is it?" she asked.

Most of our team was composed of future tennis broadcasters—Billie Jean, Mary Carillo, Julie Anthony, Fred Stolle, and Vitas.

Vitas was enormous fun. People sometimes spoke to him as if he were from some Eastern European country and might not understand English. In fact, he was a New York guy with a European name. He actually had a Brooklyn accent.

He was a disco king, a teen heartthrob, and, at 23, a millionaire, jet-setting, substance-abusing, world-ranked tennis champion who lived life in the fast lane.

He liked me because he was a Yankee fan. We'd be on our way in some van to a tennis match and he'd laughingly pick my brain about whether I thought Lyle and Tidrow were probably sitting in the Yankee bullpen at that very moment, debating whether Vitas should play men's singles and mixed doubles, or men's singles and men's doubles that night.

Vitas took me to Studio 54 and Regine's and places I had never imagined being, and all the while he was just a regular guy who happened to own the world. When he died at 40 of carbon monoxide poisoning, I had long since lost touch with him, but I always had a soft spot for this incredibly likeable guy.

Mary Carillo never played for the Apples, because a knee injury essentially ended her playing career that summer. Because of my work with the Apples, I was asked to be the play-by-play broadcaster for cable coverage of the Mahwah (New Jersey) Women's Open that year, the tournament that immediately preceded the U.S. Open.

The cable station was part of the fledgling USA Network operation, headed by the gifted Kay Koplovitz. It was an honor to be asked, particularly because my broadcast experience was limited to being interviewed on behalf of the Yankees and serving as color commentator on Apples radio broadcasts during the season. (Could anyone really have been listening to tennis on the radio?)

But I did like the microphone, and broadcasting had, of course, been an early career goal for me. One of the really fun evenings of my life had involved being a guest on a WMCA radio program on which trivia was the topic. I was a sports specialist. Talk about an interesting group— Murray the K was there doing rock and roll. Tiny Tim was there doing turn of the century music that no one had ever heard of. And, if you can believe this, Jane Fonda was there doing movie trivia. Murray, Tiny Tim, Jane, and me. What a night.

Anyway, I was hired to broadcast the Mahwah Open, and I was told that I would be working with Rosemary Casals, the retired tennis star. I was asked if I could recommend a third person, and it occurred to me that Mary Carillo was very well spoken, charming, and personable and might be terrific. So I called Mary's mother, who was all for it, and, that weekend in Mahwah, I was responsible for Mary's debut as a broadcaster. She has since become one of the great tennis commentators in the world.

We did a live open from the court—not an easy feat without a script—and we got through it as I took director's cues in my earpiece to throw to commercial or to drop in plugs for local sponsors or upcoming programming. Virginia Wade beat Tracy Austin for the title and presumably drank whatever champagne they offered. It was a great experience.

I did a few more tennis matches for that cable station and then was asked whether I would go to Washington for a major tournament that would be carried on USA Network. It conflicted with my brother's wedding, and I felt at that point that I needed to decide whether I was serious about broadcasting or whether it was just a passing thing. I decided to opt for the wedding and pretty much told the network that although I could be available from time to time, I didn't think I wanted to travel around and be their regular weekly tennis broadcaster. And so that opportunity drifted away, at my choosing.

Our super-duper star on the Apples, of course, was Billie Jean.

I was quite taken with her, to tell you the truth. I found her to be not only a fiercely dedicated, well focused woman who was a part of American history but someone with a sweet, vulnerable, and shy side. I am always a sucker for those three attributes.

She was very good to me; she enjoyed "Appel" working for the Apples and liked introducing me to people that way. I'd sit with her on flights, and she would draw diagrams on cocktail napkins about how to place shots to greatest advantage. Once, I was sitting between her and JoAnne Russell, one of our other players, and I watched her give JoAnne literally a complete lesson in ball placement right there on my tray table, on a cocktail napkin. Not only was it brilliantly taught but JoAnne was the eighth-ranked player in the U.S.! I was amazed that the eighth-ranked player still needed to learn things like this.

Billie Jean did have a fiery side. At a match in Seattle, the scoreboard operator, seated at the scorer's table, was openly cheering whenever Seattle got a point. This was very unprofessional, but he was a kid, a daily hire, and WTT was trying to encourage cheering.

At some point, Billie Jean had heard enough, and, during a court change, she got into an argument with the kid, and the next thing I knew, they were about to fight! The court umpire had to separate them, with the kid yelling obscenities at our lady. The crowd totally turned on our star, cheered for the scoreboard boy, and gave us all a good verbal thrashing as we slunk out of the arena.

The New York Times pretty much ignored the Apples, and there wasn't a newspaper more important to reaching the upscale tennis audience. So my big mission was to get the *Times* interested.

Probably, about 70 percent of all of its daily stories have PR input in them, whether it's the White House communications office or the Yankee PR director or spokespeople for corporate America. (Even the obituaries often have PR contributions; at home I always maintained biographies of the key executives I reported to, just in case I had to make a sad call during non-business hours.) The *Times* just don't like the *idea* of dealing with PR people, as a matter of principle.

The whole daily news cycle is an amazing thing to watch. The *Times* (and other papers) are full of PR-driven stories. Television and radio stations then use newspaper stories to outline their daily newscasts—a free news bureau, so to speak. If you want big coverage for a story, give it to the newspapers, and TV will pick it up. It seldom works the other way around.

For the Apples, a friend in the *Times* sports department made a suggestion to me.

"Call Arthur Gelb in editorial," he said. "He loves celebrities. He would love to have Billie Jean King to lunch in the *Times'* private dining room."

So I did, and, sure enough, he couldn't have been more receptive. I arrived with Billie Jean and we had the most exquisite private luncheon, and Billie Jean was not at all shy about pitching why the *Times* should cover World Team Tennis more.

She gave him an autographed copy of our media guide and he said he would look into the matter.

Sure enough, we soon had not only coverage but a beat reporter assigned to us, making road trips with us, and giving us great feature stories. When Chris Evert led her Los Angeles Strings into town and we drew about 12,000 people—one of the biggest tennis crowds ever—we had the main story on the sports page, with a three-column photo showing the crowd.

The problem with the league, unfortunately, was that Chrissie was attracting about fifty percent of the league's total attendance for her matches and that none of the men stars—Borg, Connors, and the rising young John McEnroe—were participating. I actually walked right up to McEnroe at the Garden one day during one of our matches—he was still up and coming, but people knew he'd be a star—and said, "John, you should be in this league next season."

But only the women players really supported it. Martina Navratilova was not yet the great champion she would become, but she was out there every day, improving her game in the uniform of the Boston Lobsters.

I really came to cherish my friendship with Billie Jean. She was very knowledgeable on the subjects she chose to care about. She had little regard for Renaissance men who knew a little bit about everything. She was a dedicated athlete, a dedicated feminist, and a great promoter for tennis and World Team Tennis.

When, during that summer, she won her 20th Wimbledon title (in women's doubles this time), she gave me her racket as a gift when she returned. I had given her a charm with a "20" before she left.

I accompanied her to a clinic in Cape Cod one morning after a match with the Lobsters and we managed to miss the flight back to New York, where another match was scheduled for later that day. So we had to scramble to rent a car, rush to Logan Airport, grab a shuttle to New York, and get to Madison Square Garden in time. It was great fun driving at high speeds, listening to music, dropping the car in a lot without turning it in to the rental agent (no time), running to make our flight, getting a lunatic cab driver at LaGuardia, and just getting to the Garden on time.

We had a nice friendship, but it was during that very summer that *People* magazine broke the story of her lesbian relationship with her hairdresser, which I knew nothing about, despite many people's insistence that she and most other women players were gay. Her husband, Larry, was frequently around our office, in fact. So too was Marilyn Barnett, her hairdresser.

Billie Jean's lesbian scandal was enormous news all during that year but hardly the first sexual issue in the league. WTT signed Dr. Renee

Richards, the transsexual, and she obviously drew attention wherever she played. The issue of her competing as a female was a compelling subject of debate all summer. Poor Renee, in the few encounters I had with her, seemed so overwhelmed by the attention that whatever sense of humor Dr. Richard Raskin had enjoyed was drained from her. I had a feeling she was a nice person but hated the attention.

Poor Billie Jean's commercial relationships all ended at once after the scandal broke, and she's never gotten them back to this day, despite regularly finishing high in century-ending polls as the most important woman athlete of our time. She never denied the relationship, and her only apology was for being unfaithful to her husband. She showed a lot of guts in dealing with it as her financial security slipped away. I wanted to be a supportive friend, but, by then, the story had taken on worldwide implications, and she retreated to a cocoon surrounded by high-powered agents and lawyers.

Working at Madison Square Garden with the Apples was a treat because of the mix of interesting shows and performances that always went on there. Except for when Chris Evert was there, we always played our matches in what was then called the Felt Forum, a smaller venue over on the Eighth Avenue side.

One afternoon, while waiting for the evening's match, Howard Freeman and I wandered through some tunnels and into the big Garden itself, the main arena.

There, on the stage, was none other than Bruce Springsteen and the E Street Band, rehearsing for an upcoming weekend show.

We looked around. We were alone except for some Garden maintenance workers. It was Bruce, the E Street Band, the maintenance workers, Howard, and me.

So we stood and watched the rehearsal. Bruce was jumping all over the arena, doing sound checks from different locations. It was a memorable afternoon to have this private show.

Bruce had a former agent named Mike Appel, with whom he was then locked in a horrible lawsuit. His fans hated Appel because the lawsuit kept Bruce from recording for a long time. I was increasingly being mistaken for Mike, or asked if we were related, but we'd never even met.

Then, about 15 years later, I was making a call from a pay phone at the Grand Hyatt Hotel in New York. On the phone next to me I could hear a man say, "Tell him it's Mike Appel."

So we were standing side by side.

I said, "I couldn't help but overhear—are you Mike Appel, Bruce

Springsteen's former agent?"

He had learned, I think, to be a little cautious about this question, so I jumped in and introduced myself. It turned out that he was often asked if he were related to me! We enjoyed the moment and the remarkable coincidence of being on adjoining phones.

The Apples folded at the end of the summer of '78. You could see it coming, because Chris Evert was, in effect, the league's only asset. A league couldn't operate like that. Sol Berg, the kindly owner of the Apples, didn't mind losing money—it was like buying a new yacht every year. He had the dough. But it was time to face reality.

I never got back into tennis again, and I lost touch with Billie Jean and Vitas and everyone else, but it was a fun summer, it made me a pretty decent tennis player for a while, and I got some broadcasting in. My trip from Cape Cod to Madison Square Garden with Billie Jean was like "Mr. Toad's Wild Ride." The whole thing was a good adventure.

As good timing would have it, the baseball commissioner's office was just then looking to expand its PR operation, and I was asked to join Bowie Kuhn's staff. This did come along at a key moment, because I had just bought my first house, a three-bedroom ranch near White Plains on a wooded third of an acre. I used to enjoy describing where it was, which was nowhere in particular—White Plains address, Fairview fire district, Elmsford school district, Hartsdale train station, Greenburgh taxes, Orchard Hill development. Forget about giving people directions.

The commissioner's office was located at 75 Rockefeller Center, in the Warner Communications Building. In my interview with Kuhn, he wanted to be certain that there were no lingering effects from my years with Steinbrenner, who was pretty much viewed as unsupportive of many of baseball's marketing efforts. On many, many issues, the Yankees would be the lone holdout. This was in part due to George's belief—quite true, of course—that the Yankee brand had a greater value to Major League Baseball than that of other teams. And, quite correct, it cost him more to maintain the value of that brand than it did other franchises in smaller markets. So there was logic on both sides of the dispute.

I, on the other hand, also needed to know that statements I had made in opposition to Kuhn over the years would not be held against me. I was assured that they would not be, that he certainly understood my role as spokesman at the Yankees, and that there was really only one spokesman there, no matter who was being quoted.

I joined Kuhn's staff in the fall of 1978, reporting to Bob Wirz, the former Kansas City Royals PR director, and then director of information for MLB. At Kansas City, Wirz had bled the town's printers dry of ink by expanding the Royals' media guide to triple the size of any other team's. He was a detail guy. He was a detail guy's detail guy.

My colleague in the department was Art Berke, a gifted publicist with a conscience (not an oxymoron), who would go on to handle PR for ABC Sports (living through the Howard Cosell period) and then for *Sports Illustrated*. He toiled through the drudgery of publicizing the annual swim-suit issue (okay, he liked that) and was slick enough to get Kathy Ireland's voice on his answering machine. He was also a wonderfully decent and honorable man and became one of my closest friends.

One of Art's assignments under Wirz was to develop baseball's first Media Information Directory, containing phone numbers and addresses of everyone in the media world who was part of the baseball scene. To take on something like this for the first time was a daunting task, but Art, a well-organized sort, did it brilliantly. He was justifiably proud of his effort when it arrived from the printer after numerous proofreadings. Bob called us both in for his morning briefing.

"Well, about the Media Directory," he said. "Art, what is this burr on page eleven?"

A burr is an imperfection, a dot, a scratch, some mark that isn't part of the text. It had appeared after the proofreading or was, perhaps, missed during the final read. It was remarkably insignificant, sort of 25 percent of a comma floating in white space, but just the sort of thing that elicited small groaning sounds from Art as he sat next to me. That was the extent of the comments on the Media Directory.

Our film division once produced a promotional piece—these were the skilled people who did *This Week in Baseball* and all of the wonderful highlights and blooper videos—and Bob sent them a friendly letter after viewing it, with his list of small criticisms.

Joe Podesta, the affable head of the division, called the staff in.

"Gather 'round, everyone," he announced. "Bob Wirz's letter has arrived. Let's all share it together."

Art and I got along famously, not only because we had much in common, but because we often seemed like the only ones around who enjoyed talking baseball. To much of the staff, it was all about attendance and revenues and the occasional infractions by players or executives that might lead to fines or suspensions. We were forever combing the national clippings to see if some general manager had publicly coveted another player or if some player (read: Bill Lee) had suggested that he might be sprinkling marijuana on his pancakes.

There was no rooting in the office, other than wishing that the World Series would be played in cities with good hotels and restaurants or that the Yankees and Mets would not be involved, because of the huge demand for tickets it would create from the networks, the ad agencies, and the New York sports community, not to mention everyone's personal friends.

Occasionally I would just walk past Mary Sotos, the commissioner's secretary, and pop into his office with some interesting piece of pure baseball news. One afternoon at Wrigley Field, the Phillies and Cubs were at something like 17–15 after five innings, and I thought he'd be interested. So I just walked in and told him.

In fact, he was very interested. He was a terrific fan who loved the game. When I would give him briefing notes about records falling, milestones reached, trivia, and oddities, he devoured it and put it into his briefing book as speech material. There was nothing false about his love of baseball. Hell, he'd been the scoreboard boy at old Griffith Stadium in the '40s!

My old friend Tom Villante was our director of marketing and broadcasting, and out of Tom's creative mind came a simple slogan, "Baseball Fever—Catch It," which was baseball's theme for a long time and was copied—and is still copied—by many other industries. Tom's great self-confidence and tremendous talents really helped to propel Major League Baseball into the era of modern marketing, even as the game continued to fight the incredible interest the NFL was achieving.

Joe Reichler, who had been Kuhn's first publicist, had moved over to Major League Baseball Properties when I was there. He was a longtime Associated Press baseball reporter, one of the most respected in the game.

When he shifted to MLB Properties, Kuhn hired Max Nichols, a Minneapolis sportswriter, as his successor. Max had reported to work on a Monday but was late arriving on Tuesday. By Tuesday afternoon, there had been no word from him and people were getting worried.

Around four, Max called. He was halfway home to Minneapolis. New York, it turned out, was just not for him.

That had created the opening for Wirz, who, although not an inspiring sort, was efficient and reliable.

When Art Berke and I needed a real baseball fix, we'd sit in Monte Irvin's office. Monte was a Hall of Famer, on staff in a goodwill capacity, and absolutely underutilized. Technically, he also reported to Wirz, who had him manning the copying machine at the All-Star Game one year. It was embarrassing for Monte, a bright, dignified man of great warmth.

Monte's most memorable time on the commissioner's staff, apart from Xerox duty, came in Atlanta on the day Henry Aaron hit his 715th home run. There was enormous controversy over Kuhn sending poor Monte as his representative so that Kuhn could fulfill a commitment to speak at the Yahoo Club in Cleveland (a group of Indians supporters). Monte had to suffer the boos of the hostile Braves fans, angered over the perceived snub by the commissioner.

Monte and his wife Dee flew down in the afternoon. The Braves, annoyed at his presence if not at him personally, delayed seating him. He had barely gotten to his seat when Aaron homered just after 9 P.M. Monte tried to make some on-field remarks during the hoopla, only to be booed by the fans. Henry patted him on the shoulder, smiled, and said, "Don't worry about it, Monte. It's not personal."

The ceremony over, Monte looked at Dee and said, "We can make the 10:40 flight back to Newark!" And they did.

Monte was a man of humility who never tooted his own horn. It wasn't his style. Some saw him as a mentor to Willie Mays, but he would laugh and say, "The next time Willie listens to me will be the first time."

Some felt he could have been Jackie Robinson, could have been "the first." Instead, he had to wait until 1949—two years after Robinson broke in. But then he became one of the league's great players and the man with the best record down the stretch during the Giants' miracle run at the 1951 pennant.

He and Jackie were never especially close. Jackie didn't see enough militancy in Monte over race issues, similar to the problem he had with Roy Campanella. Monte was much too diplomatic for Jackie's style. Campy however, was a close friend for life.

"And Jackie, well, he was a Dodger and we hated each other as Giants and Dodgers anyway," said Monte. "And don't let history distort what a tough sonofagun he was on the field. He could swear and heckle and bench jockey with the best of them. Oh, the things he'd say to Leo Durocher about his wife, Lorraine Day!"

Monte was generally acknowledged to have been the greatest school-boy athlete in New Jersey history, a four-sport star at East Orange High. He didn't reach the majors until he was 30, so a true appreciation of him at his peak was unavailable to most fans. He had his best years with the Newark Eagles of the Negro League.

One day the two of us were having lunch at our favorite spot, Kenny's on Lexington Avenue. I said, "Monte, when you were at your best with Newark, who would you compare yourself with today? Dave Parker? George Foster? Mike Schmidt?"

As I said, Monte was a humble man, the last you would ever find boasting about his accomplishments. But the question intrigued him. He was silent, ever so briefly, before he answered.

"Oh, DiMaggio," he said.

He meant it. He wasn't talking about Vince. And I am positive that it was accurate. Monte Irvin in 1941 must have been the equal of DiMaggio. I was glad he answered it that way, because I am sure he was correct; he was not given to exaggeration, let alone boasting.

Monte used to tell Art and me the most terrific stories about the Negro Leagues. About Effa Manley, his boss at the Eagles, who, it seemed, enjoyed the company of her players far more than was generally known.

Or about towns in which they would play, where they might "borrow" a local inmate who used to be a teammate, sneak him into a proper uniform under special arrangement with the warden, and beat the socks off a local team during a barnstorming mission.

Monte hated the film *The Bingo Long Travelling All-Stars and Motor Kings*, with Richard Pryor, Billy Dee Williams, and James Earl Jones. "Wasn't anything like that," he'd say. "It perpetuated the myth about the broken-down buses and exits out of town before the Klan got there. We were classier than that, and we weren't clowns."

We'd get wonderful Satchel Paige and Josh Gibson stories from Monte, but, as a college man, he was better educated than most of his teammates and maybe a better observer of their adventures than an actual participant.

His favorite story came from the Mexican League, where he played for Veracruz—owned by Jorge Pasquel, who had sought to raid the major leagues. Campy was catching for Monterrey.

On the last day of the 1942 season, a Saturday afternoon in Mexico City, Monte was coming to bat, with his team trailing 1–0, two outs, and a runner on in the ninth inning.

Pasquel called Monte over.

"Jorge, I'm getting ready to hit; I can't talk now."

But Pasquel was insistent and Monte hustled over to the owner's box.

"You hit a home run for me and win the ballgame, huh?" he said.

"Everyone in the ballpark figured out what he was saying to me," Monte would say. "It was a home run situation. When I got to the batter's box, Campy asked me what he had said, and I told him. And Campy laughed and said, 'No way, not the way Salazar's throwing, man.'

"But on the third pitch, I hit it into the bleachers, and we won the game. The place went crazy, and Pasquel gave me five hundred pesos. And he told me to give Campy half for calling the pitch, which I did. Oh, we partied that night, Campy and me, and to the end of his life, when-ever we would see each other, we'd think about that day in Mexico City and laugh and laugh."

While we worked together, we would both keep an eye on the home run progress of Texas's Pete Incaviglia. Until Pete came long, Monte was the game's all-time home run leader—for players who started with the letter I (A was Aaron, B was Banks, C was Cepeda, and so forth). He had 99. When Incaviglia finally passed Monte, he said, "Well, my 99 really stuck out like a sore thumb anyway, two digits. Just as well."

Of course, had he played in the majors during his prime, he would have been closer to 350 or 400 and would have retired, at the time, as one of the game's all-time top 20.

Another old baseball character on the staff was Harry Simmons, a longtime baseball employee and rules expert who was forever com-plaining about how "the lawyers ruined baseball." He hated Kuhn just for being a lawyer.

Charlie Finley came calling one day, probably to try to argue his way out of a fine. Someone told Harry that Finley was there; he had once worked for him.

"No kidding, I've got to say hello," he said.

So Harry went out to the reception area as Charlie was waiting for an elevator. Finley jumped.

"Harry Simmons, I can't believe it; I'd heard you passed on!" he said.

Harry, who for years wrote "So You Think You Know Baseball" for Baseball Digest, likewise recoiled at this improbable greeting. To say it was awkward all around would be accurate.

The staff was a good group of people, especially Gloria Coleman, the office assistant who also doubled as a travel agent and who was still booking my airline tickets for me more than 20 years after I last worked there. I enjoyed the company of my former Yankee colleagues, Johnny Johnson and George Pfister. But there was often scrutiny by team executives over the size of the staff, because the operation of the office was funded by the teams. The operation was much smaller than the NFL's and would likewise be dwarfed by the NBA when that league took off some years later, but still, many watched our spending and our head count very carefully.

We had a near strike in 1980, and I was on the scene as last-minute negotiations kept it from happening. I remember Peter O'Malley saying to his fellow owners, "You mean we are going to shut down our industry over a handful of average players going as compensation for lost free agents?"

And his wisdom prevailed. The strike was averted, but, by leaving a single issue—compensation—tabled for another year, the owners and the players had effectively guaranteed a strike in 1981. When you leave only one issue to negotiate, there can be no give-and-take in other areas to achieve a compromise. It guaranteed that both sides would dig in during '81 over the compensation matter, and that's exactly what happened, leading to the first prolonged, in-season strike in baseball history.

I was no scholar on labor history nor could I pretend to be a genius on labor negotiations. But I was friendly with the owners' bargaining chief, Ray Grebey, and I expressed to him my view that they had left one issue undecided, and that it was certainly a step toward an impasse in 1981.

"You could be right," he told me, "but you take what you get at the time and worry about that down the road."

Art Berke was growing increasingly discontented at work and left to go to ABC in 1980. I was also unhappy there. I wasn't getting along well with Wirz, and I was having trouble adjusting to working in the game's bureaucracy as opposed to having a rooting interest and a team involvement. My days there were winding down.

I had an offer from Tal Smith to join the Astros as PR director and, amazingly, one from Gabe Paul to join the Indians. I had never realized that Gabe respected my work.

I liked Kuhn a lot, and he arranged for an interview with Commissioner Larry O'Brien and his general counsel David Stern at the NBA, just to keep me in town, if not in baseball. Clearly, he needed to support his department head, Wirz, as a matter of good administration. And Wirz, to be sure, needed assistants who were more suited to his style.

I left the staff shortly after the 1980 World Series when a job offer came to me in television. Kuhn always kept in touch with me and, four years later, selected me to work with him on his memoirs. It was a compliment to be asked and, in a sense, vindicated my work on his staff, which I had always felt fell short of what I hoped to contribute.

With a certain irony, my spot on Wirz's staff would be taken by Rick Cerrone—not the Yankee catcher, but the publisher of a modern version of *Baseball Magazine*. Rick would go on to marry Villante's secretary. He would later leave Peter Ueberroth's staff to join the Pittsburgh Pirates as vice president of PR—the organization I might have joined years earlier had I accepted Bill Guilfoile's offer.

When budget cutting came to the Pirates, Rick and other vice presidents were let go. In 1993 he was offered a job with Topps, the trading card manufacturer, but turned it down. It wound up going to me. Two years later, while he was still on the job market but also running his own PR consulting firm, I turned down another offer to return to the Yanks as PR director, being happy and well paid at Topps. I suggested they call Rick, and he was hired, enjoying the fun and success of the Joe Torre years. In the meantime, Topps, downsizing as its industry crumbled, laid me off, leading to the start of my own business. Rick and I seem destined to leapfrog and crisscross each other's careers, and, every time one of us changes jobs, it always seems as if the other fellow has just left the room.

SANDY, I JUST DON'T LIKE WHAT I'M SEEING HERE

I had little understanding or appreciation of the enormity of the television industry when WPIX-TV recruited me to handle its public relations in 1980. It was still a time when over-the-air broadcast and network television ruled. Cable was just getting started; the three networks still dominated, and baseball games had been shown in color for a little more than a decade. It was the year CNN was born. The VCR was still a new toy making its way into homes, enabling "time-shifting" for those who could figure out how to program it.

To a lifelong New Yorker, WPIX was the rerun and movie station, loaded with *The Odd Couple* and *The Honeymooners*, along with old movies and kids' programming. As a youngster, I had enjoyed *Officer Joe Bolton* and the *Three Stooges*, *Captain Jack McCarthy* with *Popeye* cartoons, and, each Christmas, the channel 11 Yule Log—hours of uninterrupted Christmas music played over the video of a roaring fire.

They had a cute meteorologist named Gloria Okon (whose son would become the towel-receiving kid in the famous Mean Joe Greene commercial for Coca-Cola), but the news was pretty low budget.

What channel 11 really had going for them was Yankee baseball, which they had been faithfully telecasting since 1951.

I had no idea that all those reruns and children's programs and low-budget news shows had made this a bigger business than the Yankees were. The broadcast industry, I quickly learned, was an enormous revenue generator. If you had a license to run a New York City television station, you could make a ton of money, much more than by owning a baseball team. People were standing in line to buy commercial time, and salesmen were standing in line to work at a place like PIX.

They had a crafty old engineer, a true broadcast pioneer named Otis Freeman, who used to say, "You know, we should run a show from midnight to six A.M., with just an overhead camera peering down on a green felt cloth. And every sixty seconds, a hand would roll a pair of dice. It would be the biggest show in town."

He was right, but if a station was run by responsible people, conscience prevailed. And in case it didn't, the FCC was there every few years to review how you used the public airwaves when they considered renewing your license.

So there were always the public service announcements and the editorials and the community affairs programming to satisfy license requirements, and, for WPIX, they were critical because a nasty license challenge went on for over a decade, initiated by the station's simple act of running old Pentagon file footage and claiming it was same-day war footage. That little indiscretion opened a Pandora's box for the challengers and fed a lot of lawyers for a long time.

I was recruited to the station by Leavitt J. Pope, the station's president and part owner, who had himself helped to put the station on the air in 1948. Lev was an engineer by training, which was very unusual for the top man at a TV station, whose background was usually in sales or programming. He was a handsome, athletic, religious man who put 11 children through college and had great dignity and integrity. He had a gift with people; the sort where, even if he didn't remember a name, he could make a person feel important.

I sat in his office on the day he tore a personal check out of his ledger and said, "That's it, my 88th and last tuition payment." I always liked Lev, always thought he was an honorable man above all else, and, when he offered me the job, I gave it serious consideration. Considering that I had no television background and didn't speak the language of the industry, it was a gutsy thing for him to make me a spokesman for one of the industry's most important independent stations.

("Independent" means not affiliated with a network, creating its own programming 24 hours a day. With the advent of WB, Fox, and UPN, there are virtually no "indies" left.)

Lev knew me from my Yankee days, and we had had several press conferences together to announce renewal deals. He was a great Yankee fan, and a Giants fan before that—the station had also done New York Giants games before the team moved to San Francisco. He had negotiated contracts with Horace Stoneham and Chub Feeney of the Giants, and with Dan Topping, George Weiss, Mike Burke, Lee MacPhail, and George Steinbrenner of the Yankees.

The station was absolutely terrific at delivering live baseball and, in fact, had created instant replay, although the networks would take credit for it. But in 1959, director Jack Murphy, acting on an on-the-air request from Mel Allen, replayed a base hit by Chicago's Jim McAnany that fell in front of Norm Siebern, breaking up a Ralph Terry no-hitter. There was the birth of the replay. I always gave the station full credit for that, although I knew the real heroes were the engineers who invented videotape. The techies never got enough credit.

Bob Fishel was the one who prodded me to join WPIX. He was the one who told me that Lev was a great man and that the station was part of an industry far bigger than baseball with a lot of growth potential. Tom Villante knew a good thing when he heard it. "Don't think of this as a rerun station," he said. "You've got it all wrong. This is a $100 million-a-year company, part of Tribune Company, and it's a huge world out there. It's the entertainment industry!"

I began to look at it differently.

They were right, of course, about the size of the industry. In baseball I could stay up-to-date by reading the sports section and following through with *The Sporting News*, *Sport*, and *Sports Illustrated*.

In broadcasting I had as many as 15 publications to read each week, including *TV-Radio Age*, published by none other than Gabe Paul's kid brother Sol. It was fine that I knew about sports and the station's history with baseball, but to be its spokesman I also needed a crash course in every aspect of a station. I had to understand programming, sales, engineering, community affairs, news, ratings, demographics, hiring practices, commercial placement, billings, FCC regulations, graphics, advertising, and promotion. Engineering itself was huge—not only the daily operation and transmission of the station's signal, but news gathering, live coverage, the matter of moving the transmitter from the top of the Empire State Building to the top of the World Trade Center, and other such things. I had to understand how signals traveled by land line or by satellite, even how we could feed Yankee games to a limited group of stations; what transponders were and how many cameras and replay machines were needed for different events. Then there were their names, like Chyrons and Dubners and still-storers and Harrys. There were must-carry rules and superstations and distant signals; there was first-run syndication and live-on-tape programming and cherry picking, bicycling, and wheels. There were the names of the major syndicators, the names of the national sales reps, and there was always the "hit 'em where they ain't" strategy that independents used against the networks, showing news when they were in entertainment, entertainment when they were in news; women's programming while they were showing sports, children's programming while they were showing political interviews.

To help stave off the license challenge, we had to operate a New Jersey bureau and do a certain percentage of stories from New Jersey, which did not have any of its own stations. And an activist group in Long Island forced us to establish a bureau there and devote stories to that area. There were surely days that we felt besieged for the right to occupy a place on the broadcast spectrum.

Like most people, I never trusted the ratings system for measuring viewership and used to hear so many viewers say, "They never call me!" But I learned that there was enough supporting data behind them to give them more legitimacy than I had expected. One year we ran a 3-D movie, *Revenge of the Creature*, a campy old horror flick starring John Agar (Shirley Temple's first husband), with a cameo appearance by Clint Eastwood.

To view the movie, people had to purchase 3-D glasses from Burger King for a buck. So they'd made an investment that would make most of them watch—and we had a pretty good idea of how many pairs of glasses were sold.

There was no way that either of the ratings services, Nielsen or Arbitron, could have had that information, but both came very, very close to the number we estimated. It was a rare opportunity to run a large test, and the services delivered.

This was not an industry that especially cared about history. No one cared about naming the station's program managers in order, or in what years our local news might have won its time period. Everything was about today and tomorrow, and the only look back that mattered was how we were doing with return on investment compared with a year earlier. We did manage to create a two-hour special for the station's 40th anniversary—I wrote the sports portion—but I really had to resist my usual temptation to call upon the past as a PR tool.

Then there were the organizations with their endless acronyms— NATPE, NATAS, INTV, IRTS, FCC, NAB, ITNA, INN, RTNDA, NYSBA, and so forth. I was active in the New York Chapter of the National Association of Television Arts and Sciences and represented WPIX on a number of all-industry committees.

One year I even represented the station at a U.S. Senate subcommittee hearing on the intrusion of pay-cable into free sports broadcasting. An attentive listener at our Washington session who seemed very sympathetic to our cause and asked very good questions was Senator Al Gore of Tennessee.

One of the more interesting characters at the station was a sound engineer named Marc Rothstein. How many people can have three remarkable credits such as these . . . he was the grandnephew of Arnold Rothstein, the gambler who had fixed the 1919 World Series; he was the random "fan in the stands" who was pictured on the cover of the 1969 Mets Yearbook; and his mother had been a babysitter for David Berkowitz, "the Son of Sam."

The scary giant lurking on the horizon was cable television. When its penetration into households was less than 30 percent, we could somewhat ignore it, particularly in New York, where the outer boroughs—Queens, the Bronx, Brooklyn, and Staten Island—were slow to get wired. That was all politics and economics. The poorer neighborhoods would be expensive to wire, because the sign-up rates would not be cost-effective.

For viewers used to "free" broadcasts of Yankee baseball, this was a great populist issue. SportsChannel, owned by Charles Dolan, was intruding more and more into WPIX's schedule of free telecasts. We took our argument to the press as a champion of "the people," and I was the primary spokesman on the issue in the nation; everyone was watching how it would play out in New York, where fans were used to getting their baseball for free. Maybe it was one thing for an HBO to give you commercial-free movies for your buck, but SportsChannel charged for the same telecasts we delivered for free, commercials included. It just didn't sit well.

The argument was simple. Every man had a certain inalienable right of access to baseball on the free public airwaves. As programming, it was the great equalizer. The elevator operator could talk to the CEO about last night's game. Now baseball stood in danger of sinking into an elite bunker, in which only the rich—those who could afford cable—would see the games.

Games on free TV did not hurt live attendance at all. WPIX had shown that throughout its history of baseball coverage by helping to "sell" the experience of being there in person by showing crowd enthusiasm, promoting upcoming games, and developing millions of fans.

Baseball had always advanced to ever larger audiences, first on radio, then on local television, and then on network television. With the broadcast people in the commissioner's office exploring more and more cable opportunities, they were, for the first time, advancing a theory that less was better—as long as those watching were more upscale. It was not only an issue I was required to represent the station on, it was an issue I felt passionate about. I must have done three hundred interviews on the subject as cable grew to be more and more of a threat to our ownership of the broadcast rights. I became well known for a time on the New York airwaves, as even our competitors covered the battle between WPIX and SportsChannel for Yankee rights.

One of my great PR coups came the first time Opening Day was on SportsChannel and not on WPIX. The dirty truth was Opening Day was a weekday game—it might have had a 3 or 4 rating and was not one of the coveted games when we divided up the schedule. But I knew a PR opportunity when I saw it, and so, a few days before the game, I alerted all media that "This will be the first Opening Day Phil Rizzuto has missed since 1940, when he was in the minor leagues. Poor Phil is very choked up by this, and will be available at his home for photos, watching the game on cable."

Sure enough, a mob descended on his home in Hillside, New Jersey, and there he was, posed in front of his big-screen TV (a gift from SportsChannel on Phil Rizzuto Day), looking on as the Yankees played their home opener.

Newsday put the picture on page 1 under a headline HOLY COW! YANKS HOME OPENER ON CABLE! (*Newsday* was the hometown newspaper for Dolan and the SportsChannel crowd.)

Could Rizzuto have gone to the stadium to see the game in person? Of course. But the dramatic photo of poor Scooter, unable to do the game on free TV for the common man, was a PR winner for us. It was huge. It got attention.

Sometimes, I have to say, we didn't help our own cause very much. One year the Yankees announced that they were moving their starting time for night games from 8 P.M. to 7:30. They didn't even consult us.

Lev Pope immediately knew that would mean preempting our lucrative 7:30 newscast many times. He calculated the lost revenues from that newscast to be $1 million over the season. As much as he loved the Yankees, he couldn't believe they would do this without even consulting us.

So he decided to fight back. He called me to his office and said I should announce that we were going to join the games in progress at eight. Since first pitch is usually closer to 7:40, we wouldn't miss that much, and few games were decided in the first inning, anyway.

For a former Yankee PR director to go public with that position was very difficult. I pleaded with Lev to rethink it—he was a big fan, he knew that "first innings counted!" But he needed to make his point.

It caused a general outrage among fans and made us look very bad. But a million bucks was a million bucks, and eventually we compromised.

We would show the games at 7:30, but we would get some additional commercial time, the revenue from which we would not share with the Yankees. In the end, we would be made whole by the deal. Lev knew what he was doing.

One year he almost got the Mets to move to WPIX. He had me set up a meeting with Frank Cashen, the Mets' general manager and a former colleague from my time in the commissioner's office. Working with Tom Villante as a consultant, Lev crafted a revenue-sharing plan that was far better for the Mets than their arrangement at WWOR-TV. The problem was, we had another year to go with the Yankees, but the Mets were available now. Lev thought we could somehow televise both teams, and he was tired of dealing with Steinbrenner. He saw Yankee games increasingly drifting to SportsChannel, anyway. We could work out the scheduling for one year, but there would be instances of give-and-take, and Cashen simply did not want to get into a battle with Steinbrenner over who got which dates. In the end, everyone wound up right where they started, but our Yankee schedule was down to a precious 50 games, with 100 on cable.

I learned the broadcast industry quickly, came to appreciate the importance of WPIX in the broadcast world, and liked my colleagues at WPIX a lot. I was still close to the Yankee scene, and Don Carney, the producer and director of the games, was always receptive to little ideas I had for the telecasts.

When Tom Seaver was going to pitch at Yankee Stadium, in search of his 300th career victory, I suggested that we hire Lindsey Nelson for the game as a guest announcer. Lindsay had been the Mets' longtime announcer, and, as such, had broadcast Seaver's first win. I had a sense that Seaver, going for 300 in New York with his family on hand and with the possibility of a baseball strike looming, would be a sure thing.

Don brought Lindsay into the booth, and he called the ninth inning as Seaver ensured his place in the Hall of Fame. Lindsay was thrilled to be part of it and forever appreciative that I had made the suggestion. Seaver sent me a note thanking me for having Lindsay there. And WPIX won the New York State Broadcaster's Association award for best live sports coverage, on the basis of that particular game.

It was little things like that that made Lev feel I could handle Don's sports responsibilities when Carney retired in 1988. When he did, I was given the added title of "vice president, public relations and sports" and became executive producer of Yankee telecasts, as well as preseason games of the Giants and Jets and occasional sports specials.

To take this on, I really needed a crash course in the engineering side of live telecasts, which our technical people were all too happy to give me. Any innovative idea we wanted to implement, however, was thwarted by Major League Baseball, such as adding additional microphones to better capture on-field sound or miking the managers. Most of our ideas appeared later, when the networks, which were throwing a lot more money into baseball's coffers, asked for permission.

One innovation we did bring about was actually Lev Pope's idea.

"How about cameras on the roof of Yankee Stadium?" he said. "One over home plate, one in upper left field looking in toward home. It will be a great new view."

They are called "beauty shots" in production.

At enormous installation cost from Yankee Stadium maintenance people, we put up the two cameras. Our inside joke was that the home plate camera would not really be there to catch balls and strikes but would be a surveillance camera to catch Rizzuto sneaking over the George Washington Bridge in the seventh inning. He had a habit of leaving early to beat the traffic.

After I left WPIX, they decided to abandon those camera positions, and they were taken up by MSG Network, then the cable rightsholder. They continue to provide great shots, including "beauty shots" of the New York skyline, and because the cameras were unmanned and controlled only by a joystick in the control room, it was a shame WPIX couldn't maintain them. Now the users get a lot of extra credit for their great shots, which were all Pope's idea.

While we may have been slowed down on the engineering side in our attempts at fresh ideas, we were never at a loss for production ideas. John Moore, our director, joined me in some pretty innovative stuff, like recreating the full nine-inning scoreboard (complete with Stadium façade) instead of the brief runs-hits-errors summary after each half-inning. We always did a feature-driven opening, setting the stage for the game. We sought out newsmakers to visit the booth and did anniversary tributes to great Yankee moments, using vintage newsreel film. We had Broadway Video, the producers who did the opening for *Saturday Night Live*, do ours.

I learned a sociological lesson when I got players to record Mother's Day greetings to use as "bumpers" when we went to commercial. No problem getting players for that one. A month later, Father's Day failed to be as successful. Except for Chris Chambliss, I could find no black players to record Father's Day greetings.

One of my first innovations as producer was to bring Mel Allen's voice back to our telecasts. Mel had been the "Voice of the Yankees" from

1939–64. In the '70s and '80s he had returned to the booth in a less noticeable role as part of the cable TV broadcast team. He had even called Dave Righetti's no-hitter in '83. But that job was now over, and his visibility came through his work as host of *This Week in Baseball*.

As I looked at the 1990 schedule, I decided that I wanted Mel back in the WPIX booth for one game—in order to make him a seven-decade announcer! Baseball people love trivia like this. So, in April 1990, we brought Mel back to WPIX for the first time since his firing after the '64 season, and he called a couple of innings in a game against Oakland—with Mark McGwire and Jose Canseco in the lineup. Mel, who broke in doing Lou Gehrig's games, could now go out doing the Bash Brothers.

He hugged me after the stint, and I felt very good about someone paying this man back for the Ph.D. he'd given me when I was just learning the game.

I didn't quite drop it there. As long as I was the executive producer, I had Mel's recorded voice in every opening we did. "HELLO there, everybody, THIS is Mel Allen. LIVE, on the WPIX Yankee baseball network, it's the 1988 NEW YORK YANKEES!" We went through the recording ritual each year, sometimes doing it at the studio where he was hosting *This Week in Baseball*, and sometimes having him come up to the small announcing booth at PIX. He would kid me and say, "Let's record ten years at once, then you'll have them . . ." and I'd cut him off, because I didn't want to contemplate what he was suggesting.

Because we were doing only 50 games when I became executive producer, we got by just fine with two announcers—Rizzuto and Bill White. They were a terrific team, played so well off each other, genuinely liked each other, and gave an expertise and entertaining call to the games.

Now, the first thing you have to know when you begin talking about announcers is that—contrary to long-standing belief—our national pastime is not baseball but, rather, critiquing the announcers.

Try it. Ask anyone about last night's game, and see if the subject doesn't turn to the announcers within 60 seconds. Everyone has their likes and dislikes, and everyone likes to talk about them. It probably began with Mel Allen, and it certainly peaked with Howard Cosell, but it is now a daily part of our national dialogue.

I had always enjoyed Rizzuto's work, even as a kid. Sometimes I turned down the TV audio and listened to him on the radio. He had this great innocence, like the angelic choirboy with a touch of mischief in him who could get away with anything. Once, I even heard him say, "HOLY cow, what a screaming line drive into the stands that was! It's a wonder more people don't get KILLED coming to the ballgame."

Now I was his boss.

Phil was exasperating, with his endless birthday and restaurant plugs. John Moore, our gifted director, was out of his league trying to reign Scooter in, as was I. No one was up to it, because, in that way at least, he held the cards. No one was going to fire him over birthday plugs. He knew that this was one battle he couldn't lose. We'd tell him to tone it down; he'd say he would, but never did.

One year we thought we were doing our final telecast ever on WPIX. We hadn't renewed our contract, and speculation was that the Yankees were going all cable. John put together a terrific closing piece, with great scenes and players from the 40 years WPIX had covered the Yankees, set to Billy Joel's *New York State of Mind*.

Leading into this piece would be Scooter, doing the final inning of what might be our final game, and his too.

Phil always did play-by-play, never color. If he was the color commentator, you might as well not have him there at all. His concentration would be gone, he would be saying hello to everyone walking by the broadcast booth, he would be running out for cannolis, and he couldn't add much about the players because he didn't really know them. John and I always joked about Rizzuto probably never having met Don Mattingly, because he never went downstairs and he never traveled with the team.

But here he was, down to one batter, Billy Joel all cued up, and it was a fly ball to left. Perhaps on the last batter of his broadcast career, Phil said, "Oh, and before this ball comes down, time to get in one last birthday wish for Mrs. Viola Ferrazzano out there in the Whitestone section of Queens, a great Yankee fan."

Argh! We all screamed in the control room in the basement of Yankee Stadium. But that was Phil.

The thing with the Italian names was always out of control, but Bill White had a great comeback for him one day on the air.

"Something about all of these birthdays today, Scooter, they all seem to have something in common," he said.

"You mean they all end in vowels?" said Rizzuto, sheepishly.

"Like *White*?" said Bill. Then he laughed his great hearty laugh on the air, and Phil knew he'd been set up.

Bill White was a great person and a great broadcaster, but I always felt the fans came to appreciate him—or him with Rizzuto—more after he left than they did during his tenure. The two of them were a great show, and sometimes Bill would squeeze Rizzuto's wrist if he thought he was getting into something that would get him into trouble. He'd squeeze so hard he could stop the circulation in Phil's hand.

White was a man's man, a strong, bright person with little use for the politics of the game, only the justice. He would have made a great marshal at Dodge City if they'd had equal opportunity hiring back then. And he wouldn't have had to shoot bad guys, he could just have squeezed their wrists.

We had become friends almost immediately when Mike Burke hired him in 1971, on a strong recommendation from Cosell. He became the first black broadcaster for a local team (Jackie Robinson had done some broadcast work for ABC's early baseball coverage), and Bill was always well received by the fans, even as he was learning his new craft.

That first spring training, I spent a lot of time with him, helping to acclimate him to the new career and a new league. We went fishing and talked about the responsibilities of a broadcaster to his audience. We had dinner and talked about how you ease into the commercials and the out-of-town scores. He would tape his games and we would listen to them back at the hotel. Some of his mistakes were hard to believe. He would call left field right field and vice versa because he wasn't used to looking at a game from that angle. He called the Washington Senators the Redskins. He called Comiskey Park "Cominsky."

But he worked hard and wanted to know every detail and every error, because he didn't want to make the same mistake twice. He sent tapes to Vin Scully for review. He absorbed a lot from the skillful lessons of Tom Villante, who had a great ear for a good broadcast. He worked with a private voice coach and kept up a grueling schedule, driving from his home near Philadelphia to Yankee Stadium each day.

The plan was to have him do color for a few months and then ease him into play-by-play.

That strategy lasted eight innings. In our first exhibition game from miserable old Miami Stadium where we were playing the Orioles, Rizzuto spotted Joe DiMaggio outside the broadcast booth as the ninth inning was just about to begin. Naturally, he had to go out and say hello, even though he was on the air. So he just said, "White, you take it," and scooted out of the booth.

On the first pitch, Chico Salmon hit a game-winning homer, and Bill pretty much said, "Uh-oh," and that was the beginning of his play-by-play. It was also another reason why we often considered handcuffing Rizzuto to his seat.

Fishel was one of the first to tire of Phil's on-air work, although most fans loved it. It would drive Bob crazy that Phil was always talking about "a break for the Yankees," as though they weren't earning their victories on merit, only on "lucky breaks."

As the years went on, Phil's popularity was slipping. Younger fans didn't get or didn't care for his ethnic humor, and he wasn't a Yankee legend to them, either. But I still loved his work and came to respect him more than ever as a broadcaster. He could do any script in one take, and it was no coincidence that he brought out the best in everyone he was ever partnered with. He had no ego problems, never cared about hogging the mike, and played so well off anyone, whether it was White, Frank Messer, Fran Healy, Tom Seaver, you name it. Part of this was not ego, but self-confidence. He was intimidated in his early broadcast days, working with Mel Allen and Red Barber. Neither one of them, especially not Red, wanted a former player in the booth. But now, as a man of seniority, he was able to hone his innocent-little-boy act and tease his partners and still give you an entertaining call of a game.

He was fun to travel with, especially when he did his daily CBS Radio Network show. The script, written by Herb Goren, would be waiting for him at the local CBS affiliate. He would take a cab, run upstairs while the cab waited, read the script, and be back in the taxi on his way to play golf, in about 10 minutes.

"Don't ever tell anyone how easy this is," he warned me.

For years, people would tell him that he belonged in the Baseball Hall of Fame, but he would always brush it off. And, it turned out, he meant it.

"The Hall of Fame is for guys like Ruth and Cobb and Hornsby and Mathewson," he said, "I'm not one of those guys."

Even when Pee Wee Reese got in, he would brush it off. But, once Reese made it, you could tell it was more important to him. (Today, I believe he belongs in the broadcasters' wing as well.)

There were so many interesting things about Scooter; you'd never get tired of him. One year we had a new ladder installed in the broadcast booth at the stadium. It proved to be a little clumsy for me to climb down when we visited it for the first time.

"You huckleberry," he said, "watch how we do it in the navy."

And then he turned around and went step-step-step-step-step, with his back to the field, so quickly that I knew at once he had passed the ladder test during the war in fine form.

So the White and Rizzuto team went on for years, following the departure of the steady pro in the booth, Frank Messer, who always lent sanity to every broadcast. Frank's departure meant that a good friend to all of us was gone, and Rizzuto always fought to bring Frank back whenever there was an opening. Unfortunately, no matter how much we agreed, the approval always rested in the hands of the Yankees (meaning you-know-who), and it was never forthcoming. It saddened me to hear that Frank felt we at WPIX could have brought him back but didn't. He was a pro's pro, and we would have. On more than one occasion, Don Carney battled hard to retain him and triumphed.

After my first year as producer, I got a call from White. It was a call from an old friend—he had been to my wedding, talked to me about job changes, talked to me about his own kids and his divorce—but I was also his boss.

"Can we have lunch tomorrow?" he said.

"Oh, no," I answered. "They didn't offer you the National League presidency, did they!!?"

I don't know how I knew this, but I did. Bart Giamatti was moving up to commissioner, and I had a hunch they would find Bill.

"Let's talk about it," he said to me. "I need to pick your brain."

So we had lunch at the Helmsley, next door to WPIX.

"Bill, you could never stand the politics of baseball—this is as political as it gets," I told him. "Think about wearing a suit and tie every day, sitting through committee meetings, waking up at six, carrying a briefcase, living in Manhattan. It's not you!"

I cared more about Bill at this point than about losing an announcer.

He wouldn't quite say it, but the pressure was great to take the job. No black man had ever held such a high executive position. To turn it down would have been difficult, even though he hated to admit that he was part of a bigger picture. He wanted it very much to be an individual decision.

"If I take it," he said, "I want you there with me. You know how to work the hallways of the game. I would need your politicking skills."

He called me two days later.

"I'm gonna take it," he said. "It's time, anyway. I've been doing the Yankees for eighteen years. A man needs a change. I'm not as focused as I once was; I'm not doing as good a job as I once did."

I started to correct him, but I sensed that he had talked himself into this to find a rationale for leaving. I let it drop.

So Bill went off to the National League presidency, a job he never really came to enjoy. He feuded constantly with Fay Vincent, Giamatti's successor as commissioner, had the difficult task of taking calls from every old teammate who wanted a job in baseball, and had to play politics with a briefcase and a suit while dealing with Richie Phillips and the umpires. He was happy when his term ended, and, although Len Coleman succeeded him, the job soon faded away, the league presidencies no longer relevant at all.

Meanwhile, I was faced with the need to hire a replacement for Bill. This got me on the phone with broadcasters and agents all over America. The Yankee job was a coveted one, and in no time my office was floor-to-ceiling in audition tapes.

As I weeded through all of the tapes, I had a name in mind who hadn't submitted one. Tom Seaver. His agent, Matt Merola, had always been a straight shooter with me. Tom and I had done two books together, during which I had really come to admire his appreciation for baseball history and his knowledge of the game far beyond the field.

Tom was no amateur broadcaster. He had done NBC World Series telecasts, was an experienced commercial pitchman, and had a big name in New York. Of course, that was on the Mets' side of the river, but he was still a glamorous figure in New York sports history.

He had retired in 1986, and his two years out of the game had left him a little directionless. He had remained in the New York area, living in Greenwich, Connecticut, and handling endorsement assignments and the occasional broadcast gigs that Matt would arrange. The Mets kept him at arm's length. Some felt that they saw him as a threat—a guy who would want to become general manager no matter what position they gave him. When Matt inquired about a broadcast position there, they had told him, "Sure, send us a tape." The Mets needed a tape from Tom Seaver?

Seaver was a good broadcaster; the big question would be how he would work with Rizzuto and whether Yankee fans could accept him.

I discussed it with Lev Pope, who immediately loved the idea. I was confident that Yankee fans would like Tom if he gave them a good broadcast filled with his baseball knowledge. Fans were now growing accustomed to learning the inner game during a broadcast. Tim McCarver had broken through with the most insight fans had ever heard on the air. Guys like Rizzuto would never get hired anymore—fans demanded more. I knew Seaver could deliver. We negotiated a deal with Merola and brought him aboard.

At the same time, we wanted a third announcer, more of a pro. We were actually going to be doing more games in '88, and we all felt that Rizzuto and Seaver needed a third man who could give them a couple of innings off and bring his own expertise to the booth. For that we took George Grande, who had been the original *SportsCenter* announcer on ESPN. George was a knowledgeable class act who got along well with everyone in baseball. He worked hard, did his homework, and did everything asked of him.

We had a press conference to unveil our new team, then went off to spring training to make it click.

Tom, it turned out, had a shyness that made him uncomfortable in certain situations. Yankee employees were confused at times by what almost appeared to be aloofness. He could be outgoing at a cocktail party, be loud in the clubhouse, and active in the Players Association, but, with strangers, he never knew quite how to act. So he would put his head down and walk forward, his half-glasses resting on his nose, and the office people would say, "What's with him?"

But he could be full of charm at times. One year, I was coaching my son's Little League team and we were well on the way to setting an all-time Larchmont-Mamaroneck record for perfection. We were headed for an 0–19 season, and it was all I could do to keep the players showing up for each game.

I decided they needed a morale booster, so I managed to get the WPIX luxury suite one afternoon and brought the whole team. I invited the announcers down to give the kids a pep talk. And they were great—Rizzuto, Seaver, and Grande, each taking a lot of time with the kids, posing for pictures, signing autographs, and telling them to keep their spirits up.

We still went on to lose every game, which I thought might have been my coaching until a few years later, when I coached my daughter's softball team to a first-place finish.

Seaver bonded well with Rizzuto; they looked out for each other. When I had a difficult contract negotiation with Rizzuto in 1990, one which got ugly in the newspapers and found him calling me names, I knew that Seaver was coaching him on the side. "They'll give you the money, Scooter; don't give in."

That was a miserable time for me. I loved Scooter and he deserved the money, but senior management was firm that we were only going to pay him so much. Although I thought it was below market value, it was my job to negotiate with the money that had been budgeted. And that was when we went to war. It lasted several weeks, and there came a point when I was certain that it was over—Rizzuto would not sign, as a matter of pride; we would not raise our offer; and we would wish each other well. The fans would be angry, but they would get over it. Everyone does.

I received two death threats on the phone at WPIX. I considered them frivolous, but I reported them anyway.

In the end, Tribune told WPIX to give him the money he wanted. I wish it could have been like that earlier on. It left both Phil and me scarred and the friendship shaken, but I made the first road trip with the club, we had a private lunch together, and we healed the wounds. I told him that Cora had gotten me through the tense weeks by assuring me, in a conversation that took place when Phil was not home, that things would work out and Phil didn't consider this personal. They even took a picture of us hugging each other in the press box that evening.

He was still a great character, and you never knew what you were getting. I decided to fly to Boston at the end of the season for a "year end" early dinner before our final telecast. Although there are many great restaurants in Boston, I decided we'd go to the Hard Rock Café, because it would undoubtedly give Phil a lot of material for the broadcast that night.

Seaver, Grande, Moore, and I were all set to meet at four.

No Rizzuto.

"The Hard Rock Café?" he said on the phone. "Holy cow, I can't go to one of those topless places; Cora would kill me!"

I explained that it wasn't a topless place, but his excuse was in place, so he never arrived.

Boston was also the scene of another great moment, which certainly could have involved our hero.

In the early '70s everyone was talking about this risqué new film, *Deep Throat*, and of course, with a traveling baseball team, everyone had to see it.

It was playing across the street from the Sheraton, and a group of writers decided to check it out.

"Phil, want to come and see *Deep Throat*?" one of them asked.

"Are you crazy? Cora would kill me," he answered. (Cora was a wonderful person, and it was hard to imagine her running after him with a frying pan.)

Well, we were about 20 minutes into this cinematic classic when a particularly graphic scene—one that gave the movie its title—appeared on the screen. Suddenly, from the back of the otherwise silent theater, we heard, "Hol-ee cow!"

It was unmistakable. But, in fairness to Phil, we never turned around, and at the end of the movie, there was no Rizzuto in sight; so, Cora, it could well have been an imposter. Don't hit him.

Not only did Phil and I patch up our business differences, but, in 1994, long after we had worked together, when he finally made the Hall of Fame, I drove over to his house to help with the press. He was totally on his own, and I knew it would be a mob scene. I told Cora to hang their American flag outside the window. "This is going to be a big day." I took all the phone calls, gave out the directions, and organized the whole frantic day of interview requests, all out of old friendship.

That evening, exhausted, Phil asked me and John Moore to join him and Cora for a celebration dinner at one of his favorite Italian restaurants in New Jersey. He got a standing ovation when he entered, and we had a wonderful time, but John and I sat there amazed that we were sharing dinner with Phil on this amazing night. Who gets to have dinner with a man the day he gets chosen for the Hall of Fame?! Where were his three kids? In any event, it was an honor to be part of that dinner, and an unforgettable cap on our long relationship, with all of its highs and lows.

When we thought we were losing Scooter during that ugly contract negotiation, we had to begin to make contingency plans.

I called Bobby Murcer in Oklahoma City and asked him if he could take on the difficult task of "being ready" if we didn't sign Scooter. We were also shopping for a number three announcer with George Grande moving on to Cincinnati, so I was inundated again with tapes from the whole broadcast world. Bob Costas called to recommend Dave Cohen, who had done Syracuse games. Whenever Costas spoke, I listened. I respected his opinion a lot.

In the end, when Rizzuto signed, it sort of moved Murcer out of the picture. But I liked Bobby's work. His broadcast career had seemingly run out of gas a few years earlier. He had done TV (had been sensational calling the details of the George Brett "Pine Tar" incident), radio, and cable. He had been home in Oklahoma City the previous year, out of work.

I called him and said, "You were great to just stand by in case we had an opening. And you're a good broadcaster. I'd like to see if I could bring you in for that number three slot. It doesn't pay what Rizzuto's position would have paid—and you're the same guy and would be doing the same work—but the budget is only so big. I want to ask if you would take that job for these dollars, and I'd also like to say, as your friend, that you should. You need to get back in the booth, and not many people get an offer when they've been out of it for a year."

He took it. And the team of Rizzuto, Seaver, and Murcer proved to be very strong. Even without a "pro" in the booth, they would rise to the occasion when needed. We had no problem with the professional matters—the commercials, the interviews, the promos, the out-of-town scores, the disclaimer ("This copyrighted telecast . . ."), although Rizzuto would never read it, nor would he go downstairs to do prerecorded interviews.

Under Moore's strong and creative direction, we were a hit. We would still hear from some that it was hard for fans to accept Seaver in the Yankee booth, but his work was solid. Murcer was better than he had ever been. And Rizzuto got over the contract dispute and was as entertaining as ever.

In 1991 John and I were told that we could produce two half-hour specials, one on Rizzuto's 50th anniversary with the team, and one on the life of Billy Martin, who had passed away over the winter.

Billy had actually been a WPIX broadcaster for one season. Steinbrenner had insisted on it as a way for Martin to finish out his contract after he'd been fired as manager for the second, or third, or fourth time; I forget which.

Lev Pope was pretty sure he didn't want him. He simply didn't care for Billy's reckless lifestyle and was concerned about whether we could trust him to go on the air sober for live, primetime telecasts.

We found a strong reason to exclude him. Anheuser Busch was our sponsor, and Billy was a Miller Lite spokesman, part of its long-running and very clever former-athletes campaign.

We told Judge Eddie Sapir, Billy's agent, that the Miller–Bud thing was a problem. Still, they wanted a meeting, and Lev wanted to look Billy in the eye and tell him that no drinking would be tolerated when he was doing a live broadcast. And in the meantime, Sapir had gotten Steinbrenner to call the Miller people and the Budweiser people to get clearance for Billy to do the games.

They arrived for the meeting, with Billy in a cowboy hat—and a Miller Light sweater. What nerve.

Lev looked right at him and said, "We have kids watching, we are doing live broadcasts, and if you ever go on the air after drinking, this will all end for you."

Billy (who sounded just like Sonny Bono to me) did the broadcasts, and I remember only one "uh-oh" moment that I ever caught.

Andre Thornton, the black first baseman of the Indians, had said in that morning's paper that he wanted to be a manager one day.

On the air that night, Billy said, "Next they'll want to be commissioner."

I braced myself, waiting for the phone to ring. What was I going to say? What exactly did "they" mean? First basemen? Indians?

I knew exactly what he meant, and I thought we were in for big trouble. But the remark passed unnoticed. We got away with one.

Our half-hour Martin special after his death (no one used the term *untimely death* for poor Billy; it was more a question of how he had made it to 62 at all) was narrated by Phil Pepe, who had left print journalism for a career in broadcast journalism. The program was solid.

The Rizzuto special, we both felt, was stronger. First, I had reached out to my old college friend Art Toretzky, who was now a prominent Hollywood agent. I asked his advice on a narrator for the show. He got Charles Durning for us, who was just terrific to work with, even if he needed the entire backseat in the limo to spread out.

As luck would have it, both of the programs were nominated for Emmy Awards in the category "Outstanding Sports Program." And there were no other programs from any other station deemed worthy of nomination that year. So we were competing only with ourselves, and we were guaranteed a win! Not many can ever walk into the Emmy Awards feeling that confident!

My father flew up from Florida, and it was a wonderful moment when Joe Franklin, the veteran host of talk shows in New York, called out *Billy Martin—Forever a Yankee* as the winner. John and I went up on stage at the glamorous Marriott Marquis Hotel to receive our statuettes, and I spoke for us both. I thanked everyone, resisted saying, "Actually, we thought the Rizzuto special was better," and cited the supportive folks at WPIX who had helped put it together.

The Emmy awards are always attended by producers, directors, and talent. Engineers stay home and run the station, and most of them don't own suits. So I couldn't resist one final remark, which was about myself as much as anyone else in the room.

"I want to thank the engineers at WPIX who helped put this program together, and I would also like to ask if there is anyone in the room who happens to know how in the world you get a picture on your TV when you turn it on."

It got sort of an embarrassed but hearty laugh, and it was true. The miracle of the broadcast signal going over the air or through cable lines will always be a mystery to minds like mine.

In my five years as executive producer, all paired with Moore, WPIX had won "Outstanding Coverage of Local Sports" five times from the New York State Broadcasters Association. We were cooking. Ratings were improving as the team got better, Don Mattingly and Dave Winfield were performing heroic feats before our cameras, and each year we were getting better equipment to compete with the improving look of cable coverage. Those guys were putting all of their resources into sports coverage—it was all they had. We were part of a station that was still an all-purpose broadcaster. And as the station's PR director, I still had my finger on the pulse of all the other aspects of the station competing for funding.

But Yankee baseball remained the station's chief identity for the general public, the one thing we had—for more than 40 years—that no one else had on the broadcast spectrum. A big game could get us as high as a 15 or 16 rating—several million households and big revenue.

I got a copy of Alexander Cartwright's Hall of Fame plaque, which detailed his contribution to baseball: the codification of its basic rules—three outs, 90 feet, nine innings, and so forth.

I framed it and added a little of my own wisdom to the plaque copy.

WPIX SALUTES ALEXANDER JOY CARTWRIGHT, WHO IN 1845 CREATED THE CONCEPT OF 18 COMMERCIAL BREAKS.

In the '80s I served on the Advisory Committee for the "Cracker Jack Old Timers Game." Before old timers games became too plentiful, this one was pretty special. It was the one that was originally played in RFK Stadium in Washington, where the Senators had long before pulled up stakes, and this was the only taste of baseball for Washingtonians all summer. It made its mark in its very first year when Luke Appling, age 73, hit a first-inning homer into the shortened left field stands. The home run played on every newscast for days, including all of the network newscasts, and the Cracker Jack game became legendary in its first inning. You can't plan things like that, but thank you, Warren Spahn, for laying one in there for ol' Luke, who hit only 45 home runs in a 20-year career.

The Advisory Committee was a blue-ribbon panel of "formers," headed by the brilliant Dick Cecil, a former Braves official who conceived of the idea. I was honored to serve with Tal Smith, the former Yankees and Astros general manager; Cliff Kachline, the former *Sporting News* writer and Hall of Fame executive; and Jack Brickhouse, the former voice of Chicago baseball.

We were in Buffalo, New York, at the beautiful new downtown Rich Stadium, for what would be the last of these games, in June 1990. Tal ordinarily managed the National League, Chuck Stevens the AL. On this day, Tal was away on business, and Dick Cecil asked if I would manage the Nationals.

Would I! This would be like playing Strat-O-Matic with real players! It would absolutely be the highlight of my career.

Sandy Koufax, who did not attend many of these functions, was among my pitchers. The best baseball player of my lifetime, and I was going to be his manager.

It was determined that Sandy would throw only one pitch as the starting pitcher and then yield to Warren Spahn. That, at least, was the plan. (This was a necessity due to the arthritis that had ended his career 24 years earlier.)

In the clubhouse before the game, I asked Sandy if he could at least make it one full batter. There were, after all, 18,000 fans on hand, and we had put Sandy's picture on the advertising poster, and . . . well, how about just one full batter?

Reluctantly, he smiled, took a last drag on a cigarette, and agreed. He would face Dick McAuliffe, then walk off and Spahnie would come in.

Well, it took about five pitches, and I was starting to feel guilty, knowing how his arm hurt with each delivery, and hearing the words in my head from that 1966 news conference: "If he pitches again, he could seriously damage his arm for life." But he retired McAuliffe with no harm done.

Now, instead of allowing Sandy to trot off under his own steam, I knew my big managerial moment was upon me. So I walked up the steps of the third base dugout and headed for the mound. He looked at me like I was either (1) crazy or (2) going to try to talk him into another batter. Spahn stopped throwing in the bullpen and watched.

I was in my National League cap with an NL windbreaker and black slacks. Not quite Connie Mack, but civilian. I reached the mound and put out my right hand, palm up, for the baseball.

"Sandy," I said, "I just don't like what I'm seeing here."

And with that, I motioned with my left hand for Spahn to come in.

Well, Koufax starting laughing, my infielders started laughing, and I could hear the guys in the dugout laughing, especially the unmistakable, high-pitched laugh of Tom Seaver, who was one of my Yankee broadcasters in "real life." It was a moment seldom experienced by Walter Alston, Sandy's only manager.

I managed a pretty snappy game, I must say. In an old timers game, the idea is to get everyone in, and never mind strategy. But I had some strategy—I wanted my two best-conditioned players to be there for me in the last inning. That meant Bill Robinson in center field and Tug McGraw on the mound. I figured if we had a lead, Robinson could run anything down, and Tug could save it. He still threw great.

Sure enough, we had a 3–0 lead in the last inning, and I had Robinson in center. I wanted Tug to pitch the entire fifth, the last inning. I slapped the ball into his glove and said, "Take us on home, Tug."

You had to love Tug's enthusiasm. "You got it, skipper," he said, and he ran to the mound, slapping his leg with his glove as he had with the Mets and the Phillies. He overpowered the AL, with Bill Robinson catching two fly balls, including the final out. Today, Tug is better known as country music star Tim McGraw's dad, but, that day, he was my Cy Young Award winner.

I was pretty flawless as a manager otherwise, except for one small snafu. Gene Mauch, one of the winningest managers in baseball history, was one of my reserve infielders. I had the good sense to go to him before the game and say, "Um . . . if you see anything you'd like to point out, don't be shy."

My starting lineup had Charlie Neal at second, and the arrangement was Neal would play two innings, and then Mauch would replace him.

· In the third inning, I turned to Mauch and said, "Okay, Gene, you're in at second."

"Where the hell you been?" he said. "I took over for Neal last inning!"

Okay, so you can't watch everything. A little mutiny on the *Bounty*, but otherwise, I survived the test.

At breakfast the next morning I sat with Koufax and we laughed about the mound incident. He still thought it was funny; I was relieved that he didn't think I was a total jerk. We had a very long talk about marathons. It turned out that Sandy, at 54, regularly ran marathons, but seldom in the U.S. He just didn't want to draw attention to himself. So he ran international marathons in anonymity. I wondered silently how he reconciled running with his smoking but let it pass.

Back home, Seaver didn't let it go. On the air for our next Yankee broadcast, he recounted his visit to Buffalo and said to Rizzuto, "And guess who was our manager?"

When Rizzuto bit, Seaver said, "It was none other than our dandy little executive producer, Marty Appel."

"Holy cow," said the Scooter, "the same guy who lost every Little League game last year?"

About a week after the Old Timers Game, I got a handwritten note from Lee MacPhail, now retired president of the American League. He made note of my old mentor, Bob Fishel, another AL loyalist:

6-26-90

Dear Mr. Appel—

It has come to my attention that, at a recent event in Buffalo, NY, you not only allied yourself to the group that opposes all we hold dear, but actually led that group—and even worse, led them to victory against us! Poor Bob. I am glad that he is not around to witness the defection of one whom he trained and educated. Alas, 'tis a sorry day.

LSM

17

WILD GOOSE CHASE

I was never a guy who enjoyed writing term papers very much in school. If the project called for 12 pages, my margins would be nice and wide, and I would agonize and groan until it was finally done—to the word count. Not one sentence over. It was a chore. I'd stop and count every 100 words to see how many more I had to eke out.

So when I was first approached about a book project, my reaction was similar—ugh.

But you couldn't do journalism and political science and public relations without writing a lot, and I had acquired certain skills.

First was my ability to type very fast. I was often my own secretary when I wanted things out in a hurry because I could type more than 60 words a minute. I could think my sentences right onto the page. The mechanics of typing never slowed down my thought process. That was a great asset. I could never have developed the patience to be a writer in the pre-typewriter days. Even the days of pre-electric would have tested my patience, although from 1970–74 I did an annual preview of the American League for a paperback release, with my counterpart from the Mets—their assistant PR director, Matt Winick—doing the National League portion.

In 1973 I was approached about doing a "definitive book" on the Baseball Hall of Fame for McGraw-Hill. It was called *Baseball's Best: The Hall of Fame Gallery*. I was to write the text—1,500 words on each Hall of Fame member—and someone else would do the photo research and design.

I carried my typewriter around the country with me throughout 1974 and interviewed whomever I could for this project. The chance to talk to the older generation of sportswriters was too good to pass up. John Carmichael in Chicago, wonderful Mo Siegel and Shirley Povich in Washington, and even the novelist James T. Farrell, who created Studs Lonigan (and who grieved over the Black Sox), were fair game for me.

Moe Berg, the old catcher who was an OSS spy in World War II, was helpful, but, true to form, fairly tight lipped. It would not have broken defense secrets to share a bit more about Babe Ruth, but Moe, always gray from head to toe, complexion and wardrobe included, was pretty secretive.

My favorite Moe story (and he visited our press box a lot) was that he was an accomplished linguist—something like 20 languages—but when he was assigned to Europe during World War II, it was discovered that neither German nor Italian were among his talents.

In spring training I spent time with Roger Peckinpaugh, who had played and managed from 1910 to 1933 and who knew many of the long-deceased men I was writing about.

It was a little awkward to interview Roger in that he was not himself a Hall of Famer, something I discovered was a sore point with him. This was around the time that the Hall began electing members of the Negro Leagues, which really set him off.

"So they say, hey, Satch, how many would you have won in the big leagues? And he says, oh, I don't know, four hundred maybe. And they say, 'Great, you're in!'"

To win his favor, I naturally offered the opinion that he certainly belonged in the Hall of Fame.

"Whattaya mean?" he said. "I *am* in the Hall of Fame."

I didn't know what to say.

He got up, walked into his bedroom, and brought back a yellowed newspaper clipping from 1920, 16 years before the Hall of Fame was founded. He gingerly unfolded the fragile clipping, which read, OUR MAN PECK—A HALL OF FAMER FOR SURE.

Good enough for me. And obviously good enough for him.

I spent two days with Fred Lieb, a legendary New York sportswriter who wrote many baseball histories and who covered the Yankees as far back as their Highlander days in 1911. He was a fountain of great remembrances, but, after each story, he'd say, "It's all in my book." I guess I could have saved myself all the recording and transcribing, but I would have missed the great time with Fred.

I spoke to as many of the living Hall of Famers as possible. The biographies were interesting in that I made sure to include their pre- baseball days (father's occupation, things like that), as well as what they did after their career ended. Whitey Ford, who was traveling with us as pitching coach while I was doing the book, was the only one who actually proofread his own chapter, correcting "34th Street Boys," one of his youth teams, to "34th Avenue Boys."

"People will think you've never been in Queens," he said.

The book was also unique in that it was the first to offer full biographies of the executives, managers, and umpires in the Hall.

I was pleased when it was warmly received by the baseball community, particularly by the Hall of Fame people, who later had me send it to President Reagan as overnight briefing material before a White House reception for Hall of Famers. It helped begin a friendship with the Cooperstown folks that has lasted more than a quarter century, and I always feel at home in their presence.

I still see the book in the offices of baseball officials, and I did manage to get my own copy signed by more than 50 Hall of Fame members. It was published in 1977 and was named the outstanding sports reference book of the year by the American Library Association. We updated it in 1980, and I am told it is still the place to go for obituary writers planning their sendoffs.

After Thurman Munson won his MVP Award in 1976, it occurred to me that he was now a likely candidate for an autobiography. You win one of those in New York—and you have the kind of popularity that he enjoyed—and such a project seemed logical.

The problem with Munson was that he had a miserable relationship with most of the likely co-authors, the New York sportswriters. He didn't talk to most of them, and they made wide circles around him. That was a credit to his fairly gruff personality, and the fact that he never felt they got things right.

So in the year in which I was working with Joe Garagiola Jr., I called him and asked if he'd like to do a book.

"Naw," he said, "I'm twenty-nine. Who writes a life story at twenty-nine?"

I told him a lot of sports figures did. "And when you win an MVP with the Yankees, a lot of people want to know about you."

"Well, I don't care, I don't want to do it."

I tried a different approach.

"You know," I said, "someone else can go out and write a book about you, and pretty much say things the way they want to say them. You would have no approval on it, you'll hate it because you'll think it's all wrong, and you won't get a nickel for it. If you do your own book, it's less likely that someone will do a book *about* you."

"So it will be sort of like an insurance policy, you're saying?"

"Yes, that's right. Do your own story and publishers won't care very much about unauthorized versions."

That appealed to him.

"I don't want this to be an expensive hardcover book, though," he said. "I want kids to be able to buy it."

I explained that a paperback version often followed a hardcover version and that the hardcover versions were the ones that made it into libraries, where kids could read it for free.

So, he was set. And in 36 hours, I sold the project to Coward McCann Geoghegan, and we had ourselves a writing project.

I did most of the taping with him at his rented home in New Jersey, not far from Teterboro Airport, from which he could fly in and out after night games to get home to his family in Canton. He was filled with stories about his aviation experiences and his real estate investments, and a little about baseball too.

What he didn't want to talk about very much was his father, who, he said, played hard. "He would hit me grounders, and if one took a bad hop and bloodied my nose, he'd just keep on hitting. Tough guy."

Diana Munson would ask me, "Did he tell you about his dad?" And I'd say, "Yes," thinking I was getting the whole story.

Diana loved that he was doing the book. She kept him on schedule with me and made sure he proofread it as we went along. He was going through a whole "trade me to Cleveland" thing at the time, mostly fueled by salary disagreements with Steinbrenner but also by a desire to be near his home and to spend more time with his family. On that, he was sincere, and it was touching. Diana and his three children represented a family life that he never had as a child.

The book came out in spring 1978. As Yankee books went, it was not very controversial at all. Sparky Lyle's *The Bronx Zoo* had charted new ground in that area, and thus the Munson story, by falling far short of that, was not a high-impact book.

I was sitting at my desk in Bowie Kuhn's office late on the afternoon of August 2, 1979, when I answered the phone and heard George Steinbrenner's voice.

"I've got to speak to Bowie," he said. "We've just gotten a call from the airport in Canton. Thurman's been killed in a plane crash."

The news seared us all.

He was the captain of the Yankees, the first since Gehrig, and he didn't even live to be 37, Gehrig's age when he died. He was only 32. He had a wife, three children, stardom, success, money, and friendships. He had it all.

I accompanied Kuhn to Canton and sat with tears in my eyes as we looked at the coffin, knowing that his body had burned on impact, and then at an oil painting above it of him in his glory, in his Yankee uniform. It was so shocking, so sudden. It was the biggest "death of an active player" story since Roberto Clemente.

It was so touching to see the Yankee team assemble in Canton for the ceremony, including some former Yankees like Mickey Rivers, who came in from Texas. I flew to Cleveland the night before the funeral (Kuhn would arrive the next day) and picked up Lou Piniella and Bobby Murcer at the airport, along with Mike Heath, then with Oakland, who had been one of Thurman's protégés. In the back seat, as we drove to Thurman's home, Lou and Bobby began to prepare the eulogies they would movingly deliver the next day.

At Munson's home that evening, many family members were speculating about whether Thurman's father was still alive, whether he had heard the news, and whether he might show up. It seemed he had disappeared after Thurman's mother had suffered a stroke some years earlier. It was clear he was not held in very high regard, and that his presence would not be well received.

He did show up. He arrived in a bizarre Mexican sombrero and proceeded to hold an impromptu press conference just a few feet from the coffin, wildly explaining to the media that "I was a better player than he was, I just never had his breaks."

He was behaving so poorly and so inappropriately, was causing such a disruption, that eventually Diana's father had to literally move him out of the hall before the service began. I will never see a stranger scene at a funeral than I did that day.

We drove to the cemetery, just past the Pro Football Hall of Fame, with people lining the streets as the cortege passed. Diana, in all of her grief, while standing at the cemetery, said to me, "Thank God he did the book. His children will always have that."

I could only nod and put my hand on her shoulder.

The book wound up giving me a link to Thurman forever. I was a founder of the Thurman Munson Dinner, held each year by the Association for the Help of Retarded Children. I was the moderator of a memorial tribute to Thurman on the 20th anniversary of his death on August 2, 1999, when we did a program at the Yogi Berra Museum with Diana, Murcer, and Gene Michael, his old roommate. Usually, on the anniversary, some writer does a remembrance and checks in with Diana, Bobby, Stick, Lou, and me. Diana is a great lady, a grandmother now, and I cherish the fact that we have remained friends for all these years.

The book was reissued with an updated, final chapter, and became a bestseller and a Book of the Month Club selection. I was pleased by that but felt that by withholding the full story of his screwy father, we had missed an important part of his life. I wished he had been more open about that, but it obviously embarrassed him.

We sold movie rights to the book but it was never produced, and, although there is periodic interest, it does not appear that it will ever be developed as a film. But the Yankee fans continue to love Munson, and when his image appears on the scoreboard during a retrospective of great Yankees, the cheers are always loud for the guy with the dirtiest uniform, the guy who wouldn't accept losing, no way, no how.

A couple of years after the Munson book, I was approached by my agent, Bill Adler, about doing a book with another hot Yankee, Goose Gossage. He was a colorful, dominating relief pitcher with a great New York following—myself included—and I was happy to entertain the idea. You had to love Goose if you loved the Yanks.

I called Gossage, and he was agreeable. I described the manner in which I worked with Munson, and it sounded okay to him. It being the offseason, we would need to work out of his home in Colorado Springs, but that was what the publisher needed in order to get this out quickly for the summer. Goose and I agreed to a split of the money and to divide equally the travel costs involved, and we made plans for me to fly out to Colorado Springs on a Friday evening, work through the weekend, and see how far we got.

This was in November 1980. I had literally just begun work at WPIX, so I didn't feel I could steal any time other than weekends. Gossage and I confirmed on Thursday, and he said he'd meet me at the airport on Friday night, and that I could stay at his home.

It was one of those bitter cold nights when I took off from LaGuardia and headed into a snowstorm in Colorado. It was a white-knuckle flight, but we landed pretty much on time.

I went to baggage claim, where we were to hook up, but no Goose. I had been around ballplayers long enough to know that they were not always the most reliable, so I gave it some time.

There was no answer at his home, so I waited as the airport emptied of the people arriving for ski weekends, and I sat alone in baggage claim.

Finally, after about 90 minutes, a four-wheel drive pulled up outside and the unmistakable figure of Gossage appeared. He was with an old buddy, and it appeared they had been celebrating the arrival of the weekend.

We shook hands and he said, "Oh, yeah, by the way, I changed my mind about the book. I don't think I want to do it."

"But Goose, we just confirmed this yesterday; what happened?"

"Aw, shit happens," he said.

I didn't really know what to say. I assumed this meant I wouldn't be staying at his home, which he confirmed. He told me of a nearby hotel I could book, and then, "There's probably a flight out early in the morning."

He was right; there was a 6:30 A.M. flight, and I booked it before I left the airport. I was furious at his insensitivity—not having the decency to call before I took off. I had been at my office all day. Bad enough to cancel the project, but totally thoughtless to not give a damn about my flying cross-country.

He turned to leave, probably satisfied that he had done more than he needed just by showing up to tell me in person that there would be no book. The next Coors seemed to be calling him.

"What about my cost to come out here?" I said. "We were supposed to split this."

"Hey, that's your problem, man; that was only if there was a book."

And off he drove.

I got back to New York the next afternoon, and, instead of being totally disgusted, a couple of drinks on the flight east had made me surprisingly calm about the whole incident. I decided that that was the price you paid in dealing with players—now and then, this would happen. I even decided I would probably still root for him as long as he was the Yankees' closer. I thought to myself, "Well, this may not show much character, but I guess I'm an insufferable Yankee fan to the end."

The matter of the cost of my trip still bothered me, and I made a couple of attempts to recoup the money.

A year later, I got a check for $210—half the airfare and hotel—signed by his wife, Cornelia. And I said to myself, "Well, he should have paid for the whole thing, but someday I'll have an extra anecdote for a book."

In 1984 I did a children's book with Tom Seaver in which we picked "all-time teams," from before his playing days and during them. It gave us a chance to put together a lot of short biographies with comments from Tom, who was becoming a real student of the game.

We did the work in the backyard of his converted barn, on his property in Greenwich, and how much better can it get than sitting there talking baseball with Tom Seaver on beautiful afternoons with his wife, Nancy, pouring unlimited lemonade refills. The book found a young audience and, seven years later, we teamed up again for a book on great moments in baseball history, with me providing the details of the events, and Tom giving a modern perspective. My original manuscript, with Tom's extensive hand-written comments, is probably one of my best baseball keepsakes.

We later did a syndicated radio program together—my writing, his narration—but it was short-lived, a victim of the 1994 strike.

My most historically important contribution to baseball literature was my collaboration with Bowie Kuhn on his autobiography, *Hardball: The Education of a Baseball Commissioner.*

Bowie was perfectly capable of writing this by himself. He was a skilled, extremely knowledgeable writer. I came to think that he never missed a day of school and never forgot anything he learned. During the course of more than 100 hours of taping, he could be found recalling scientific principles, Shakespearean quotations, the starting rotation of the 1943 Washington Senators, and which Supreme Court justice wrote which majority opinions. He had an amazing mind.

He needed me to organize the book, pepper him with questions, research things, and remind him of all the events of his 17 turbulent years in office.

We were a good team. I brought no ego into the project, and he followed my day-to-day work schedule rigorously. I would conclude each session by telling him what we would cover in the next session. I was a good devil's advocate and wasn't shy in badgering him about the more controversial decisions of his term, even if they were sore points for him. Night World Series! No overcoat! Halting Finley's sales! Scolding Jim Bouton! I let him have it, and he gave it right back. It was healthy, and I think it helped make the book an important part of the game's history. Jerry Holtzman, the Chicago columnist who was no fan of Bowie's administration, thought it was one of the best books on the game he had ever read. *The New York Times* named it one of the Notable Books of the Year, and our favorite review called it "so well written as to be almost believable."

We generally worked on Fridays and Saturdays in the basement of his home, on a pretty cul-de-sac in Ridgewood, New Jersey. It was a home straight from a Currier and Ives Christmas card, complete with a library in which we had cocktails before dinner.

Luisa Kuhn went about her daily routine upstairs, but around one each afternoon, from the top of the basement steps we'd hear, "Boooo-eeeee, Mar-tee . . . lunch!" And she would have a wonderful soup and sandwich meal waiting for us.

His love and knowledge of baseball were totally genuine. He was a true fan, and nothing gave him as much pleasure as the company of the old players in Cooperstown each summer, especially the elderly Negro Leaguers.

For about six months we sat across a large table, my tape recorder rolling. We wore casual clothing, kicked off our shoes, and squared off for up to ten hours a day. We were surrounded by his notes, briefs, files, clippings, reference books, and, for good measure, a very impressive Bowie knife—a gift recalling his distant ancestor, Alamo hero Jim Bowie. He spoke in perfectly developed paragraphs. If I surprised him with a fact he'd forgotten, he would always raise his eyebrows and utter, "You don't say."

I would write the first draft and send it to him. He would keep some paragraphs, rewrite others, and send it back. We were behind our deadline, and, in fact, more than a year late in getting the book out. But in the end, we had a book we were enormously proud of—an important record of his era, 17 years of remarkable events. No one ever found a single error of fact in the book, which was one of my chief responsibilities. No one, except Marvin Miller, whose own autobiography a few years later was essentially a rebuttal to *Hardball*, and questioned almost everything in it.

I will be forever proud of being associated with it, and of the fine relationship I maintained with Kuhn during the project and after. In my own copy, he wrote, "To my faithful critic and treasured friend," and in his introduction he added ". . . my drill sergeant and fount of knowledge."

I followed that by editing and serving as agent for Lee MacPhail's memoirs, a project done mostly as a family gift and handed over to a small publisher. He cared little about its sales, but I thought it was a nice overview of the MacPhail family, his time in baseball, and his thoughts about the future. It was called *My Nine Innings*.

I was pretty good at catching errors big and small, and would occasionally get consulting jobs to review baseball books or film projects, such as the HBO docudrama on Mantle and Maris and the magical year of 1961, directed by Billy Crystal.

When my son, Brian, was eight, he was getting birthday invitations almost every weekend, and that perfect baseball book for 8-year-olds never seemed to exist as a gift option.

Brian liked baseball, had his trusty Don Mattingly poster over his bed, and always had interesting questions to ask about the game, such as, "Why is the ball so hard?"

With the ever-present need for birthday gifts and his curiosity as an impetus, my wife suggested that I simply write an appropriate book "which we could give as presents."

I sold the idea of *The First Book of Baseball* to a publisher, who liked it so much that it had John Madden do a companion book, *The First Book of Football*. Mickey Mantle was nice enough to give me a quote for the cover, and the book was a pretty good seller for a number of years.

Eric Gregg was an oversized umpire from West Philadelphia, who, as a black umpire, was pretty easy to pick out among his colleagues, most of whom were crew-cut, conservative types who might be working construction or serving as firemen had they not been umpires.

When I was offered a chance to do a book with Eric, I wanted to meet him to size up what we had here.

What a character he was, and what a delight. He was bigger than life—well over 300 pounds—but he had a terrific sense of humor, a great outlook, and, as a guy who overcame enormous odds to break out of the ghetto, a terrific story.

His father was barely a part of his life. His sister died of an overdose. He had a brother in jail for a long stretch who had been horribly burned in a prison riot, his life a total ruin.

Eric, a great baseball fan, was watching TV one day when Curt Gowdy mentioned umpiring school. Eric suddenly recognized his calling, and he managed to get himself to Barney Deary's umpire school and learned the trade.

He married a wonderful Dominican woman, had four great children, and made a life for himself as an outsider among his colleagues, but a guy who made friends wherever he went.

I used to love getting on the train in New York and going to the 30th Street Station in Philadelphia to spend a day working with him on the book. He was a great storyteller, and he would drive me around his old neighborhood and point out all the sandlots he had played on, the rickety old house he had lived in, the street corners where he had hung out with his friends, and the police station where his ice cream pop had melted in his pocket while awaiting discipline for skipping school.

His weight was a continuing concern for him, for his friends, and for the League office—including my buddy Bill White, his boss. Several times he was taken out of action and hustled down to Duke University's weight reduction clinic. Never was it more serious than after John McSherry, another greatly overweight umpire, died on the field in Cincinnati, his heart failing. That scared Eric a lot.

Our book was called *Working the Plate*, which had a double meaning, of course. It was one of the few books covering the life of an umpire; his life was both a happy one because of his gift for making friends, but also a troubled one, fighting his weight battle and trying to make it in a redneck world.

A loyal supporter of umpire union chief Richie Phillips, a fellow Philadelphian, he found himself among those fired in 1999 when he foolishly submitted his resignation and didn't rescind it in time.

Michael Joseph "King" Kelly was baseball's first matinee idol, its first super-hero. When I wrote my book on the Hall of Famers, his bio had stuck with me. He was a guy I had known little about, but I fell in love with his story.

A King Kelly biography would depict the early days of baseball, of how a ballplayer became a national celebrity before the days of mass media, and what his impact was on those who followed him.

I loved his story. And on the 100th anniversary of his death, in 1994, I wanted to honor him with a long overdue biography.

My agent wasn't interested, nor were any of the major publishers. So I found a small publisher in Maryland to produce the book, and it went on to win the Casey Award as the best baseball book of 1996. I was as proud for Kelly as I was for myself, because through the project I felt we had become like brothers. I even visited his gravesite outside of Boston a few times, a site that had found 10,000 mourners on that fateful day a century before. When I visit, I always leave a miniature whiskey bottle at the simple stone in the Elks Lodge plot.

Finding time to write these books around my full-time employment was not always easy. I generally limited my writing to Saturday and Sunday mornings, from about seven to 11 each day, and tried to work straight through. I was well disciplined, and usually pulled it off.

Occasionally something would come along that was too much fun to resist, and I'd steal a few days of vacation time for it. Such was the case early in 1984 when I saw a small ad in Variety reading, "Extras needed for new Woody Allen film project." It gave an address of a casting agency.

So I thought, *Hey, I love Woody Allen films, I'm 35, I'll be a grownup soon, I need to do these things while I can.*

So I sent a letter to the agency and introduced myself as a guy who once stood in front of a Yankee Stadium press conference and announced that we were banishing underprivileged kids from the bleachers.

I was hired.

The movie was *The Purple Rose of Cairo*, and I had to report by 6 A.M. each day for makeup and costume in the building behind the landmark Camel cigarette sign in Times Square. Not only did I get to experience a film production, and to observe Mia Farrow, Jeff Daniels, Ed Herrmann, and Van Johnson, but I was plucked out of line as a stand-in because I was the right height. So I got to be directed by Woody, his hands on my shoulders, moving me around like a prop. What an experience. In the final edit, I was the one seated behind the potted palm in the nightclub.

18

NO MORE
MR. WHITE GUY

One Friday afternoon in November 1991, my phone at WPIX rang. It was a woman from the Atlanta office of Heidrick & Struggles, the executive recruitment firm.

"Your name," she said, "has been given to us as someone who might be able to recommend a candidate to head up public relations for the Olympic Games in Atlanta. If you know of anyone, would you be good enough to call?"

That is the common language used by search firms when they actually have you in mind.

Almost from the moment I hung up the phone, I had a feeling that I was going to be headed for Atlanta.

I called back on Monday and expressed my own interest in "learning more." I met with Heidrick & Struggles people in their New York office and then was flown to Atlanta to meet with Billy Payne, A.D. Frazier, and Ginger Watkins, three of the major players staging the games.

The interviews went very well. I wasn't sure if I was prepared to make this move, but they liked my background because it covered not only sports but television. Furthermore, they liked that I had worked for George Steinbrenner, who was on the board of the U.S. Olympic Committee. They felt, I learned, that anyone who could stand up to Steinbrenner would be able to work with Billy Payne. Even Payne liked that.

Where they heard that I had stood up to Steinbrenner was left unasked.

In New York I felt I was being pulled in many directions. I was attending to football—WPIX televised the annual PSAL football championship each year, and it occurred to me that this could be the last time John Moore and I would work together. In addition to the Yankees, we had been through five years of Giants and Jets preseason games, plus this high school championship, which required every bit as much work as the NFL games, perhaps more.

The calls continued to come from Atlanta. An offer was made which was nearly fifty percent more than I was earning in New York. Yes, the job would end in 1996, but where did it say I had any guarantees of more than five more years at WPIX?

Inevitably, the station was going to lose more games to cable, or cable was going to handle the production. My role would diminish. Would WPIX keep me on under those conditions? It was hard to say. Many of "Lev Pope's people" had moved on after he retired. I got along well with our new GM, but if I wasn't doing baseball production but only PR, I was probably going to be considered overpaid.

I began to reveal the offer to my friends. They all thought it was the opportunity of a lifetime, something that every stage of my career had set me up for. I had, at this time, taken on an agent (TV production people generally had one), and he was the only one who heard my story and said, "Sounds like you really don't want to do this."

I was not only happy with my job, but I was very happy with my life. My children were enjoying good schools and great recreational programs in Larchmont, where I was active in coaching, had many friends, and served on the local cable-TV oversight committee.

I was a very "New York" kind of guy. I loved the excitement of the city, loved living in the suburbs, and enjoyed my friendships, professional and otherwise.

I was actually sitting at my desk eating a sandwich in December when Billy Payne called from a payphone in New York. He was meeting with network television executives and took the time to make this "recruiting call" while he was in town. "We gotta have you," he said. "What will it take?" When I named a figure, he said, "That's at the high end of what I pay my senior staff; I can give you five hundred less to make it work."

The man who had charmed the entire International Olympic Committee was charming me. No city had ever won the Games in its first attempt. He did it. People thought Athens had to have the Centennial Games, because they had the first modern Olympics. Payne overcame that. People thought it could never come back to the U.S. so quickly after Los Angeles, but he pulled it off. He told the IOC that the average temperature in Atlanta in July was only 79 degrees. He included the hours of midnight to 6 A.M. He was driven to win these Games, and he did it. I felt almost powerless against his overtures.

I discussed it endlessly with my wife, who was completely encouraging. She saw it as a great adventure, a chance to be involved with one of the great events of the century. "Think of the people we'll meet, the social events associated with it, the travel, the excitement."

I took the job. I knew that I was halting my career in television production and electing to go forward as a public relations specialist, but it was, after all, the centennial Olympic Games, or, as Payne often said, "The greatest peacetime gathering of nations in the history of the world."

My son, Brian, who was 12, thought it was terrific. Debbie, who was only nine, was heartbroken over leaving her friends. Her reaction was very difficult for me; I almost wanted to call it off just because of her tears. But I knew it could be a wonderful learning experience for the kids, too.

I had a nice sendoff from my coworkers at WPIX. In television, if you haven't been fired, you're usually leaving to work for a competitor, so warm farewells are unusual. It was very special to me.

The *Daily News*, the *Post*, and the *Times* all published nice columns wishing me well. Bob Raissman in the *News* wrote, "Appel, definitely not a grits kind of guy, had these parting words to his friends: 'Send pastrami!'"

Phil Mushnick in the *Post* wrote of the time that I chastised him for reporting that we had taken a camera shot of a seagull in the Toronto outfield. "By writing that," I had said, "you only encourage other seagulls to fly out onto the field."

Murray Chass in the *Times* wrote that I would be reunited with Atlanta native Ron Blomberg, who had been an usher at my wedding, and give the South a more Yankee glow.

Maury Allen, now writing for the Westchester papers, said I'd resigned to accept "the hottest position in sports."

I had for several years served as a trustee for the fledgling New York Sports Museum and Hall of Fame. I attended a final meeting just days before I left, in a conference room at the World Trade Center. The meeting broke up around eight, and I walked by myself across the massive plaza before the twin towers, heading for Broadway to catch a cab. Although New Yorkers tend not to stare at tall buildings, I found myself looking back over my shoulder at the power of these buildings, of how they represented the city that I loved. I was talking myself into a genuine depression over this next step in my life. But it was my heart talking.

My family would stay behind in Larchmont until the school year ended, and I would come back to see them every other weekend. That would be almost 20 weeks during which I would live in hotels and executive apartment rentals. I would miss them terribly, but we felt it was best to keep the kids in school for the balance of the year, and then give them the summer to acclimate. Besides, the summer was going to provide one of the great bonuses of the job—we would be off to Barcelona to observe the '92 Games, and I would make a family vacation out of it, adding London and Paris to the itinerary.

Billy Payne was, indeed, a heroic figure in Atlanta. His accomplishments will forever place him in history books. He was a University of Georgia football star who had gone into commercial real estate. Active in his Dunwoody church, he had helped with the fund raising for a new building. The success so inspired him that he sat in the church and felt he needed another calling.

At about that time, he read that another southern city was thinking of preparing a bid for the '96 Games. And he thought, "We're the capital of the South—if they could bid, we could surely mount a better bid."

So he rounded up eight close friends—all moneyed—and the group began to talk up their idea. They raised funds and began to travel to Olympic gatherings to make themselves known. They made friends, using that legendary southern charm, and showcased all the positives about Atlanta— the infrastructure of luxury hotels, world-class airport and highways, the concentrated athletic facilities including Georgia Tech, the World Congress Center, Atlanta-Fulton County Stadium, the Omni, and the planned Georgia Dome, the sense of volunteerism that was endemic to the south, and the support from corporate giants like Coca-Cola and Delta Airlines.

"We're going to have an army of eighty thousand volunteers by the time the Games are here," said Payne. And I would look at him and say, "Eighty thousand volunteers? In New York, I think you'd get twenty-five, and they would want to know how much they were being paid!"

The Gang of Nine went out and wooed the IOC voting members. As was revealed amid much controversy, years after the Games had ended, there was some gift giving that exceeded acceptable standards, and the actions of the Salt Lake City people, far greater in excess, came to reflect on the Atlanta bunch. I thought this was a bit unfair. The excesses were few, and the practice of gift giving was not only a gesture of southern hospitality but seemed to me to be appropriate within the existing climate at the time. These were not government officials, after all. This was a group of private citizens bidding for a commercial venture, promising to stage it without a dollar of public money, and if it took some gifts to win some votes—and no guarantees were attached to the gifts—it did not seem to be felonious.

The Games would be funded by ticket sales, television rights, licensing rights, and corporate sponsorships. And after all of that, the committee would be leaving behind incredible facilities, including Olympic Stadium, which would become the new home of the Atlanta Braves. And all without any taxpayer money.

About a year before I was hired, Juan Antonio Samaranch had moved to the podium to announce the winning city. Thousands were standing by in Underground Atlanta—the downtown gathering place—before heading for work, awaiting the announcement on a big-screen television, live from Tokyo.

"The 1996 Olympic Games are awarded to . . . the city of . . . Atlanta!" said His Excellency, and the city went crazy. Even for me, arriving a year later, the excitement of that moment was still the driving force behind the nuts and bolts of getting the games moving. I would make many speeches around the South in my new role, and when I would tell the story—"The Ballad of Billy Payne," I would call it—I would get goosebumps.

Making speeches, establishing friendships with the Atlanta media and its public relations community, attending sessions with special interest groups, doing radio and television interviews, were all things I was thriving on, and enjoying.

When we hired Dick Clark Productions to stage a gala to mark the arrival of the Olympic Flag in Atlanta and the first event in the new Georgia Dome, I was able to bring my television production expertise into the mix, and was brought in as the principal liaison to Dick's production team when they found themselves unable to work with the woman who had been their primary contact. Everyone in Hollywood wanted to produce this show, because they felt it would be an entree to stage the glamorous opening ceremonies. This really was quite a show, featuring Gladys Knight, James Brown, TLC, Carlos Santana, Trisha Yearwood, Alabama, and a special appearance by President and Mrs. Bush.

I learned a lot about Atlanta from many transplanted New Yorkers in the Atlanta sports community, including friends at Turner Sports, Coca-Cola, the University of Georgia, the Braves, CNN, the PR and ad agencies, and the local media. Lee MacPhail's brother Bill, who ran CNN Sports, was a frequent breakfast partner with wise counsel. I studied Atlanta history, came to know its political workings, mastered its geography and its neighborhoods, and grew to admire the support we were getting—all free—from the top communications professionals in town.

Atlanta was surely a town struggling with its identity. Any city that spends so much time proclaiming itself to be "a great international city" is struggling to back it up. When I was there for the Super Bowl in 2000, a forecast of snow (none developed) forced the afternoon newspaper to cancel publication two days before the game. That doesn't happen in "great international cities."

I was hardly a cultural snob, but it wasn't long before I arrived in Atlanta that the Atlanta Ballet was still performing to recorded music.

And although most people took life in stride, I had a sense that there was a huge number of people who still harbored anger, bitterness, and the embarrassment of defeat over the outcome of the Civil War. I know that back in my neighborhood in New York, no one spent much time thinking about the victory.

The Braves gave me more than a strong dose of baseball, because they were just plain spectacular, and it was a pleasure to watch them execute the game under my old friend Bobby Cox. My friend Dick Cecil, who ran the Cracker Jack Games, had a season box right behind home plate, which was not only available to me often but was the same seat Bill White, then National League president, offered to share with me during the NLCS.

Bob Cohn, a founder of Cohn & Wolfe Public Relations, was the first to welcome me to Atlanta, inviting me to be his guest for dinner even before I moved south. He was one of the great Olympic memorabilia collectors of the world, the creator of the pin-trading centers at Olympic venues on behalf of his client, Coca-Cola, and to have the Games in his backyard was heaven for him.

I began saying "y'all" despite myself and even lifting my voice at the end of sentences that weren't questions. The speech patterns were interesting. "I surely can't" would always catch me by surprise.

Andrew Young—the former advisor to Dr. Martin Luther King Jr., UN ambassador, congressman, and mayor—was co-chairman of the Olympic Games and proved to be a wonderful friend, not only because of his interesting background, but because he was sincerely interested in my adjustment. We had a mutual friendship with Paul and Carol Muldawer, who had been active in first promoting Governor Jimmy Carter as a long-shot presidential candidate 15 years earlier, and, at Carol's introduction, Andy embraced me warmly as an important part of the team.

Andy Young's contribution to winning the Games was vital, particularly with voters from third-world nations, who respected his standing in the international community.

But some would tell me that in the end, the votes had as much to do with the comfort of the luxury hotels in downtown Atlanta—and the chance to spend two weeks in the U.S. with all of its comforts—as opposed to the other bidding cities that weren't quite as famous for being so state-of-the-art.

I was even told that some of the IOC members thought they were voting for Atlantic City.

I genuinely enjoyed meeting with the special interest groups, who had their own agendas and that was fine. Everyone wanted their piece of the pie, this promise of economic growth that the Games might bring.

I met with people with disabilities who wanted to make sure that the Games were fully accessible to them. I met with the art community, which wanted to make sure that local artists were well represented in the look of the Games. I met with the gay community, which who threatened to make the Games the "Queering of the Olympics" if the issue of AIDS research wasn't addressed. It was outside of the Olympic agenda, but everyone was feeling that the Olympics were to wield enormous political power and that any goals might be achieved by hooking on to the Games.

My great sympathy went to the inner city black people who lived in the neighborhoods near Atlanta–Fulton County Stadium. These people had been displaced in the '60s by that ballpark's construction, and now, with the Olympics headed for town, they were hoping to reap some benefit from the economic boom. They had eloquent representation, as would befit the city that launched Dr. King, but it was evident to all, including them, that not many of their wishes would be granted. All Olympic officials could do was to show concern for their needs and promise to do what could be done to see that they were not left displaced or shut out of the process. (In the end, Mayor Bill Campbell agreed to grant street-peddler licenses, which destroyed the hoped-for lofty look of the city, but which did give the common folk a chance at the riches. I don't think any of them really made out very well.)

Shirley Franklin was a dynamic Olympic vice president who was a perfect liaison to the black community because, as a feisty black woman who took no prisoners, she could tell them how it was going to be, not give them any false promises, and win their confidence and support. She emerged as one of the most dynamic people I met there. But in fact, Payne and Frazier had really put together an all-star team of executives, persuading each to put his or her career on hold until this great adventure was done. I worked with some of the most brilliant people I had yet encountered, and we thoroughly enjoyed the mission we were on.

Maynard Jackson was the high-profile mayor, who sometimes butted heads with Billy Payne before Campbell succeeded him. I attended numerous meetings at City Hall and once presided over the unveiling of the city's official "Countdown Clock," which would measure the days, hours, minutes, and seconds until opening ceremonies.

A lot of what we did in those days was ceremonial. I represented the Olympics at the dedication of an Olympic postage stamp, accompanying Hank Aaron and others for its unveiling. I was in the beautiful city of Savannah to receive the Olympic Flag, which had flown in Barcelona and been passed to our care.

I flew in the Goodyear blimp and photographed all of our venues, some of which were as far as 60 miles outside Atlanta.

I surveyed Stone Mountain and its multiple venues, only to learn that it was, historically, the scene of KKK gatherings, and as such was considered a politically incorrect sight to host these gatherings.

Governor Zell Miller was a big Yankee fan, as it happened, and was delighted to find out that Mickey Mantle had moved to Georgia. Mickey was living with his manager and girlfriend, Greer Johnson, and the couple was frequently invited to the Governor's Mansion for dinner, where Miller loved to hear Mickey's stories. Greer and I became friends, and later, after Mickey's passing, we went through some early stages of a book of her remembrances. In Mickey's final days he had returned to Dallas, where he died in the presence of his wife and his three surviving sons. Greer had been banned from the hospital and the funeral (although she went and sat in the back with Pat Summerall), and I always had great compassion for her difficult situation at the end. She was a decent person who suffered greatly through Mick's years with alcohol; but she provided him with companionship and love and caring after his marriage had effectively ended. She deserved a better fate, but perhaps only in France, where the wife and mistress of Francois Mitterand were pictured together at his funeral, could such a thing be possible.

The original core volunteers at ACOG had divided key executive posts among themselves, hired banker A.D. Frazier as the chief operating officer, and then began to recruit other key executives.

The first two "outsiders" were Jim Millman and myself. We were both, coincidentally, from Larchmont, although we did not know each other well. Millman had operated a sports marketing company with great success and was brought in to handle Olympic sponsorships, a critical job.

Millman lasted only a few weeks. Payne sensed that the chemistry wasn't right. I had been there for only a few days when I was summoned into Payne's office. Harvey Schiller, head of the USOC and an interested party on the sponsorship side, was there.

"We're gonna let Jim Millman go, give him a chance to go home before his family moves here, and before his business is dissolved. The chemistry just isn't right between us, and we've got to be able to work closely together. We're gonna hire a local fellow to take the job. How do you think we should announce this?"

I hadn't been there long enough to understand the politics involved or whether the local community would read this as more of the "ol' boy network," or how they might react. I think Payne was disappointed that I didn't—*bang, bang*—say, "This is what to do." I had been there for about seventy-two hours.

Billy liked it when you were forceful with advice, but he was clearly his own man and was going to have things his way. When I sensed that there could be controversy over his choice of our insurance carrier—an old buddy of his from UGA—he winced at my suggestion that we should consider opening this up for bid. "No way," he said.

His style was perhaps best exhibited when it came time to choose the Olympic mascot.

All of the major design firms in Atlanta submitted artwork. Some nationally recognized firms did as well, although some refused when told they would not be compensated. Everything was considered a volunteer act for the good of the "Olympic Movement," a somewhat cultlike, scary term.

The mascot would be a long-reigning symbol for the Games and would sell a lot of merchandise—millions of dollars' worth. In modern marketing, such a decision would be made by committee. There would be focus groups, consultation with sponsors, input from marketers, and, ultimately, decision by committee.

"I'm picking the mascot," said Billy, making it quite clear. And sure enough, one Saturday morning he walked into a room and saw about a dozen possibilities stretched out on tables, the floor, and video screens. He walked around like the judge at the Westminster Kennel Club dog show, walked around again, and then stopped, pointed to one, and said, "That's it."

What it was remains in doubt to this day. It was called Whatizit, later shortened to "Izzy." It was some sort of blue blob with huge eyes that was expelling stars out of a tail. It was unveiled in closing ceremonies at Barcelona to gasps of horror, and within days we knew it was a total loser. Even those of us from Atlanta were embarrassed when this thing ran on the field at closing ceremonies, as the cute Barcelona mascot, Cobi, sailed up to mascot heaven in a balloon.

But Billy was determined to make it work. "It morphs into all sorts of figures; wait until you see it in action," he said.

When it was apparent that it was universally hated, and we still had three and a half years to go, I suggested that we simply "morph" it into a different mascot, with our tongues firmly in our cheeks. But he wouldn't hear of it. And since local interests designed it, it was insulting to suggest that the locals had failed. There was much local protest when a San Francisco firm had done the handsome and elegant logo. Now Atlanta would have to live with Izzy. It was a disaster of Olympic proportions.

Another disaster was adding golf to the Games. Golf was big in Georgia, and it was decided that it would be played at Augusta National, home of the Masters. Just convincing the bluebloods of Augusta in their green jackets to allow this was a miracle.

Samaranch endorsed it, and it looked like an important Atlanta legacy would be golf. But controversy immediately swirled around Augusta's restrictive membership policies, hardly indicative of the way the Olympics should be perceived, and golf wound up being scratched, to everyone's continuing embarrassment. Not only did this expose the restrictive nature of Augusta, but it also showed that despite the endorsement of both Payne and Samaranch, you couldn't count on anything.

It didn't have to be. There was any number of magnificent courses in the area that could have hosted it. But, to Billy, if it wasn't going to be Augusta, it wouldn't be anything.

It was hard to believe that he couldn't foresee the problem that Augusta would create.

We were keen on creating things unique to Atlanta that would be viewed as our legacy to the Games. Among Olympic people, it was sacrilegious to suggest that Munich—site of the horrid massacre of Israeli athletes in 1972—had any positives, but it was considered the breakthrough Olympics in terms of marketing and presentation.

I had a few ideas for legacies that didn't make the cut, one of which I still love. I thought that in addition to the traditional torch lighting at opening ceremonies, smaller replicas of the torch could be placed at each of the more than 25 venues, with each simultaneously lit at that same moment. It would be a spectacular sight for worldwide television and would make fans at all venues, not just those at the main stadium, feel part of the ceremony.

Furthermore, because these were the centennial Games, I thought we could even light torches simultaneously in all past Olympic cities.

Rejected.

We tended sometimes to lose sight of the fact that this was an athletic competition. When athletes did visit our headquarters—and we had

Jackie Joyner-Kersee, Edwin Moses, Nancy Hogshead, and others—it would remind us of what this was all about. A visit from Peter Ueberroth, who had made himself *Time* magazine's "Man of the Year" for his leadership of the 1984 Los Angeles Games, was a special event. He gave the staff an inspiring talk, the theme being "sometimes you just have to say no."

But so much of the daily work involved politics, venues, special interest groups, publications, transportation, housing, food, licensing, signage, security, drug testing, hospitality, construction, zoning, and so forth that it was almost overwhelming to watch that Olympic clock count down. And there was barely time to think of the sports aspect of the games, although Dr. Leroy Walker, who was running the competition plans for us, kept our eyes on the ball in that area.

There could be no delays. We had to be ready to go on July 20, 1996. We couldn't say "We need more time." The world would be watching.

Billy had helped to craft a mission statement that was properly lofty, given the enormity of the event. It read, "To host the greatest peacetime gathering in history, to bring honor and pride to the Games of the Centennial Olympics, and to forever enhance the standing in the world of Atlanta, of Georgia, of the American South, and of the United States."

In fact, we all sort of knew that we had two missions: break even, and no massacres.

When we visited Barcelona in August 1992, a gathering dominated by the presence of USA basketball's "Dream Team," we were humbled by the magnificence of this breathtaking European city. We were well prepared, with video cameras, checklists, specially created guidebooks, and plenty of pins for trading. But we were not prepared for the majesty of the city and the manner in which it lent itself to accommodating visitors. Amid all of its plazas, fountains, cathedrals, and public gathering places, we realized that we had none of that in Atlanta. Our venues, our transportation, and our hotels would all be fine, but our visitors would soon come to realize that there was no place to gather. Peachtree Street (actually, there were 41 streets with the word *Peachtree* in it) was no Las Ramblas for a stroll. Piedmont Park was not really near anything and was rather uninteresting. Underground Atlanta had some charm, but it was small and essentially a mall.

So, with that, Billy decided we needed a park, and by sheer force of his will, Centennial Olympic Park was carved out across the street from our offices in the Inforum building. It was practically a last-minute thought, but it would be one of the legacies. (There's a statue of Billy in there today, holding a torch.) And, as history would demonstrate, it would be memorable for another terrible reason as well.

I wasn't doing as well within ACOG as I had hoped. I was viewed by some as an "outsider"—a mercenary, so to speak. An import from—of all places—New York, and, unlike the other executives, I hadn't spent years as an unpaid volunteer. When I submitted my first expense report for a trip to Savannah and dinner with a journalist, I was told that I was expected to pay for such things myself, sort of my "contribution."

We got that policy reversed in a hurry.

Bob Brennan, an older fellow who had been the PR director for MARTA, the rail system, was our press spokesman and a former volunteer. He was polite to me but greatly resented that I was brought in at a higher salary and with a vice presidency to follow, with him reporting to me. Bob was also a bit on the curmudgeonly side. He was gracious and suave with the international press and the media people in Lausanne, Switzerland, the IOC headquarters, but sarcastic, gruff, and impatient with the local press. The *Atlanta Journal-Constitution* writers were quickly very skeptical of almost everything he released and would spend the better part of the '90s criticizing the Olympic planners.

Things started off poorly with the *Journal-Constitution* almost from the time the Games were won. The paper immediately put out T-shirts carrying their front-page headline, IT'S ATLANTA. But because the front page included the five-ring Olympic logo, the committee decided to go after the paper for unauthorized use of the logo. A bad way to begin an important five-year relationship.

Media was not directly part of my responsibilities, it was Bob's, but it got back to me that there was disappointment that we were getting such bad local press and that Billy's salary, quite high, was being questioned. It was an impossible situation for me, because Bob handled media, media disliked him, and he was making it impossible for me to have any input there. It was clear that he was not only unhappy about reporting to me, but was spending as much time as he could winning Billy's confidence.

Ginger Watkins, who ran something called "Trees Atlanta" each Christmas, was effective in developing the "look of the Games," but she was going through her own growing pains as the plans unfolded. This was her first test in a high-profile, high-management position; she was going through a divorce; and there were some people she just plain couldn't dictate to.

One such person was a woman named Cassandra Henning. One night I had been in an edit studio cutting a promo for the show and had to decide whether to include a particular artist. I had heard the artist was out of the show.

A call to Cassandra resulted only in an answering machine. The cost of the studio being as high as it was, I called the West Coast and was told that the act was, in fact, out. So we cut the promo without naming that group.

Cassandra hit the roof, even though the spot came out correctly. Confronting Ginger, she demanded to know on whose authority I had called Dick Clark Productions. I didn't think that any authority was needed—I had to get the spot right, I was involved in hiring Clark, and a simple phone call cleared it up. It was ridiculous, but Cassandra was very insecure and very territorial. She practically resigned over this issue until Ginger brought us both into her office to "iron it out."

When Cassandra left, chastised, Ginger and I looked at each other and both exhaled together over what tension had been in the room. It was the one moment in which the two of us actually bonded, bound together by this impossible situation with Cassandra.

But the bonding didn't really hold.

I was talking with my friend Phil Pepe on the phone one day about the things I missed back home. "Ronzoni pasta! You have to buy it here in specialty import stores at three-fifty a box! And the *News* and the *Post*! I can't follow Woody and Mia and the Buttafuccos! And my God, they bombed the World Trade Center and I wasn't there to watch the local news coverage! And Cousin Brucie on the radio! I miss New York radio!"

Phil was now doing sports at WCBS-FM, "Cousin" Bruce Morrow's station. About a week later I got a cassette in the mail from him. I was delighted—I assumed he had taped a portion of the station's broadcast just to remind me of home.

So I popped it into my car cassette deck and heard the voice of ol' Cousin Brucie, in his distinctive, top-40, 1960s patter. "EE-ya, and say, cousins, tonight is the start of the World Series down in Atlanta, and we know a big baseball fan down there who'll be watching . . . our old cousin Marty Appel, the former Yankee PR chief; and so, Marty, this goes out to you . . ."

And on came the unmistakable notes of an instrumental that never quite made the top 40 but sounded so great that night . . . the theme *Here Come the Yankees*, used at the start of every Yankee radio broadcast.

There wasn't a dry eye in the car.

In November 1992, during our weekly staff meeting, I matter-of-factly announced that I would be heading back to New York on Thursday, where my son was having his bar mitzvah, and that I would be back on Monday.

There were a few congratulations around the table, but silence from the others. They had known I was Jewish, but the term *bar mitzvah* was, well . . . sooooo Jewish.

We returned to Larchmont as a family for the weekend. It was a very moving time. All of our families and old friends were with us at Larchmont Temple. The rabbi spoke of how good it was to have us "home." I felt a lump in my throat, telling me how much I missed "home."

While home, I met with Bob Tisch, co-owner of the Giants. Bob was new to the pro football world and was wondering if I might become his personal assistant, travel the country with him, introduce him to the sports media, and get him more involved in the sports community.

I was appreciative but not ready to pack it in just yet.

When we got back to Atlanta, I found myself off the social calendar. Ginger had a big Christmas party at her home, honoring local heavy-weight champion Evander Holyfield. I was off that list.

So too was I off the lists for social galas at the High Museum of Art, the Fernbank Museum, Zoo Atlanta, the Botanical Garden, and the Woodruff Arts Centzer. The "Cultural Olympics" were an important adjunct to the Games, but they were becoming social gatherings for seventh-generation Atlantans, not for me.

I was also excluded from the weekly staff meeting. I was supposed to have been promoted to vice president at this point, per my contract, but instead I was beginning to feel as if I was on the outside looking in.

I was running public relations, but I was learning about us in the morning paper. This was definitely going off track. Decisions were being made by the good ol' boys over Jack Daniel's late at night, and I was out of the loop.

In the meantime, my kids were unhappy in school. Brian, in seventh grade, was two years behind where he had left off in New York. He had found a lacrosse league, was venturing into the city on his own, and was playing tennis. But we were very concerned about his schooling, and private school was not really an option because all of the private schools were Christian. In the end, we sent Brian home to live with a friend in Larchmont and to return to his old school. It was a difficult but necessary decision.

Debbie, to our delight, had adjusted nicely to Atlanta; was playing Little League baseball with her trusty Bobby Bonilla mitt, competing in tennis, winning swimming medals, making friends, and doing well in school.

We had a big house in the northern suburbs, which I absolutely hated. Every room produced echoes, and it was too big to ever feel like we were together. The development, like so many in Atlanta, was based on electric garage door openers. You would drive in and out and never see a neighbor. There was the video rental store, where I would spot John Smoltz from time to time, but the culture of the community was to let everyone be. It was not the southern hospitality I had been told about.

Because MARTA was designed *not* to go to the northern suburbs (lest undesirables move there), everyone had to drive to work. Even at 6 A.M., when I hit the road, the traffic was horrid. In the chill of winter (which surprised me), with rain falling, wipers running, headlights on, nothing on the radio but reports of all the local "wrecks," I would sit, bumper-to-bumper on I-285, and I-75 or I-85 and wonder what in the world was going on here.

There were some that tried to tell me it was a Jewish issue. "We have 435 employees," I was told, "and three are Jewish. And Atlanta has a large Jewish community!" Steve Selig, a prosperous local land developer who came out of the University of Georgia with Payne, expressed his anger to me over not finding a single Jew—himself included—on ACOG's Board of Directors.

I had been raised as a white male in New York. I had never felt any prejudice, and it had never once been an issue for me. It was hard for me to accept that it could be an issue now.

I did confide my concerns to some. A friend in New York, a noted civil rights lawyer named Mel Leventhal (who had once been married to Alice Walker), gave me good counsel.

Andy Young indeed proved to be a friend. When I explained what was happening, he laughed and said, "You've been niggered." Although he was co-chairman of the committee, he was a valuable counsel during the unfolding weeks.

Shirley Franklin was sympathetic and wise, and I managed to get the name of the lawyer who had helped get Cassandra Henning, of all people, out of her contract. I felt the time had come to extricate myself from mine.

Getting a lawyer was no easy feat. Nobody was interested in taking on the power of ACOG in Atlanta in 1993. But I was steered to one who was very effective in bringing about negotiated settlements, and, in a matter of a few weeks, the matter was successfully resolved.

I lasted 15 months. I received a settlement on my contract and avoided the unpleasantness of suing ACOG or of having the matter covered by the papers. I sought only to get myself back home, to restore the happiness my family had lost, and to resume my career.

I received several nice job offers in Atlanta, notably one to join Cohn & Wolfe, who reminded me that what I had experienced at ACOG was not a reflection on either my abilities or on doing business in the South. "We like your easy style, the way you get along with people," said Jim Overstreet, when he made me an offer, car phone to car phone late one night. It was tempting, but it was time to go back to New York.

If I had one failing, it was that I was never able to really "stand up and tell Billy Payne what to do." That was what they thought they'd found in me—a guy who had worked for Steinbrenner. Well, I never did that with George, and I never did that with Billy. He went out and hired as my replacement one of his own, a lifelong Georgian named Dick Yarbrough, out of BellSouth, who was no more successful at directing Billy than I might have been, and who in the end became a vocal critic of how Atlanta had "blown their big opportunity to impress the world."

I did return for the Games in '96 as a guest of Ogilvy & Mather and its chairman, Neill Cameron, one of the many good friends I made there. Debbie came with me, and we attended a number of the events and walked through Centennial Olympic Park the day before a bomb went off there, which forever defined the Games in the memory of the world.

I am not sure that the Games enhanced Atlanta's standing as an international city. I think by the time opening ceremonies came along and they rolled in pickups with gun racks as part of the festivities, they had conceded that all of the street merchants had pretty much taken away any chance of this being more than a big southern jamboree.

The emotional moment of Muhammad Ali lighting the torch was brilliant, but it was an NBC idea, not an ACOG idea, and Ali no more represented Atlanta than did Rocky Balboa.

Different people express different feelings to me about Atlanta's legacy. They broke even, but they were a laughingstock over the mascot and looked inept with the bombing, the false arrest, and the inability to solve the crime. Payne, who many thought would remain a major figure in the city, retreated into private life. He took his hits defending the gifts during the bid process and certainly wasn't *Time*'s Man of the Year as Ueberroth had been in '84. The lordly Samaranch insulted everyone by pronouncing the games "excellent" in his closing remarks, when it was expected that he would follow custom and pronounce the Games the best ever. (One letter writer suggested that he have an "excellent" flight home.)

This was surely a professional setback for me, but yet, it was a growth experience. I had fared well far from the sports arena, dealing with so many divergent and complex issues. I was personally pleased with my performance and didn't second-guess my overall effort at all. I had published a beautiful magazine about the Games, had taken command of the Dick Clark concert, had integrated a lot of special interest groups, had provided a lengthy study of the PR operation in Barcelona, had begun a weekly radio show on WSB previewing the Olympics, and had won many, many friends for the Games through my work on the air, in conference rooms, and through speeches.

My personal legacy would be in the friendships I maintain to this day, and in knowing that I'll probably never cross the George Washington Bridge again in pursuit of a job.

Now I found myself at a very low point in my life. I was out of work. We couldn't return to our own home, which had been rented. My mother had been stricken with cancer, which would take her life within the next two years. My children had interrupted their lives and their friendships.

And my marriage was ending.

Pat and I had fallen into a relationship where we were more a president and a chairman of "Appel Industries" than a loving couple. We ran the upbringing of the children and the management of the home well but had grown apart. Pat had encouraged the move to Atlanta but was, naturally, disheartened by the way it had played out and angry at being displaced, having given up her social-work practice.

We had met in London when I was vacationing there in 1971 and had married four years later when she returned to the U.S. We had two wonderful kids in Brian and Debbie, and I enjoyed fatherhood more than anything I ever did in life. But we never were very interested in each other's careers, and the strength of our long marriage was really in the raising of the children under common values.

I went back to New York to take a consulting job for Major League Baseball while I looked for something permanent. I was offering PR counsel to Richard Ravitch during the hopeless labor negotiations of 1993, which predated the inevitable strike of '94. While I lived in Manhattan and worked on this assignment, once again Pat and Debbie stayed behind, determined to let Debbie finish out her school year.

Brian, meanwhile, was living with his friend in Larchmont. He would come in to stay with me on alternate weekends; I would fly to Atlanta to be with Pat and Debbie on the others. It was a mess.

On July Fourth weekend, we were all together in Atlanta, preparing for the move back. I don't know what was going through Pat's mind, but she cried when she dropped me off at the airport. I asked if she wanted me to come back on the 15th to help her move, but she said no, it wouldn't be necessary, the movers would be doing all the packing.

Brian was with me when we rented a house in Larchmont for a year until we could get back into our own. Rentals were few in the area, and we were lucky to get it. It was smaller than our own home, but it was well kept, in the neighborhood, and would do the job. But when Pat returned, she took one look at it and started to cry. She hated it.

I was not as sympathetic as I might have been and was, in fact, not as sensitive to her feelings throughout this period as she needed me to be. The move back had not gone well logistically, and she was strung out from the whole experience. The next day she announced that she wanted a divorce.

We've never talked about all that had transpired, not to this day. The process, by its very nature, became so unpleasant that we never had the opportunity to step back and discuss all of the good things we'd shared and all of the obstacles that befell us. And I was in the communications business.

The children were, of course, devastated. Debbie was only 10.

In the ensuing months, I plunged into the research and writing of my book on King Kelly. It was my therapy after the kids went to sleep. I would lose myself in the 19th century, and it gave my days purpose, got me away from the lawyers and mediators and accountants. I always view that book as the project that got me through 1993–94.

My mother died in September 1994. The kids accompanied me to Florida for her funeral. A few weeks later, after reaching a mediated agreement with Pat, I moved out, taking an apartment a half mile from my home in order to be close to the kids. It was the lowest point of my life.

The loss of living with my children, being with them at dinner, hearing about their day, helping them with their homework, watching TV with them, explaining the news of the day, and just enjoying the ease of a normal relationship with a family, was very difficult and never got better. Even though I lived close by, the burden on the children of adhering to a visitation schedule, their friends not knowing where to find them, their stuff invariably at the other home, made it awful for them. Brian lived with me for a few months, but out of a suitcase. Debbie finally expressed great relief when I simply called off "the schedule" and said, "Let's just get together when it works for both of us."

I don't know if the Olympics had brought all this about. It might have happened anyway, I suppose. But the Olympic period of my life had surely been a difficult period; one I needed to move beyond.

Seven years after I left Atlanta, the *Journal-Constitution* ran an eight-part summary of the Games, uncovering old memos and letters from buried files. Some of mine were included, and they tended to be memos urging the committee to beware of certain conflicts of interest, to seek better relations, or to maintain a lighter touch. I sent the author, Melissa Turner, a thank you note for including these. She sent me back a note that will forever brighten my experience:

> *Marty, you should feel vindicated. Even Colin Campbell [a frequent critic of ACOG] has said you sound "so professional, so reasonable." Several people have written or called to ask what happened to you, where did you go, and comment that maybe things would have gone so much better with the media if you had been around.*

TOPPING
IT ALL OFF

When I returned from Atlanta, I took a job at Ogilvy, Adams and Rinehart Public Relations as a consultant to Richard Ravitch, chief negotiator for Major League Baseball with the Players Association.

I was foolish enough to think I might find it within me to come up with some good idea, but greater minds than mine had tried and failed before. Ravitch no doubt had the same thoughts, and he was a brilliant guy.

I got on well with Ravitch but thought that his constant complaining about the intellectualism of the owners was inevitably going to get back to them and make unneeded enemies. He would have to be a consensus builder, but I didn't get the sense that it would come easily for him. He had been charmed by some players during a spring training visit and pronounced them a "collegial bunch." I had a feeling he was a bit starstruck himself while visiting spring training camps.

I set up briefings for him with baseball journalists who came to town. I got him on talk radio and positioned him as a reasonable man with no ax to grind, just someone who liked baseball and was looking to bring about an equitable solution. I was careful to never position him in an antagonistic stance, thinking that diplomacy would win out in the end. It didn't, but at least I didn't burn any bridges—the Players Association would later turn to me for select projects, and I was happy to be able to work well with both sides.

Baseball was paying good money for this PR counsel, but when it was apparent that it wasn't accomplishing much, the checks were slow to arrive. Jonathan Rinehart and John Margaritis, who ran Ogilvy, Adams and Rinehart, hoped to find a way to retain me full-time and put me on another account—doing PR for the heiress Doris Duke, who was being sued by her adopted daughter, Chandi Heffner Duke (whom she was now disowning), for a large chunk of her huge fortune. But Doris died, the butler fired us, and it was time to find another job.

David Stern, brilliantly running the NBA, and a former seatmate on the Metro North Railroad during commutes to the city, gave me some advice.

Drawing a square with his fingers, he said to me, "You think like a baseball person! Learn to think out of the box! There is a lot more out there than you are allowing yourself to see!"

I got together with John Moore again to produce a series of home shopping shows out of the old Boston Garden for the New England Sports Network, and we even did a few infomercials with the author of bestselling romantic novels. The only thing I got out of either show was the pleasure of working with John again and of renewing my enjoyment of television production. Then the client stiffed me when neither show produced a profit.

The break in this professional downswing came when Rick Cerrone, who had been the Pirates' PR man but was now unemployed, called to tell me that he had been offered the PR position at The Topps Company, the legendary trading card manufacturer, but had decided it wasn't for him.

I asked if he had any problem with my looking into it, and he said, "Of course not."

So I talked to Sy Berger, the legendary creator of the modern day card and a Topps vice president, and soon was hired as the first in-house public relations director this venerable company would have. Although the office was in a horrid warehouse on the Brooklyn docks, I was assured by J Langdon, the president, that we would be moving later that year to lower Manhattan.

Actually, with that in mind, I didn't object to Brooklyn at all. It was nice to see the company's roots, to be part of where it all began, as a gum company in 1938. Old timers there remembered that they would leave work each day covered with the sugar dust from Bazooka bubble gum. A PR man should be able to speak as though he is part of the company's history, not just this week's hired gun. I didn't have sugar residue on my shoes, but I did know about life in the 36th Street warehouse in Industry City, Brooklyn.

Topps had been an important part of my youth. Baseball cards had been, for me, and for generations to follow, the gateway to the players. David Halberstam had used me as the prototype for his young Yankee fan of the '50s in his book *October 1964*, and, to any typical fan, it all began with the cards. Those 2½-by-3½ pieces of cardboard were treasures, not just for trading, but for learning the game. To this day, if a player from that period dies, the image of his card flashes before me. And my mother, unlike most mothers (including Barbara Bush, whose son George W. was a major collector), never did throw away my cards.

The term *chase card* was part of the language of the industry when I joined Topps. It meant an insert card, scarcer than the regular issues, coveted by collectors. But when I was a kid, even without that term, I knew a chase card when I saw it. When I got a Yankee—that went into a special pile. Zach Monroe, Harry Simpson, Virgil Trucks, Al Cicotte, Bobby del Greco, Jim Pisoni—I didn't care, as long as it said "Yankees" on the card. I chased after all of them.

And when I got a Mickey Mantle card—well, I can remember the very street corner or playground I stood upon for every Mantle card I ever found in a pack. There was no finer childhood moment, and cash value had nothing to do with it.

The company began issuing trading cards in 1950, actually doing All-American football players before they did baseball in '51. Sy Berger had written, designed, and done the stats for those early baseball cards on his kitchen table, effectively creating the modern prototype for what a card contains. He never anticipated that by 1994—when I arrived—he would be witness to a $1 billion industry in new card sales, and even more in the sales of old cards, the so-called secondary market. But he did know that the original concept—inserting cards to sell more gum—was backwards. He knew kids would love the cards from day one, and he was right.

Topps had been the only manufacturer of note between 1956 and 1980. Fleer and Donruss entered the picture in 1981, Score in 1988, and Upper Deck in 1989, setting the industry on its heels by proving that people would pay more for a better-quality card.

One of my favorite projects was bringing the noted artist Peter Max and Topps together for a series of both baseball and football cards in one of our high-end brands. Peter was still filled with the loving spirit of the '60s, but still thriving as one of America's most commercially successful artists. We threw a grand party at his studio to introduce the baseball set, and had Derek Jeter, the hottest player in town, on hand to unveil his own painting. It was a glamorous night in the baseball card game, and Derek was a perfect gentleman, calling Peter "Mr. Max," just as he continued to call his manager "Mr. Torre."

But, although competition was forcing better products into collectors' hands, it was also creating too many companies and too many brands. Factoring in all four sports and all the brands, a collector walking into a card store might find more than 240 products a year—more than four new ones each week.

Furthermore, just as I had coveted Mickey Mantle's annual card, and his total of 18 when he retired, a player like Ken Griffey Jr. was pictured on more than 2,500 different cards in the first 10 years of his career. To say this was out of control would be accurate, except that Topps had a great sense of marketing, knew that each brand was intended for a specific audience, and positioned its products well.

Sadly, the bubble gum came out in 1991, when collectors said it was marring the cards it was touching and lowering their values. Yes, values were critical, and everyone read the price guides published by Beckett and Krause Publications.

As if overproduction wasn't enough of a problem, baseball as an industry shut down in 1994, the strike even canceling the World Series. It was a devastating blow to card sales; without the heroes performing heroic deeds, essentially promoting themselves each night on *SportsCenter*, the kids were turned off and the "free marketing" of the product—the players playing—was gone.

The billion-dollar industry became a $400 million industry. Companies merged or folded. People who bought 100 Jose Canseco rookie cards for $125 each were looking at cards now worth $15.

To the rescue came Mickey Mantle. The late Mickey Mantle.

Mick had been the first hero of the modern card industry, the impetus for kids like me to buy cards. One could say that he almost created the craving for cards. (I would often be asked why his cards were so much more valuable than Willie Mays', and I always suspected that the questioner was digging for a racial angle. But Michael Jordan and Griffey cards outsell other players'; I don't think it was racial so much as the fact that Mantle was a more national figure, appearing in 12 World Series in his first 14 years with the Yankees. Mays was in three.)

In the late '70s, when an old Mantle card went for big bucks at something called a "card show," he gave rise to the secondary market, triggering the phenomenon of these weekend card shows, national conventions, and price guides.

Mick died in Dallas in 1995. Even today, it is hard to believe that this forever-youthful symbol of strength and speed could be gone. His best days were his final ones, in which he faced up to his demons and made amends for his life. He was a symbol of courage at the end and, finally, in saying "Don't be like me," a true role model through his honesty.

At a staff meeting at Topps a few weeks later, while we were looking to see what might help sales in what was still a strike-bound situation, I suggested that we think of paying tribute to all that Mickey meant to the hobby.

"Why don't we reprint his old cards, the eighteen of them, put a commemorative logo on them, and insert into new packs?" I said.

It was a marketing idea, but it was also intended to be a genuine tribute. I thought that baby boomers might now buy these cards for their kids, and the kids might open a pack and get the same thrill I got out of finding a Mantle.

I was asked to call Mickey's agent, Roy True, in Dallas, a man I had had many conversations with over the years. We made a deal, and the cards were issued.

The hobby magazines reported that "Mickey Mantle, for the third time, has jumpstarted this industry."

The reprints were a terrific hit. With the 1995 season again delayed due to continuing labor strife, the Mantle cards drove what card sales there were. It could have been a disastrous year, but Mick saved it. And Topps enjoyed a fine year after all.

I was enjoying all of this tremendously. It was the first time I had worked for a company that put products on shelves. I learned about the distribution system and visited stores with our salespeople.

And, because Topps also made Bazooka and candy products, I learned about the confectionery field. And boy, did America love Bazooka. We had one stint in the mid-'90s when Bazooka was used as a punchline or a storyline on the television programs *Seinfeld*, *The Simpsons*, *Mad About You*, *Third Rock from the Sun*, *Beacon Hill*, Jay Leno, and David Letterman within a matter of two months. When we made slight changes to the look of the red, white, and blue wrapper, the story ran across the nation with before-and-after photos, many on page 1.

I hosted a number of press conferences in which we brought the likes of Brooks Robinson, Bubba Smith, and Willie Stargell to conventions and, at one memorable dinner in Anaheim, had a small group of about 20 licensors and journalists sit and chat sports through the evening with Bill Walton and my old employee Tom Seaver, to whom I passed the wine list for his expertise.

I had arrived at Topps as the downward curve was beginning for the industry. The good days were ending. To cut costs, Topps decided to shut down its production facility in Pennsylvania and lay off hundreds of workers. It was unpleasant, but I was the spokesman for the company during the downsizing and participated in several planning sessions with former governor Mario Cuomo of New York, who was now serving as Topps's counsel on this matter through his office at Willke Farr.

Business was not good. The factory closing wasn't sufficient to stop the bleeding.

I was having lunch with my book agent, Bill Adler, early in 1998 when my beeper went off. Arthur Shorin, the company's chairman and son of one of its founders, wanted to see me.

I took the subway back to our office on Whitehall Street, and something told me it was trouble.

Arthur had three guest chairs facing his desk. I sat on the one to his right. Behind him the windows overlooked the historic U.S. Customs House, with Battery Park and the Statue of Liberty in the distance.

"Marty," he said, "we are in very serious trouble here. We're nearly bankrupt. Effective tomorrow, we are going to be laying off fifty-seven people. I need for you to handle the announcement. And then, when you're done, you're going to be number fifty-eight."

I was silent. I was stunned, despite my premonition. It wasn't as if I hadn't contributed; the company was going broke. Our stock would shortly drop to 1½ from a high in the early '90s of 21.

Arthur was a good businessman with a great sense of humor, and to know him is to know where Garbage Pail Kids and Wacky Packages came from. He wasn't like a lot of CEOs. I could take him to breakfast with a journalist and he would say, "Take vomit! Kids love vomit!" in explaining the success of Garbage Pail Kids.

I had nothing against Arthur's decision nor did he have anything against my work. At that moment, as he offered me some bottled water (I would have accepted something harder), we both knew the reality of the situation.

I tested the New York job market for sports positions and public relations agencies but found, as many have before me, that a good job is not always there when you need it, no matter what your background or reputation.

So, in a few weeks, I went back to Arthur, who had designed a plan under which I would be phased out, first at three days a week, then two, and, after six months, *poof*.

"I have an idea," I said. "Topps still needs PR, perhaps more than ever. I have done this effectively for you for almost five years, and the media trusts me and likes me. What if I was to start my own business? Would you be able to afford me on a consulting basis?"

He never hesitated.

"Absolutely," he said. "Just tell us when you're fully launched, really up and running, and we'll work out arrangements for you to become a consultant for us."

It was a great gesture, and who wouldn't start a business under those circumstances? We shook hands warmly.

A quick call to Villante, of course.

"Are you serious? Do it! And we'll have a power lunch at Walter's Hot Dogs in Mamaroneck once a week!"

My girlfriend, Marge Teilhaber, a court reporter, who was bright, witty, caring, curious, and owner of a good business sense, was ecstatic. "What an opportunity!"

Brian and Debbie checked in approvingly, Brian from UMass in Amherst, where he was majoring in management (and interning for the Red Sox over the summer), Debbie from her perch at Mamaroneck High School, where she still had the best instincts in the family. The team was supportive.

Leaving the corporate umbrella was a big step for me—no health benefits, no 401(k), no bonus, none of those nice things. I would be on my own. I hadn't done this since 1977 with Joe Garagiola Jr.

Bill Goff, an old friend who ran a hugely successful business in Kent, Connecticut, selling fine-art lithographs and calendars of old ballparks, not only added encouragement but said, "I want you to do PR for me. Starting on the first day you are in business."

We shook hands and it was a go. Marty Appel Public Relations opened for business on March 8, 1998, operating out of Topps and out of a well equipped home office, complete with fax, e-mail, copier, scanner, and printer, with Hydrox cookies just steps away. For assistance when needed, I had a network of friends all over the country, from more than thirty years in the business, that I could call upon, to either help out personally or recommend top people.

Within days, we were hired by Major League Baseball Properties and Major League Baseball Players Association to handle the PR for a rare joint venture, in which players distributed free cards to kids during spring training. I might not have helped bring those two organizations together while advising Ravitch, but the spirit of cooperation in which I was serving both was abundant on this one. And we scored nicely with great photos of Tony Gwynn handing out cards in USA Today. In 2000 the Players Association asked me to assist with Big League Challenge, a renewal of the old Home Run Derby concept at which all of the game's greatest sluggers would compete in an ESPN series taped in Las Vegas.

We put Goff together with Topps to create a series of 20 portraits of modern stars, done in the style of 1953 cards, which was a hit both as a card product for Topps and as lithographs for Bill. It also launched a period in which "throwback" cards in old designs would be big hits with collectors, leading to a successful campaign to celebrate Topps baseball cards' 50th anniversary in 2001.

My friend Bob Aniello of Topps went to Vancouver to become marketing director of EA Sports, the hot video game company. We were hired to help launch their new basketball and baseball products, setting up a major press event at the NBA Store in New York with Willis Reed and Earl Monroe and a spring training party in Phoenix with Sammy Sosa.

We helped a first-time author find a publisher for a book on Billy Martin.

We worked with Boys & Girls Clubs of America in running a campaign to identify their 3 millionth member and ran a press conference at the Kingdome with Ken Griffey Jr. to make the announcement. Then we did a follow-up at Yankee Stadium with Roger Clemens and Mo Vaughn, old Boston teammates. And we brought in Cal Ripken Jr. and Chipper Jones to announce a physical fitness program with The Sports Authority.

We worked with the New York Giants and the New York Rangers to develop media coverage for the fundraisers they did for Ronald McDonald House of New York City.

The Sporting News became a client in the summer of 1999.

I hadn't missed an issue since 1962, had enjoyed it throughout college when my roommate, Buddy, and I had two subscriptions. When John Rawlings, the editor, called, I was proud to take it on and honored by the phone call. And I found it to be a willing recipient of public relations ideas. Not long after the assignment began, I suggested that we might get a lot of attention with a "100 Most Powerful Sports Figures of the Century" list. *The Sporting News* had been doing an annual list since 1990.

Not only did they like the idea, it developed into a cover story, which led to a major press conference in New York at which all four commissioners—Paul Tagliabue, Bud Selig, David Stern, and Gary Bettman—were present to honor the number one man on the list, Pete Rozelle. It was an enormous event for the magazine, and Selig mentioned to me that the four had never before been together in the same room. I can't say that the high visibility of the event made a difference, but the magazine was for sale at the time, and a few weeks later it was sold by Times-Mirror to Paul Allen's Vulcan Ventures. And, in 2000, Vulcan purchased One-on-One Sports Radio, renaming it The Sporting News Radio Network, and *bang*, we had not only a major magazine but also 425 radio stations to work with.

Leland's Auctions was a client. Three times a year it produced magnificent catalogs of absolutely fascinating sports collectibles. Joshua Leland Evans, the company's founder, was the son of antiques dealers and had been wheeling and dealing since he was eight. Now he had founded a company that was among the most recognized authorities in sports collectibles and was a master at creating interest in his auctions.

He had achieved fame by selling the "Mookie Ball," the one that rolled through Bill Buckner's legs in Game 6 of the 1986 World Series; by auctioning off the "Greer Johnson Collection" of Mickey Mantle treasures; by selling off the contents of the old Boston Garden, and by selling the first home run ball ever hit in Yankee Stadium—hit by, and signed by, Babe Ruth. That item was the first we handled for Josh, and we splashed it all over the front page of the *Daily News*.

Each auction seemed to produce something of great interest—the jersey Lou Gehrig wore on Lou Gehrig Appreciation Day, or the first Heisman Trophy ever awarded, or Carlton Fisk's home run ball from the 1975 World Series, or Bobby Jones' green jacket from August National. Twice in a matter of months we got Josh on the *Today* show to show Matt Lauer his latest goodies. Jerry Schmetterer, one of the most respected and sharpest newsmen in town, worked with me in identifying the right place for each story. I did more and more projects with Jerry and we began operating as informal partners. Together we handled the PR for the most ambitious Webcast ever attempted—two weeks of live coverage of the 2000 Paralympic Games from Sydney, Australia, for WeMedia, an Internet site for people with disabilities.

In '98 Josh was planning to auction off the original Howdy Doody marionette, which would have been another part of my childhood to resurface in my adult professional life. That would have been huge.

I had to call Buffalo Bob himself to coordinate the public relations for the sale. I called in the summer of 1998. My first call to him was taken by his wife, who informed me that he had just been in the hospital for tests and that I should call back in a few days.

When I did, we spent 45 minutes talking of mutual baseball friends like Ernie Harwell and our time in Westchester County. I told him he had been like my second father during those Howdy Doody days, and I think our conversation gave him a terrific lift. He loved recalling the old baseball acquaintances. And his voice was unchanged—I was thrown back to my youth on St. John's Place.

He needed the lift. It was the first day of chemotherapy for him.

I told him we would plan a media tour for the time of the auction and that we would keep in touch.

Ten days later, he was dead. I would like to think I gave him a happy 45 minutes of baseball talk near the end and made him feel that one of his peanut gallery rejects was still a fan.

Like so many things in my life, a childhood connection had come full circle.

In 2000 I was honored to be asked by HBO to serve as a script consultant on its movie project *61**, the story of the Mantle-Maris home run race, directed by Billy Crystal. Working with Billy was a great thrill, and he was no slouch in the baseball knowledge department. He knew his stuff, but I got a great kick out of seeing all of my nitpicks come to life in the final screen version, small things such as taking "batting in the fourth hole" out of Ralph Houk's dialogue, because people didn't use that expression in the '60s. Or telling them that the actor playing Hoyt Wilhelm (actually the knuckleball pitcher Tom Candiotti) had to tilt his head to one side as he came in from the bullpen, just like Hoyt did.

We did PR for the reissue of Jim Bouton's *Ball Four*. And we did PR for a pitching machine called ProBatter that could throw up to 100 mph with eight different pitches.

And then there was Yogi Berra.

I don't think I ever spent a day around Yogi when I didn't feel better about life itself. What a wonderful person he was, so full of humility and decency and honor, but so natural. He was one of the most successful, celebrated, and admired people in the nation, yet he had been a fifth-grade dropout during the Depression who overcame people's beliefs that you had to look a certain way to achieve success in baseball.

People always underestimated Yogi. He won three MVP Awards and 39 rings; was listed eight times in *Bartlett's Familiar Quotations*; had his number retired by the Yankees; had, in Carmen, a great wife; had three sons who became pro athletes; and had nine grandchildren, including one, Lindsay Berra, whom I helped land a writing position at *ESPN Magazine*. He was on the Hall of Fame veterans committee, was still a highly sought commercial spokesman, and, with the death of Joe DiMaggio in 1999, became the greatest living retired Yankee player.

He had it all. Except, of course, a museum in his name, and that became a reality in 1998 when friends, fans, and admirers raised enough money to build the Yogi Berra Museum and Learning Center on the campus of Montclair State University, which had bestowed an honorary doctorate on him a few years earlier.

My company was hired to do the public relations for the museum, and this little 7,200-square-foot building became an enormous hit, instantly a site for newsworthy events and important gatherings, brilliantly directed by Dave Kaplan, a former *Daily News* sports editor. Later I was honored to be asked to join the board of directors.

The museum drew some sixty thousand visitors in its first year, a remarkable accomplishment. Mayor Giuliani came out several times, once to present the museum with the Yankees' world championship trophy for display.

For me, the best part was always the time with Yogi, who, living just 10 minutes away, liked to come over and hang out at "his" museum. Carmen Berra said she "finally has a place for all of his B'nai B'rith plaques," but it housed far more than that, including two of his MVP Awards, his glove from Larsen's perfect game, more than 50 magazine covers, great old photos, and exhibits on to the development of baseball in New Jersey, the evolution of catcher's equipment, the Negro Leagues, and baseball during World War II.

Yogi had been a sailor, providing cover for troops landing at Normandy on D-Day, the only major league player to see action at Normandy. In early 2000 he was awarded a French medal for his participation there, and my media advisory said, "It is not certain whether Yogi will be kissed on both cheeks when he receives this medal." He wasn't, but he did cry.

Yogi and I went back to not only his Yankee coaching days but to a project we did in the '80s called "Yogi at the Movies." They were short reviews in his own style, produced by Tom Villante, and I did the public relations. Yogi was a great movie fan, and although he didn't always get the names right (Glenn Close was "Glen Cove," Cary Grant was "Gary Grant"), he knew what he liked. *Eight Men Out* was his favorite baseball movie.

You never knew what you were going to come home with after a day with Yogi. His "Yogi-isms," some invented by Joe Garagiola, some real, were all true to the way he spoke, the way he thought things through.

One day, as Joe DiMaggio lay dying in Florida, we were listening to his DiMaggio stories. I happened to mention Marilyn Monroe.

"I had dinner with him and Marilyn in Florida once, during spring training," he said.

"You did? With Marilyn? Yogi, I have to know every detail about this. Tell me everything about that evening!"

"Well," he said, "you know how when you order a shrimp cocktail they usually bring you out four or five of them? That night, we got eight."

The purity of Yogi was wonderful. Right to the point. Only the important stuff really mattered.

It was never more evident than during his 14-year feud with George Steinbrenner, which dated back to the day he was fired as manager in 1985 after the team started off 6–8. He was furious with the manner in which it happened, with Clyde King being designated to tell him.

"Hell, all managers get fired," he told me. "I'd been fired before. But be a man, tell me face to face, don't send someone else."

Yogi was very serious about this and vowed never to return to Yankee Stadium as long as George owned the team. In truth, he did cheat a couple of times, running over to see Nick Priore in the clubhouse to get some equipment or some such, but he was never there when anyone would notice him, nor did he ever visit his plaque in Monument Park.

The long-running feud finally ended in early 1999. Suzyn Waldman, the Yankee correspondent for WFAN radio and the first woman to ever do play-by-play for Major League Baseball, brokered the detente, using the opening of the museum as a perfect venue for a Steinbrenner visit.

She was assisted by Yogi's son Dale, who appealed to his family feeling. "Dad, your grandchildren have never seen you cheered at Yankee Stadium."

Arrangements were set for the George visit, and we did our best to make it a non-media event, although Suzyn would do a live broadcast with the two of them over WFAN from the museum. Yogi was pacing back and forth as we waited for George.

"You think I'm doing the right thing?" he asked me. "I don't know about this. I'm still pretty pissed off."

"Yogi, fourteen years is a helluva feud," I answered. "Yankee Stadium is as much your place as his. I think you've made your point."

"I guess so, but I'm not really happy about this."

But, when George came, it was a very emotional moment. George can be warm and charming, and he was very much so on that day. The two of them went into Dave Kaplan's office and George admitted that he had made a mistake. A whopper. "Biggest mistake I ever made," he said.

Yogi, class all the way, put an end to the feud with four words.

"I've made mistakes, too."

And they hugged and shook hands and emerged friends. And usually, when Yogi went to Yankee Stadium, the team won.

Yogi Berra Day was so remarkable that every history of the Yankees had better mention it, lest readers think it is a contrived story. On Yogi Day, Don Larsen threw out the first ball to Yogi, who borrowed Joe

Girardi's glove for the catch.

And then David Cone went out and pitched a perfect game, with Yogi and Don looking on.

It was as if Girardi's glove were blessed. I was there, and I will never forget how supernatural it all seemed. I also loved the comment from Montreal manager Felipe Alou (an old Yankee player from my PR days), when he was asked when he first thought it might be a perfect game.

"When I was making out my lineup card," he said. He added that it was because his hitters had never faced Cone before. But, like many good quotes in history, it works better out of context.

"Out of context" is a good way for a public relations man to wind up a book. It is one of those 30 or so catchphrases that we might tell a client in trouble to use, whether it *was* out of context or not. That buys a little time to think out a bolder strategy.

"Haven't had a chance to review the document" is a good one. "We don't wish to debate the matter in the press" is another.

I have been a lucky guy to witness so much, to know so many extraordinary people, and to make a living doing something that people tell me I was "born to do." I never took it for granted. I have made it a practice to return every call I have ever received, even from wacky fans looking to settle a bet. I have had a historian's curiosity when I've met significant personalities from the world of sports, be they athletes, executives, or media. Or Little Ray Kelly, Babe's mascot. I have appreciated unfolding events as history in the making and have been blessed with a pretty good memory for details.

If I can be so presumptuous as to offer advice to young people coming into the field—in all likelihood, much better prepared than I was—I would say, take nothing for granted, be a good listener, read everything you can, and respect everyone you deal with. The suburban journalist deserves as much respect from the public relations person as the New York Times columnist. The journeyman ballplayer as much as the star. The $2,500-a-month client as much as the $15,000-a-month client.

Earlier in this book, I said it was all an accident, that I was never supposed to be a Yankee fan. Well, I don't think I was supposed to do a lot of what I've done, but, as Yogi himself would say, "When you come to a fork in the road, take it."

INDEX

New from SPORTClassic Books

Darryl Dawkins and Charley Rosen

Now on sale

CHOCOLATE THUNDER
The Uncensored Life and Times of the NBA's Original Showman
Darryl Dawkins and Charley Rosen

Long before The Answer, there was Chocolate Thunder. Before Kobe, before Shaq, before Air Jordan and even Magic, there was this man-child who understood that, above all, basketball was entertainment. Darryl Dawkins' signature move during a colorful NBA career was bulldozing to the basket and smashing the glass backboard to smithereens. On the court or on the prowl, the former NBA star was a seven-foot showman who charmed teammates with ribald humor, fans with outlandish antics and women with irresistible charm. Here, he revives that swashbuckling persona in this tell-all autobiography.

Dawkins invites you to join him in the locker room, on the court and at the parties. He recounts rampant drug use, speaks bluntly about racism, and explores the differences between "black ball" and "white ball," and offers frank appraisals of several NBA stars of the 1970s and '80s.

TOTAL TENNIS
The Ultimate Tennis Encyclopedia
Bud Collins

Total Tennis is the fourth book in the successful series of *Total* encyclopedias, following *Total Baseball*, *Total Football* and *Total Hockey*. It is a comprehensive reference book comprising player profiles, Grand Slam, Davis Cup and Federation Cup tournament results, world rankings, Hall of Fame listings, insightful essays, a player statistical register and other statistics, photographs, plus a complete tennis history from 1874 to today, presented by Bud Collins, the dean of tennis journalism.

Available May 2003

www.sportclassicbooks.com